THE FUTURE OF CONTINENTAL
PHILOSOPHY OF RELIGION

INDIANA SERIES IN THE PHILOSOPHY OF RELIGION
Merold Westphal, *editor*

THE FUTURE OF CONTINENTAL PHILOSOPHY OF RELIGION

Edited by
Clayton Crockett
B. Keith Putt
Jeffrey W. Robbins

Indiana University Press

Bloomington & Indianapolis

This book is a publication of

Indiana University Press
Office of Scholarly Publishing
Herman B Wells Library 350
1320 East 10th Street
Bloomington, Indiana 47405 USA

iupress.indiana.edu

Telephone 800-842-6796
Fax 812-855-7931

© 2014 by Indiana University Press

All rights reserved

No part of this book may be reproduced or utilized in any form or by any means, electronic or mechanical, including photocopying and recording, or by any information storage and retrieval system, without permission in writing from the publisher. The Association of American University Presses' Resolution on Permissions constitutes the only exception to this prohibition.

⊖ The paper used in this publication meets the minimum requirements of the American National Standard for Information Sciences—Permanence of Paper for Printed Library Materials, ANSI Z39.48-1992.

Manufactured in the United States of America

Library of Congress Cataloging-in-Publication Data

The future of continental philosophy of religion / edited by Clayton Crockett, B. Keith Putt, and Jeffrey W. Robbins.
    pages cm. — (Indiana series in the philosophy of religion)
    Includes bibliographical references and index.
    ISBN 978-0-253-01383-5 (cloth : alk. paper) — ISBN 978-0-253-01388-0 (pbk. : alk. paper) — ISBN 978-0-253-01393-4 (ebook) 1. Religion—Philosophy. 2. Continental philosophy. I. Crockett, Clayton, [date] editor of compilation.
    BL51.F88 2014
    210—dc23

2013046586

1 2 3 4 5   19 18 17 16 15 14

Contents

Acknowledgments   vii

Introduction: Back to the Future /
Clayton Crockett, B. Keith Putt, and Jeffrey W. Robbins   1

Part I. The Messianic

1   Is Continental Philosophy of Religion Dead? / John D. Caputo   21

2   Friends and Strangers/Poets and Rabbis: Negotiating a "Capuphalian" Philosophy of Religion / B. Keith Putt   34
     Response by Merold Westphal   45
     Response by John D. Caputo   51

3   On Faith, the Maternal, and Postmodernism / Edward F. Mooney   59

4   The Persistence of the Trace: Interrogating the Gods of Speculative Realism / Steven Shakespeare   80

5   Speculating God: Speculative Realism and Meillassoux's Divine Inexistence / Leon Niemoczynski   92

6   Between Deconstruction and Speculation: John D. Caputo and A/Theological Materialism / Katharine Sarah Moody   108

Part II. Liberation

7   The Future of Liberation / Philip Goodchild   127

8   Monetized Philosophy and Theological Money: Uneasy Linkages and the Future of a Discourse / Devin Singh   140

9   "Between Justice and My Mother": Reflections on and between Levinas and Žižek / Gavin Hyman   154

10 *Verbis Indisciplinatis* / Joseph Ballan   167

11 Overwhelming Abundance and Everyday Liturgical Practices: For a Less Excessive Phenomenology of Religious Experience / Christina M. Gschwandtner   179

12 Countercurrents: Theology and the Future of Continental Philosophy of Religion / Noëlle Vahanian   197

PART III. PLASTICITY

13 The Future of Derrida: Time between Epigenesis and Epigenetics / Catherine Malabou   209

14 On Reading—Catherine Malabou / Randall Johnson   219

15 Necessity as Virtue: On Religious Materialism from Feuerbach to Žižek / Jeffrey W. Robbins   229

16 Plasticity in the Contemporary Islamic Subject / John Thibdeau   242

17 From Cosmology to the First Ethical Gesture: Schelling with Irigaray / Lenart Škof   253

18 Prolegomenon to Thinking the Reject for the Future of Continental Philosophy of Religion / Irving Goh   263

19 Entropy / Clayton Crockett   272

List of Contributors   283
Index   287

Acknowledgments

The Editors want to thank Dee Mortensen at Indiana University Press, and Merold Westphal, editor of the Indiana Series in the Philosophy of Religion, for their interest in and commitment to this book. We also want to acknowledge the origin of this project, and many of the chapters, at the Postmodern Culture and Religion 4 Conference held at Syracuse University in April 2011. Thanks to everyone who presented at, participated in, and attended this conference, and special thanks to Jack Caputo for asking us to form a committee to read and evaluate paper submissions, as well as put together the conference program. As the final PCR conference, it is a fitting culmination of Caputo's conferences at Villanova and at Syracuse, and a genuine turning toward a future for Continental philosophy of religion, if there is one. Finally, we want to thank Deborah Pratt for her tireless work before, during, and after the conference and David Matusek for his work on the index.

THE FUTURE OF CONTINENTAL PHILOSOPHY OF RELIGION

Introduction
Back to the Future

Clayton Crockett, B. Keith Putt, and
Jeffrey W. Robbins

THE FUTURE HAS always figured prominently in Continental philosophy of religion. Indeed, we might even say that the (relatively short) history of Continental philosophy of religion has been defined by the future. So by way of introduction, our task will be to chart the concept of the future that has animated, inspired, and propelled this burgeoning discourse, which, by our reckoning, has both come into its own and reached a turning point, if not a terminal point or a fork in the road. Put otherwise, by posing the question of the future of Continental philosophy of religion, we are posing not only the possibility of a different future than the specific conception of the future that has heretofore been determinative, but also the possibility of overlapping futures, and thus, an alternative conception of time—not only a future structured by *différance,* but a plurality of temporalities that makes genuine change and difference possible.

We are asking this question now because now is precisely the time when different futures are appearing on the horizon with the intention of sparking still different thoughts about what the future might hold, and what hold the future might still have on what is a relatively young discourse. So, for instance, what comes next after the death of the generation consisting of Derrida, Deleuze, Foucault, and Levinas—the so-called 68ers? Is there a future afterlife for those thinkers who have left such a deep impact on Continental philosophy of religion? Or after the 68ers, or even after the afterlife of the 68ers, what new constellations of thinkers or movements will be most determinative in shaping the future of Continental philosophy of religion? Secondly, is there a politics of Continental philosophy of religion? Does Continental philosophy of religion have its very own political theology? It is with this question that the concepts of liberation and sovereignty get embroiled with money and capitalism, or with Western culture more generally, leading inexorably to the question of whether there is a home for postcolonialism within Continental philosophy of religion? Or is Continental philosophy of religion still awaiting its own liberation, and maybe even its own decolonization? Thirdly, with whom or what is Continental philosophy of religion in conversation? In what ways do the burgeoning discourses on speculative realism, the new materialism, and the new findings in the neurosciences and evolutionary psychology open new pathways for thought?

The above sentiment and questions give this volume birth. By speculating on the future, the volume is marking the time of the present as a time of transition—a time of overlapping and, frequently, contesting futures. What we can tentatively say about this future is that it is both radically open and highly determined. This is not a contradiction. On the contrary, it is because the future is overly determined that it can be understood to be open. The future is not a blank slate and does not open up into an empty void. Instead, what we will see is that the future of Continental philosophy of religion has a determinate past. We might even say that it has a pedigree—a DNA that is known by its names, styles of thought, and problems both known and unknown. This pedigree opens up future possibilities even as it determines access. Continental philosophy of religion has heretofore has been largely a deconstructive and post- (if not anti-) metaphysical philosophy. Its preferred methodology has been that of phenomenology, its ethics an ethics of radical alterity, and as for its politics, or whether there could even be a politics of Continental philosophy of religion, that was a question left to others.

The above situation explains why it is only now that the future of Continental philosophy of religion can be asked, now that that single determinate future has been punctured. To put it bluntly: if deconstructive philosophy has been the de facto philosophy of Continental philosophy of religion, that path forward will now have to be forged *without Derrida;* it must become a thinking of what deconstruction left unthought. And so we observe that while the theological turn in phenomenology continues to be disputed, there are new figures and schools of thought ranging from Alain Badiou to Radical Orthodoxy that have effected their own metaphysical becoming of Continental philosophy of religion. Likewise, whether it is from the aforementioned Badiou or Radical Orthodoxy, their frequent interlocutor Slavoj Žižek, or even the Italian triumvirate of Giorgio Agamben, Antonio Negri, and Gianni Vattimo, there has also been a political becoming of Continental philosophy of religion, a growing recognition that any philosophy of religion that does not take up directly the omnipresence and apparent omnipotence of global capital is a philosophy of outmoded religiosity, if not necrotic theology of a dead God.

What we are suggesting, therefore, about the future of Continental philosophy of religion is that we have come to a time when it is more about its many different futures—from the single to the plural, and from the indeterminate to the multitudinous. These are not just different futures, but a different conception of what it means to be open to the future. The future is open not simply because it is unknowable, but more because it is overlapping and contested. The future contains its own excess, a doubling of its own determination. It is punctuated not just by different visions of what is to come, but different temporalities. Surely this time of transition will contain as many false starts and mis-starts as it will generate the various futures that are being envisioned. It will not be up to us here to decide. After all, this volume is meant not as an authoritative last word, but as an invitation to journey back to the future—and more specifically, to the variety of alternative considerations of what the future might hold for, and what hold the future still has on, Continental philosophy of religion.

This collection of essays is organized into three distinct sections, each oriented around a particular touchstone or image of the future: the messianic, liberation, and plasticity. In the introduction that follows, we will provide an orientation and explanation for each with a specific focus on how they have collectively given particular shape to the question of the future of Continental philosophy of religion. The three sections are each headed by a representative figure, and the other chapters offer snapshots of a possible future oriented around these three themes.

The Messianic

The future that has, heretofore, been most clearly articulated and most determinative in shaping Continental philosophy of religion is the notion of the messianic as drawn from Derridean deconstruction. John D. Caputo has been its principal proponent. It is a formal messianicity that is distinguished from the determinate content of particular messianic faiths. To speak of the messianic is to speak of a messianic promise to come. Even more, as Caputo has taught us, to speak of the messianic is to speak of "the messianic form of the promise itself, messianicity itself, which goes to the heart of a promise, which is the form of any promise of something to come."[1] This formal messianicity, in contrast to any particular messianism with a determinate content, is always already future-oriented. It is about the coming of the other in and as time. As such, it disrupts or opens up the horizon of time itself. Time deconstructed is time structured by a promise, time pledged to an open and indeterminate future. The twist offered by Caputo's groundbreaking work on Derrida is that this deconstructive opening of the horizon of time may be a *religious* rendering of time—deconstruction is driven by an affirmative religious passion, and this passion may, and indeed has, become the resource for a rich and probing phenomenological description and analysis.

The messianic promise of the future is concerned not just with any future, but in the words of Caputo, with the "absolute future," which is to be distinguished from what he calls the "future present." In contrast to the future present, the absolute future is unforeseeable. It shatters our normal horizons of expectation. It comes as a complete surprise, as if from outside, an inbreaking of transcendence that cannot be prepared for, or even accounted for, by our normal immanent frames. In Derrida's words, it is "without horizon of expectation and without prophetic prefiguration," and it "can only emerge as a singular event when no anticipation *sees it coming.*"[2] For Caputo, it is precisely with this absolute future that we enter the sphere of the religious. It is religion's proper concern. "With a notion like the absolute future," Caputo tells us in his book *On Religion,* "we move, or we are moved, past the circle of the present and of the foreseeable future, past the manageable prospects of the present, beyond the sphere in which we have some mastery, beyond the domain of sensible possibilities that we can get our hands on, into a darker and more uncertain and unforeseeable region, into the domain of 'God knows what' (literally!)."[3]

As something that is unforeseeable as a complete surprise, that which is past the prospects of the present and beyond the domain of sensible possibilities, the absolute future is linked with the impossible. It is something that happens, but we do not know why or how. It is something we might pray for, or hope for, but never reasonably expect. Shifting idioms, the impossible is what Caputo will later call the "event," a radically destabilizing point in time that opens time to its other. It is in this way that the messianic is conjoined with an ethics of alterity and a religion without religion. By combining deconstructive philosophy, ethics, and religion together in this way, Caputo helped to define what would come to be known as Continental philosophy of religion, with the paradoxical effect of renewing a future for religion. This effort to write the affirmative implications of various strands of postmodern theory into a constructive religious discourse, and in so doing, engender an alternative (in most cases more pious, if not orthodox) mode to that of radical theology, defined this first wave of Continental philosophy of religion led by Caputo. While this affirmative spirit within Continental philosophy of religion was appreciated by many, its covert theological aspirations gave others pause. Noteworthy here is the critique of the theological turn in phenomenology by French phenomenologist Dominque Janicaud.[4] Likewise, in the introduction to the volume *After the Postsecular and the Postmodern,* editors Anthony Paul Smith and Daniel Whistler link Caputo's (Christian) brand of deconstruction with the theological turn in phenomenology and the British school of Radical Orthodoxy as examples of the contamination of philosophy with theological thinking. Their volume of collected essays on Continental philosophy of religion is then set up as an attempt to liberate philosophy of religion from this "theologisation of philosophy."[5]

From our perspective, there is much more that distinguishes and separates Caputo's variant of Continental philosophy of religion from either those associated with the theological turn in phenomenology (e.g., Levinas, Marion, Henry, Chrétien, et al.) or most certainly with Radical Orthodoxy. What cannot be denied, however, is that the "Continental Philosophy" in the Continental philosophy of religion that has been led by Caputo has been virtually synonymous with phenomenology. Derrida has been employed so as to enact a distinctly Kantian philosophy of religion-delimiting knowledge in order to make room for faith. Indeed, Caputo's rewriting of Kant's famous formulation of the transcendental understanding of the proper relationship between faith and knowledge can be read as the hermeneutical key to how Caputo successfully reintroduced Derrida into postmodern religious thought in such a fashion as to revalorize the affirmative nature of religious belief. "Derrida has found it necessary to limit and delimit *voir* and *savoir*," Caputo tells us, "in the interests of making room for *croire*." And later, Caputo uses this formulation to define the quasi-transcendental condition of faith: "delimiting *savoir* in order to make room for the passion of *non-savoir*, impassioning the desire for the impossible and the unforeseeable."[6]

But between his *Prayers and Tears* (1997) and *The Weakness of God* (2006), Caputo undergoes a conversion of sorts, or what he describes as a coming out as a theologian. This conversion or coming out from Caputo marks itself in several key registers, each opening new, uncharted or obscured pathways for thought as can be seen in the essay that opens up this volume: "Is Continental Philosophy of Religion Dead?" With this question, Caputo envisions a future beyond the first wave of French 68ers whose work invigorated Continental philosophy and whose influence inaugurated a Continental philosophy of religion.

First, whereas Caputo's phenomenological reading of a religion without religion took its lead from a Kantian reading of Derrida wherein faith and knowledge are opposed, Caputo now announces a turn from Kant to Hegel. The Kantian path in postmodernism employs deconstruction as a means for theological apologetics. Caputo does not pull his punches on this matter: "Kant was engaged in damage control," Caputo tells us. Those who employ Kant are interested in only a "half-hearted epistemological postmodernism." In Caputo's mind, this justifies the charge from Quentin Meillassoux and others that this Kantian mode is merely "a cover for fideism." The Hegelian mode of postmodernism, by contrast, is the more radical one because it links faith with knowledge.

Second, Caputo's new commitment to this "more radical Hegelian mode" aligns with his retrieval of the American radical theological tradition. Just as Hegel provides a way of thinking faith without fideism, radical theology provides a way of thinking theologically without ontotheology. Caputo's theology is not a confessional theology or, more certainly, not an orthodox one. Instead of operating as an ontic science and proceeding according to a self-explicating logic wherein its end is already known from its beginning, Caputo's theology makes faith unsafe. It is a faith that cannot be immunized against un-faith. It is neither safe nor saving, he tells us.

Third, and finally, these first two points provide the basis for Caputo's theological intervention into the burgeoning discussion over the so-called new materialism, here represented by Ray Brassier's *Nihil Unbound*. Where Brassier sees nihilism, Caputo sees grace—not a grace that somehow fills the nothingness of being with some divine purpose, but precisely the opposite. Caputo sees grace in nihilism precisely because nihilism is the defining condition of grace. It is a "being-*for*-nothing." He writes, "The very thing that makes life impossible—that makes life a gratuitous and temporary episode in a vast cosmic narrative without purpose, a tale told by the idiot of entropy—is what makes life possible. The very thing that destines life to impermanence and extinction makes life precious."

With this affirmation, Caputo returns to certain themes about the future that have been with him both before and after this turn from philosophy to theology we have charted here—namely, the future remains a messianic future wherein time encounters its other in a future unknown and unknowable. In this way, his intervention here makes clear that whatever the future of Continental philosophy of religion holds, it will remain beholden to the future as its theme. Along the way, as Caputo models a new kind of theological engagement with the new science of the new materialists, he dares to give a name to a desire whereby entropy gets reconfigured as the nihilism of grace.

To rework Caputo's concluding paragraph, perhaps the coming Continental philosophy of religion will be no Continental philosophy of religion at all, or at least none that we today can recognize. It is a Continental philosophy of religion that has suffered its own theological becoming, and as such, is now poised to realize its own radical promise. The other contributors from part I likewise engage with the very figures and themes that have been largely determinative of Continental philosophy of religion heretofore, where questions about deconstruction and messianicity are crucial, even as speculative realism emerges to challenge these presumptions.

In chapter 2, "Friends and Strangers/Poets and Rabbis," B. Keith Putt suggests that the future of Continental philosophy of religion is "Capuphalian," or a blend of Caputo's philosophy with that of Merold Westphal. Westphal is one of the most important founders of Continental philosophy of religion, but he is less Derridean than Caputo. Putt uses the theology of Paul Tillich to bring Westphal and Caputo together, offering a portrait of Caputo that is more poetic, and one of Westphal that is more rabbinic. Together, however, they constitute a rabbinal poetics of philosophy of religion, which allows Putt the option of not choosing between these two important philosophers. Westphal and Caputo themselves each offer a short response to Putt's chapter, as well, affirming and resisting Putt's characterization of them as mirror images of each other.

From Caputo and Westphal as American Continental philosophers of religion, we move to two European philosophers, Derrida and Kristeva, in Ed Mooney's chapter "On Faith, the Maternal, and Postmodernism." Just as Putt reads Caputo and Westphal via Tillich, Mooney coordinates Derrida and Kristeva with Kierkegaard, suggesting that the pseudonymous author of *Fear and*

Trembling, Johannes *de silentio,* gives birth in a way to both Kristeva and Derrida's religious reflections. Mooney traces Derrida's reflections on *Fear and Trembling* in *The Gift of Death,* but then supplements them with Kristeva's conception of the semiotic *chora* as a site of natality that gives birth to embodied human existence. Kierkegaard talks about childbirth and weaning at the beginning of *Fear and Trembling,* and it is this maternal register that Mooney emphasizes as a way to draw together Kristeva and Derrida as offspring of Kierkegaard and as potent resources for the future of Continental philosophy of religion.

In chapter 3, "The Persistence of the Trace," Steven Shakespeare begins with the biblical character of Abraham in his interrogation and critique of speculative realism, specifically focusing on Quentin Meillassoux's concept of the "arch-fossil." Speculative realism, associated with Ray Brassier, Graham Harman, Levi Bryant, and others, follows the critique of correlationism developed by Meillassoux in *After Finitude,* and claims that the arch-fossil is an example of an object that exists before or without any human consciousness to know it. Correlationism is the name for the opposition to idealism and neo-Kantianism in Continental philosophy, and the return to or rehabilitation of objects over against this circular subjectivism. Shakespeare shows how Meillassoux's critique of correlationism proceeds on the grounds of opposing the religious turn of Continental philosophy and deconstruction, but it issues in a strange divinology when Meillassoux speculates about the "inexistent god" who is not but could appear or occur at some point in the future. Shakespeare goes on to show how Derrida's philosophy is not neatly correlationist, in Meillassoux's terms, and he then goes on to take up other issues at stake in the opposition between deconstruction and speculative realism. He ends up, again, with Abraham, intimating a spectral messianicity that is speculative but not obviously realistic.

Leon Niemoczynski puts speculative realism to more productive use, showing how it is more compatible with Caputo's philosophy when read in terms of process theology. In chapter 5, "Speculating God: Speculating Realism and Quentin Meillassoux's Divine Inexistence," Niemoczynski argues that the ethical motivations of Caputo and Richard Kearney are also implicitly speculative or metaphysical in a positive sense, and there is room to compare their views with the speculations of Meillassoux. The God who does not currently exist but can conceivably come to be has resonances with Caputo's emphasis on the weakness and more recently insistence of God as well as Kearney's anatheism. It is a process relational ontology and theology, Niemoczynski claims, that allows us to perceive the resemblance between Meillassoux's speculative realism on the one hand, and Derrida and Kearney's ethical messianicity, on the other.

The last chapter in part I, by Katharine Sarah Moody, also situates itself in the space between speculative realism and deconstructive messianism. In chapter 6, "Between Deconstruction and Speculation," Moody compares and contrasts Caputo's philosophy with that of Slavoj Žižek by invoking but side-stepping Žižek's more well-known debate with Radical Orthodox theologian John Milbank. Although Žižek is not often considered a speculative realist, he is sometimes seen as a fellow traveler due to his criticisms of stereotypical postmodern deconstruction and his emphasis on political ontology. Here Moody suggests that St. Paul mediates a constructive encounter between Žižek's Christian atheism and Caputo's theology of the event. Caputo and Žižek converge on an a/theological materialism that is expressed in more popular form in the work of the iconoclastic theologian Peter Rollins, where the Church enacts a betrayal of itself as substantialized form in its "fidelity to the universal Christ event of unconditional justice, hospitality and love." This is a paradoxical relationship that places theology, in its messianic deconstructive materialism, in the service of liberation rather than conservation.

Liberation

Next to Caputo, Philip Goodchild has done more to define the field of Continental philosophy of religion than any other contemporary figure. He proved to be one of the first to have his finger on the pulse of the emerging field of Continental philosophy of religion by hosting an early conference under that moniker. In his introduction to the volume that was produced from that conference, Goodchild says that "philosophy of religion stands at the threshold of an extraordinary transformation and emancipation."[7] This bold pronouncement comes at the conclusion of his genealogy of the modern emergence of philosophy of religion. Like Caputo, Goodchild shares an orientation toward the future, defining Continental philosophy of religion by its liberation from its modern rationalist bearings. But while Continental philosophy of religion marks a break from the past, it also reawakens and transforms the original animating purposes of the modern philosophical reflections on, and eventual critiques of, religion. So in this case, in order to appreciate Goodchild's bold vision for the future, we must return to our own modern history wherein philosophy of religion was born.

The story of the modern Enlightenment elevation of introspection and reason over authority and tradition is well known. But Goodchild adds an important and often neglected piece to this history; namely, he situates the emergence of the modern philosophical critiques of religion within a matrix of theologico-political concerns. In other words, it was decidedly "not an abstract love of disembodied reason for the sake of its own purity" that motivated the rational exploration of religion and the modern emergence of philosophy of religion.[8] Take René Descartes, for instance, the father of modern philosophy and both the culprit and the caricature of the disembodied mind: his methodology of radical doubt is too often seen as being strictly an experiment of the mind, a mind-trick even, stripped of any theologico-political concerns. But we forget that this mind-trick was being played during a crisis of authority every bit as political as it was philosophical and/or theological. As the moral philosopher Jeffrey Stout has persuasively argued, Descartes's concerns were more of a pre-philosophical nature than they were philosophical per se. He was more concerned with the crisis of authority than he was with the problem of knowledge.[9]

What this means for Goodchild is that when contemporary philosophy of religion seeks to retain the early modern valorization of reason and rationality, it is a twisting of reason and rationality beyond, or over against, its original animating purposes. Put otherwise, reason stripped of its theologico-political context loses its claim on rationality. Or, as Goodchild explains, "Continental philosophy has transformed philosophical reflection through a critique of reason itself."[10] Beyond the modern Enlightenment critique of religion, this philosophical critique of reason is one of the primary contributions Continental philosophy has made to contemporary thought. The original context for the modern emergence of philosophy of religion was in a world of virulent religious division and open warfare, wherein the assertion of any authority heightened, more than resolved, conflict. By emerging in this modern context, philosophy of religion also helped to contribute to shaping modernity itself. By its "attempt to purify passions, counteract dominant interests, expose hypocrisy, or discover 'true religion' or 'true piety,'" modern philosophy of religion accomplishes a flight, or a self-distancing, from existing authorities and traditions.[11] In so doing, it was, in the words of Richard Rorty, "fighting (albeit discretely) to make the intellectual world safe for Copernicus and Galileo."[12] At the same time, of course, it replaced one form of authority and one set of traditions with another. Now autonomous reason reigned supreme.

What must be understood here is how the law of unintended consequences is in effect. It makes perfect sense that if a truly indubitable foundation for knowledge could be found, then the wars that are sparked over the conflict of authorities and traditions might be ameliorated. As superficial a reading of Descartes as it might be, there must be some end to the Protestant appeals to scripture and the Catholic appeals to the pope. And when Protestants battle fellow Protestants over conflicts of interpretation, to whom or what can they appeal? Philosophy of religion emerges as a grappling less for an independent arbiter than for a universally binding and self-authenticating means of arbitration.

The irony, of course, as Goodchild explains, is that while "contemporary philosophy of religion may carry forward the heritage of these eighteenth-century debates, it carries little of the theologico-political concerns."[13] As history teaches us, reason made autonomous takes on a life of its own. While it most certainly has been employed to mount a sustained attack on religiosity, more recently, with the demise of logical positivism, it has carved out a safe—we may even say sacred—space for religious ideas by its insistence that philosophy must shield itself from any and all presuppositions, even those regarding religious truths. In other words, that religion might operate according to its own logic, its own rationality, and its own coherence, is also a product of the modern reign of secular reason. The problem, then, as Goodchild writes, is that contemporary philosophy of religion "is often used as an attempt to justify religious beliefs that have their origin in the very conceptions of authority and revelation that early modern philosophers were attempting to exclude from reason."[14] This historical irony may have freed religion, or at least relegitimated it (to the extent that religious ideas and practices are in need or want of philosophical legitimation). But what we see here is another way of getting at the problem of fideism that was at least partly the source of Caputo's turn from Kant to Hegel. If philosophy of religion is merely providing cover for faith, then has it lost its way? Does it even have, or deserve, a future?

It is with this question in mind that we may return to Goodchild's pronouncement that "philosophy of religion stands at the threshold of an extraordinary transformation and emancipation." With this statement, Goodchild was laying out an agenda for a specifically *Continental* philosophy of religion. The emancipation is a liberation from philosophy of religion's analytic restraints. Religious truth must not be allowed to be reduced to that of just another logical problem to be solved. This objectification of religious life makes the mistake of reducing religion to propositional form. But further, this liberation is a transformation by being resituated into a theologico-political matrix. Continental philosophy of religion distinguishes itself from what otherwise passes for philosophy of religion by adding a further dimension to reason—reason must be thought together with, and in the context of, "its social preconditions, its psychological motivations, its gendered and embodied locations, its strategies of domination and violence, its passions, its symbolic structures, its fundamental presuppositions, its ethical responsibilities, its incompletions, its aspirations, its creative becomings, and its religious modes."[15]

It is with this transformation and emancipation in mind that Goodchild's turning from a metadiscourse about philosophy of religion to the doing of a new and different kind of philosophy of religion illustrates its timely and *critical* task. "Philosophy of religion must remain a critical discourse," Goodchild insists.[16] And like Caputo, this turning has involved a shift within his own thinking from a philosophy to a certain kind of theology, but all the more, a *critical* theology that takes its lead not from traditional faith communities and forms of theological thought, but from the contemporary world as presently lived. His is an immanent critical theology that pursues the thought of how money has come to function as God in today's world. And thus, it is by Goodhild's critical inquiry about, and intervention into, what he calls the "theology of money" that he has cemented his influence and authority as one we must hear from when considering the future of Continental philosophy of religion.

His first foray into this subject was his 2002 book, *Capitalism and Religion: The Price of Piety*, a book that was at once a genealogy of modern philosophy, a social and ethical analysis of the nihilism of contemporary society, and a survey and immanent critique of the reigning orthodoxies in economic theory and policy. Goodchild writes in the voice of a prophet invoking an alternative piety, shattering the illusions of the infinite expansion of economic globalization and exposing how the failure of capitalism is revealed by the almost constant state of crisis that is as much ecological as it is existential, a crisis of capitalism that has both philosophical and theological significance. Even more, any philosophy or theology that does not recognize money as the value that determines all value is, in a manner of speaking, an exercise in futility, a sticking of one's head in the sand.

And so, *Capitalism and Religion* bequeathed *A Theology of Money*.[17] Its argument is that money is predicated on faith, and that as an elaborate global system, it binds us all in an inescapable web of debt and obligation functioning as a system of social control that carries with it its own morality, its own piety, and that thus is ripe for its own theological analysis and critique. In a world still reeling from the global economic collapse of 2008, where the incessant desire for cheap labor is remaking the world's demographics, where the need for cheap energy is remapping geopolitics, and wherein almost everything, from clean air and clean water to public airwaves and education, has been already successfully commodified, there is no one better equipped to speak to us about the future of Continental philosophy of religion than he. It is with this context in mind that his contribution to this volume must be understood.

"The Future of Liberation," he tells us in chapter 7, requires a way of thinking otherwise, a new and different practice of philosophy that reclaims philosophy as a spiritual exercise. This is a breaking down of the artificial walls between philosophy and theology, between the secular and the religious, and as Goodchild first pronounced to us over a decade ago, between an ahistorical conception and employment of reason within and on behalf of philosophy of religion and one rooted in its theologico-political matrix. Goodchild's exercise in thinking as a form of spirituality and as a possible mode of liberation sets the context for the rest of the contributions in part II.

In chapter 8, "Monetized Philosophy and Theological Money," Devin Singh follows Goodchild's lead, developing some theo-political reflections on money and how it shapes our past, our present, and our notions about the future. He suggests, however, that Goodchild is a little too quick to oppose Christ's theology to money, and he also supplements Giorgio Agamben's work on *oikonomia* in *The Kingdom and the Glory* with some analysis of money's role in the emergence of Christological discourse. Money is associated with equivalence, exchange, and sovereignty, and Singh argues that we need to attend more closely to these entanglements to have any hope of achieving liberation.

In chapter 9, "Between Justice and My Mother," Gavin Hyman provides different coordinates to think about liberation by developing a tension between Slavoj Žižek and Emmanuel Levinas. By opening with Albert Camus's decision to preference his mother over an abstract justice in his Nobel Prize speech, Hyman affirms a kind of particularity of the face of the Other in Levinas's thought, and contrasts it with the universality of justice in Žižek's philosophy. If Levinas decides on the priority of ethics (the particular relation to an other) over politics (the third person who instantiates justice), then Žižek champions the political over ethical in his "plea for ethical violence." Hyman wants to resist the premature resolution of the tension between universal political justice and the specific ethical call of an other (which in its extreme case is my mother). Liberation involves the refusal to make a forced choice.

Along with Žižek and Alain Badiou, Jacques Rancière has emerged as an important contemporary political philosopher. Joseph Ballan offers a more methodological liberation of philosophy of religion from the constraints of disciplinarity as well as the seductions of interdisciplinarity. In chapter 10, "Verbis Indisciplinatus," he appeals to Rancière's idea of "indisciplinarity" as a way to be more sensitive of the role of ideology in the construction of our discourses, and as a tool to break them open in the name of a radical equality. According to Ballan, indisciplinarity is relevant for the study of religion, because it "is about inventing new ways of presenting and re-presenting, which is to say narrating, knowledge about religion that dissent from the established ways of dividing up kinds of human activities and modes of existence in the same strokes by which kinds of knowledge are divided and kept safe from contaminating each other."

For Christina Gschwandtner, liberation is less about ideology critique and more about an everyday practice of liturgy. In chapter 11, "Overwhelming Abundance and Everyday Liturgical Practices," she sketches a nuanced phenomenology of liturgy, which is not the merely purview of a particular religious practice, but a liturgy of everyday life. Resisting the extreme formulations of religious phenomenologists such as Jean-Luc Marion and Michel Henry, and to a lesser extent Ricoeur and Caputo, Gschwandtner argues for a less excessive phenomenology of religious experience. This phenomenology is based on a notion of liturgy, which is experiential, cyclical, and communal, and requires hermeneutical discernment. Gschwandtner gives a phenomenological reading of an Eastern Orthodox service of Theophany, suggesting that liberation need not be quite so excessive, in theological or political terms.

The last chapter in this section is by Noëlle Vahanian, and in "Countercurrents" she argues that philosophy is exhausted, and there is no future for philosophy of religion, unless thinking is inherently theological. This theological thinking is not what ordinarily passes for theology, but a radical thinking to-the-limit that takes place immanently within finite beings. She invokes Rousseau,

Feuerbach, Nietzsche, and Freud as forerunners of this theological countercurrent. This form of theological thinking may be more excessive in Gschwandtner's terms, but for Vahanian only a genuinely radical theological thinking can liberate Continental philosophy of religion.

Plasticity

The contemporary French philosopher Catherine Malabou, author of chapter 13, heads the third and final section of this book. In his book entitled *On Futurity,* Jean-Paul Martinon identifies Catherine Malabou (along with Jean-Luc Nancy) as one of "the two central figures of French philosophy in the wake of Derrida."[18] The concept of plasticity is her "original, signature idea."[19] Unlike Caputo and Goodchild, she can make no claims on Continental philosophy of religion. She has never used this terminology to describe her own work, nor has she been invested in defining its meaning, whether in the past or for the future. Nevertheless, in many important respects, by her neurological concept of plasticity she has changed the future of Continental philosophy of religion. Plasticity not only is one instantiation of the so-called new materialism in religion and philosophy that enacts the serious engagement between philosophy and the hard sciences so desperately needed, but also is a new and different conception of time that opposes messianicity, and thus suggests a new and different future of and for Derrida and deconstruction—and thus, of Continental philosophy of religion.

The title for her contribution to this volume is "The Future of Derrida," a theme she acknowledges was given to her by Caputo. But her "Derridean" future is totally at odds with Caputo's. We must stress this point of difference in order to accentuate the diversity and contestation that exists within Continental philosophy of religion. And to repeat, it is not simply that the future direction of Continental philosophy of religion is open and contested, but actually how Continental philosophy of religion itself conceives of the future is in question. That is to say, there are different and overlapping futures that actually puncture time and temporality as once conceived. By offering us with yet a third conception of the future of and for Continental philosophy of religion, Malabou enacts a doubling and tripling of time that forces us to rethink the very concept of temporality itself.

The problem with starting the discussion of Malabou with Derrida, however, is that it might mislead the reader about the critical distance that Malabou takes from Derrida, specifically on the concept of time and on the question of the future. In his book-length study of Malabou, Nancy, and Derrida, a study that focuses precisely on the question of the future, Martinon correctly places Malabou alongside Nancy and Derrida as three figures who have employed and expanded the French notion of *l'avenir* in order to displace and disrupt the commonplace presumed linearity of space and time. The conclusion he then draws from this variety is that what Malabou, Nancy, and Derrida share in common is a persistent, though varied, "endeavor to evade the principle of figuration," or that "it is impossible to figure (the) à-venir."[20]

Yet, when Martinon explores the shared philosophical heritage of Malabou, Nancy, and Derrida, he includes the figures of Husserl, Heidegger, and Benjamin, but excludes Hegel. Indeed, the only mention of Hegel is how his philosophy of history is the obvious case of the traditional or vulgar understanding of one-dimensional and unidirectional time that Malabou, Nancy, and Derrida effectively deconstruct each in his or her own way. The result of this exclusion of Hegel is that Martinon comes to the conclusion that "none of the three philosophers explored in this book—Jacques Derrida, Jean-Luc Nancy and Catherine Malabou—attempts to propose *another* way of *thinking* the future. . . . Their works focus instead, each in different ways, on deploying a number of strategies of *displacement* of traditional views of the future."[21]

Based on Malabou's contribution to this present volume, it is our contention that Martinon misses the distinctive contribution that Malabou makes when it comes to thinking the future differently. First of all, Malabou makes it clear that she is not satisfied merely with the various strategies of displacement of the traditional views of time. On the contrary, she is offering up an entirely different conception of the future that promises to restore time to philosophy after its displacement by Heidegger and its radical disruption by Derrida. Second, this restoration of time to philosophy provides a decidedly nonmessianic conception of the future. What is more, this is not just an alternative conception of the future, but an overt rejection of the messianic in lieu of an alternative founding notion of the epigenesis of reason. In light of this, it is inaccurate to say that Malabou is in basic agreement with the conclusion that "it is impossible to figure (the) à-venir." Instead, an epigenesis of reason testifies to reason's self-formative power, its power to fashion its own possibility. We are dealing not with the unknown and unknowable, but with that which is malleable and transformable. It is not only possible to figure the à-venir, but it is always already figured and being refigured. In this way, Malabou's rendering of time is like the double meaning she ascribes to plasticity—plasticity is that which is capable of receiving and giving form.

This is the critical break that Malabou makes with Derrida, a break that reverses time's withdrawal. If Heidegger declares, "Time *is* not," and Derrida declares that the gift is more originary than time, Malabou provides a new and different perspective, one we might call the materialization of time by virtue of her neurological concept of plasticity. By this materialization of time, she makes it possible to (re)figure the future, with the added irony of providing a renewed future to deconstruction. Once time is restored to philosophy, and the future is no longer conceived as the vast unknown or the unthinkable, then nothing is undeconstructible. This brings us to our third and final point: not only does Malabou promise to restore time to philosophy by providing a nonmessianic conception of the future, but she also provides a new and different future for Continental philosophy of religion. Hers is an immanent, secular, and explosive philosophy of religion wherein nothing is sacred and everything is deconstructible.

She achieves this by her employment of Kant, an employment that differs significantly from that of Caputo. Recall that Caputo's early phenomenological reading of Derrida's religion without religion relied on the basic Kantian formulation of the limitation of reason in order to make room for faith. However, after Caputo's self-avowed theological turn and as a consequence of the gathering concerns over fideism, he has rejected Kant in favor of Hegel. Malabou, by contrast, does not pit Kant in opposition to Hegel, but instead, reads Kant by way of Hegel. Whereas Hegel is central to Malabou's discovery and explication of the concept of plasticity, it is through Kant's *Critique of Pure Reason* that she comes to the expression of the "Epigenesis of Reason," a fortuitous expression that resonates with her already existing interest in epigenetics. The significance of this different Kant is that it suggests a different philosophy of religion than that which has prevailed in Continental philosophy of religion. Faith is not presented as outside the bounds of reason, as that which reason cannot think, or as reason's other. This is not a blind faith, in other words. "An epigenesis of reason on the contrary," as Malabou insists, "supposes that there cannot be any other origin than reason." This is what Malabou calls "the plasticity of the transcendental," wherein "time would not be the opening of a messianic horizon but the immanent development of the transcendental."

This epigenesis of reason also conforms to a plastic epigenetics, and suggests a nonreductive biological materialism that is resonant with but also importantly different from contemporary Speculative Realism. When there is no outside or no elsewhere, when nothing is sacred and everything is deconstructible, the plastic future may be (re)figured as part of time's own horizon just as faith is fashioned as the very own possibility of reason or even *bios* itself. This is not only a new space for deconstruction, but a new and different future for Continental philosophy of religion.

The remainder of the contributions from part III share this basic orientation with Malabou, either by engaging her work explicitly, or more generally, modeling a nonreductive engagement between Continental philosophy and science that charts a new materialism for Continental philosophy of religion. This section opens Continental philosophy up to non-Christian or Jewish religious traditions, as well as post-humanist possibilities. In chapter 14, "On Reading—Catherine Malabou," Randall Johnson offers a more discursive and interpretive piece that assists readers in opening up Malabou's own oeuvre. Johnson shows us that reading possesses its own plasticity and its own materiality. He references the significance of motor neurons in primates, suggesting that our brain reminds us how to think and how to read. Following Malabou's shift from Hegel to neuroplasticity, Johnson emphasizes that understanding how our brains work gives us vital insight into belief, how we believe. Malabou does not simply provide methodological perspectives on contemporary science; she shows us "how to make use of the findings of science for thinking" and living. Here religion would implicitly be a praxis of care for *how to live*.

From a specific focus on Malabou, we open up to a broader materialist perspective on religion as such in Jeffrey W. Robbins's essay. Chapter 15, "Necessity as Virtue: On Religious Materialism from Feuerbach to Žižek" allows for a more plastic, nonreductive, but still materialist reading of religion. Robbins accepts the classical materialist critique of religion, but claims that it does not go far enough. We need a materialist critique of materialism, and we need to understand materiality itself more in terms of dynamic plasticity and less as a stable reductive entity composed of bits of matter. Robbins focuses on how Žižek's religious materialism represents a shift beyond conventional materialism, while still being profoundly materialist.

A religious materialism produces or recognizes new forms of subjectivity. In chapter 16, "Plasticity in the Contemporary Islamic Subject," John Thibdeau reads Malabou's philosophy together with Saba Mahmood's study on Egyptian women in *The Politics of Piety* to show how their subjectivity is plastic. This means that subjectivity does not take the form of a simple either/or: either a free autonomous subject that is modeled on Western liberalism, or a subject completely determined by biology, psychology, or culture. We need more careful, nuanced, and engaged studies of non-Christian religions in Continental philosophy of religion, and Malabou's work helps conceptualize how that might be done, as Thibdeau adroitly carries it out.

Another non-Christian religious tradition considered in chapter 17 is Hinduism, and Lenart Škof brings together the Vedic tradition and the philosophy of Luce Irigaray, showing how they intersect in part via Schelling. In "From Cosmology to the First Ethical Gesture," Škof offers a mediation about cosmology and breath that is both materialist and spiritual. A new philosophy of spirit emerges vitally out of breath, and although this is not developed in terms of plasticity, and proceeds via Schelling rather than Hegel, it opens up our vision of what Continental philosophy is and can be.

From cosmology and breathing we turn to the animal, and animality. As is well known, in his late work, Derrida wrestled with the question of the animal, and much of post-humanism confronts and contests the boundaries between humans, machines, and animals. In chapter 18, "Prolegomenon to Thinking the Reject for the Future of Continental Philosophy of Religion," Irving Goh offers a sustained reflection on the concept of the reject. In this essay, Goh engages in a critique of Badiou's resurrection of the Pauline subject and shows how in a profoundly postsecular way the reject *replaces* the subject. Goh draws on Deleuze and Bataille and gives a provocative reading of Balaam's donkey in Numbers 22. He concludes by suggesting that "perhaps the *reject* or *auto-reject* that one should follow is the animal."

The final chapter concerns energy, and entropy. In chapter 19, Clayton Crockett offers a reformulation of energy based on contemporary non-equilibrium thermodynamics, which he reads in relation to Deleuze's *Difference and Repetition*. Entropy is not just the loss of order, but more importantly the reduction of gradients, which actually produces order in specific situations. He suggests that contemporary Speculative Realism is helpful in its attention to the physical sciences, but it is not nuanced enough in its desperate attempt to eliminate subjectivism. Being is energy transformation, and this is a better perspective than linguistic constructivism or an object-oriented ontology. Finally, energy avoids the simple duality of material versus spiritual; it is a material process that is also importantly spiritual, and here the Chinese conception of *qi* as vital energy is an important resource. The essays in this section pursue questions of materiality in plastic and spiritual ways that open Continental philosophy of religion up to new and different possible futures.

Notes

1. John D. Caputo, *The Prayers and Tears of Jacques Derrida: Religion without Religion* (Bloomington: Indiana University Press, 1997), 117–118.
2. Jacques Derrida, "Faith and Knowledge," in *Religion,* ed. Jacques Derrida and Gianni Vattimo (Stanford, Calif.: Stanford University Press, 1998), 17.
3. John D. Caputo, *On Religion* (New York: Routledge, 2001), 9.
4. See Dominique Janicaud, "The Theological Turn of French Phenomenology," in *Phenomenology and the "Theological Turn": The French Debate,* ed. Dominique Janicaud, et al. (New York: Fordham University Press, 2000).
5. See Anthony Paul Smith and Daniel Whistler, "What Is Continental Philosophy of Religion Now?" in *After the Postsecular and the Postmodern: New Essays in Continental Philosophy of Religion,* ed. Anthony Paul Smith and Daniel Whistler (Cambridge: Cambridge Scholars Publishing, 2010), 2.
6. Caputo, *The Prayers and Tears of Jacques Derrida*, 312, 313.
7. Philip Goodchild, "Continental Philosophy of Religion: An Introduction," in *Rethinking Philosophy of Religion: Approaches from Continental Philosophy,* ed. Philip Goodchild (New York: Fordham University Press, 2002), 38.
8. Ibid., 6.
9. Jeffrey Stout, *The Flight from Authority: Religion, Morality, and the Quest for Autonomy* (Notre Dame: University of Notre Dame Press, 1981), 62.
10. Goodchild, "Continental Philosophy of Religion," 2.
11. Ibid., 7–8.
12. Richard Rorty, *Philosophy and the Mirror of Nature* (Princeton, N.J.: Princeton University Press, 1979), 131.
13. Goodchild, "Continental Philosophy of Religion," 7.
14. Ibid., 8.

15. Ibid., 38.
16. Ibid.
17. Philip Goodchild, *Theology of Money* (Durham, N.C.: Duke University Press, 2009).
18. Jean-Paul Martinon, *On Futurity: Malabou, Nancy and Derrida* (New York: Palgrave Macmillan, 2007), 26.
19. See Clayton Crockett, "Foreword," in Catherine Malabou, *Plasticity at the Dusk of Writing: Dialectic, Destruction, Deconstruction* (New York: Columbia University Press, 2010), xi.
20. Ibid., 12.
21. Martinon, *On Futurity*, 18.

Part I
The Messianic

1 Is Continental Philosophy of Religion Dead?

John D. Caputo

JACQUES DERRIDA IS dead. Now they are all dead—all the *soixant-huitaires*.[1] So, is it over? Is Continental philosophy—and by extension, Continental philosophy of religion—as we know it dead? For a younger generation of philosophers, the so-called theological turn is the last straw. If the religious turn is where Continental philosophy ends up, supplying a final place for religion to hide before the "singularity" arrives,[2] then Continental philosophy is dead. If it is not, the first order of business is to kill it off. What good is Nietzsche's death of God, if we still have to deal with religion? This critique goes well beyond the familiar attack on Continental philosophy by analytic philosophy. It seeks to replace both "unconcealment" and "language games" with a more ruthless realism, a more materialist materialism, a more uncompromising objectivism, aiming to put an end to Continental philosophy as we know it. When I say "as we know it," I mean the program announced by Kant when he says "I have found it necessary to deny knowledge in order to make room for faith." That is what Quentin Meillassoux, who is spearheading this attack, calls "fideism," delimiting the reach of the mathematical sciences in order to leave the door open for religious faith,[3] resulting in Continentalists who wear thick glasses and find their way with a stick, moving about in the shadows where religion carries out its dark business.

I think there is a legitimate complaint here. The Kantian path in postmodernism is an abridgement that reduces it to apologetics. That is why I pursue a Hegelian route, even as I criticize the lingering alliance of Hegel with classical theology.[4] What is called the death of God by Hegel, unnerving though it be to classical theology, is really a moment in the infinite life of God. God's plasticity, *pace* Malabou, cannot possibly include explosion, annihilation, or extinction. But if the new cosmology proposes the death of the universe in total entropic dissipation, and if God's life is inscribed in space and time, as Hegel insisted, then God's death, too, is final. The entire history of the universe *is* an explosion (the Big Bang) of which we are the debris. Nonetheless, I think the new critics do not see what they have stumbled upon. They are like someone who finds a Picasso in the attic but does not know anything about painting. Their nihilism is not without value, and it is not for nothing—but they know nothing about that. They identify our being-nothing, our cosmic precariousness, but they are know-nothings about the value of nothing, about what I call here the grace of nihilism or the nihilism of grace. My hypothesis then is this: there is a religion without religion in Continental philosophy that is articulated in a radical theology of grace, of the grace of chance and the chance of grace, which I will call being-for-nothing. The new critics are a nail in the coffin of Continental philosophy of religion in the Kantian mode, but not in its more radical Hegelian mode.

Physics as Metaphysics and the New Wonder

These new critics cannot be answered in the standard way, by cupping our ears and shouting "scientism," for two reasons. First, physics is the new metaphysics. It is the study of the universe as if there were no living things.[5] The difference between the sun, the figure of the good in Plato's allegory, and the flittering shadows on the wall is only a matter of velocity—its transience is so drawn out that we do not notice that it too is flaring up and dying off. Physics is the study of a real without a good, a real we have no reason to presume has any care for us, and all the metaphysics we are likely to get. Continental philosophy has made a profitable living out of the critique of metaphysics, but if metaphysics means an account of things beyond *physis* ("life," "birth"), a world without life, before or after life, then physics is more and more doing the heaving lifting in what was called metaphysics in the past, and metaphysics never gets any further than physics. When contemporary theoretical physicists speculate that at bottom what we call the physical universe is composed of vibrating filaments called superstrings, I very much doubt that the traditional metaphysicians, unequipped with either mathematics or experimental evidence, have anything to add. The cosmic schema to which contemporary physics at present subscribes is not far from the youthful Nietzsche's fable about a distant corner of the universe in which proud little animals invented words like "truth."[6] I will call the fantastic voyage from the Big Bang to entropic dissipation the "basic schema," the largest overarching context, the ultimate setting or, to employ an expression Laruelle picked up from Marx and Engels, the context "in the last determination" of human life. Not that it really *is* the last, but that it is the latest. The most likely hypothesis, according to physicists today, is that the universe is headed for total destruction, when a "trillion trillion trillion years from now," as Brassier says, the "implacable gravitational expansion" will have pushed the universe "into an eternal and unfathomable blackness."[7] The lights will have gone out in Heidegger's *Welt* even as Wittgenstein's language games will prove to have been played with dead languages, resulting in a wordless, worldless void, eerier than the one with which Genesis began.

Second, physics is the new wonder. Contemporary cosmology is stealing philosophy's wonder. It has taken possession of the very ground in which philosophy is supposed to plant its roots—wonder and the imagination. We do not need to be swept up in the Tao[8] or the "wow" of physics to concede that contemporary physicists are out-imagining, out-wondering, out-wowing the philosophers. Not only do physicists know more mathematics than the philosophers, but they also have more imagination and produce more stunning views of reality. Our desire for *the impossible* (whose aporetic structure is Derrida's central intuition) is more and more satisfied by the counterintuitive advances made by the special and general theory of relativity and quantum theory. Michio Kaku's *Physics of the Impossible* is well named.[9] The events of quantum mechanics are "absurd," says Richard Feynman, and the strange results of speculative cosmology today quite outstrip the extraordinary events recounted in the Scriptures, so that what is impossible for human beings is possible in the quantum world. The thirst for an "other world"—of which the literary-imaginative structures of heaven "above" and hell "below" are almost irresistible figures—is alive and well. This thirst, however, is being quenched today by other means. The Platonic "super-sensible," the theological "super-natural," and the mystical "super-essential" are giving way to super-strings. Heaven is giving way to the heavens, to the extraterrestrial, to the galaxies far, far away. The mythic structure of two-worlds metaphysics and its Platonic metaphorics is becoming increasingly incredible with each passing revolution of the earth around the sun.

Coping with Correlation

When it comes to natural science, Continental philosophy has spent most of its energies in a Kantian mode of critically delimiting science—trying to contain it, not to study it, and trying to deny knowledge (science) in order to make room for phenomenology or cultural analysis (or whatever we are doing that year). Consequently, it is badly positioned to deal with the current criticism that the "outbreak" of religion has brought to a head. I emphasize that I am *not* describing the new physics in terms of scientific "reductionism." Science is not reductionism but an explosion of wonder and imagination, of the possibility of the impossible. I am not trying to reduce theology to science or science to theology. I am not trying to *reduce* anything but to *adduce* the work of imagination in the collaboration between the theological and the scientific. I want to do so by examining what has sparked the sell-off in Continental philosophy, that is, "correlation" and "fideism."

Suppose that physics is metaphysics in the sense of dealing with the real, where the real is taken to mean what is there as if we were not there—as if we had never been born or had all perished in some cosmic catastrophe. Even so, when we are there, when we are real, the real has, for precisely that time, acquired another stratum of reality with a texture and complexity all its own that merits and requires our attention. That may seem too obvious for words, but it bears repeating in view of Meillassoux's criticism of "correlation," a view so "fundamentalist" about objectivism as to accuse the likes of Foucault and Derrida of creationism![10] If the speculation about superstrings is experimentally confirmed, that will be the much sought-after "theory of everything" (TOE), uniting relativity and quantum theory. But physics will remain in an important way "incomplete," and we must be careful about how we understand its incompleteness and not fall into the egregious mistake made by Meillassoux. Physics is related to the study of life at large and of human life in particular, *not* as "being" is related to "appearance" or as the "thing in itself" is related to some supposedly subjectivist "correlation," but as the physical basis of things is related to everything that is built upon that basis, as the founding stratum is related to the strata that are founded upon it. Physics provides the basic schema of what everything is *at bottom*, but not of every relationship found within the real. It is the theory of everything material but not of everything that matters. Physics may well seek the theory of "everything" but not of everything about which we need a theory. Granted, physics governs everything, but it does not give an account of every way in which things can be approached. The basic reason the roof leaks when it rains ultimately goes back to string theory. But by the time you got from string theory back to the roof, the house would be soaked. Life and human life are no less real than the subject matter of physics. Even if human and animal bodies are short-timers in the cosmic scheme of things, they are fascinating moments in which the universe shows what it is made of, what we are made of. I advocate not a reductionistic materialism but an open-ended materialism, just as Žižek thinks that matter is all, but the all is a non-all, and as Malabou describes a "reasonable materialism" that does not turn life into a cybernetic or neurological program.[11] Derrida, Žižek, Malabou, and I are all "materialists" in the sense that we do not think there are two worlds, one in space and time, the other transcending space and time.[12] That is why I would supplement physics with a "poetics," while Malabou emphasizes transformational "plastics," and Žižek introduces "parallax shifts."

The real is the "absolute" in the sense of the world that is there whether we mind it or not, but it is not a world without minds. Physics opens its doors for business by means of a decontextualization (removing us from the picture), but decontextualization is followed by recontextualization. The "absolute" is drawn into a "relation," a perplexing situation that is well described (as the realists to their credit recognize) by Levinas (of all people) when he speaks of a relation whose terms are continually absolving themselves from the relation, a conundrum familiar to any Jewish theologian—ever since Yahweh told Moses to mind his own business (Ex 3:14). Derrida called it a relation without relation, which we might extend to a "correlation" without correlation. "Correlation" does not, *pace* Meillassoux, "reduce" the universe to the dimensions of our "world" or dissolve its autonomy. On the contrary, the ever-expanding universe becomes the ever-widening "world" of which we are an irreducible, if increasingly minuscule, part, a point first noticed by Pascal. Correlation means not that the universe belongs to us but that we belong to it. Correlation does not "reduce" the world to us, but releases us from our contraction to ourselves, and the more we learn about the universe, the less contracted we are. A medieval realist like Aquinas said that a knowing being differs from a non-knowing being because the latter is contracted to itself and the former is expanded into and "becomes all things" (an Aristotelianism that Meillassoux reads backwards, as if Aristotle has said all things become us). I distinguish "cosmos" or "universe" from "world" or "life-world," that is, the place where we live. The universe is the ultimate or widest sphere of decontextualization, while the world is the widest context. The universe is the determination in the last instance in its order, just as the world is the determination in the last instance in *its* order, and these two orders are not adversaries but correlates. I think that Hegel saw this but, as the young Hegelians complained, in an upside-down way.

The problem of epistemological "correspondence" cannot in principle arise in any adequate account of correlation, because "we" are the very *issue* of the correlation. As Heidegger (no "worldless subject") and Wittgenstein (no "private language") well realized in strictly philosophical terms, we do not have to "build a bridge" to the world. In fact, we cannot. If the bridge were not already there, we would never be able to build it because we would not even exist. We do not construct a correlation, because the correlation constructs us. We are plants, sprouts shooting up from the local conditions in which we have been produced, in just the way that vegetation started to shoot up when the ozone layer grew thick enough to shield the earth from the ultraviolet rays of the sun, and in just the way that that the color spectrum available to our vision has been fixed by the astronomical composition of our sun, which has set the terms of light sensitivity that we call "sight." Anyone who asks whether or why what is going on "in us" correlates with what is going on "out there" is asking the wrong question. We *are* out there, and we *are* the correlation. "*Immer schon*" as Heidegger liked to say. Accordingly, physics needs to be supplemented by biology, and biology by the study of *anthropos*, not in cleanly separated strata, but in a continuum of complexity that allows for gaps when thresholds are surpassed, following along the lines described by Žižek's notion of parallax gaps. "Matter" is all, but this all is a "non-all," admitting of countless complexifications all the way from supposedly "inert" bodies—an intolerable notion if mass and energy are simply different expressions of the same thing—to human-animal bodies, in which the "energy" of so-called inert bodies is "intensified," as Deleuze would put it.

What we call in English the "humanities" belongs to the study of the real, of human reality, and its subject matter is as real as real can be. The humanities cultivate the disciplinary eyes and ears to follow the tracks of human life's finer, more complex correlations, these more deeply contextualized strata of reality, in their finer lacings and interlacings—as when Husserl spoke of a need for a vocabulary describing things that are "notched, scalloped, and lens-shaped."[13] The authentic notion of "correlation" lies in the relations among the anthropological, the biological, and the physical strata, requiring us to understand the finer and nonformal features of the relationships that emerge among human beings and between human beings and the nonhuman universe that precedes and engenders them and will survive their demise. That is why we require the collaboration of neuroscience and Continental philosophy of the sort we see in Catherine Malabou.

Derrida's work is crucially situated *between* physics and *anthropos*, between nature and culture. The most fundamental point made by Derrida—superficially the most "literary" of the Continentalists—is that life is structurally inhabited by death, not only by being shot through by an inescapable mortality, but by being already marked and inscribed by the neutral, automatic, and technical structure of *différance*. Derrida's earliest philosophical argument was made against Husserl's phenomenology of the *Lebenswelt*, where he insisted precisely upon the impersonal-anonymous structures of "spacing" that inhabit the life of living speech. *Of Grammatology* is a deconstruction of the nature/culture divide in Rousseau and his modern anthropological followers where *différance* is shown to be the "dead" differential technology in living speech. If the very *physis* of the human *zoon* is *logos*, and if *logos* presupposes *différance*, and if *différance* is *techne*, then human "nature" is from the inside out always already technological. He adduced a "materialist" point in Husserl against Husserl, when Husserl made the "Origin of Geometry" dependent upon the technology of writing.[14] We have never been purely human; there has never been any pure human life. The "principle" of life in living things is not the *anima*, the soul, but death, that is, a structure of anonymity. There is nothing about *différance* that restricts it to the human. Indeed, as a structure of spacing and timing, *différance* also provides a way of thinking about the nonhuman "merely" physical universe. The "correlation," then, is the chiasmic intertwining of the human and the nonhuman.

From Fideism to Faith

I agree with Meillassoux's critique of Kant, and I count myself among those who practice a "philosophy of religion" that descends from Hegel (through Tillich), not from Kant (through Barth).[15] Kant was engaged in damage control, a retrenchment that staves off knowledge in order to keep ethics safe (ethics being as much religion as Kant could abide). Kant opens the door to a half-hearted epistemological postmodernism, an "apologetic" use of Continental philosophy,[16] keeping the powders of faith dry as the waters of modernist critique rise. Kantian postmodernism is a skepticism that provides a cover for fideism,[17] illustrated in the saying of Kierkegaard's Johannes Climacus, who claims that just because the world is not a system for us does not mean it is not a system for God.

I prefer not to take this Kantian/Kierkegaardian approach to keeping faith safe but, on the contrary, to approach faith by exposing it in all its insecurity and vulnerability. Indeed, I prefer to go back to Hegel's critique of the rationalists,[18] who debated about the existence of God and the immortality of the soul while maintaining that the juicier theological doctrines, like the Trinity and the Incarnation, are matters of faith and revealed theology. For Hegel, all the life of religion lies in the so-called contents of revelation. Philosophy is above all nourished by a reflection upon the meaning of the Trinity and the Incarnation, which are the real or absolute truth in the form of a *Vorstellung* of the truth, a truth whose head could be cleared only by the philosophical Concept (*Begriff*). But I am a Hegelian without the Concept, who thinks we need to take religion lock, stock, and barrel in all its theological richness, but without the guidance of a Concept capable of decoding *Vorstellungen* into the absolute truth. What I call "radical" hermeneutics means that the *Vorstellung* goes all the way down. Religion, in my view, *is* a *Vorstellung*, a work of imagination,[19] not of the Concept no more than of a supernatural being in the sky but of the "event." Religion gives narrational form and flesh to underlying events—like the promise, forgiveness, hospitality, justice, hope, expectation—and to faith. I treat religious beliefs and practices as a theopoetics, a poetics of the *theos*, or the *theios*, a way of describing what is going on in our lives under the name of "God," the "gods" and/or the "divine." The several "religions" are for me so many ways to poetize the world, similar to the way Merleau-Ponty said that the several languages are so many ways to "sing the world." As a result, it makes no more sense to ask what is the true religion than to ask what the true language is. What Francois Laruelle calls non-theology, *using* theology to give it a human meaning, is analogous to what I am calling "theopoetics."[20] The landscape of human experience is for Laruelle a plane of immanence, against the dualism of the Gnostic world that he is trying to "reinvent," to put it in Derridean terms. His use of the categories of "heresy" and "Christ," his attempt to find their human meaning, is, if punishingly opaque, I think highly instructive and belongs to the structure of what I would call a "radical" theology.

So I rise to the defense of faith, but not of fideism. Fideism is a negative and apologetic strategy, a way of saying "you cannot prove me wrong so I am free to believe _____," whereas faith is an affirmation. Faith, *foi*, is not a confessional belief (*croyance*), not a creedal assertion, and has nothing to do with having faith in a world behind the scenes. I confess a circumfessional and primal faith in what I call the event. The philosophy of religion is an explication of the event, a radical theology (and a form of "radical hermeneutics"), a theology of the event, above all of the *theos,* of the name of God, while the various confessional and historical religious traditions are so many *Vorstellungen* of events.

A Nihilism of Grace

Now let us turn to the cold, disenchanted, demythologized, disappointed, scientific, realistic, rationalistic, materialistic brio of Brassier's *Nihil Unbound* in all its apocalyptic fury. Let us unbind nihilism and let it all hang out. Let us expose ourselves to the terrible trauma of the real, our heads bloodied but unbowed by this degree zero of being-nothing, which boils away both substance and subject, dissipating everything fideistic and correlational. Let us leave behind the luxurious plenitude and lush planes of the *Lebenswelt* for the thermal equilibrium of unbound entropy, where being-in-itself is nothing-for-us, nothing to us and we nothing to it. What is being degree zero to me or I to it that I should weep for being-nothing?

Now what? At this point, I am inclined to say that Brassier is too much of an Augustinian for my tastes, specifically a *City of God* Augustinian I hasten to add, not a praying-weeping circumfessional *Confessions* Augustinian. Like Augustine he believes that if a thing does not last forever, it has no true (or lasting) reality, and if it perishes, it has no true (or lasting) value, thereby embracing classical metaphysical assumptions that go back to Plato and the *City of God.* Like John Milbank, he thinks anyone who denies the existence of the God of Augustinian theology is a nihilist. They both agree that the only thing that could seal the bond of being is the God of classical metaphysical theology, and they differ only in their assessment of nihilism, in their contrasting desire to bind or unbind nihilism, to bind nihilism with the bond of being or to unbind the nihil from being's bonds.

I think the truth is exactly the opposite. The only things that can be valued or treasured are mortal, finite, transient and temporal, their very impermanence being the reason we hold them dear.[21] We hold them dear by holding them fast, and we hold them fast because we know that we cannot hold on to them forever. Their transiency intensifies their existence. The impermanence of things gives them a haunting bittersweetness, casting a patina of mortality over what is held closest to our heart. If something lasted forever, it would soon enough lose its fragrance, be drained of meaning and emptied of value, and we would be exposed to something worse than a sickness unto death, namely, a sickness unto *un*death, what Blanchot and Levinas call the impossibility of dying. Where the youthful Nietzsche concludes his sketch of cosmic nihilism by saying "and nothing will have happened," the Zarathustra of the mature Nietzsche responds, "Was that life? Well then, once more!" Life elicits the joyful affirmation of Nietzschean *Jasagung*, a Franco-German *oui, oui*, a joyful Joycean "yes I said yes."

So the faith whose cause I take up is neither the fideism that rankles Meillassoux, nor the ethical faith that Kant tried to make safe, nor especially the confessional faith that the orthodox believe will save them, but it is the unsafe faith, the *foi*, that animates or, I should say, that haunts what, following Derrida, I call a religion without religion. This faith, which cannot immunize itself against unfaith, fails to be either safe or saving. It begins and ends in the circumfession that nothing keeps us safe, that the stars do not know we are here. It does not deny the law of entropy and makes no pretense of being the secret word that wins the prize of a trip to the "other world" outside space and time. This faith confesses that we are all disasters, dis-astered. This little star of ours we call the sun is not the image of the Good or the "One" but one among many, only one of innumerable suns in countless galaxies, in a universe that may be but one of many universes. But unlike Brassier, I take this very final setting of the sun to be at the same time the setting of a certain faith. I take this impossible thought that the earth and sun and galaxy and universe are hurtling to entropic death to be the condition of the possibility of faith.[22] Here faith functions not in opposition to un-faith but in utter dependence upon it, so that there would be no reason for faith if we were not so deeply unbelieving, in just the way that hope is hope only when things are hopeless. But faith in what? In life, which is never simply life, but life-death, and in resurrection, of which the magical resuscitation of Lazarus, the resurrection of Jesus, and the various versions of reincarnation scattered around philosophy and religion are so many *Vorstellungen*. Resurrection, as Cixous says of Derrida after his "death sentence" of pancreatic cancer, is a "reprieve," being given more life, more time, being reborn when all is lost, which, being temporary, is all the more precious. Faith means faith in the grace of the moment, of the hour, of the day, of the lifetime. The menace posed by the prospect that time is running out is what constitutes its value. The very thing that makes faith in life possible also makes it impossible. This faith is a "believing in life." The word "belief" comes from love, *lieben*. So belief means what we love to think. We believe in what we love, and what we love is life, more life.

But why do we love life?—because life is mortal, a transient gift, a lily that lasts but a day, a lily of the field that is adorned with the very glory of God. The songs lovers sing are beautiful precisely because the lovers know they will die. The great aporia faced by love is whether the beloved should be blessed with the longer life or spared the pain of surviving, of having to live through the pain of separation death brings. The realization that life lasts but a moment makes life precious, not only personally but cosmically. The reality that there are long stretches in the universe devoid of life, long eons before life existed, and that there will be even longer eons when life will be no more suggests that to be alive, here and now, is a gift, like a miracle. If you ask life, "why do you live?" Meister Eckhart said, life would answer, "I live in order that I live," I live "without why," without an end or telos, "unbound" from the need of an end or telos.[23] Life is not teleological, because life is its own "because." Life is lived for itself not for an end. I live because I live; I life in order to live; I live *weil* I live, as Heidegger says about the blossoming of the rose, with *weil* meaning "because" but also "while," "for the while." Life is "headed" nowhere other than life, seeking nothing more than more life. We are not trying to get through the day for the sake of getting to the *end*, which is what is known as "wishing your life away." When we come to the end of our days, even the bad days will look good, each of them a grace. The meaning in life is found at the point that every day is found to be a grace. There is not anything you would want life "for," or for which you would exchange life, which is confirmed not contradicted whenever individuals sacrifice their life for the life of others. Contrary to Brassier, the ateleological structure of life does not mean it is being-nothing, but that it is "being-*for*-nothing," for nothing other than itself. I understand nihil unbound to mean being unbound from purpose and freed for itself, being-for-itself. I propose a kind of joyous and gratuitous nihilism, a nihilism of grace, where life is lived for nothing other than itself. Life is for free, not because it is without cost, but because it is "for" nothing, for nothing *else*. It is an excess, a gratuity, a graciousness, a grace.[24]

To speak of life as a "grace," a "gift," or a "miracle" in which we have "faith and hope and love" is to take up a "religious" discourse. Religious discourse—which has caused panic selling in the market for Continental philosophy—is liminal discourse, addressing a limit-situation. The limit of all limits is life/death, the extreme situation par excellence, the *ne plus ultra* beyond which we cannot see, from which no one returns. At that point, our faculties are driven to the limit, we gasp for air, seeking to represent the unrepresentable horizon and presupposition of everything we think and do, to think the unthinkable, to account for the unaccountable, to put a price on what is priceless, asking what life is for when there is nothing for which we would exchange life. We turn to a religious discourse *faute de mieux*, out of desperation, other categories having collapsed. Religious discourse arises at that precise point when the legs of sense give way beneath us, when we run up against the limits of sense and non-sense, the point that divides sense from non-sense, when we lack the categories we need to make sense. Then we set out in search of a vocabulary of excess, of the limit and the excess of the limit, words to describe the slash between the limit and what lies beyond the limit. Religion is one of our most venerable vocabularies of excess (and certainly not the only one), a vocabulary of grace, of the gift, of the gratuitousness of life, of the "for nothing else," the "for nothing more" of life. It is because life is a grace that life can be a curse, that there is nothing worse than a ruined life, ruined time, for which there can be no compensation. If life is priceless, there is no possible payment that can compensate for ruined life, whether it has been ruined by the ravages of injustice, or by a perfectly innocent shift of the earth's crustal plates, or by the unraveling of our telomeres.

Brassier is a limit-thinker and thus far, for all his antireligion, a religious thinker (almost). Brassier leads us up to the limits of nihil unbound, of being degree zero, of being nothing, one short step away from the intuition of being-*for*-nothing, which is what we mean by life. Life is living for nothing else than life, about which the proper discourse is both a logos and a poetics, for it presupposes a logos—physics—which provides the "basic schema," which draws the lines of the limits, and which in turn provokes a poetics, having both an ear for the voices that call from the limits and also an eye for its non-formalizable features. The very thing that makes life impossible—that makes life a gratuitous and temporary episode in a vast cosmic narrative without purpose, a tale told by the idiot of entropy—is what makes life possible. The very thing that destines life to impermanence and extinction makes life precious. The very thing that makes life meaningless gives it meaning. Life is a complete "accident," a totally fortuitous event, so that if we rewound the universe back to the Big Bang and set it off again, it might very well never have produced life, and it would certainly not have produced this life, the one that we ourselves have, here, at this moment, in this moonlight, with this spider, as Nietzsche's Zarathustra puts it so perfectly. But what seems to Brassier the gratuitousness of a great cosmic stupidity seems to me the stupid luck of grace, the gratuitousness of a grace, of a gift, made precious by its episodic, accidental, impermanent, and mortal destiny, by its *destinerrance*.

God, Perhaps

When Brassier says, in effect, that Nietzsche's *Lebensphilosophie* is just religion all over again, merely another way to re-enchant the world, and when Peter Hallward says that Deleuze's philosophy is just more theophany, I agree. But I do not regard that as a criticism of Nietzsche and Deleuze. We have every reason to believe that life is an interim phenomenon, which means that religion is as well. Religion is meant to address the interim that is life, the interim of life, to a sing a song to an event, to the outbreak of life in the midst of a cosmic play. Religion provides precisely the vocabulary of excess we require in the face of life—carnal, mortal, bodily life. The next challenge, the one whose measure it is difficult to take, is what happens when carnality, mortality, and embodiment undergo a transmutation at the hands of techno-science, when these limits, what we mean by limit-situations, are put into question by the "singularity," if it ever comes or even comes close. Any possible (Continental) philosophy (of religion) will be put in question and profoundly challenged precisely insofar as life itself is questioned and transformed. As a theopoetics of the event, of the limit situation, it will be forced to expand its horizons beyond the limits of strictly defined bio-life, beyond any strictly biologically based and, therefore, biodegradable life, beyond any notion of life that entertains the illusion that it is absolutely distinct from *techne*.

Perhaps, by the same token, God, the name of God, the "event," the possibility of the impossible, harbored in and by the name of "God," will be transformed. God, perhaps, in virtue of everything *tout autre* that stirs within this name, will be reinvented, reconceived, and reimagined, unless it is simply dropped, which is another way that the impossible is made possible. Perhaps the coming life will be no "life" at all, none that we today can recognize; the coming God will be no "God" at all, the coming philosophy no "philosophy" at all, and the coming "religion" no religion at all, not as we know it. Then we shall require an entirely new vocabulary of excess, one for which we today are unprepared, when life and religion and philosophy as we know it will be transformed, perhaps beyond recognition, when the only God and the only religion will hang by the thread of this "perhaps." Perhaps, what we mean by God, the event that is harbored in the name of God, is the perhaps itself. Perhaps all that will remain of religion will be the chance of an unforeseeable future, and religion will have meant clinging to the grace of perhaps, hanging on by a prayer.

Notes

1. The present essay is an earlier version of the material found in John D. Caputo, *The Insistence of God: A Theology of Perhaps* (Bloomington: Indiana University Press, 2013), 186–263, where many passages in this paper can be found in a more elaborated form.
2. I refer, neither to the Big Bang nor to Derrida's singularity, but to Ray Kurzweil, *The Singularity Is Near: When Humans Transcend Biology* (New York: Penguin Books, 2005).
3. Quentin Meillassoux, *After Finitude: An Essay on the Necessity of Contingency*, trans. Ray Brassier (London: Continuum, 2008), 28–49. For a robust rebuttal of Meillassoux, see Adrian Johnston, "Hume's Revenge: À Dieu, Meillassoux," in *The Speculative Turn: Continental Materialism and Realism*, ed. Levi Bryant, Nick Srnicek, and Graham Harman (Melbourne: re.press, 2011), 92–113.
4. Derrida refers to this alliance in his preface to Catherine Malabou, *The Future of Hegel: Plasticity, Temporality and Dialectic*, trans. Lisabeth During (New York: Routledge, 2005), xlvii.
5. See Caputo, "As If I Were Dead," in *The Insistence of God*, ch. 9, 180–196.
6. *Philosophy and Truth: Selections from Nietzsche's Notebooks of the Early 1870s*, ed. and trans. Daniel Breazeale (Atlantic Highlands, N.J.: Humanities Press International, 1979), 79.
7. Ray Brassier, *Nihil Unbound* (London: Palgrave Macmillan, 2007), 228.
8. Fritjof Capra, *The Tao of Physics* (Boston: Shambhala Publications, 1999).
9. Michio Kakum, *Physics of the Impossible* (New York: Anchor Books, 2009).
10. Meillassoux, *After Finitude*, 18.
11. Catherine Malabou, *What Should We Do with Our Brain?*, trans. Sebastian Rand (New York: Fordham University Press, 2008), 69.

12. That does not mean that there cannot be many universes *in* space and time.

13. Edmund Husserl, *Ideas Pertaining to a Pure Phenomenology and to a Phenomenological Philosophy*, First Book, trans. Fred Kersten (The Hague: Martinus Nijhoff, 1983), §74, 166.

14. Jacques Derrida, *Edmund Husserl's Origin of Geometry*, trans. John Leavey (Boulder: John Hays, 1978), 87–93.

15. I have spent a lot of time repeating the postmodern critique of Hegel in terms of "totalization," which I do not mean to retract, of course, while neglecting the resources of his *Lectures on the Philosophy of Religion*.

16. Caputo, *The Insistence of God*, ch. 5, "Two Types of Continental Philosophy of Religion," 87–116.

17. See a similar criticism of philosophy in Friedrich Nietzsche, *The Will to Power*, trans. Walter Kaufmann (New York: Vintage Books, 1968), no. 446, 246.

18. *Hegel's Lectures on the Philosophy of Religion*, One Volume Edition: *The Lectures of 1827*, ed. Peter Hodgson (Berkeley: University of California Press, 1988), 84–85, 92, 402–404.

19. This is not far from the hypothesis of Jonathan Z. Smith, *Imagining Religion: From Babylon to Jonestown* (Chicago: University of Chicago Press, 1982).

20. François Laruelle, *Future Christ*, trans. Anthony Paul Smith (London: Continuum, 2010).

21. This is a central point of agreement between me and Martin Hägglund, which complicates our disagreements, which I have spelled out in "The Return of Anti-Religion: From Radical Atheism to Radical Theology," *Journal of Cultural and Religious Theory* 11, no. 2 (Spring 2011): 32–125, http://www.jcrt.org/archives/11.2/caputo.pdf.

22. This very theory is itself a form of faith, since the "Big Crunch" is also a possibility, not to mention some young PhD in physics, unable to find a job in academe and working in a patent office, who might transform everything next week.

23. For the relevant texts and a discussion, see John D. Caputo, *The Mystical Element in Heidegger's Thought* (New York: Fordham University Press, 1982), 118–127.

24. See the remarkable account of grace in Adam S. Miller, *Speculative Grace: Bruno Latour and Object-Oriented Theology* (New York: Fordham University Press, 2013), which I find completely congenial to my own project.

2 Friends and Strangers/ Poets and Rabbis

Negotiating a "Capuphalian" Philosophy of Religion

B. Keith Putt

JOHN D. CAPUTO and Merold Westphal—a binary that, *pace* negative prejudices toward metaphysical polarities, simply sounds appropriate, a dynamic duo that one truly feels no duress to displace.[1] Personally, I cannot refrain from comparing this pair to other distinctive dyads who have achieved fame in Western history and literature. Cain and Abel, Romulus and Remus, Augustine and Pelagius, Bernard and Abelard, Pope Leo X and Luther, Batman and the Joker, Harry Potter and Lord Voldemort all come to mind whenever I contemplate the deep respect and affection that Caputo and Westphal have for each other. Well . . . perhaps that is not the best list of comparables!!

Allow me to begin again. Whenever I think specifically about the Heraclitean strife that unifies Caputo and Westphal in their somewhat volatile varieties of postmodern hermeneutics and theology, I honestly cannot avoid reflecting on a pair of different intellectual pairs, two couplets of classification that offer an intriguing horizon from which to examine the hetero-homogeneity—or homo-heterogeneity—that characterizes their respective skepticism toward the unholy bond between ontotheology and Continental philosophy of religion. I am thinking particularly of the theologian Paul Tillich and the philosopher Jacques Derrida, each of whom details a fascinating distinction between alternatives for discoursing about God. Interestingly enough, both theorists posit a certain *chorismos* as the nonoriginary, quasi-transcendental *Ungrund* for any use of "God" language; that is, both maintain a structural alienation or exilic estrangement as the grounds for the possibility and impossibility of speaking/writing about God.

In Derrida's case, the estrangement is the silence of God that provokes commentary and exegesis. The "word" becomes operative only because God breaks the tablets of the law, thereby fragmenting speech into the dissemination of "desert" writing, leaving language as interrogative and interruptive.[2] This linguistic *etsi deus non daretur* results in a bifurcation of interpretation, an irreducible tension between two approaches to the linguistic lacuna marked by the exiled God.[3] East of Eden, where all hermeneutics takes place, commentary becomes a necessity, since exiled speech denotes the trespass of the sign as symptomatic of a depravity of discourse, a fallenness sans reconciliation, leaving only the "spectral errancy of words."[4]

The "interpretive imperative" then gets interpreted in two ways—rabbinically and poetically. Derrida argues that the rabbi desires to return to the original text, longs for the journey west back to an Eden of direct communication with God, a semantic paradise void of the risk of meaninglessness and the slippage of misrepresentation. In other words, the rabbi dreams of a return to Truth and to the Sabbath of a Transcendental Signified that offers a rest from linguistic labors.[5] The poet, on the other hand, considers such nostalgia to be quaint at best and potentially violent at worst. The poet suspects any attempt to arrest the play of signification as a pretension to totalize one particular set of dogmas. Poetic interpretation celebrates the decentered play of infinite substitution and translatability and has no yearning to recover the literal objectivity of a decisive *bath kol*. The poet knows how to leave language to speak for itself, to function as a "diaphanous element" through which language goes forth. Surprisingly, Derrida himself goes farther and claims that in doing so, the poet acts like God![6] Consequently, even divine discourse, *s'il y en a*, cannot escape the *différance* and undecidability of exiled speech. Derrida concludes his interpretation of the two types of interpretation by insisting that the rabbi/poet binary remains disjunctive and irreconcilable, although one may "live them simultaneously."[7] There will always be rabbis and poets, and there will always be two interpretations of interpretation.

Tillich's polarity of difference and alterity centers on what he terms the two types of philosophy of religion—the ontological and the cosmological—precipitating out of different perspectives for approaching God. The ontological concerns the intimacy of overcoming estrangement; that is, in this type of philosophy of religion, the individual approaches God as one desiring reunion, motivated by a passion for reconciling the divine/human friendship. In this approach, the individual comes to know herself in the very realization of knowing God. The cosmological type, on the other hand, depends upon an extrinsic and detached situation between humanity and God, one in which God is more a stranger than a friend, more distal than proximal. In this approach, God remains recondite, leaving the individual with only probable inferences void of any assurances that a divine/human connection obtains.[8]

Tillich explicitly associates the ontological type with Augustine and the later Franciscans, both of whom recognize that God is as intimate to the individual as the self itself. For Augustine, that intimacy comes to expression in the association of God with Truth, by which God serves as the presupposition for the question of God. For the Franciscans, it means that wisdom is the self-evident recognition of the truth of divine ontological identity with the soul.[9] Clearly, Tillich does not balk at engaging in a certain ontotheology by which *Deus est esse* continues to serve as a valid maxim for expressing the self's elemental connection with the Unconditional *prius*.[10] He sounds quite metaphysical when he insists that the "presence" of the Unconditional may be experienced through a mystical "awareness," by which he means an affirmation of God's demand to overcome existential estrangement and restore the divine/human friendship. This awareness cannot avoid the cognitive; however, it cannot be reduced to mere intuition or knowledge.[11] Correlatively, one should never confuse the awareness of the Unconditional *prius* with the belief in God as an entity, as an "existing" something that may function as the object of the intellect. He acknowledges that atheism is the only religiously proper response to the metaphysical claim that God is *a* being of any sort.[12]

The alternative approach of the cosmological type, which comprehends God as a stranger, someone unknown and functionally unknowable, derives primarily from the Thomistic and Nominalistic traditions. Tillich chides St. Thomas for his empirical, "scientific" approach to faith that results in God's never being known *an sich* but only as analogously indicated through divine effects. Ultimately St. Thomas reduces knowledge to the level of authority, turning the Bible into a book of propositions and theology into nothing more than linguistic approximations of some infinite being. These approximations mean that faith and knowledge are severed and cannot reunite.[13] As a result, God remains a stranger—ineffable, unnamable, and unapproachable in God's transcendent Otherness. The legislating question, then, for Tillich becomes whether one will privilege the ontological over the cosmological or vice versa. That is to say, will God be a friend whom one can love, or will God remain a stranger separated by cognitive and linguistic *chorismoi* that can never be spanned?

The Poet Caputo and Reb Westphal

Applying the Tillichian and Derridean taxonomies to the task of prosecuting the homo-heterogeneities in the Caputoan and Westphalian critiques of ontotheology appears to result in rather obvious identifications. Who would seriously question associating Caputo with the ontological and the poetic and Westphal with the cosmological and the rabbinic? After all, is it not endemic to Caputo's radical theology of the event that God be understood from the perspective of a structural reunion of estranged friends? Tillich accentuates the Augustinian provenance of this conceit, separating it from the Thomistic pedigree of the cosmological, and anyone with merely a passing knowledge of Caputo's literary corpus will recognize the centrality of Augustine for his postmodernism. Caputo, himself, states quite explicitly that it is "in Augustine, not Aquinas . . . that Continental philosophers can find an antecedent."[14] For example, he agrees with the Bishop of Hippo that God and truth correlate, that one must understand both specifically through the verbal "definition" of veracity as *facere veritatem*, as the "doing" of truth, not the identifying of truth as the sterile cognition of adequation.[15] So, too, one should connote "God" as an event, as an action more than an entity, as naming what takes place in various occurrences of justice, forgiveness, or giving.[16] Likewise, he acknowledges the conjunction in Augustine between questing after God and questioning the self; indeed, Caputo constantly invokes the supplementarity of inquiring into both the question of what is loved when God is loved and also the question of who exactly I am.[17]

As with Tillich, so, too, *mutatis mutandis,* with Caputo, the relationship between self and God remains entangled—especially regarding the issue of love. The notion of the love of God forms a central motif in Caputo's weak theology, especially as it formally indicates the inescapable "restless heart" of all individuals, that is, Augustine's *cor inquietum,* which has been translated as the heart "tilted" toward God.[18] Yet, for Tillich, love denotes union and reunion, the intimate connection between estranged subjects. Consequently, although Caputo does not focus on love as reconciliation with the same urgency, his agapic-centered theology tracks Tillich's "friend" approach quite well. Furthermore, Tillich's idea that the "presence" of God and self is immediately "known" through an awareness of an originary demand bears a surprising harmony with Caputo's Derridean affirmation of an originary promise, a quasi-transcendental *oui, oui,* "yes, yes," that operates as something of a *prius* to every encounter—certainly to every linguistic encounter.[19]

If the cataloguing of Caputo as an example of Tillich's ontological approach needs one more piece of evidence, perhaps their agreement with reference to an existing God would suffice. Both reject the traditional metaphysical confusion of God with a being, of the divine as an entity, an object, or an anthropomorphic subject. Although they would disagree concerning how they choose to talk about God as non-entitative—Caputo would certainly brook no "ground of Being" nomenclature—they do agree that the old God of classical theism is dead. Nevertheless, Caputo does not shy away totally from following Tillich's ontotheological ploy to associate God and Being in some linguistic manner. Just as Tillich continues to use the sentence *Deus est esse,* Caputo also affirms that its converse, *esse est deus,* is a "beautiful idea" that fails as an argument for God but does provide a provocative idiom for life.[20]

Conversely, is it not apparent that Westphal endorses the cosmological approach with its insistence that God remains a transcendent stranger to us immanent creatures? He routinely declares that here in the lower elevations of finite existence, "we breathe the oxygen of language rather than the ether of silent union" with the divine."[21] As a result, our "holiness has halitosis,"[22] to such an extent that our epistemic distance from God disallows our making any theologically realistic statements about the divine predicates. Westphal explicitly affiliates with St. Thomas, who, as Tillich claims, confines human knowledge to God's effects and never to God qua God. In Westphal's paraphrase, "language, even biblical language, can never mirror, master, grasp, or encompass the divine reality."[23] God, as the "Thomistic" stranger, cannot escape something akin to a Kantian antirealism whereby the noumenal awareness of God as friend remains always beyond reach. For Westphal, there can be neither a Cartesian foundation of certainty nor a Hegelian *telos* of Absolute Knowledge when it comes to theological discourse.[24]

Quite clearly, Westphal boldly confesses that there *is* a God to be the Stranger. Nevertheless, he also testifies that although the word "God" may name an absolute transcendence, any relative intellect using that name is not, thereby, "cognitively transubstantiated" into an absolute itself.[25] Again, Westphal is too Thomistic, too Kantian, and too Kierkegaardian to abbreviate the infinite qualitative distinction between humanity and the divine. Correspondingly, he remains cosmological in his approach to God, which, for him, ensures that he may successfully overcome ontotheology. He criticizes the latter for erring in its arrogance of believing that one can manipulate the divine as an epistemological apparatus for constructing a totalized conceptual system.[26] Metaphysical theology always considers God to be its friend, someone joining it in its building project of constructing a comprehensive epistemological edifice. Westphal much prefers a "stranger" God!

Now I shall not take coals to Newcastle and argue extensively for the validity of designating Caputo as a Derridean poet. Even a reader who consistently misinterprets Caputo cannot fail to appreciate that he most assuredly celebrates the semiotic and semantic play that characterizes the influences of *différance, khôra*, and undecidability.[27] The essence—*s'il y en a*—of Caputo's radical hermeneutics has always been an honest concession to the flux of existence, to the messianic dynamic of discourse in which meaning is never totalized but always remains "to come," deferred to some future perfect invention of linguistic truth.[28] No interpreter can ever recollect the glory of a past original meaning, nor can he or she anticipate the teleological appropriation of absolute knowledge. Instead, one never escapes the inevitability of *hermeneusis,* of having to confront the slippage and fluidity of signification, that perpetual motion that never outruns the risk of meaninglessness and loss.[29]

The decentered play of signification does not diminish once one moves into theological hermeneutics, since no language is safe from the differing and deferring jouissance that characterizes the ambiguity of all discourse. As a result, Caputo contends that even when one speaks about God—and who can truly avoid doing that?!—one must admit that the name of God is endlessly translatable, substitutable, and countersigned by every "theologian" who speaks or writes about God.[30] Accordingly, Caputo has consistently engaged in various "poetics" as the proper way to do hermeneutics, from a poetics of obligation in ethics to a poetics of the kingdom in a Christian theology of the event to a poetics of the impossible in a more general theory of religion.[31] In truth, he goes so far as to argue that the poetic play of dissemination and *différance* may be a cipher for the event inherent in the very name of God—an event that always portends the transformability of life, the open-ended play that redemptively suggests the metanoetic.[32]

I shall shake off the coal dust once again and attempt brevity in presenting Westphal as hermeneutically rabbinical. Reb Westphal most assuredly believes, notwithstanding his more cosmological approach, that one can return to the horizons of the biblical texts and speak about God according to the classifications of classical theism.[33] His faith can, indeed, seek an understanding of God as a personal creator and redeemer, as displaying all of the "omni" traits that a traditional dignified deity should, and as being the subject of a predicative "meganarrative."[34] Not surprisingly, therefore, Westphal concludes, as any good Derridean rabbi should, that some "literal" meaning obtains, that one can participate in some good theological realism and predicate some specific attributes of the divine. The play of signification may not come to a complete stop for Westphal; however, it does slow to such a crawl that it appears static.

Reb Westphal most assuredly does not agree that the name of God frolics poetically through the fields of discourse; on the contrary, it stands still and resolute in naming a distinct agent who acts, at least who "speech-acts," and who interacts with humans through various media of revelation.[35] Despite the fact that even rabbis reluctantly capitulate to hermeneutics as exilic, Westphal attenuates the extent of the exile by claiming that through the disciplines of *lectio, meditatio, oratio,* and *contemplatio,* one can read the biblical texts and "hear the very voice of God!"[36] For a poet such as Caputo, the *very* idea of the rabbinic ratification of hearing the *very* voice of God is so shocking as to leave even his poetic voice veritably speechless.

A Poetic Westphal and a Stranger Caputo

I, too, now find myself speechless—under such penitential conviction that only silence seems to secure me against a surplus of self-incrimination. If Caputo and Westphal truly are my philosophical patriarchs, then I must genuinely genuflect before them and say, "Fathers, forgive me, for I have sinned!" I confess to being in the rather embarrassing position of the "perhaps," as in "perhaps" I was wrong earlier in this essay when I somewhat apodictically proclaimed that plugging Caputo and Westphal into the Tillichian and Derridean binaries may be done "obviously." Yet, I simplistically assumed that no one would gainsay that Caputo is both friend and poet, while Westphal is both stranger and rabbi. Well, now it seems that *I, myself,* must gainsay that. Nonetheless, in the spirit of self-absolution, I should also testify that "perhaps" my reevaluation is not so embarrassing after all; "perhaps" the "perhaps" is a good Derridean ploy for keeping any pretension toward totalization open, or, as one might say, "in play." Moreover, this "perhaps" leads me to another Derridean motif, one that factors significantly in any attempt to overcome ontotheology—that is, the idea of inversion. One of the necessary prophylactic prescriptions for minimizing the contagion of metaphysics is to invert every established polarity. Consequently, I now want to recant (a bit) and recount how Caputo should actually be classified as a rabbi adhering to the cosmological approach of the stranger, while Westphal, as a poetic friend of God, honestly desires to spend his time in play.

A broader reading of Caputo certainly evidences that the name of "God" functions in his thought as a mark of the ineffability and anonymity of God. God is the *es gibt,* the *il y a,* an impersonal, esoteric *je ne sais quoi*—or as Derrida would say: *"Je ne sais pas; il faut croire."*[37] Caputo believes, but he does not know what—or whom—he believes. His passion for God, then, is a passion for the unknown, for the mystery that cannot be identified.[38] The awareness or affirmation of the originary promise may come from God, but he does not know that. The structurally infinite translatability of the name of God results in a perpetual motion of signification without any discernible signified operating as merely a "bathroom break" from the flux![39] Is it God or love? God or justice? Or is justice God? Do we hear God's call? Or is it more Heideggerian—simply the call of our own conscience? Caputo does not have a head for such heady conclusions, claiming that we can never genuinely "know" if what we talk about is God or not. In other words, he does not know what he loves when he loves his God.[40] As a result, as per Tillich, Caputo's God is always a stranger, and we can only wager, as good "Thomists" do, that we encounter the effects of the event occurring in the name of God.

Of course, in order to add impetus to the inversion, I should announce that Westphal loves Augustine! In particular, he loves the Augustinian idea of the "inner word," the notion that something akin to an internal testimony of the divine Spirit manifests a divine/human intimacy that yearns for a friendly reunion.[41] Westphal believes that God acts as a "voice beyond my own who calls me to a life beyond my own," a phrase that Tillich might consider a translation of his concept of the awareness of an ontological demand.[42] Such awareness for Westphal could well be what motivates the loving response of praise and adoration—not to mention of obedience.[43] Westphal does, indeed, know what he loves when he loves his God; he loves a deity who loves him and relates so intrinsically to him that "predication must yield to praise" and theological discourse become doxology.[44] This is a God before whom one can sing and dance, a God of/as Truth, a "personal God on whom we are dependent for the whole of our life . . . [whose] highest priority is love."⁴⁵ Undoubtedly, the "ontological" Westphal would have no hesitation in singing "What a *Friend* We Have in Jesus"—preferably a cappella!

Still, the inversion must continue of course, which requires that Caputo drop the mantle of the poet and wrap himself in the *tallith* of the rabbi. But is that truly possible? Could he ever be associated with a hermeneutical perspective that seeks to rediscover some semblance of literal meaning, to restrain the poetic play in order to predicate, in some manner, something correspondent to reality? Could Caputo accept both the interpretation that God is a stranger *and* the propriety of rabbinic hermeneutics? The answer to all of these questions is "yes." Reb Caputo does decidedly engage in a certain apo-kataphasis, a negatively positive theological discourse through which he does not hesitate to tell us what God is by telling us what God is *not*. He prophesies of a God who is not an entity, who does not intervene in the world, whose name can be legion because it identifies no divine attributes, and who functionally has no effect on reality.⁴⁶ To believe otherwise is simply to be in error. Now in the interest of full disclosure, I must admit that Reb Caputo does undeniably tolerate those who hold a contrary determinate faith in a more personal or entitative deity; however, he considers them to be theologically incorrect, which logically entails that there *is* a theologically *correct* interpretation—specifically Caputo's! As I claim in another recent essay, he allows for others to hold a view of God contrary to his own; yet, he thinks they should be ashamed of themselves! One might claim, therefore, that it is he, as rabbi, who holds the power of the shibboleth allowing entry into theological truth.⁴⁷

The poetic mantle does not lie discarded for long, since Westphal picks it up and wraps it around himself, and, in doing so, completes the inversion of the two sets of polarities. Yes, he does join in the lively sport of semiotic and semantic play, and not as a reluctant participant. He contends that hermeneutics is inescapable, is systemically radical, and is incorrigibly risky. Humans never cavort with an objective meaning but always with one value-laden and immersed in the flux of traditions, saturated by Gadamerian prejudices and Derridean textuality.⁴⁸ Westphal concedes that the naïve acceptance of interpretive intuition, the notion that one does not need hermeneutics but should simply "just see" the obvious meaning manifested transparently through discourse, may be motivated by "respectable reasons"; however, he considers such intuitive *non*-interpretation to be an epistemological immediacy impossible to obtain.⁴⁹ He argues that no one can ever hope to occupy some Archimedean position outside the limiting strictures of language, tradition, history, and culture in order to get absolute leverage on truth and meaning.

Westphal joyfully reminds us that we are not God; consequently, we remain poets, fated to admit our linguistic exile and to resign ourselves to the plurality, difference, and uncertainty that typify existence east of Eden and west of the New Jerusalem. To be sure, his poetics of facticity results in his playing the game of relative humility, even to the extent that he must accept the real possibilities that the world is godless and that theological language is nothing more than a differential play of semiotic surfaces, mere verbal veneers that cover nothing objective or factual beneath them.[50] He cannot escape being haunted by the specter that poetic play may entail running around linguistic circles in some Dionysian dance of *différance* without the benefit of an identifiable center. He thinks, of course, that his theology *does* play with God, but, in reality, it may simply be a play with/on words.

Toward a "Capuphalian" Rabbinical Poetics

Were this essay adhering strictly to deconstructive protocols, now would be the time to begin the process of displacement; after all, the inversion of polarities functions only as a propaedeutic, a way of breaking them up in order to sweep them away. Yet, as professed in the first sentence of this chapter, I have no intention of displacing Caputo and Westphal. On the contrary, my *vouloir dire* throughout all this little fragment of methodological musings on philosophical theology has been specifically to celebrate the creative tensions that agitate the interstices between a Caputoan and a Westphalian approach to ontotheology. Although it is impossible ever to achieve a nice Hegelian synthesis of these two perspectives, I must declare my passion for the impossible and my bipolar commitment to a "Capuphalian" philosophy of religion. For only by holding both of these irreducible, yet irreconcilable,[51] interpretations of theological interpretations do I find my own personal and professional professions of faith: "I believe; but help my unbelief"—"I disbelieve; but help my belief."

Westphal believes that ontotheology addresses the issue of *how* we speak of God more than *what* we say of God. Playing off of the Heideggerian gloss on the term, he insists that overcoming ontotheology in no way requires the total rejection of the classical theistic traits of God as the eternal, immutable, omnipotent, omniscient, omnipresent creator of heaven and earth. Nor does he stutter when pronouncing the Latin derivatives of these metaphysical marks of divinity, such pithy little phrases as *Actus Purus, Ipsum Esse Subsistens,* or *Causa Sui.* Of course, he prefers the more personal categories that address God as agent, as one who loves, promises, commands, and acts within the physical, historical, and cultural structures of reality. He contends that those qualities are more consistently biblical. He will not support, however, the ontotheological ploy of subordinating God under the conceptual idolatry of philosophical categories in order to enhance human domination over nature and other humans.[52] He contends that overcoming ontotheology is less about God and more about us—specifically about instilling within us a genuine epistemic humility, the recognition that we are finite and fallen.

Caputo, on the other hand, emphasizes that overcoming ontotheology concerns not only two of the three constituent concepts in the term but all three. Whereas Westphal may focus on the *ontos* and the *logos* more than the *theos,* Caputo pronounces ontotheology as equivalent to metaphysical theism, and, consequently, overcoming the former requires rejecting the vocabulary of the latter.[53] One must silence the claims that God is a being who exercises a strong force over reality, privileging some people over others, performing magic for one group but ignoring others by arbitrarily micromanaging and manipulating events in the world.[54] Caputo insists that a non-metaphysical theism would speak about God with the idioms of a weak theology of the event, with a poetics of faith that comprehends God as the endlessly translatable name for what we most desire but cannot identify, with a passion for the impossible that is always to come, and with a yearning that deciphers God as a call and a promise instead of as a being or an agent—and certainly instead of Being-Itself or Self-Caused Cause. Ironically, Caputo prefers these non-metaphysical categories of the divine because he considers them to be *more biblical*!

For Westphal, Caputonan non-metaphysical philosophy of religion may be a passion for the impossible, but that passion could be only the residual heat from the fiery stream of a superficial semantic theism, a quasi-Feuerbachian linguistic projection of what we value most in humanity.[55] Consequently, Caputo rightly passes for an atheist with his contention that "God" names those events astir in what occurs when there is really no one, or no thing, doing *any*thing for *any*one in *any* way. For Caputo, alternatively, Westphalian non-metaphysical philosophy of religion uses the old bait-and-switch tactic. It advertises that in *non*-ontotheology, one will ostensibly witness the humility of discursive play, the ongoing comedy in which no one can determine decidedly who we are or what we love when we love our God—or even if we do love God. But in reality, when you buy your ticket, you look behind the curtain and there is the same old strong theology hawking the same old ontotheological God. Caputo, therefore, regards Westphalian epistemic humility as vulnerable to the humiliation of camouflaging the arrogance of objective certainty behind the façade of faith.

So the questions remain: "Whose interpretation? Which ontotheology?" You are all free to choose this day whom you will follow, but as for me, I will follow both. I choose to shuttle to and fro between both positions, since both Caputo and Westphal convince me that faith is the substance of perpetual play *and* the evidence of existential conviction. It is both positional and peripatetic, both indecisive and decisive, both credulous and incredulous, both certitude and insecurity. Westphal's God often appears to be a bit too much for me, while Caputo's God appears to be not quite enough. Westphal's personal God of creation and redemption seems more biblical to me than does Caputo's poetically quasi-personal God of the event; however, Caputo's theology of the weakness of God seems more biblical to me than does Westphal's classical theism of an omnipotent deity.

I cannot choose between the two; yet I am constantly choosing between the two. One might say that I put the possibility of solving this disjunction into an *epoché,* consign the either/or to a steadfast suspension. But Derrida would call this "suspended" response a "negotiation," a word that etymologically signifies "un-leisure" or "dis-ease." Negotiation references a constant movement among several positions, a reciprocal shuttling between multiple stations without the stasis of inertia. Negotiating for Derrida means "no thesis, no position, no theme, no station, no substance, no stability, [and] a perpetual suspension."[56] Subsequently, I cannot escape negotiating a "Capuphalian" philosophy of religion, tapping into my postmodern "Luther" nature and confessing that here with Caputo I stand; I can do no other—except here with Westphal I stand; I can do no other—except . . . well, except that maybe negotiating such a "Capuphalian" philosophy of religion allows me to see God, if only through a prism darkly.

Response by Merold Westphal

On Being a Rabbi and Poet

I am grateful to B. Keith Putt for his thoughtful and illuminating comparison of the point of view for my work as an author with that of my good friend Jack Caputo. Notwithstanding a few quibbles and caveats, I acknowledge that he has me pegged just about right. But for the record, let me add that he did not fool me one bit. The dogmatic obviousness with which he assigned me to the cosmological and rabbinic side of the fence and Jack to the ontological and poetic side made me suspect, almost immediately, that his approach would become more dialectical and that he would reverse the assignments as well. Nicely done.

So now the "quibbles and caveats!" I must begin by questioning one of the two grids on which Putt seeks to locate us, that is, Tillich's distinction between "cosmological" and "ontological" types of philosophy of religion. Personally, I think Tillich's polarity is three ways confused. In the first place, the distinction strikes me as conceptually false. It sets up an either/or between God as stranger and God as the overcoming of estrangement; however, one could argue that the God of, say, Abraham, and thus of the Abrahamic monotheisms, is simultaneously both a friend and also a stranger. Rather than an either/or relation, there is a dialectical relation in which the God who was a stranger becomes our friend and in doing so remains a stranger, transcendent to and disruptive of our desires, our plans, and our ideas. Only as we gain a new identity (and in Abraham's case a new name) through our encounter with this stranger is estrangement overcome and we can then be at home as nomads in the world. Ironically, biblical faith is a stranger to Tillich's "stranger" God, who is more a source of estrangement than a site of its overcoming.

In the second place, it seems to me that Tillich also has it historically wrong. For example, like Abraham, Augustine is one whose faith can be described as making friends with a stranger. Although his God is immanent and discoverable within the inner spaces of the self, on the dialectical flip side, that same God is also transcendent and can only be found in the Bible and in the catholic church. The strong apophatic dimension in Augustine's thought keeps God an epistemic stranger, while the new identity and agenda Augustine finds in God, rather than in his own desires, keep God transcendent to his will as well as to his intellect. In other words, Augustine appears to fit Tillich's scheme quite badly. As, too, does Aquinas. If one reads him past the Five Ways that traditionally get into the anthologies, I believe one gets a more balanced, indeed more dialectical picture. The participation motif in St. Thomas's thought makes it clear that his God is not *merely* a stranger but also the ground for overcoming estrangement and becoming who we truly are.

Finally, I find Tillich's scheme theologically problematic. It is closely related to his rejection of the notion of God as *a* being in distinction to Being itself, whatever those two "beings" may mean. The God of the Abrahamic monotheism as Creator, Lawgiver, Judge, and Redeemer, however, *is* a being, though surely not one of the finite beings that constitute the created world. To infer that God is not a being in any sense from the fact that God is not a finite being is simply to define the God of the Bible out of existence without argument. A God personal enough to love, to make promises, to issue commands, to enter into covenants, and so forth, is surely *a* being in a sense theology must try to articulate rather than to deny. In making this denial, Tillich shows himself to be a pantheist rather than a theist. That's fine if he simply wishes to be another Plotinus or Spinoza. But he purports to be a Christian theologian, and this puts him, in my view, somewhere on a spectrum that runs from confused to fraudulent.

If the ontological/cosmological distinction is not an either/or for Augustine or Aquinas, neither is it for me. On the one hand, I belong to Tillich's cosmological approach insofar as it involves the epistemic transcendence of God that Putt emphasizes. By virtue of our created finitude and sinful fallenness, our representations of God always fail to be adequate to the divine reality. I would certainly want to give equal time to God's alterity to our wills as well as to our intellects. This means that the essence of estrangement is sin, and its overcoming requires a forgiver and not Being itself. But on the other hand, I see the life of faith as one in which, by virtue of revelation and grace, we become friends with the God who was and will ever be a stranger. When it can be said of us, as it was said of Abraham, that we are called friends of God (Jas 2:23), we will have overcome estrangement. Clearly, Putt eventually acknowledges the "Augustinian/ontological" dimension of my thought that thinks of a "friendly reunion" with God.

Well then, am I also a Derridean rabbi? Yes, given that the point of departure for my thinking is a "*sacred text surrounded by commentaries.*"[57] And yes, given that I see the necessity of commentaries as exiled speech, of the inevitability of hermeneutics, and of the risks of interpretation haunting secure intuition and sheer presence.[58] But no, I do not have a nostalgia for "the immediate proximity of the garden [of Eden],"[59] nor do I "reluctantly capitulate" to hermeneutics as exilic. For I think it is quite possible for God to speak to us through scripture east of Eden. The result will not be Absolute Knowledge as specified by some philosophies, especially modern. Yet, we do not require that for loving relations with our parents, spouses, children, and friends, so why should we require it for our relation with God? If "every other is wholly other," as Derrida tells us, following Levinas,[60] then our most immediate relations with other persons exhibit the transcendence in which their presence to us occurs within a horizon of absence. So we inevitably must take the risk of interpreting their words and actions. Why should the claim that God speaks to us especially in a particular book and that God has acted in history make us think that it should be different with God, that we must have sheer presence? In seeing the rabbi as nostalgic, has Derrida confused the rabbi with certain (modern) philosophers?

Putt also sees me as Reb Westphal for believing "that one can return to the horizons of the biblical texts and speak about God according to the classifications of classical theism." Let's take these one at a time. Do I want to return to the horizons of biblical texts? For the sake of precision, I have to say, "No." I do not and cannot live in Samaria in the time of Jeroboam or in Corinth in the time of Paul. I am a Christian, and I want my life-world to be grounded in and grow out of biblical revelation. But my hermeneutics is a double hermeneutics, asking two questions: "What did the biblical author say to the original audience back then?" and "What is God saying to us today through those ancient locutions?"[61] This means that I do not aspire to "return to the horizons of the biblical texts," becoming, as it were, interchangeable with contemporaries of Moses, or Jeremiah, or Jesus, or Paul. I remain with the horizons that are already my home; nevertheless, I open them to the truth claims addressed to me in and through those ancient texts. In this encounter my horizons are changed, but I continue to live in the twenty-first century.

In Gadamerian terms, this is to say that "temporal distance is not something that is to be overcome."[62] To repeat, the fusion of horizons in which my faith seeks to be an authentically biblical faith does not mean that I return to the horizons of biblical actors and authors, their language, their culture, their history. It rather means that I seek to open my world to theirs, to understand, as best as I can from where I am historically and culturally located, what was meant and understood back then, and then to understand what it might mean for me in a very different world. Thus understanding is both reproductive (the first hermeneutic, what did it mean?) and productive (the second hermeneutic, what does it mean to me today?)[63] It is through this double process that I open my world to the truth claims of the text and possibly revise or replace elements in my own world.[64]

Do I believe we can "speak about God according to the classifications of classical theism"? Once again, for the sake of precision, I must say "No." By the language of classical theism, I understand the abstract, impersonal, metaphysical attributes of God such as omniscience, infinity, atemporality, simplicity, and so forth. In the first place, I think that the biblically derived personal descriptions of God as agent and speaker are primary and privileged. Second, and here's what's right about Putt's suggestion, I do not simply dismiss the impersonal, metaphysical attributes. There is a place for them if (a) they remain subordinate to the personal categories rather than replacing them and (b) they can be justified biblically as qualifiers that protect the personal categories from a univocal anthropomorphism.

I regularly say that there is a legitimate debate over the metaphysical attributes associated with God, which means that I neither automatically reject them nor immediately incorporate them into my own God-talk. I am skeptical about some aspects of classical theism. I confess that talk about the simplicity of God leaves me mystified; I do not see its importance. I confess that I am intrigued by open theism and its limitations on God's omnipotence and omniscience.[65] I confess that I hope Nicholas Wolterstorff is right in arguing that God is temporally everlasting rather than atemporally eternal.[66] I do not devote much of my time to reading and thinking about these issues, much less writing about them. I would rather spend my time thinking about the implications of a personal God, such as the inversion of intentionality that implies for phenomenology.[67]

So, with these caveats, I acknowledge that I am a Derridean rabbi. Am I also a poet? Putt thinks so by virtue of holding that "hermeneutics is inescapable, is systemically radical, and is incorrigibly risky." Indeed. I do not understand hermeneutics in terms of deciphering a text to find a single meaning fixed once and for all at its origin (in or by the mind of the author). Accordingly, I see the author and the subsequent readers as coproducers of textual meaning, which means that texts legitimately give rise to a variety of meanings in a variety of contexts. But I do not join the hermeneutical bandwagon reluctantly, frightened by the vertigo of relativity and the bugaboo of "anything goes." As Gadamer puts it, hermeneutics is productive (poetically creative) as well as reproductive (exegetical). It renders the indeterminacies of the text more fully concrete while remaining faithful to the text's determinacy. But I would not describe this as joining "in the lively sport of semiotic and semantic play." I understand Derrida to see play as something that happens in texts and traditions more than as something we (are invited to) do. We cannot produce texts without ambiguity and open-endedness. Our task is to recognize this play and thus the indeterminacy of meaning that makes hermeneutics risky. But texts are determinate too, and they provide constraints that the image of "lively sport" might all too easily lose. They call for a "doubling commentary" (reproduction) that serves as an "indispensable guardrail" without which interpretation "would risk developing in any direction at all and authorize itself to say almost anything."[68]

So it isn't as if the rabbi is completely predetermined by the text and the poet completely free to say anything whatever. That is why, when discussing the two interpretations of interpretation in another context, with specific reference to play, Derrida denies that the task is to choose between them.[69] The freedom of the rabbi gives to him (masculine because we are talking about Caputo and me) a poetic dimension, while the constraint of the poet gives to him a rabbinic dimension. Here we have a dialectical dimension supplemental to the heuristic that we did not find in Tillich.

Finally, a few brief comments on Putt's placement of Caputo. How well does the latter fit Tillich's ontological model? Well, both Caputo and Tillich leave God as a personal being out of the picture, but I'm not sure that Caputo is very deeply into overcoming estrangement. Rather, it seems to me that his Derridean world is one in which we are always strangers ourselves, always disrupted, dislocated, and disseminated by *différance*. East of Eden we remain estranged. I find no gospel in Caputo's theology. He talks a lot about "the promise"; however, without any promises more reliable than human promises, I see little basis for hope. Conversely, Caputo is surely a Derridean poet. But that raises the following question: "Does he follow Derrida in finding any determination that places constraints— that is, a 'guardrail' against the subjective and arbitrary—on what the poet can say?" Derrida himself does not always seem to ride the guardrail. He writes, "Language has started without us, in us and before us. This is what theology calls God."[70] Really? The only theologians I know who substitute some significant feature of human experience for God are Feuerbachian atheists, and they hardly qualify as the voices of "theology." Just as Spinoza freely stipulates that by "God" he will mean "mechanistic nature," so Derrida may freely stipulate his own uses as he wishes, but don't both "God" and "theology" have determinacy that renders his stipulation subjective and arbitrary?

Again, Derrida says, "God is the name of the possibility I have of keeping a secret that is visible from the interior but not from the exterior." Elsewhere God is the name of "the absolute singularity of the other."[71] Here again Feuerbachian atheism assigns the name of God to important structures of human existence. In the context of the first of these formulas, Derrida makes clear that for all his talk about undecidability, he has decided for atheism and against theism. "We should stop thinking about God as someone, over there, way up there, transcendent, and ... capable ... of seeing into the most secret of the most interior places."[72] Derrida is free to be an atheist, but is he entitled to claim the name of God for such beliefs in any but a purely stipulative and idiosyncratic sense? Are the critics right who say that for deconstruction, anything goes?

Caputo says that the name of God is endlessly translatable and substitutable, and he does not challenge Derrida's translations. Of course, it is true that theology is caught up in an infinite hermeneutic that precludes any fixed and final formulations. But consider this analogy. There are an infinite number of integers that can be substituted for three as an example of an odd number. But the number four is not one of them. It is just wrong. So the question about Caputo as a Derridean poet is this: "Does he follow Derrida's hermeneutical theory, according to which there is a constraining guardrail to protect against just any old hermeneutical substitutions; or does he follow Derrida's practice in which it seems that the historical-linguistic determinacy of such terms as 'God' and 'theology' is simply ignored in favor of an utterly free poet?"

I've been virtually equating Derrida and Caputo in this last questioning, which brings me to my last point. Putt holds Jack to be a Derridean rabbi because, in holding some theologies to be wrong, he implies that there is "theological truth," marked by its appropriate shibboleths. I want to suggest another way in which Caputo is a rabbi. He lives in a world of *"sacred text surrounded by commentaries."*[73] Just as Harold Bloom famously tells us that Shakespeare is his Bible,[74] so Jack shows us that Derrida is his Bible.[75] He practices a double hermeneutics, giving wonderfully lucid exegesis of the textual meaning and going beyond this to develop its application to our religious and political lives. Of course, he uses the Bible, just as I use Derrida. But perhaps the difference between us can be expressed by saying that the Bible is my Bible and Derrida is his. We both gladly confess that we are trying to think our ways into, through, and out of the texts that have the highest normative significance for us. Still, however poetic (or prosaic) our God-talk may be, we remain ineluctably rabbis. No doubt that is what Gadamer means by the authority and power of tradition. We all think into, through, and out of a complex canon—which may imply that we all are rabbinical poets and poetical rabbis.

Response by John D. Caputo

One Slight Tweak

I am grateful to B. Keith Putt for having adroitly drawn the lines that join and separate me from Merold Westphal, my venerable partner in dialogue over the years, and for the invitation to respond to his paper. I think that Putt is quite right about the ways in which the Tillichian categories of the ontological and the cosmological and the Derridean categories of the rabbinic and the poetic both apply and do not apply differently to Westphal and me. If it is not too confusing to say so, I must confess that Westphal and I do, indeed, cross the lines of both distinctions, and I find this a nuanced way to construe the differences. Consequently, allow me to propose an explanation—slightly tweaked—of why Putt is right about this, and to do so by playing on Tillich's "Two Types" essay still one more time. I contend that there are also two types of Continental philosophy of religion, one descending from Kant and the other from Hegel. As a result, I think Westphal descends from Kant through Kierkegaard and Barth, whereas I descend from Hegel through Kierkegaard and Tillich. Furthermore, if Westphal's immediate (that is, recently deceased) hermeneutical prototype for philosophy of religion is Paul Ricoeur, mine is Jacques Derrida.

Westphal's approach is broadly Kantian and apologetic, directed primarily toward the delimitation of knowledge in order to make room for the traditional faith. The strong point of the Kantian approach Westphal takes is to circumscribe all pretensions to dogmatism, whether expressed by the militant atheists so popular today (Dennett, Hitchens, and Dawkins) or by the no less militant religious fundamentalists who think that by believing in God they have the authority of God. For Westphal, postmodernism does not mean that there *is* no God but only that *we* are not God. It does not mean that the world is not a system (it is for God) but only that it is not a system for us. His view turns on the infinite qualitative difference between how things stand for God and how they stand for us, and his postmodernism means we should acknowledge that we are defined by the latter and deprived of the former. He agrees with the fundamentalists in terms of the fundamentals of *what* they say—that God is the sovereign creator and the scriptures are the word of God in a recognizable sense of the word "word." As Putt says, they both sign on to the same list of omni-attributes. That is Westphal's rabbinic side. His main complaint about them, however, is *how* they say what they say, the way they end up confusing themselves with God and confusing God with the idols of literalism. That is, they leave no room for a poetic side. But Westphal is happy that the fundamentalists are unwilling to negotiate away the fundamentals, because he, himself, is orthodox ("rabbinic") in a broadly Barthian sense.

I, on the other hand, am intractably heretical and heterodox ("poetic") in a broadly Tillichian sense. If Westphal wants to delimit knowledge to make room for faith in transcendence, I want to delimit transcendence and redescribe faith. Like Tillich, I agree with the atheists about the "entity-God," and, therefore, I disagree with the fundamentalists about both the "what" and the "how." I think that there is only one world, that of the flux unfolding in space and time, the flux that *is* spacing-timing, which James Joyce called the "chaosmos." But I overtly chide the atheists for having a tin ear, for hamfisted and insensitive renderings of religion. They are like computer geeks trying to read a poem, like the tone-deaf writing music criticism, or the color-blind in an art museum! They are oblivious to what is going on *in* religion, what I call the "event," which I contend undermines the distinction between theism and atheism and the endless ensuing battle between the two. What "we" call in Christian Latin "religion" is a way of celebrating the flux, of singing a song to the world. Religion is a way to respond to the events that stir within the world, within history and language, within our bodies and the universe, by which we are always already addressed, to which we are always already attempting to respond. Religion is a way to answer what is calling. There are, of course, many ways to do this, both with or without "religion" and with or without what the great monotheistic traditions variously call *Elohim, Allah, theos, deus, Dieu, Gott,* or God.

As we always require both poets and rabbis, I must admit that I, too, have a rabbinic side myself. We require a "rabbinic" fidelity when attending to what is happening in "religion." We need a rigorous scholarly study of religion outside the reach of the police who all too frequently patrol its study in seminaries, divinity schools, and confessionally administered institutions. We need a rigorous study of "religion" even as we also need to approach religion with a poetic ear for the event that is going on *in* religion, which I call a "poetics of the event." My quasi-Hegelian version of the "philosophy of religion" proposes an account of the events of justice and promise, of giving, forgiving, and thanksgiving (the list is long) that are going on *in* religion. Its work is to construct a poetics of the form or shape these events assume in religion. Hegel called these forms or shapes *Vorstellungen,* noting specifically how they set themselves (*stellen*) forth (*vor*) in concrete historical form, which for him is the way the "Absolute" sets itself forth within history. On this point I am a heretical Hegelian, since I break with any such metaphysical Absolute and settle for feeling around in the dark for the underlying "events." The latter are not absolutes but quasi-phenomenological structures that admit not to a logic but to a "poetics," issuing not in a theologic but a theopoetics, a poetics of what stirs *within* the name of God, within what "we" call "God." Since these quasi-phenomenological forms of theopoetics never reach the stasis of a fundamental Absolute reality, one must acknowledge that religion is *Vorstellungen* all the way down!

Now as Putt quite insightfully points out, my work has taken the form of a poetics in three parts: (1) a poetics of "obligation," where obligation is the event and what we call "ethics" means the response to that event; (2) a poetics of the "Kingdom of God," which is a hermeneutics of the "event" that takes place in Christianity; (3) and finally—the first two are instances of a common structure—the poetics of the impossible, of the possibility of the impossible, the horizon-shattering arrival of the event that reopens and reinvents our world. Heroes of the poetics of obligation (say, Nelson Mandela) and heroes of the poetics of the Kingdom (say, St. Francis) are heroes of the impossible, people who make the impossible possible, who go where they cannot go, which is what we mean by the event.

Although I do have poetics aplenty, there is also, again as Putt rightly insists, a rabbi in my house, which I myself locate in the careful scholarly study of the history and texts of the various religious traditions. Because such scholarship exposes the contingency of confessional doctrine and confessional authority, it is always carefully supervised in confessional institutions, where one's scholarship can cost someone his or her job. Scholarship means the right to ask any question, a right with which confessional authorities have limited patience. They have no stomach for letting the chips fall where they may when it comes to scholarship. Putt, on the other hand, centers my rabbinic side not around the scholarly study of religion but around the question of the existence of God. In a certain sense, Westphal would agree—the way Karl Barth would agree—that religion is a *Vorstellung*; however, by that nomenclature Westphal means that religions are human constructions that can never do justice to the absolute transcendence of God (Westphal's theological "rabbi" keeps his "poet" in check). But I must reiterate that for me it is *Vorstellungen* all the way down, so that God and transcendence too are *Vorstellungen*, not of the absolute (Hegel) but of events; that is, they are the particular forms that events take in religious discourse. So my "poet" necessarily haunts any possible theologically minded "rabbi" with darker hauntological possibilities; in other words, the theopoetic spooks the theologic and keeps it up at night.

Personally, I prefer to say that God does not "exist" but "insists," meaning that the name of God is the name of an event that lays claim to us, to which we are called upon to respond. I treat the name of God as the name not of an existent being (Aquinas), a Ground of Being (Tillich), or a Hyper-Being (Pseudo-Dionysius), but of an insistent claim made upon us. God *in*sists, while it is we who *ex*ist and are responsible for giving God such existence as God has in the "world." I do indeed think the event is an event of "truth" and that the truth of the name of God is the becoming-true of the event that this name harbors. But this truth takes place in us, in our response. Hence the truth of the event is not the truth of a proposition, whether it propose theism or atheism. I am accordingly not trying to decode religious discourse into its unvarnished propositional truth in the manner of the rabbi-hermeneut Derrida is describing. I am not trying to establish as a metaphysical result the nonexistence of an entity called God, as if that were the "transcendental signified" that arrests the play of religious signifiers. I am adhering rigorously to the structure of the event, of the call and response, of insistence and existence, which I think nourishes and gives content to religious discourse. I think that by responding to the event that insists in this name, our existence draws strength from the weakness of God and the weakness of God (insistence) draws strength from our response (existence). The truth of the name of God is found in our response. The name of God is the name of a deed.

I leave it to the metaphysicians, and I leave the metaphysicians to themselves, to conduct their irresoluble debates about the existence or nonexistence of invisible entities, even as I forecast the gradual withering away of the old two-world theology. I make no metaphysical arguments against there being some invisible Hyper-Being or *Hinterwelt*. I just think that such beliefs are the result of hypostasizing an event, that they are part and parcel of a theology of the world behind the scenes according to which, after we die, we will flit about in airy weightless bodies in another world. This I regard as party to a pre-Copernican imaginary "heaven" "above" and "hell" "below," which Tillich called "supernaturalism." I philosophize not with a hammer but with a stylus. I do not set out to "refute" two-world theology so much as I try to ignore it on the premise that eventually it is going to look so bad that we will just give it up. That is what Putt is referring to when he chides me for thinking that people who sign on to the two-world theory should be ashamed of themselves. Putt calls this my rabbinic side, but I just consider it my healthily incredulous side, in the Lyotardian sense. I agree I have a rabbinic side, but I would locate it in taking a long hard and rigorously scholarly look at the history of the texts and institutions that have appointed themselves the guardians and administrators of the name (of) "God."

Employing Putt's overall schema, I would sum things up as follows. My "rabbinic" side is that I am all for a rigorous scholarly inquiry into "religion," but I am more interested in a "poetics" of a concrete religious figure like the "Kingdom of God" that attends to the play of events going on in such a figure. I am "ontological" about events, since events are what we love and are most interior to us, as the other in us, but as my ontology is a hauntology I am "cosmological" about the names we give to events, treating them as so many contingent figures, historical formations, or substitutable constructions, in short as *Vorstellungen*, for underlying events. Given my explanation of how Putt is explaining me, which I have slightly tweaked, I find myself in complete agreement with his explanation. I couldn't have said it better myself.

Notes

1. Perhaps a brief caveat might aid anyone who either takes too literally Derrida's notion of the absolute future or fails to appreciate the nuances of his contention that "*il n'y a pas de hors-texte*" and questions why a chapter examining John Caputo and Merold Westphal should be included in a book on the future of Continental philosophy of religion. Obviously, in the first case, if the future of Continental philosophy of religion is an impossible event, then it will have had no antecedents or horizons of expectations; consequently, there will have been no reason for another investigation into Caputo and Westphal. In the second case, however, given Derrida's idea of textuality, there is no future of Continental philosophy of religion that will not continue to bear the marks of those significant theorists who have influenced its development. As a result, Caputo and Westphal will continue to inspire and provoke the reevaluations and new directions that will "determine" that future. In other words, whatever the future of Continental philosophy of religion might be, it will not be devoid of "Capuphalian" resources; therefore, I do not hesitate to continue this investigation into their various pertinent positions.

2. Jacques Derrida, *Writing and Difference*, trans. Alan Bass (Chicago: University of Chicago Press, 1978), 67–68.

3. Ibid., 67.

4. Jacques Derrida, *Sovereignties in Question: The Poetics of Paul Celan*, ed. Thomas Dutoit and Outi Pasanen (New York: Fordham University Press, 2005), 105.

5. Derrida, *Writing and Difference*, 292.

6. Ibid., 70.

7. Ibid., 293.

8. Paul Tillich, *Theology of Culture*, ed. Robert C. Kimball (New York: Oxford University Press, 1959), 10–12.

9. Ibid., 12–15.

10. Mark Taylor certainly agrees that Tillich fails to escape ontotheology and suggests that his "two types" of philosophy of religion should be supplemented with a third type—an approach that attempts to move *beyond* ontotheology. Obviously, for this essay, Caputo and Westphal offer just such a third type—in their varying ways, of course. See Taylor's *Tears* (New York: SUNY Press, 1990), 83–84.

11. Tillich, *Theology of Culture*, 22–23.

12. Ibid., 24–25.

13. Ibid., 13, 16–19.

14. John D. Caputo, "What Is Merold Westphal's Critique of Ontotheology Criticizing?" in *Gazing through a Prism Darkly: Reflections on Merold Westphal's Hermeneutical Epistemology*, ed. B. Keith Putt (New York: Fordham University Press, 2009), 111. It should be noted that Caputo, himself, explicitly references Tillich's article on the two types of philosophy of religion in a brief discussion on Heidegger and Meister Eckhart in *The Mystical Element in Heidegger's Thought* (New York: Fordham University Press, 1986), 231–235.

15. John D. Caputo, *The Weakness of God: A Theology of the Event* (Bloomington: Indiana University Press, 2006), 16.

16. John D. Caputo, *On Religion* (New York: Routledge, 2001), 130.

17. "The question that I am made unto myself (*quaestio mihi factus sum*)—rather than one that I abstractly 'pose'—is what do I love when I love you my God?" (John D. Caputo, "Laughing, Praying, Weeping before God: A Response," in *Styles of Piety: Practicing Philosophy after the Death of God*, ed. S. Clark Buckner and Matthew Statler [New York: Fordham University Press, 2006], 253).

18. John D. Caputo, *Philosophy and Theology* (Nashville: Abingdon Press, 2006), 72. See also Garry Wills, *Saint Augustine's Childhood: Confessiones Book One* (New York: Viking, 2001), 29. Clark M. Williamson also interprets Tillich's ontological approach in language reminiscent of the Augustinian *cor inquietum*, calling it a "yearning, a discontent, a restlessness . . ." ("Tillich's 'Two Types of Philosophy of Religion': A Reconsideration" *Journal of Religion* 52 [July 1972]: 206).

19. John D. Caputo and Gianni Vattimo, *After the Death of God*, ed. Jeffrey W. Robbins (New York: Columbia University Press, 2007), 54, and John D. Caputo, *Deconstruction in a Nutshell: A Conversation with Jacques Derrida* (New York: Fordham University Press, 1997), 195.

20. John D. Caputo, *Against Ethics: Contributions to a Poetics of Obligation with Constant Reference to Deconstruction* (Bloomington: Indiana University Press, 1993), 70.

21. Merold Westphal, *Transcendence and Self-Transcendence: On God and the Soul* (Bloomington: Indiana University Press, 2004), 117.

22. Merold Westphal, *Suspicion and Faith: The Religious Uses of Modern Atheism* (Grand Rapids, Mich.: William B. Eerdmans, 1993), 284.

23. Westphal, *Transcendence and Self-Transcendence*, 117.

24. See for example, Merold Westphal, "Onto-theo-logical Straw," in *Postmodernism and Christian Philosophy*, ed. Roman T. Ciapalo (Washington, D.C.: Catholic University of America Press, 1996), 264–265.

25. Merold Westphal, *Overcoming Onto-Theology: Toward a Postmodern Christian Faith* (New York: Fordham University Press, 2001), 289.

26. Westphal, *Transcendence and Self-Transcendence*, 103.

27. See for example, John D. Caputo, *More Radical Hermeneutics: On Not Knowing Who We Are* (Bloomington: Indiana University Press, 2000), 211.

28. John D. Caputo, *The Prayers and Tears of Jacques Derrida: Religion without Religion* (Bloomington: Indiana University Press, 1997), 246.

29. John D. Caputo, *Radical Hermeneutics: Repetition, Deconstruction, and the Hermeneutic Project* (Bloomington: Indiana University Press, 1987), 271.

30. Caputo, *On Religion*, 128

31. Caputo, *The Weakness of God*, 103, 112.

32. Ibid., 88.

33. Westphal, *Overcoming Onto-Theology*, 5–6.

34. Ibid., xiii, 273; Merold Westphal, "Hermeneutics and the God of Promise," in *After God: Richard Kearney and the Religious Turn in Continental Philosophy*, ed. John Panteleimon Manoussakis (New York: Fordham University Press, 2006), 81, 85.

35. Merold Westphal, *Whose Community? Which Interpretation? Philosophical Hermeneutics for the Church* (Grand Rapids, Mich.: Baker Academic, 2009), 38–40.

36. Ibid., 144–145, 156. Westphal, himself, admits that when interpretation seeks to "retrieve the divine voice in the written word," it cannot avoid being labeled "rabbinic" (*Overcoming Onto-Theology*, 72). But he argues, in good Derridean fashion, that rabbinic interpretation can no more be accomplished or abandoned than can metaphysics itself (ibid., 73).

37. Jacques Derrida, *Memoirs of the Blind: The Self-Portrait and Other Ruins*, trans. Pascale-Anne Brault and Michael Naas (Chicago: University of Chicago Press, 1993), 1, 129.

38. Caputo and Vattimo, *After Death*, 54.

39. John D. Caputo, "Without Sovereignty, Without Being: Unconditionality, the Coming God, and Derrida's Democracy to Come," in *Religion and Violence in a Secular World: Toward a New Political Theology*, ed. Clayton Crockett (Charlottesville: University of Virginia Press, 2006), 147.

40. Caputo, *Prayers and Tears*, 25.
41. Westphal, *Transcendence and Self-Transcendence*, 95.
42. Ibid., 224.
43. Westphal, *Whose Community? Which Interpretation?*, 43.
44. Westphal, *Overcoming Onto-Theology*, 274–276.
45. Ibid., 277.
46. Caputo, *The Weakness of God*, 39; Caputo, *Against Ethics*, 245; Caputo and Vattimo, *After the Death of God*, 65. Joseph G. Kronick actually claims that Caputo's understanding of God as "the secret without truth [and] the name of passion" to be "a little too theological!" He questions whether Caputo's perspective does not in the end smuggle in some divine attributes when naming God as "addressee." See his *Derrida and the Future of Literature* (Albany: SUNY Press, 1999), 12.
47. Derrida says that the rabbi is the one who guards the covenant and allows entry through the proper shibboleth. This is another version of "circumcising the word." See Derrida, *Sovereignties in Question*, 61.
48. Westphal, *Overcoming Onto-Theology*, 65.
49. Westphal, *Whose Community? Which Interpretation?*, 20–22.
50. Merold Westphal, *Levinas and Kierkegaard in Dialogue* (Bloomington: Indiana University Press, 2008), 72.
51. This nomenclature comes from Derrida (*Writing and Difference*, 67, 293).
52. Westphal, *Overcoming Onto-Theology*, 4–6.
53. Caputo, "What Is Merold Westphal's Critique of Ontotheology Criticizing?" 108–109.
54. Caputo, *The Weakness of God*, 79.
55. Surprisingly, Feuerbach does sound a little Caputoan when he details his own brand of the Euthyphro Problem. He specifically connects "God" and "justice" and claims that God must be considered just because justice itself is divine. See Ludwig Feuerbach, *The Essence of Christianity*, trans. George Eliot (New York: Harper and Row, 1957), 21.
56. Jacques Derrida, *Negotiations: Interventions and Interviews 1971–2001*, ed. Elizabeth Rottenberg (Stanford, Calif.: Stanford University Press, 2002), 12–13.
57. Jacques Derrida, *Writing and Difference*, trans. Alan Bass (Chicago: University of Chicago Press, 1978), 67.
58. Ibid.
59. Ibid., 68.
60. Jacques Derrida, *The Gift of Death*, trans. David Wills (Chicago: University of Chicago Press, 1995), ch. 4.
61. See Nicholas Wolterstorff, *Divine Discourse: Philosophical Reflections on the Claim that God Speaks* (New York: Cambridge University Press, 1995), chs. 11–12.
62. Hans-Georg Gadamer, *Truth and Method*, 2nd. ed. rev., trans. Joel Weinsheimer and Donald G. Marshall (New York: Crossroad, 1991/2004), 297/297.
63. Ibid., 296/296.
64. Ibid., 267/269.
65. See, for example, John Sanders, *The God Who Risks: A Theology of Providence* (Downers Grove, Ill.: InterVarsity Press, 1998).
66. Nicholas Wolterstorff, "God Everlasting," in *Contemporary Philosophy of Religion*, ed. Stephen M. Cahn and David Shatz (New York: Oxford University Press, 1982), 77–98.
67. See Merold Westphal, "Inverted Intentionality: On Being Seen and Being Addressed," *Faith and Philosophy* 26, no. 3 (2009): 233–252. Inverted intentionality is an important theme in Levinas, Derrida, and Jean-Luc Marion.

68. Jacques Derrida, *Of Grammatology*, trans. Gayatri Chakravorty Spival (Baltimore: Johns Hopkins University Press, 1976), 158. For my reading of "play" in Derrida, see "Deconstruction and Christian Cultural Theory: An Essay on Appropriation," *Pledges of Jubilee*, ed. Lambert Zuidervaart and Henry Luttikhuizen (Grand Rapids, Mich.: Eerdmans, 1995), 107–125.

69. *Writing and Difference*, 90–93.

70. Jacques Derrida, "How to Avoid Speaking: Denials," in *Derrida and Natural Theology*, ed. Harold Coward and Toby Foshay (Albany: SUNY Press, 1992), 99.

71. *The Gift of Death*, 108, 66.

72. *The Gift of Death*, 108.

73. See above, note 56.

74. Harold Bloom, *Shakespeare: The Invention of the Human* (New York: Penguin Putnam, 1998), xvii, xx, 3.

75. The three Bibles mentioned here have this in common: they are complex totalities of texts that can be read on their own but demand to be read in relation to each other.

3 On Faith, the Maternal, and Postmodernism

Edward F. Mooney

We know our futures from our adopted pasts. The Ur-text for Continental philosophy of religion is penned by the elusive Johannes de Silentio, sometime freelancer in the employ of Søren Kierkegaard, in 1843 in the Danish market town, Copenhagen. Surprisingly, the first really *intelligible* figure of faith in *Fear and Trembling* is not the grotesque, or shall we say, monstrous father who binds Isaac at God's command, but an unassuming mother weaning her child. De Silentio announces that his approach will employ resources both "dialectical" and "lyrical," both philosophical and poetic. In the event, however, even these rival measures do not make Abraham a figure he—or we—can understand. At issue, of course, is faith, and Abraham is the father of faith.

Why does a *mother* of faith, a weaning mother, make such a startling early appearance—as if *she* is the key to the tale? Abraham is opaque, elusive, a nightmarish apparition. The weaning mother seems transparently familiar. After the mother, the second ordinary figure of faith is an unassuming shopkeeper—simple, like a tax collector, nothing like the fearful Abraham. Later, among our transparent figures of faith will be a silent woman knitting by the window.

The elusive author Johannes de Silentio writes at the prompting of the elusive Søren Kierkegaard, who in turn prompts and is midwife to Heidegger, then to Levinas, Derrida, Kristeva, and Caputo—figures without whom we have nothing like Continental philosophy of religion.[1] *Fear and Trembling*, it follows, is mother and father to Continental philosophy of religion, its Ur-text and womb. But what exactly *is* Continental philosophy of religion, after all? In a nutshell, it's marked by labor under the shadow of Nietzsche's death of God, under the associated threats and realities of loss of unified authors, selves, texts, and ethics, and under the loss of confidence in epistemology, ontology, and representation. All of this labor can be filed under the headings of absurdity, impossibility, and aporia. Take it on faith if you must, all of this arrives newborn and wailing in the labored but joyous deliveries of *Fear and Trembling*.

I give an account of *Fear and Trembling* and the role of the maternal and midwifery. Then midway through my essay, I turn to Derrida and Kristeva as writers born with assistance from Johannes de Silentio. Derrida's *The Gift of Death* is *Fear and Trembling*'s offspring, despite its wayward reading of Abraham.[2] Kristeva also is an offspring. She can guide our understanding of natality—of the significance of de Silentio's lyrical evocation of a weaning mother. Finally, I turn from the moment of birth to prospects for the future, short of death. If we can't know what the future will bring, what can we *want* Continental philosophy of religion to become?

A Role for Fear and Trembling

We can work forward and backward in establishing these genealogical connections. The cultural DNA is transmitted forward from *Fear and Trembling* via Heidegger and Levinas to Derrida, Caputo, Kristeva, and many others. The descendants of *Fear and Trembling* are identified as such because we can trace forward transmissions of style and insight even as we look backward, altering the past through present acts of adoption and caretaking.[3] How can we adopt this Ur-text from our present position? Do we observe this birth clinically, or do we *proclaim* the birth? Both, of course.

A courtroom judge brings a neglected point of law, long dormant, into present (and future) prominence, thus changing the significance of the past as well as the future. He proclaims it decisive, letting it become powerful by present adoption. Just so, with no legal but perhaps tribal authority, I invite you to find this little non-book by a non-author to be henceforth a common ancestor for Continental philosophers of religion. I declare this to be so. And what do we welcome into the world, thereby? In adopting *Fear and Trembling* as an Ur-text, we welcome as a progenitor a motley of figures, heroic and antiheroic, paternal and maternal—a shifty-but-marvelous cast of players in a piece of theater still infinitely interpretable, an infinite poem.

The "Book"—Lyrically Considered

Fear and Trembling is a basket of false starts and marginalia, of fantasy, fairy tale, and farce.[4] It undermines and blatantly distains any pretense to display a unified or stable text, author, or self. Also absent is a sense-making God. In the early "Attunement" (sometimes translated "Prelude" or "Exordium") we have Abraham embark on four ascents of Mt. Moriah.[5] Interestingly, each depicts a failure of faith—at least a failure to portray it, tune to it, properly: a warning about expecting representation to carry much of a burden in matters of faith.[6] But then we are thrown into disarray, for each failed attempt at portraiture has a tag, a caption that changes the subject. The easily dismissible tags sketch what? A *mother blackening her breast, weaning her child.*

And *why* this intrusion?

Could it be, God forbid, that the horrendous trial Abraham, the father, undergoes is but a variation on the trial any weaning mother undergoes, as she blackens her breast, making it repulsive? Could it be that the uncanny Abraham is *weaning* Isaac, or an uncanny God is weaning *Abraham*?

Retreating, for a moment, to the issue of representation, the mother seems to be the first unproblematic, canny portrait of faith. And Johannes de Silentio, Kierkegaard's delegated messenger, seems to let the maternal, or feminine, upstage the father for a moment. She promises intelligibility, where Abraham does not.

We have to await a later section of the lyric introduction to *Fear and Trembling* to find another portrait of faithful existence as canny, or graspable, as the mother. The mother usually takes a back seat in commentaries to Abraham, and equally overlooked is the apparent tax collector, that unassuming, nonchalant churchgoer who strides home from work. We're tuned to his world in "Preamble from the heart" (badly translated, "Preliminary Expectoration").[7] The shopkeeper/tax-collector imagines a fine head of lamb prepared by his wife. (Comic echoes of Abraham, offered a lamb.) He notes, bemused, a scurry of rats under a board over the gutter. He finds the sublime in the lowly, every day, and pedestrian. And where Abraham fails every test of representation, these knights of faith, mothers and shopkeeper, pass with flying colors.

Monstrosity and the Simply Ordinary

Why must representation of Abraham fail? Simple objects (trees, flagpoles) are easily represented; faith and knights of faith are not. De Silentio offers credible portraits of tax-collectors, mothers, knitters, and young men caught in unrequited love. Abraham defies description because he is no simple person or object or concept. He leaves us speechless the way a *spectacle* or the *sublime* leaves us stammering. The sublime or the spectacular can be *defined* as that which in its arresting significance nevertheless defies adequate description, gives portraiture an impossible task.[8] Abraham is like a wild storm that just can't be caught in a simple, single snapshot.

As a "freelance" reporter, Johannes "de silentio" is silenced, because the spectacular and the sublime are silencing. If he approaches Abraham along the route of the spectacular or sublime—which he mistakenly does—he will be confined to silence about faith. He only half believes his important *aperçu*, that there's another route to take. A weaning mother or a jaunty tax collector—ordinary and unspectacular humans, far from Abraham's monstrosity—can embody faith. De Silentio becomes *unsilent* as he voices these "ordinary" knights of faith. This lets the diction of faith move from the spectacular to dance steps, or leaps, to walking jauntily home—to giving up and getting back an object of love. His ordinary knights give us simple actions and sufferings that speak of grace, courage, trust, and delight in the *simple* shimmers of a life.⁹

The simple tremors and shimmers of life do not obviously elude representation. To all appearances, they are what they are, not what they try to dramatize on the stage of the Terrible and Holy. Dance embodies faith, and the faithful dance with graceful ballet leaps through life. Think of the damage done in thinking of a "leap of faith" as akin to a daredevil piece of base-jumping from high cliffs. Faith is not a daredevil circus leap from a tower into a flaming tub, nor is faith endorsing a true or false proposition, or explication. A knight of faith dances, just as Socrates dances solo before the Divine in the *Postscript*.¹⁰ Dancers are articulate through bodily gestures that "speak"—not *about* anything. They bespeak what they are. We are there to behold, but we behold the simple, not the spectacular or monstrous or wild sublime.

The taxman and weaning mothers are as inconspicuous in their faith as Abraham is conspicuous. No drama! But the drama of Abraham is mesmerizing, even as every representation of him fails. Johannes is ingenious and outrageous in depicting him fail: he runs up the mountain too fast, he stays home too long, he decides he'll avoid the journey and raise the knife at home, he decides he'd rather kill himself, he passes the knife to God, saying, in effect, if you want Isaac, YOU kill him, he decides he misunderstood, that his God could never ask such a thing, he raises the knife but feigns being a murderer (not a man of faith), he raises the knife but sinks in despair, unwilling to forgive God for asking.¹¹

The jaunty burgher, in contrast, more squire than knight, shows us faith's double movements, resigning the world, and then receiving it back as gift.¹² In releasing one's claim on the son, one is open to receive him. There is no terrifying near-murder on Moriah. We see the "movements" first in terms of a walker, and then of a dancer, whose lifts and falls become leaps up (in resignation of grounds), and sure landings (in groundless faith). Dancer and burgher are at home, always on the *way* home, bodies ever in motion, like the quiet good woman of faith stitching: no drama.

We want the glorious, spectacle of an impossible Abraham, not the simplicity of knitters, mothers, burghers, or dancers. We are tornado chasers. Tivoli Gardens, one of the first theme parks in the world, opened in Copenhagen the year *Fear and Trembling* appeared.¹³ Abraham is the main attraction in this literary Tivoli, a grotesque. We line up for tickets. Faith is a carnival distraction, a spectacle to gawk at and applaud.¹⁴

Dreams, Births, and Infinite Poetry

This Ur-text is neither theology nor scholarship but art: poetry, collage, many panels and portraits stitched loosely together; or theater, scene after scene loosely stitched. It is a dreamy, sometimes scary carnival and circus, a poetics of life and death. It is *dreamy* art. Johannes de Silentio frames his Abraham portraits as moments in "a beautiful dream," a childhood dream of a man who recalls it in old age. Biblically, and for Freud and so many others, remembering dreams is a key to faiths, salvations, and revelations. One gives up waking life for a dream, and gets waking life back, the dream included, life now modulated by dream. We're told dreamily, as an aside, that in such remembrance the faithful give birth to their own father. The faithful wield powers of the maternal. They are immersed in natality, in motherly openness to a possible intervention of gratuitous good. They know a capacity and potential for birth and rebirth, for the newness of "repetition," and, strange to say, for the dream and reality of giving birth to one's father.[15] This quiet story of faith is missed by Levinas, who sees only the monstrosity of Moriah, and an invitation to killing or violence.[16] The quiet story is the weaning of a child who lives to give birth to its father in a faithful stride, at home in the world, watching rats scamper under the gutter planks, accepting them heartily as a gift of life.

Kierkegaard lets the story provide other critical lessons of interest to Continental philosophers of religion. The little non-book gives a critique of bourgeois market society (Preface); a critique of direct communication (Epigraph); a critique of religion as bible-based hero worship (Speech in Praise); an attack on rule-based and bureaucratic conventional morality (Problema); an appreciation of domesticity (mothers weaning, shopkeepers strolling home for dinner, knitters by the fire). (NB—Aspiring sovereigns need not apply.) Furthermore, it provides a pornographic peephole into dreamlike blood and violence; a critique of the Spectacular City; a range of polyphony (the voice of terror, of praise, of detached analysis); a display of thematic variations (Abe might have dallied, rushed, stabbed himself, asked God to do it, refused, done it in despair, in deception). Finally, this little non-book by a non-author gives us a striking panoply of genres: the carnivalesque and bawdy; the fairy tale or fable; the satirical or farcical; the tragic; the labyrinthine unfathomable; the grotesque, the sublime; the dialectical, the lyrical; the fantastical and dreamlike; the antinomian and apophatic; the eucatastrophical (an unexpected finish that's marvelously good).

Hamlet, about to catch the conscience of king and queen, gets a preview from Polonius of the little play about to be performed. We are now about to watch the play performed by Kierkegaard–de Silentio. We should be prepared to witness *"the best actors in the world, either for tragedy, comedy, history, pastoral, pastoral-comical, historical-pastoral, tragical-historical, tragical-comical-historical-pastoral, scene individable, or poem unlimited."*

Derrida's Daring Misreading

Derrida devotes a chapter and more to the Abraham-Isaac scenario in *The Gift of Death*.[17] In other works, he mirrors Johannes de Silentio's extravagant experiments with style and genre, adding his own striking improvisations. Both thinkers, it seems, prefer literary seduction and ornamentation to abstract demonstration; they prefer philosophical tease and exploration. They both abjure the classic Cartesian quest for certain knowledge and come to stress the responsibility of singular agency over the acquisition of objective knowledge. Kierkegaard's "Truth is Subjectivity" is better rendered "Truth is Responsibility," a *troubled* responsibility. But Derrida parts ways with Kierkegaard—whether knowingly or from inattention to the text, I cannot say.

As Derrida would have it, the troubled responsibility in *Fear and Trembling* is the troubled knowledge that I sacrifice *many* in taking up responsibility for *some*—that I sacrifice *Isaac* in being answerable to *God*, or that in being answerable to God, I compromise my answerability to Sarah. Silentio is focused on Abraham's *troubled* responsibility, and also on the faith prerequisite to spiritual survival. Can Abraham weather this agony of crossed responsibilities? And it is not only his responsibilities that are crossed and apparently canceling in their conjunction. There is his faith that God will *give Isaac back*. (That God has demanded Isaac is never in question.) He must survive crossed responsibilities, and also the mind-shattering tension between the assurances that Isaac will be lost and that Isaac will be returned, that without qualification, God demands Isaac, and that God is to be trusted to return Isaac, without qualification. Talk of "love of the impossible"!

Faith is to weather a storm of intermixed joy and terror—joy in the expectation of Isaac's return, and terror in the expectation that Isaac will be lost. Abraham's faith is akin to a faith that God must harbor. He can order Isaac to be sacrificed and—quite incredibly—have faith that Abraham will keep loving Isaac and keep loving God. Superimposed on this is the faith that he can order Isaac up and expect Abraham still to hold on to the promise he will father a people through Isaac. Abraham is served a concatenation of impossibilities; God has faith he will joyfully, fearfully, impossibly, hold on.

In *The Gift of Death*, Derrida takes the Abraham-Isaac scenario to exemplify what he takes to be a universal and terrible boundlessness of responsibility. In answering God, Abraham sacrifices Isaac. So much is incontestable. But then Derrida launches this fact into an Enlightenment-style universal principle—every responsible response wreaks endless irresponsible harm. He illustrates: in answering the needs of my daughter, I irresponsibly sacrifice the needs of endless other daughters; in feeding my cat, I irresponsibly abandon thousands of others. Kierkegaard and Derrida agree that on Moriah, it is not knowledge of God or of the authenticity of his voice that is the issue, but rather a difficult, impossible, surely *troubled* responsibility. But then they part company.

Derrida's Miscues

First, for Kierkegaard not all responsibilities are universal, nor are they all simultaneously binding. The Abraham-Isaac scenario raises precisely this possibility, the possibility of a nonuniversal responsibility. This is a possibility Derrida never considers, though it is the centerpiece of the text he is reading. Kierkegaard asks the question: is there a "teleological suspension of the ethical" (where "the ethical" means "the universal")? If Abraham is bound to sacrifice his son, then there must be a unique, *nonuniversal* responsibility that singles him out. Whether we call this a religious responsibility or a (revised) ethical one—where "ethics" now incorporates particular, nonuniversal demands—the result is the same: to sacrifice Isaac *carries no commitment whatsoever either to assume or to abandon a responsibility to sacrifice every son, anywhere.* Abraham is not asked to bring every son to Moriah. He does not model the universal principle that fathers should always honor God's demand for sons, whenever. *Fear and Trembling* suggests, on the contrary, that a responsibility can be singular, targeting only *this* person, at *this* time and place. *God* may care equally for all, anywhere, at every moment, but finite creatures are not universally bound in that way. They find the needs of a specific neighbor sufficient unto the day.

There is something metaphysically melodramatic, grandiose, and false about Derrida's understanding of responsibility. It's rather grandiose to believe that each instance of felt-responsibility is also a principled demand requiring immediate *universal* fulfillment—as if we were *God*. To attend even in thought to absolutely *all* in need (present and future, here and everywhere) erases the full attention that neighbors and family and friends deserve.[18] If we are to "love thy neighbor as thyself," surely the neighbor is not an abstract class of all-in-need any more than loving myself is loving an abstract infinite multitude of "me." The motherly knight can't—and shouldn't—believe that in weaning her infant she is—or ought to be—weaning, and abandoning, all others. To be anxious about the thousands of infants she neglects would make her less than a mother, pitiably grandiose, and hardly of a mother of faith.

Derrida's reading fails in a second respect. He has conflated *resignation* (the thought that I must abandon my love) and *faith* (the thought that I will receive my love back). Faith requires trust that I *won't lose* those at risk as I act. A "knight of infinite resignation" lives in the pain that the object of his love eludes him. Derrida lives in the pain that he will never answer the needs of every claimant on his heart. But faith is the trust that I will get Isaac back, that in weaning the child, the child will not be lost, that in feeding my cat, others will not starve. To lament inattention to endless others is a counsel of despair, not the hope (*espoire*) that is faith. For de Silentio, faith is a double movement, a relinquishing and a receiving back, the trust that he who loses (gives up) his life shall regain it. Abandoning my Isaac opens the portal to regaining him. Giving up my grandiose hold on the whole world of cats, I get them back, undead, and I am released to feed mine, responding to a singular responsibility. He has not read Kierkegaard closely enough.

Espen Dahl puts the point more generally:

Postmodern accounts of the sublime, in Derrida and Lyotard, have focused on how the sublime surpasses our comprehension, and there is no doubt that the sublime is supposed to remind us of "the event" or "the trace" that metaphysics loves to suppress. What is symptomatic, however, is not only that such accounts have so little to say about the ordinariness of the sublime, say its vulnerability to being missed or rejected, but more importantly that they have nothing to say of the sublime's power to *return* us toward the everyday. It is indeed telling that in Derrida's reading of Kierkegaard's *Fear and Trembling*, nothing is made of the fact of the return. It is as if Derrida can see the sublime as figuring in the first movement, indeed its stroke of madness. But he does not attach significance to the *double* movement that arguably makes up Kierkegaard's prime concern: the infinite resignation must be succeeded by faith enacted in the recurrence of the everyday.[19]

Kristeva: Silent Approvals

In the 1930s in Paris, Kierkegaard, Hegel, Heidegger, and Marx were placed in many-sided contestations. At stake were a minimal social order and stable institutions; the imperative of liberation from suffocating bourgeois conformity and fascist regimentation; the emancipatory imperative of social change and political revolution; the rational imperative of science and critique in the formation of a viable society; and finally, the imperatives of art and religion as these intersect social, political, and scientific imperatives.[20]

If Kierkegaard was center-stage in the 1930s, after 1950 his presence began to diminish. Heidegger gave us anxiety; Sartre, radical choice; Arendt, the critique of a stifling public "blob." These are Kierkegaardian themes, but the Dane went into partial eclipse. However much their thinking leaned on his, the intellectual celebrities spoke for themselves rather than from a figure from a century past. Forms of phenomenology, poststructuralism, and after 1946, the influence of Lacan, Derrida, and Foucault came to dominate the French milieu. And they wrote in a milieu deeply suspicious of religious thought. It's not hard to paint Kierkegaard as overzealous, wild, and dangerous.

Kristeva entered the Parisian scene in the 1960s with a dissertation in hand on Bakhtin, who famously argues that the polyphony of voices in a novel like *The Brothers Karamazov* marks a polyphony of authorial standpoints.[21] Accordingly, the assumption of a unitary authorial voice becomes problematic. "The" author disperses in a multiplex spread throughout the voices of characters.[22] The absence of a unified authorial identity has its parallel in the absence of a unified self, agent, or subjectivity.

It seems unlikely that a single authorial voice underlies Kierkegaard's pseudonymous and veronymous works. Kristeva brings Bakhtin to her psychoanalytic writings, transporting a multiplicity of voices inward; Kierkegaard would approve.[23] We are a fragile polyphony, reminiscent of the polyphony in the lyric sections of *Fear and Trembling*. Johannes is both garrulous and silent about many things, including his true center (if he has one). "The" self, for Kristeva, becomes a Kierkegaard-like ensemble of dialogical internal relations, reflecting an unfolding matrix of interpersonal child-parent and self-other relations.[24] Kristeva's early work on Bakhtin also takes up his theme of the carnivalesque, a literary mixture of the grotesque, sensational, satirically comedic, and unblushing showmanship. These are striking features of the first third of *Fear and Trembling*. Copenhagen's new amusement park, Tivoli Gardens, was meant to outdo Paris, and opened in 1843, the year *Fear and Trembling* was published. Johannes de Silentio does not spare us the theatrical and macabre, the sensational, horrific, burlesque, and grotesque. Perhaps he is a carnival barker for a kind of freak show—as if Abraham were a three-headed monster, providing an occasion for gawkers to scream on the cheap, and crowds to line up for a view.[25] Here, we *see* faith!

It is not that Bakhtin *found* the carnivalesque or a loss of a unified author in Kierkegaard. De Silentio can be claimed as the ancestor who establishes the carnivalesque and disestablishes the unified substantial self as a matter of present identification—just as an adult might claim as a father someone other than his biological father. Kristeva claims Bakhtin as her father, and we can claim Kierkegaard as *his* progenitor. In this vein, *Fear and Trembling* is dubbed the now-acknowledged mother of Continental philosophy of religion—quite apart from having to trace precise influences, a path of cultural DNA transmission, as it were.

This is not backward causality but renewing the present through new and creative adoptions of the past—what Robert Pogue Harrison (in *The Dominion of the Dead*) calls "Choosing your Ancestors."[26] Similarly, the actual knowledge Kristeva has of the four mothers weaning in *Fear and Trembling* is irrelevant to my interest. My claim is that Kristeva's thinking is so attuned to what we might call the deep meaning of religious separation, trauma, and the possibilities of rebirth, or birth itself, that we *cannot but* see her continuing Kierkegaard-Silentio's depictions of the trauma and promise of weaning as homologous with faith.

Mine is not an invitation to speculate on a possible direct influence of Kierkegaard's portraits on Kristeva (perhaps such an influence will be established). Mine is an invitation to see Kristeva commenting on those portraits the way we might see my neighbor's struggles with affliction as commenting on the Book of Job. If Job can address my neighbor across centuries, Kristeva can address 1843 mothers weaning. I invite readers to an occasion of mutual address and acknowledgment.

Embodied Significations

As she proceeds into a career in psychoanalysis, Kristeva elaborates what we could call the carnivalesque of inner life; carnivals are full of nonverbal pranks and tumbles. Her two faces of signification has a striking resemblance to Kierkegaard's two faces of communication. Her semiotic signification, the embodied speech and gesture that imparts a particular individual's feeling and passion, resembles Kierkegaard's indirect communication.[27]

The contrast to semiotic signification would be abstract words reporting banal facts or objective directions, where an embodied speaker is inessential to the message. Kierkegaard would call this direct communication, and Kristeva would call it symbolic signification. Both Kierkegaard and Kristeva affirm the centrality of embodied communication, the non-propositional imparting or transfer of affect, pathos, and individualized perspective.

Neither Husserl nor Saussure has a place for embodied speech, for the voice of *this* person, speaking in *this* tone of voice—in *this* physical posture, with *this* gesture, among just *these* attentive, embodied, listeners.[28] To give language a sort of theoretical and abstract sheen excises the dramatic, even theatrical, context of living speech and expression. Speech has its genesis in a baby's coos, eyes fixed on its mom, who returns the look and the coo. It emerges later in an orator's sweating or calming exhortations. To insist on passion and embodiment does not denigrate the symbolic but resists the loss of particular speaking beings who avail themselves of the symbolic *and* the semiotic, the abstract *and* the corporeally enacted.

Kierkegaard uses pseudonyms, dramatic narrative, and a variety of genres to set words in living motion in particular contexts, uttered by singular, passionate souls.[29] He valorizes the singular individual, and it is a virtually embodied individual to whom he gives voice in the figures of Judge Wilhelm, Don Juan, the young man of *Repetition,* the seducer, and the professorial anti-professor, Johannes Climacus. Kierkegaard addresses the embodied individual as "My dear reader." Kristeva has no use for a theory of language that leaves language "removed from historical turmoil," floating "midair," words uttered, as she puts it, by "a sleeping body."[30]

Tremors and Traumas

We live episodically, our time punctuated by intrusions of the horrific. As a psychoanalyst, Kristeva is exquisitely attuned to the generative and dangerous drama of interlocking fathers, mothers, infants, and children.[31] Thunder awakens us to mortality, finitude, and grandeur, and the chaos of cities awakens us to loss of place. Outbursts and communions can awaken us to the horrific and rejuvenating powers of family-ensembles. We can see Kristeva's schemas of familial tensions played out in *Fear and Trembling*'s schema of trauma, near-death, and rebirth.[32] The Abraham stories, as well as the quieter images of knights of faith, give us theatrical performance of our familial constraints and possibilities. They are dreams for our therapist that awaken us to nightmarish undercurrents in father-son, mother-infant, God-subject relations—and hold out an "absurd" hope for survival.

An old man remembers a childhood story. To whom does he tell it? Perhaps it's offered to the attentive ear of a confidant. Each of the early tableaux has a caption reflecting a weaning mother. The terror of the father in the act of severing is transposed to the anxiety of the mother severing. A nightmarish fright as Abraham raises his knife is transposed to an anxious nurturing calm. However difficult the severing of infant from mother, this scene of the mother will domesticate the horror of the near-sacrifice on Moriah. Yet even as the knife is partially blacked out, its afterlife transfers a minor horror to the act of weaning. Does the maternal severing now seem more like the paternal severing (and vice versa)? If Abraham becomes more like a mother, a mother becomes more like an Abraham. The trauma of severing, maternal or paternal, can live on.

A dreamy mother-infant scenario matches a dreamy father-son scenario—both dreamed under the demanding gaze of God. Isaac's trust that his father will protect him, Abraham's trust that God will protect him—a nursing infant's trust that its mother will protect her—are all placed at catastrophic risk. A person's moral sensibility—sense of up and down, good and bad, God and subjects, faith and reason—can be thrown into disarray. Do we awake from these nightmares to a world more or less restored?

Kristeva's writes on "the imaginary father" (colloquially, a "father figure") and the powerful yet expelled "mother figure." Both are larger-than-life impostors with counterparts in Father-God, weaning-Mother, and knife-wielding Abraham. Viewed from the positions of an infant or Isaac or Abraham as under duress, the near-destructions and wondrous escapes imply a divine Wholly Other. The nightmare of God's demand is the fright of mammoth waves, and the release from terror mimics awakening from a bad dream, awakening, in the best of times, to a rejuvenating wonder and delight—*jouissance*.

In *Fear and Trembling*, the tale is framed as a childhood memory of a beautiful fairy tale—by such modulation of register we handle our fears. But the possibility that God could make such a demand and that a father could heed it, remain disgusting, taboo, like mangled flesh. These are thoughts to vomit out, but they remain powerfully there, as what Kristeva will call *abjects,* marking a pollution of meaning, a fate to which any self is heir. Expelling the horrific is fantasized protection—casting it out.

Abraham's freedom might require casting off his internalized Isaac, setting Isaac free of him, and freeing him from Isaac. It might require that God cut off Abraham from God—temporarily suspending that relation. The survival of a son requires a father's and a mother's ever-greater relinquishment of control and sovereignty—without relinquishing love. It is as if these difficult relinquishments were collapsed into three days approaching Moriah—and a moment of restoration, freedom, and independence. Just so, an infant's independence rests on a mother's casting off at weaning.

Johannes gives initiative to the mother who blackens her breast. Kristeva unabashedly defends the necessity of matricide—surely hyperbole.[33] Yet that is exactly the hyperbole at work in the Moriah tales of near-infanticide. Matricide is the necessity that the child separate from its mother in the name of independence: there is the necessary severing of the umbilical cord, and the later severing at weaning. However, each of these cuts is initiated not by a matricidal child but by a mother.

Abraham takes initiative at the behest of a Father who is in a position to order fathers. But we might wonder whether this Father is a model of constancy. It might seem that God capriciously flirts with the death of Abraham, at least with Abraham as father of faith. Isn't it plausible that Abraham will die of grief whether he obeys or disobeys, whether he loses Isaac (and retains God) or loses God (and retains Isaac)? Yet there is method in this madness. In *Postscript*, Kierkegaard says God wants to give independence to persons over against Himself.[34] God's apparent withdrawal of all succor might be a gift of independence.

The widescreen drama of Isaac and Abraham haunts as a moment of *death*. But there are also moments of *birth:* the infant's cord is severed, and new life emerges in weaning—not to mention *rebirth* at Isaac's restoration.

Natality, Mortality, and Chora

We can figure separation not only as mortality but as natality, as coming to birth and independence. Then the infant's weaning, though awakening tremors, is also a foretaste of life. The weaning of Isaac from Abraham, and of both from God, is miraculous rebirth, as in the return of Isaac from the dead, and the return of Abraham to the ordinary world of fatherhood.

Speaking of natality, it is striking that Kristeva ventures beneath language, signification, psychoanalysis, and politics, to hazard an image of primal womb. She ventures beneath discourses, disciplines, cultural practices, and institutions that crystallize, articulate, or edit a world. There in that under-world she imagines a place holding and giving birth to all levels and strands of the above-world. Lifting Plato's term, she calls this site of primal natality simply *Chora*.[35] Not the stuff of the world—cultural, psychological, or otherwise—that becomes edited, organized, or constructed, *Chora* is whatever holds or contains that stuff, whatever "stuff" and its processes are "placed in." Of course, in the ordinary, above-world, a piece of "stuff" is born from its earlier, predecessor stuff. But infinite regresses are terrifying, and Plato and Kristeva venture that "stuff" and its processes are born from a womb that is held by nothing deeper, and so is absolute or primordial.

Socrates is midwife, male and female. He brings souls to birth, helps them emerge as individuals, emerge, that is, from wombs. Kristeva is enough a Bakhtinian and Socratic dialogical thinker to take psychoanalysis as a midwife's art. Insight comes as she helps readers or clients trace a genealogy of formative mothers, fathers, siblings, teachers, and neighbors—that is, trace generative ensembles working in embodied, speaking space. These deeply rooted familial and wider ensembles are all held in play in an unnamable place—of fright, but also of birth and nurture. Kierkegaard would call it the place of God, while Kristeva has it the place of natality or *Chora*, in its own way, divine. Therein the pain of dispersal and mortality's abyss are joyously, affirmatively, answered.

What Is the Future for Continental Philosophy of Religion?

We could say that the future is unknown and so it might be that the future is rosy, or we could say that the future might be rosy but also might be dismal. I'd say that a future worth having lies in cherishing little things, even snippets of song, or flashes of imagery. So let's begin.

Why the future? Why wonder what lies ahead? No doubt we need to be reassured that the projects we have undertaken as writers in this tradition in fact *have* a future. We want the future to be rosy, to know that our efforts are not the last gasp of a dying historical moment.[36] I wrestle with images from the start of *Fear and Trembling*, images of nurturing mothers and forbidding fathers. They lie with life's grittiness; I'm *invested* in them; I want them to live on. Like a tune that won't go away, like the Byrds' "Turn, Turn, Turn," I carry them in memory, and they carry me. Each time that tune sings my imagination (or sings in it?) I know it has a kind of immortality. It doesn't die as I fall asleep but is there in the morning, singing me into the world. Of course I join in, so I create its future in letting it sing. Continental philosophy of religion will survive into the future because it sings in my past, and resonates in my present, and I know I will carry its tunes into a rosy future. That's faith, the future is faithfully kept (or not), it's mine, and maybe yours, faith as *desire for a good to survive, and the full assurance that it will*.

No one has a crystal ball. Kierkegaard said that we understand backward, and live forward.[37] The future is not understood but we live into it anyway, like nightwalkers, *feeling* our way. Our feelings are modulated as desires, hopes, and fears for the next moment and the morrow. There is no third-personal objective standpoint from which to forecast the shape of my life or of a philosophical tradition. I speak first-personally of *my desires* for the future. I have faith in the survival, the continuance into the future, of what's good in life. One thing that's good is immersion in the strangeness of loving and weaning. I desire that thrill (and shudder) of contact with those alluring and forbidding images of conflicted fathers and mothers. It's inseparable from the thrill and shudder of contact with life.

I desire, and find myself fully assured, that a rosy future for Continental philosophy of religion lies ahead. This is not, in the first instance, a desire that something as general as a historical tradition should have an upbeat future. It's a desire for the specific ride these particular Kierkegaard images give. They arise from the dark of memory into my present and burst forward to shape my next moment, that moment where I sing them—and they sing me. So a future may not be as dismally opaque and unmusical as the image of nightwalkers feeling their way suggests. It's opaque only if we crave the impossible, the hard-and-fast grip of impersonal knowledge. But if we want not knowledge but *life*, then the futures can be rosy, as upbeat as "Turn, Turn, Turn." The question of the future of Continental philosophy becomes enticing if I transpose a futile *searching for the facts* (what will the future bring?) into *savoring my desires* (what do I *want* my future attractions to be?).

"Turn, Turn, Turn" starts as a snatch of melody that grows into a song that can join forces with Ecclesiastes, and with the world of '60s and '70s pop music, and the troubadours since who sustain and advance a tradition on the back of this tune. Continental philosophy of religion starts, for me, as a snatch of images from *Fear and Trembling* that grow into sentences and passages and on into texts from Derrida or Kristeva that form and are formed by a historical movement and its canon. In my own case, desire for a tradition rests on my being *struck by an image*, and *wishing it well*, and *yielding to its work*.

It's easiest to savor things close at hand: a sea view, a good cappuccino. The more distant and abstract the target of my desire, the harder it is to savor. Do I want to dive into something as diaphanous and slippery as Continental philosophy of religion? Who knows! I *do* want, no question, to dive into *Fear and Trembling*'s "Attunement," into its haunting images and captions, and I *do* care for the future of those images and sentences. Do I thereby dive into a tradition and its canon?

Perhaps Continental philosophy has no frozen canon to cherish because one of its motifs is that canons must be repeatedly deconstructed and dissolved, left to the elements like footprints washed by the sea. I savor what Kierkegaard says on joy, or what Nietzsche says on disquietude, and I hope for their good health in the morrow.[38] I hope for the survival of single sentences, just as I hope for the survival of "Turn, Turn, Turn." I hope for longevity for Thoreau's "Joy is a condition of life," and for his deathbed whisper, "One life at a time."[39] I savor slender strings of words and the life that they bring and sustain. My nurturing attention to these new strings, shoots, and branches of meaning, as Kierkegaard delivers and nurtures them, is my living into their meanings, and elongating their presence, letting their life be seminal. Thus do words, worlds, and writers, in virtue of my attention—and the attention of countless others—move into a future *defined*, brought to birth, by such attention.

Possibilities for the Future

I characterized Continental philosophy of religion in historical generality as working under the shadow of the death of God, under associated losses of unified, substantial authors, selves, texts, and ethics, and under the shadow of lost confidence in epistemology, ontology, and representation.[40] We can't have *knowledge* of what such a basket of motifs foretells, but I have vague and speculative thoughts on the matter, not reflecting a desire but a hazard of possibilities.

Continental philosophy might just fade away, becoming of only archival interest. Political theology might dethrone once-dominant interests in the death of God, texts, authors, or ontology—though those motifs might leave their marks in a subdominant register.[41] This might be a *continuation* of present trends or a radical break. Then again, there might be *more* to say about the death of God or the volatilization of texts, either because the lessons need restating or because there are new twists to the theme to grapple with. The once-dead God may rise yet again.

The historian's *philosophical movement* is something about which I have at best only tepid hopes or fears. I don't want a philosophy that finds intimacy with weaning mothers and fearsome fathers repulsive or irrelevant. I think *Fear and Trembling* is the Ur-text of Continental philosophy of religion, historically considered, but that matters less to me than the impact of Johannes de Silentio's images and captions. They draw me in, and draw me to ask why I ascend Moriah with Silentio, and why *this* mother gets paired with *this* father—and no one is aghast or thrown into wonder.

I hope for a rosy future for these sentences and texts and images, but I said the future might turn dismal. I don't *want* that, or *predict* it, but at times I *fear* it. Continental philosophy will turn dismal if it turns scholastic or merely fashionable. In self-infatuation, it can rebuke the gritty textures, tastes, and fabrics of life, tender and terrible.

Philosophy is best as it plays close to the grain and grittiness of life. Of course it can be legitimately practiced as impersonal forensics or construction of worldviews and systems. It can be practiced as deconstruction or microanalysis or cultural critique, or as argumentation within its glorious traditions. Thus practiced, it is more or less impersonal or "objective," and a regal splendor. Philosophy becomes starkly inglorious, as I see it, when it becomes scholastic, irrelevant to the tastes and contours of ordinary (and extraordinary) life, and abandons a search for truths. It can want to be à la mode, basking in cliquish notoriety, exchanging passwords with a knowing wink. I'm attracted to thinking that risks dialogue at close quarters on matters of visceral, existential concern. I savor philosophy that can take a singular thought, image, or vignette, and deliver it compellingly to nonspecialists. I want it to move informally, dialogically, face to face, in a dance of loves, aversions, and uncertainties. When Thoreau says, "joy is a condition of life," I respond.

Johannes de Silentio gives me images with visceral impact. Derrida and Kristeva expand the impact. They carry them to their further significance. When it comes to the future, the deck is stacked in favor of images with captions, and *against* the dismal alternatives of a scholastic philosophy, or one hawking idioms that baffle the uninitiated. Things get dismal when idiom serves only its own sophistication and glitter. Life is erased by a text excessively crosshatched by *aporia, the impossible, materiality, the other, the body, the auto-destructive, the Eventual, the spectral, affect, repetition, sovereignty, colonizing, intersectionality, or singularity*. If philosophy is an intimate dance with life, it's hard to feel it beneath some of these garments.[42]

Exuberant, Dancing Wisdom

Nietzsche famously loves a dancing philosophy. Emerson, our American continental, anticipates Nietzsche: "I think the peculiar office of scholars in a careful and gloomy generation is to be (as the poets were called in the Middle Ages) Professors of the Joyous Science, detectors and delineators of occult symmetries & unpublished beauties, heralds of civility, nobility, learning & wisdom . . . who should affirm it in music or dancing."[43] I hear these words addressed to our own "careful and gloomy generation," calling for thinking and writing at the visceral level open to the uninitiated. Poetic professors model thought to be absorbed (in joy or in tears) in public squares, as well as on solitary walks.

I have at hand an instance of a writer following the grittiness of life rather than the glitter of eviscerated theory, the novelist Zadie Smith. In a recent *New Yorker,* she writes strikingly of attunements in *Fear and Trembling*.[44] In a companion piece that follows, in the *New York Review of Books,* she writes on joy. Her informal reflections become philosophical as she characterizes joy as a troubling mix of rapture, affliction, and terror, as perhaps a kind of extraordinary Dionysian seizure, though it can triggered by something as pedestrian as love of a child. Perhaps we thought we knew something about joy. She tells us otherwise, for joy is not just happiness, its opposite is not suffering or melancholy, and it is not just delight. We ought to fear it as well as cherish its irruption into ordinary life.[45] (If we've been reading philosophy of religion with our other eye, we can ask, what is it to have both delight and terror in the otherness of God's presence?[46])

Joy overtakes us, takes over, leaving us naked. It is a gift, as wonderful and terrible as our humanity. She raises the possibility that simple, pedestrian joy can also be the terrifying, extraordinary sublime, like the joy-terrors of Abraham. She lights up a space, and lets questions percolate without answers, inviting our fledgling philosophical responses. There's a coy directness to her account that invites comparison with Johannes de Silentio's terrible and loving images. Abraham is not joyous ascending the mountain, but neither is he melancholy, depressed, or in despair. The shop-keeping knight of faith is "happy every moment," but is he joyous? Is the mother happy to release her child?

Smith starts us thinking, providing grist for philosophical imagination and for those well outside (as well as inside) academic mills: two points in her favor.

She writes: "Occasionally the child . . . is a pleasure, though mostly she is a joy, which means in fact she gives us not much pleasure at all, but rather that strange admixture of terror, pain, and delight that I have come to recognize as joy, and now must find some way to live with daily."[47] Learning to live with this daily must be a task and gift not of faith as clinging to propositions, but of a dancing faith. A weaning mother feels some of the terror of Abraham, even as she is overjoyed to have brought life to the world and set it free. Then Smith offers a wildly discordant conjunction of images:

> Real love came much later. It lay at the end of a long and arduous road, and up to the very last moment I had been convinced it wouldn't happen.
> I was so surprised by its arrival, so unprepared, that on the day it arrived I had already arranged for us to visit the Holocaust museum at Auschwitz.

Love's joy arrives on the way to . . . *Auschwitz?* Of course Abraham's faith arrives on the way to Moriah! (Perhaps horror hollows us to make room for love.) Then this summation of paradox: *"We were heading toward all that makes life intolerable, feeling the only thing that makes it worthwhile."* What but love—and joy—makes the journey to Moriah and its awful separations worthwhile? Love among the ruins.

She adds:

> [Joy] doesn't fit with the everyday. The thing no one ever tells you about joy is that it has very little real pleasure in it. And yet if it hadn't happened at all, at least once, how would we live? . . . Isn't it bad enough that the beloved, with whom you have experienced genuine joy, will eventually be lost to you? Why add to this nightmare the child, whose loss, if it ever happened, would mean nothing less than your total annihilation? . . . Joy is such a human madness. . . . Surely if we were sane and reasonable we would every time choose a pleasure over a joy, as animals themselves sensibly do.

The most horrendous loss and most wondrous gifts are inextricably wed. So say the opening images and captions of *Fear and Trembling*.

Is Zadie Smith's Kierkegaardian riff a small leap forward, philosophically speaking? She invites us to reconsider a commonplace opposition between pain and joy. She invites us to begin a long haul of philosophical revision and refinement. What is it to mix joy and terror, pain and transport, all with a dash of delight? She rings a hopeful bell that invites us to savor enigmas not only at the heart of a life worth living, but also at the heart of a religious way of living.[48] The same enigmas tempt Kierkegaard (from one angle), and Derrida and Kristeva (from another). Smith's philosophical riffs emerge from immersion in the fine-grained structure of living, free of scholasticism, pretension, or fashionable jargon. They point toward religious sensibilities that deliver worlds one can delight in, live with, and struggle through haltingly, close to the marrow, close to the heart.

Notes

1. It is apparent from even a quick glance at John D. Caputo's *Against Ethics* (Bloomington: Indiana University Press, 1993) that he is indebted to *Fear and Trembling*.
2. Jacques Derrida, *The Gift of Death*, trans. David Wills (Chicago: University of Chicago Press, 1995), 70–77.
3. For discussion of choosing a progenitor, see Robert Pogue Harrison, *The Dominion of the Dead* (Chicago, 2003), ch. 6, "Choosing your Ancestor."
4. On *Fear and Trembling*, see my *On Søren Kierkegaard: Dialogue, Polemics, Lost Intimacy, and Time* (Burlington, Vt.: Ashgate, 2007), ch. 8; *Knights of Faith and Resignation: Reading Kierkegaard's Fear and Trembling* (Albany: SUNY Press, 1991); and *Selves in Discord and Resolve: Kierkegaard's Moral-Religious Psychology from "Either/Or to Sickness Unto Death"* (New York: Routledge, 1996), chs. 4 and 5.
5. The Hannay translation is superior here. Søren Kierkegaard, *Fear and Trembling*, trans. Alastair Hannay (New York: Penguin Books, 1986).
6. I document these multiple failings in *Knights of Faith*. In addition to the four "Attunement" versions, additional "false-lead" variations occur (in the Hannay trans.) at 21, 32, 36, 52, 119.
7. I follow the Hannay translation, once more.
8. Jack Caputo is in love with *the impossible*—but among knights he does not, as I see it, claim the impossibility of *representing* weaning mothers or dancing knights. And rightly so. But plenty of impossibility remains: the impossibility that a weaning mother or a jaunty tax collector *is* a knight of faith, or that both are somehow *equivalent* to the father going up Moriah, or that Abraham can survive his trial, or that God could stage it.
9. Espen Dahl writes of the possibility of an *ordinary* sublime in Kierkegaard, Cora Diamond and Stanley Cavell. This is what de Silentio calls, with regard to the shopman, discovering "the sublime in the pedestrian." See Espen Dahl, *Stanley Cavell, Religion, and Continental Philosophy* (Bloomington: Indiana University Press, 2014), especially chapter 1. We might say that Kierkegaard exhibits an astonishing flexibility in projecting the image of Abraham on Moriah into the new, ordinary, everyday context of a weaning mother.
10. Socrates dances before the divine: Kierkegaard, *Concluding Unscientific Postscript*, trans. Howard Hong and Edna Hong (Princeton University Press, 1992), 1:89. Climacus dances with death in the preface of *Crumbs*, last sentence: Søren Kierkegaard, *Philosophical Crumbs and Repetition* (Oxford World Classics, 2009).
11. See note 6, above.
12. For a fine discussion of how the tax man's simple faith can sustain his joy and delight amidst a world of cruelty, boredom, and sin, see Sheridan Hough, "What the Faithful Tax Collector Saw (against the Understanding)," *International Kierkegaard Commentary* 18, ed. Robert L. Perkins (October 2006): 295–311.
13. I show how Tivoli and Moriah are homologous in *On Søren Kierkegaard*, ch. 8.
14. I discuss the Abraham scenarios as distractions from faith, in *On Søren Kierkegaard*, 140–141.
15. I discuss de Silentio's allusion to giving birth to one's father, of being mother to one's father, and hence to oneself, in *Knights of Faith*, 40.
16. For Levinas's brute reading, see his 1963 lecture on Kierkegaard that pinpoints a dangerous "violence" in Kierkegaard's willingness to praise Abraham as someone "transcending the ethical." See "Kierkegaard: Existence and Ethics," in *Proper Names*, trans. Michael B. Smith (London: Athlone, 1996), 66–74. Of course Levinas has other passages that seem less appalled at Kierkegaard, and a rapprochement between the two can be constructed around the notions

of love and responsibility, starting from the premise that Kierkegaard's "Truth is subjectivity" is better rendered "Truth is Responsibility." For a wonderful exploration of Kierkegaard, Levinas, and the maternal, see Claire Elise Katz, *Levinas, Judaism, and the Feminine: The Silent Footsteps of Rebecca*, (Indiana, 2003).

17. Derrida, *The Gift of Death*, 70–71. See John J. Davenport, "What Kierkegaard Adds to Alterity Ethics: How Levinas and Derrida Miss the Eschatological Dimension," in *A Conversation between Neighbors: Emmanuel Levinas and Søren Kierkegaard in Dialogue*, ed. J. Aaron Simmons and David Wood (Bloomington: Indiana University Press, 2008).

18. Patrick Stokes has suggested that Derrida may be making a less extreme claim. "Derrida's point is perhaps more that in attending to the neighbor, we thereby fail to help others—we can't help everyone who we *could* help. Thus it's not necessarily that we have to attend to or focus on *everyone*, but that every moral act represents a failure to help someone else." My sense is that we can often distill a "reasonable" reading from points Derrida delivers with seductive hyperbole. But shouldn't we *challenge* hyperbole—if that's what we have?

19. Espen Dahl remarks: "In Derrida's reading of Kierkegaard's *Fear and Trembling*, nothing is made of the fact of the return. It is as if Derrida can see the sublime as figuring in the first movement, indeed its stroke of madness. But he does not attach significance to the *double* movement that arguably makes up Kierkegaard's prime concern: the infinite resignation must be succeeded by faith enacted in the recurrence of the everyday." Dahl, *Stanley Cavell*, ch. 2, "The Ordinary Sublime."

20. See Samuel Moyn, *The Origin of the Other* (Ithaca, N.Y.: Cornell University Press, 2005), 164–194. In *An Atheism That Is Not Humanist in French Thought* (Stanford, Calif.: 2011), Stefanos Geroulanos gives an eye-opening account of "anti-humanism" in France—a perspective that was dead set against "liberal" views that put individual consciousness (or subjectivity) center stage. This move against Socrates, Descartes, and even a Kierkegaardian subjectivity started in the 1930s and resurfaced after World War II, especially in evidence in Heidegger's "Letter on Humanism" and Derrida's privileging of *texts* over contexts, persons, or authors.

21. For a longer account of Kierkegaard and Kristeva, see my "Julia Kristeva: Tales of Love and Horror," in *Kierkegaard Research: Sources, Reception and Resources*, vol. 13: *Kierkegaard's Influence on the Social Sciences*, ed. Jon Stewart (Burlington, Vt.: Ashgate, 2011), 177–194.

22. See "On Style and Pseudonymity," ch. 3 in my *Excursions with Kierkegaard: Others, Goods, Death, and Final Faith* (New York: Bloomsbury, 2012).

23. Mikhael Bakhtin, *Problems of Dostoyevsky's Poetics*, trans. C. Emerson (Minneapolis: University of Minnesota Press, 1984). In the late '60s as she first entered Parisian intellectual circles, Kristeva read a much-discussed paper that focused on Bakhtin's themes of the carnivalesque and polyphony in Dostoevsky's novels.

24. On a relational self, see "Self, Others, Goods and Final Faith," ch. 2 in *Excursions*.

25. I pursue the Tivoli / Fear and Trembling comparison at length in ch. 8, *On Søren Kierkegaard*.

26. Harrison, "Choosing Your Ancestor."

27. Kristeva, *Desire in Language*, trans. Leon S. Roudiez (New York: Columbia University Press, 1980). And on indirect communication, see my "Style and Pseudonymity," in *Excursions*, ch. 3.

28. See *Revolution and Poetic Language*, trans. Margaret Waller (New York: Columbia University Press, 1984), 13.

29. See "Style and Pseudonymity," in *Excursions*.

30. *Revolution*, 13.

31. See Kristeva's *Black Sun: Depression and Melancholia*, trans. Leon S Roudiez (New York: Columbia University Press, 1989).

32. *On Søren Kierkegaard*, ch. 8.

33. *Black Sun*, 27–30.

34. On a God who above all gives independence against himself, see Kierkegaard, *Concluding Unscientific Postscript*, 1:260–261, note.

35. Kristeva, *New Maladies of the Soul*, trans. Ross Guberman (New York: Columbia University Press, 1995), 204, and *Revolution*, 25.

36. One of my favorite graduate students confides, "As one of those entering Continental philosophy, I want to know that I have a future that includes employment; and, more importantly, one that has a rich interaction of images and ideas that speak to and enrich my life. That's what drew me into CPR in the first place."

37. "It is perfectly true, as philosophers say, that life must be understood backwards. But they forget the other proposition, that it must be lived forwards. And if one thinks over that proposition it becomes more and more evident that life can never really be understood in time simply because at no particular moment can I find the necessary resting-place from which to understand it backwards." See Kierkegaard's *Papers and Journals*, selected and trans. Alastair Hannay [43 IV A 164] (Hamondsworth, UK: Penguin, 1996), 161.

38. When I'm asked if I want Kant or Nietzsche to survive, then I'm on surer ground than if I'm asked if I want the German Enlightenment or Postenlightenment German Romanticism to survive.

39. For "Joy is a condition of life," See Henry David Thoreau, "On the Natural History of Massachusetts," in *Essays of Henry David Thoreau*, ed. Lewis Hyde (New York: North Point Press, 2002); on Thoreau's last words, see Lorraine Loviglio, et al., "One World at a Time," *Concord Saunterer* 19/20 (2011–2012): 250–263.

40. With regard to the death of God, or the volatilization of texts, authors, and selves, I see no turning back from Kierkegaard's disruptions. Though he announces his writer (in *Fear and Trembling*) as a man of silence, he is finally not suspicious of words and truth and morals, and refuses to utterly volatize them. He *proliferates* morals and truths, so we move from "Is ethics suspended?" to "What sort of ethics fails, and what sort survives?" We move from "Is truth dead?" to "What sort of truths does the weaning mother enact?" From the question "Is the world only present to men fixated on death?" we move to "What is the world of the maternal, of natality, of new life?" Kierkegaard doesn't leave classical epistemology in shambles: rather, he shifts to the sort of self-knowledge that underlies (or fails to underlie) action and reception, being and becoming. Ontology expands to include the being of moods and possibilities. We have less "onto-theology" and more "onto-anthropology." He shows the *limits* of ontology: It can't give a definitive answer to whether Abraham (or the mother) are "real-life," or rather figures in an old man's dream, or instead, only figures in the lyrics in a poet's song, or just illustrations in an argument about teleological suspensions of ethics. And if acting and undergoing in time is our mode of becoming, we must have reliable *representations*—of *this* wave about to sweep us away, *this* rifle about to fire. (See my *Excursions with Kierkegaard: Goods, Others, Death, and Final Faith* [New York: Bloomsbury, 2012]). On his place in the "death of God" tradition, let me only say that Kierkegaard claims, provocatively, that he is not a Christian, that his vocation is Socratic, and that God does not exist. I can't expand on these remarks, but let me say that God does not exist because only humans have existential status, that a Socratic vocation is part of a collaborative identity, the other part being the task of becoming a Christian, and he is not a Christian, also, because no one in Christendom is. See my *On Soren Kierkegaard: Dialogue, Polemic, Lost Intimacy, and Time* (Burlington, Vt.: Ashgate, 2009).

41. My colleague Carson Webb reminds me, "The cadence from the subdominant chord (i.e., based on the fourth tone of the major scale) to the tonic is the famous 'Amen' cadence that

concludes so many old hymns and chorales." The implication, previously unbeknownst to me, is that the death of God remains a theme only as we give an "Amen" to close down the requiem.

42. Not every new-minted idiom paraded on fashion's runway is worth buying. Philosophy, like any art, courts innovation, but the pace and multiplicity in the bloom of idiom can block out insight and radiance. I find in Sartre, Camus, Merleau-Ponty, the late Foucault, a relatively jargon-free contact with life. Of course Sartre has forbidding terminology, but he bundles the grit of old age, pretension, sexuality, or self-deception without overwhelming it in terminology. Idiom should serve life and its shattering, joyous vicissitudes. De-defining, re-defining, deconstructing what only yesterday were "religion," "ethics," "technique," "person," "animal," "friendship," "charity," "gifts," "dependence," "honor," "violence," "stranger," "obligation," can have salutary effect. Yet it takes time to learn and absorb these new idioms, time to see the difference they make, time to know the cost of unlearning the old, and time to know if an innovation is worth its salt, beyond signaling clique membership. Inflation in the treasury of terms can mean deflation in value all around. An instance of falling for the fashionable comes from a recent call for papers for an important meeting of a Kierkegaard group I shall not name. The call asks contributors to consider how Kierkegaard's thought could inform issues relating to postcolonialism, neoliberalism and global economics, cross-cultural philosophy and religion, national identity and cross-border ties, denationalized citizenship, global warming, transnational political theology, or non-Western cultures that do not privilege the self.

43. See Emerson's "The Scholar," in *The Early Lectures of Ralph Waldo Emerson*, ed. Stephen Whicher, Robert Spiller, et al. (Cambridge, Mass.: Harvard University Press, 1964–).

44. Zadie Smith, "Reflections on Attunement," *New Yorker*, December 17, 2012, 29–32; "Joy," *New York Review of Books*, January 10, 2013, 1–3. Smith has this to say about Kierkegaard, literature, and philosophy more generally: "To me philosophy *is* writing. I curl up with a philosopher in the same way I would curl up with a novel. I don't recognize the distinction between the forms, really. I never was an academic philosopher, so I'm sure I read philosophy badly and with a great deal of ignorance, but I read it with enormous pleasure, and my favorites are meaningful to me as if they were characters in some enormous novel. Kierkegaard is a *character* to me (actually, many characters, because that's how he liked to write), and I read him thinking of him like an old friend." http://www.goodreads.com/interviews/show/806.Zadie_Smith. This marks a goal of one kind of philosophical writing, that it be a pleasure to read, and that readers—even nonphilosophers—be able to walk with the thinker like a friend.

45. Carson Webb, at work on Kierkegaard's concept of joy, reminds me that "Absurd Joy" is a theme of Kierkegaard's "The Gospel of Suffering."

46. In fact Gary Gutting is moved to bring together Smith's "hip" account of joy's difference from pleasure and its affinity with suffering with Aquinas's metaphysical ruminations on the difference. See, "The Joy of Zadie Smith and Thomas Aquinas," *New York Times*, Opinionator, "the Stone," January 20, 2013, http://opinionator.blogs.nytimes.com/2013/01/10/the-joy-of-zadie-smith-and-thomas-aquinas/?_r=0. Alternatively, we could link Smith's account to what Cora Diamond calls "the difficulty of reality," a phrase evoking "experiences in which we take something in reality to be resistant to our thinking it, or possibly to be painful in its inexplicability, difficult in that way, or perhaps awesome and astonishing in its inexplicability" (*Philosophy and Animal Life* [New York: Columbia University Press, 2009], 68).

47. Smith, "Attunement," 30.

48. Stanley Cavell's work straddles the continental divide. It has affinities with Levinas and Derrida. See Peter Dula's *Cavell, Companionship, and Christian Theology* (Oxford University Press, 2011). See Espen Dahl, "On Morality of Speech: Cavell's Critique of Derrida," *Continental Philosophical Review* 44 (2011): 81–101.

4 The Persistence of the Trace
Interrogating the Gods of Speculative Realism

Steven Shakespeare

A%%BRAHAM STOOD ON%% a hill above a wide plain. It was familiar, but he was rather surprised to be there, as he had been dead for three thousand years. A voice spoke from behind him. "I assume you remember our previous conversation here?" Abraham shuddered. "Oh. It's you," he said. "I might have known. I do remember now. I remember that I haggled with you for the lives of the people of Sodom and Gomorrah. You said that you would spare them if there were fifty righteous among them. I bargained you down to ten. Not that it stopped you." By this time, the Lord stood at Abraham's side. He smiled, but did not answer. Abraham cleared his throat. "So why am I here now?" "Things have become interesting once again on the plain of Sodom and Gomorrah," said the Lord. "Look down there." Abraham looked. There was a multitude of tents and awnings scattered among trenches and quarries and piles of earth. God sniffed. "Archaeologists. They're digging, mining for answers. Going below ground to get the dirt on yours truly." Abraham asked, "What do you mean?"

"Oh, they think they'll find the real history of Sodom and Gomorrah. Some proof that I was wrong to . . . judge them the way I did." The Lord grunted. "Look at it—like a scene from Raiders of the Lost bloody Ark."

Abraham frowned. "What?"

"Sorry," said God. "I guess even dated pop culture references are lost on you."

"Why am I here?" Abraham was beginning to get impatient. God replied: "Because I willed it. I am the possibility of the impossible, after all. I bring the dead back to life. It's what I *do*. And I wanted a witness." Abraham did not understand: "A witness to what?" Just at that moment, a cry rose up from the plain. Abraham could just make out the figure of a man climbing out of one of the trenches. He held in his hands something that glowed amber in the light of the setting sun. Abraham squinted. "What is that?" God smiled. "I left a little something for them to find. A surprise. You could call it a kind of fossil. I think the fashionable word these days is 'a trace.' Or 'an event.' Or possibly 'an object.' I lose track so easily; there are so many blogs, you see." Again, Abraham did not understand: "And what in God's name is a blog?" At that moment, somewhere behind him, Abraham could just make out the sound of a woman laughing.

Abraham is well known as the father of faith, the one who leaves his home and binds his son at God's command. A terrible, silent figure inspiring admiration in the shallow believer, but fear and trembling in those on the borders of faith. But Abraham was not always lost for words. He was also the original interrogator of God: "what will you give me?" (Gn 15.2); "how am I to know?" (Gn 15.8); "can a child be born to a man who is a hundred years old? Can Sarah, who is ninety years old, bear a child?" (Gn 17.17). Before Sarah, Abraham was the first to laugh in the face of God (Gn 17.17). Then just a bit later, while overlooking the plain and the cities of Sodom and Gomorrah, Abraham challenges God's plan to destroy the cities. He challenges God by invoking God's own justice. He speaks to God in the name of God, with the authority of God's own nature: "Shall not the Judge of all the earth do what is just?" (Gn 18.25). To borrow a phrase from John Caputo, I would suggest that, in this story, something stirs in the name of God: a justice that is not wholly exhausted by the God who appears, who speaks, commands, creates, judges.[1] God and God's nature fail to coincide. God's name does something more than, something other than, naming God.

Abraham's question is as much a source of fear and trembling as are his silence and obedience. The question provokes the negativity that divides the essence of God from itself. It sends a shudder through the good conscience of all the Euthyphros of the world. The interrogative is what makes God possible as appearance but also irreducible to that appearance. All of this might seem to be a familiar Derridean move. I make no particular apologies for that. I am aware that Derrida's gravediggers have been whetting the edge of their shovels, but I wager that he still has something to offer contemporary debates about what is real and what is absolute. Of course, these debates have been intensified by "speculative realism," a phrase that functions as an umbrella term covering a number of thinkers who reject the dominant form taken by Continental philosophy since Kant. Briefly stated, one might characterize this dominant form as correlationism and antirealism. A correlationist believes that being or objects or nature can only be known as the correlate of a human subject, a human act of knowing. Epistemology, thereby, supplants a realist ontology, that is, any account of how things are independent of any human knowing.

In this chapter I will begin by exploring and critiquing the explicit interest in God shown by Quentin Meillassoux. I will then suggest that rumors of Derrida's demise have been exaggerated by arguing that his work can be put into critical, constructive dialogue with the new speculation. And I will suggest more fruitful connections with another branch of speculative realism, the object-oriented approach of Graham Harman.

Of Fossils and Finitude

In *After Finitude,* Meillassoux advocates a new thinking of the absolute: a mathematicized absolute devoid of secondary qualities, an absolute that escapes the wicked embrace of the correlation.[2] His argument sets out from what he calls the arche-fossil. Science is constantly making claims about events that occurred billions of years before there was any life, before there were any subjects, and, therefore, before there was any correlation between a knowing subject and the world. The arche-fossil is any material that *indicates* or *manifests* the existence of a reality or event anterior to terrestrial life.[3] Those words—*indicates* and *manifests*—are pretty direct translations of the ones used by Meillassoux in the original French. Consequently, Meillassoux poses a challenge to thought: how is it that the arche-fossil manifests an anteriority prior to manifestation? Correlationist thinking is unable to account for how it is that science can successfully refer to the realities that these arche-fossils make manifest. These realities lie, not just outside any human cognition, but prior to its emergence. Meillassoux is not content with establishing this, however. Canny correlationists could cheerfully admit that there is a reality beyond our cognition; nonetheless, they would respond that we can only think that reality in relation to, or via, the mediation of our structures of knowing. Epistemology would remain the royal road of philosophy.

Meillassoux has to show how the correlation breaks down when it is pushed to its conclusion, how it can be outwitted from within its own logic. He argues that the correlationist must remain strictly agnostic about reality as it is in itself, apart from cognitive mediation. Correlationism insists that we cannot know the absolute, which, etymologically, means a reality absolved or severed from mediation—what Meillassoux also calls rather quaintly the "great outdoors." The great outdoors, however, turns out to be not a wholesome realm of woodland rambles and birdwatching, but a lawless hyper-chaos that threatens every stable reality with dissolution. By remaining agnostic about reality as it is in itself, the correlationist must admit the real possibility that it could be radically different from anything we know now. Using the example of a debate about life after death, the correlationist cannot rule out any of the options: immortality with God, annihilation, or the real possibility of either alternative.[4] In short, the correlationist is forced to accept the conceivability of both my radical transformation and my nonexistence after death, neither of which can be the correlate of an existing human subject. Moreover, the correlationist cannot supply any reason for preferring either option.

Of course one reason Meillassoux despises correlationism is that it has opened the door to a return of religion in Continental philosophy. If we can't know reality in itself, nothing prevents us fideistically projecting religious meaning onto the void. Meillassoux's speculative move, however, is that when we push the correlation to its limits, we find that we are able to think an absolute that is not a correlate of a human subject. The absolute is precisely the capacity of things to be radically other than they are for no reason. This becomes Meillassoux's principle of unreason, "the equal and indifferent possibility of every eventuality."[5] We can know that the absolute is this: that anything can be otherwise than it is, and there can be no reason for this—in the more lyrical language of a hyperchaos, one might call it something akin to time, a "menacing power" "capable of destroying both things and worlds, of bringing forth monstrous absurdities, yet also of never doing anything, of realizing every dream, but also every nightmare." It is like a terrible God, "an omnipotence that has become autonomous, without norms, blind, devoid of the other divine perfections, a power with neither goodness nor wisdom."[6]

Meillassoux's position comes with a price. Having set out to establish the validity of scientific statements about an ancestral past, we are left with a world of chaos in which there is no reason for anything to happen or not happen. The fossil dissolves into abstract possibility. Now as we know, the world seems pretty regular, which seems mildly surprising if there is an infinite possibility of lawless chaos. Meillassoux has an answer to this, however: Cantorian set theory has supposedly demonstrated that what is conceivable is not totalizable.[7] In other words, we cannot say that it is improbable that we live in a stable universe, because we have no way of calculating probabilities in a non-totalizable universe. I am not alone in finding this tenuous, to say the least, but let's accept it for the sake of argument.[8] Meillassoux still has no reason to suppose that the laws governing the universe have not, in fact, changed from day to day, and our memories erased and restarted; he has no reason to expect the world to continue in any recognizable form in the next few seconds. He has no reason to doubt that the world was created six thousand years ago by God, who cunningly hid fossils in the earth to test our faith.

Ah, but wait! As far as God goes, Meillassoux is off the hook, since the one thing we can be sure of is that there are no necessary beings. The only necessity is the necessity of contingency. This raises several difficult questions. Is the principle that all things are contingent itself necessary? Is the premise that the absolute must be thinkable as absolute possibility itself not just a tiny bit correlationist? After all, to draw strong ontological conclusions from what is or is not supposedly "conceivable" by a human subject does seem to be a position with a few wisps of idealistic *Geist* still clinging to it.⁹ But back to God. We have to rid ourselves of the knuckle-dragging precritical assumption that there could be a necessary being, so goodbye God, don't call us! And yet, as Meillassoux's essay "Spectral Dilemma" makes clear, the door is never shut. God is still possible. There may never have been a God; there may not be one now; but, hey, there could always be one in the future.¹⁰

I find myself in some sympathy with Meillassoux's starting point, which is the acknowledgment of tragic deaths, of suffering and dying that seem unjust and unredeemed. At least wounded bodies are getting on the stage now. According to this essay, the religious believer responds by claiming that God will sort it out and eventually provide justice for the dead. But any God who lets these things happen in the first place would be a monster, a nightmare being whose justice is not worth anticipating. Atheists, however, fare no better. They offer no hope for the dead, and so we are left without the possibility of mourning them. The spectral dilemma—how to mourn the unredeemed dead—cannot be answered. Yet, I continue to wonder why we should ever think it must be answered? Why should mourning be something that is resolved or resolvable? Is that not what makes it mourning in the first place: that something singular is lost, that we are torn between nursing the wound and betraying the lost one by moving on?

Yet, we shall remain with Meillassoux, because he does have an answer, or rather, he possibly knows someone who might. In a world of hyper-chaos, there is nothing to prevent a being with the characteristics of God coming into existence, even if there is no God now. So we can have our God without the tiresome necessity of a theodicy, since this God would be blissfully innocent of all crimes. A happy ending for all! Except it is not, of course. Such a God is only a possibility. And even a possible God who becomes actual would not be a necessary being, so there would be no guarantee that God would not pop out of being as quickly as he popped in, in a puff of unreason, which could, for all we know, leave us and the unredeemed dead in a worse hell than ever.¹¹

At the end of his essay, Meillassoux leaves us with the task of a divinology—of imagining the kind of God we would like to come into existence. But constructing an idea of God in the midst of hyper-chaos appears to be the worst kind of wish fulfillment, not least because it engenders no agency and no politics. The possibility of this God is entirely out of our control. Redemption is subject to the arbitrary fiat of a blind absolute. The miraculization of hope is no answer to worldly despair. Hope morphs into abstract fantasy or salvation ex nihilo. Meanwhile, the suit-wearing gods of this world carry on sharpening their knives. According to Meillassoux, the question we must ask is what God would we like to come? Which God, which offspring of Chaos, would be the most singular, noble, and interesting?¹²

Interesting? I can clearly hear Kierkegaard turning in his grave. He considers the category of the interesting to be the highest achievement of the aesthete, whose enjoyment of the world must pass through an ever-revolving machinery of distraction. And what should save us from our own boredom, and from the "vortex, which is the world's core principle" but the interesting?[13] Through staging the fantasy of his own life, the aesthete celebrates and dreads the "universal law" that is "the downfall of everything."[14] Irony is the only absolute, and possibility is only the "infinite possibility for confusion."[15] God save us from an interesting God. Such a God cannot be questioned or wrestled with, only passively admired or feared. The mode of waiting for this God is not like that of one who waits or labors expectantly through the night for a birth or a death; it is the abstract waiting for an abstract novelty, a novelty that is not qualitatively different from the arbitrary instances before it.

How did we get here? It was the fault of the fossil. It signaled to us by indicating and manifesting something. But the message got confused. So it is time to invoke the specter of one who specialized in messages that failed to arrive. In "Typewriter Ribbon," Derrida reads Rousseau again.[16] I know, with all the great outdoors around him, Derrida is inside reading books. But let's be patient with him. His topic is forgiveness and excuses, specifically the strange performative logic that affects both. If what I forgive is forgivable, then it requires no forgiveness. If what I excuse myself for is excusable, I need to offer no excuses. Furthermore, both of these topics relate to the question of the archive: what apparatus, what material body, and what inscription are required to record a singular act or event? Is this singular event betrayed by being archived, being made repeatable?

In the course of his reading, Derrida mentions an incident a few years before that happened during the time he was preparing a seminar on forgiveness and perjury. In Picardy, an insect had been discovered preserved in amber at the very moment of sucking the blood of another creature. He connects this with another report of two midges "immobilized in amber the color of honey when they were surprised by death as they made love."[17] He adds: "fifty four million years before humans appeared on earth, a *jouissance* took place whose archive we preserve. It arrives/happens to us again, it is still arriving to us. We have there, set down, consigned to a support, protected by the body of an amber coffin, the trace, which is itself corporeal, of an event that took place only once."[18] A little later, Derrida emphasizes again this anteriority, a scale that dwarfs human history: "when I was not there, when an 'I' and above all an 'I' saying 'me, a man' was not there."[19]

These fornicating insects trapped in amber constitute a kind of fossil. Not strictly an arche-fossil, since they do involve living beings. Nevertheless, what constitutes the trace is its inorganic support, the amber coffin. The singular event requires an archive, if it is to survive and be read. This archive always has something "machinelike" about it: a capacity for iteration that exceeds or, rather, precedes the formation of conscious intentionality. This is the cut, the wounding of the present that ensures the possibility of survival.[20] A kind of thinking of the cut, of the absolute—and of God—because this machinelike structure that presupposes itself, that causes itself, is strangely akin to God. Indeed Derrida understands the "question of the technical as question of the theological. Question of the 'machine for making gods' in which Bergson recognizes, at the end of *The Two Sources of Morality and Religion*, the 'essential function of the universe . . . on our refractory planet.'"[21]

The absolute is severance, but a severance that cuts itself, a stigmatized God: "Before any other possible suffering or any other possible passion, there is the wound, which is at once infinite and unfelt, anesthetized, of this neutralization by the 'as if,' by the 'as if' of this quasi, by the limitless risk of becoming a simulacrum or a virtuality without consistency—of everything."[22] We are here quite close to Meillassoux's hyper-chaos; and, yet, this thinking of the absolute is as different from Meillassoux's as it is from any dogmatic metaphysics. There are no wounds in hyper-chaos. There are no bodies, or at least no bodies are required. There is no risk in any meaningful sense, since there is no reason for anything to be, no reason to hope, or even to wager. There are fossils, but they were never anything other than mathematizable points. To be sure, nothing resists chaos.

In contrast, Derrida's absolute cut does not absolve itself of risk. The absolute absolves itself of its own impossibility by becoming incarnate as trace. It is, therefore, the opposite of a dogmatic assurance: "The vulnerability, the finitude of a body and of a corpus is precisely the limit of all performative power, thus of all assurance."[23] No God or forgiveness or politics without severance and without bodies, or without risk. When Derrida writes in this context of a "materiality without matter," it is to deny a certain concept of matter as a given and comprehended entity.[24] Rather, there is a force of resistance as resistant to correlationism as any speculative strategy. More so since it is does not shrink from our touch. Derrida has nothing to do with linguistic idealism or antirealism. The trace is not coextensive with human language. Fifty-four million years ago, before an I, before it was thinkable, there was the trace. To put it crudely, to make the point, the trace is a structure of reality, albeit one that makes reality real by destructuring it into forces of resistance. Who ever thought that difference and temporality depended on language? Time was always becoming space, becoming fossil, becoming archive.

To that extent I welcome Martin Hägglund's reading of Derrida in *Radical Atheism*, where he argues that the trace is the condition for all life.[25] In his contribution to *The Speculative Turn*, he states, "Without temporalization a trace could not persist across time and relate the past to the future."[26] This persistence, this survival, is the very possibility of desire, of anything mattering. The persistence of the trace is also its utter precariousness: "it is precisely the radical destructibility of life that makes it a matter of care."[27] It is not the "interesting," then, as mentioned above, but what Kierkegaard's pseudonym Johannes Climacus calls *inter-esse:* the "between being," the relation between thinking and being that resists abstraction, because it is actuality itself.²⁸

Of course, a speculative thinker might challenge this privileging of life and of interest. Geology, not theology, is the way to go. As Daniel Whistler suggests in his advocacy of a Schellingian speculative geology of religion, words are not like rocks, they *are* rocks.²⁹ But by the same token rocks are never just rocks. They are structured traces, sedimentations, transformations, obstacles overcome. Even the arche-fossil, even this matter that predates life, still indicates and manifests. And it does so aporetically: a manifestation of what is prior to manifestation. Surely there is common ground here between speculative and deconstructive approaches. The *inter-esse*, the "being between," of the trace is never limited to life, much less humanity. Otherwise, the appearance of life and consciousness would never be possible. Perhaps rather than the relation between thinking and being, we must talk simply of the becoming of being, the nonself coincidence of being, the very things that make the absolute communicate itself and simultaneously make it questionable.

There is an intriguing parallel here with object-oriented philosophy of the type championed by Graham Harman.³⁰ Harman's position takes Heidegger's analysis of tool-being as its point of departure. For Heidegger, there is an aspect of the tool that is not exhausted by our practical or theoretical interaction with it. The object is neither exhausted by its relations nor by how it appears to or affects other objects or subjects. Harman argues that the interior of the object has its own life, which withdraws from view, inaccessible to any interaction or gaze. He, therefore, seeks to rehabilitate talk both of substances, which exceed their properties, and of occasionalism, in which objects have no direct relations with one another. Causation happens only vicariously through the sensual images that arise from objects within the intentionality of other objects.³¹

Harman recognizes Leibniz's monadology as a key forerunner of this position. An important distinction is that, for Leibniz, the occasion for indirect interaction between objects is God. God alone knows and relates the otherwise enclosed worlds of the monads. Harman does not accept the need for a single binding divine occasion but instead argues for a polytheistic occasionalism; every object withdraws into a kind of divine inaccessibility, and every object is able to be the occasion for indirect interaction with others. Referring to his use of an offshore drilling rig as an image of how objects suck up images of other objects, Harman writes: "The entire cosmos is in fact a dystopia filled with trillions of miniature deities, each of them a platform in a hurricane infested gulf."³² Still, there is a tension in Harman's approach. It lies in the concept of translatability, which is the process by which an object takes up and transforms the sensual images of other objects. Real entities make contact only with phenomenal or translated objects.³³ Now translation is an interesting trope to employ, a highly textual one given the disdain for Continental philosophy's supposed obsession with textual mediation that Harman and other speculative realists deploy.

I have two proposals to make for an ongoing dialogical exploration of these issues.[34] First, there seems to be a significant link between the divine withdrawnness of objects and Derrida's notion that God is the name of the secret, or of the possibility I have of keeping a secret that no one else can access. If one extends this sentiment from subjectivity to the realm of objects, something interesting emerges: objects keep secrets because there is something of the wholly other about them. *Tout autre est tout autre;* however, remember that for Derrida, the secret is not a specifiable content, something that can one day be discovered. It is a secret without a secret, because the other cannot be resolved into their relations, or into a substantial interior self-presence. In other words, the withdrawnness of objects depends upon a logic of the trace, a non-coincidence with self.

Second, the translatability of objects makes the connection between objects both possible and impossible. To put it bluntly, translation is always interpretation; it always transforms its object in order to make it available. The singularity of the object translated is always betrayed. But for Derrida, this is not simply an event that resides on the outside of objects. Harman himself suggests that we should not think that objects first make direct contact and then an operation of translation takes place. Translation is intrinsic to the object relationship. Derrida pushes a bit at the object-oriented approach because the target object is always already translatable. This does not reduce the object to its relations, since translation will never capture the singular idiom of things; however, if it is to be translation at all, rather than a completely equivocal relationship, it presupposes that the simplicity of objects is compromised from the outset. Objects are always partial results of translation and always translatable. Again, this is not to say that objects are reduced or made transparent to translation; but the very possibility of translation depends upon the prior operation of articulation, of the trace within the object itself. The persistent trace calls for an unavoidable interpretation, not as an external operation, but in the solidarity of the question. And every trace is mortal, since if it disappears, it takes its translatability with it, and the world suffers an irredeemable loss. Translation is the condition for an unending mourning.

The language of God returns as this dispersed otherness, a withdrawal that not only severs objects but offers a fragile and mortal connection. The absolute absolved itself of simplicity to let things be, to let them be in secret, hidden even from the eyes of God. The labor of the negative becomes a labor of love, not simply of comprehension. Where I would differ from Hägglund, therefore, is in identifying such a speculative deconstruction as radically atheist. It lands certain conceptions of God in hot water: the God of impassible simplicity and omnipotent beatitude, for instance. But is that all that is going on in the name of God? When Abraham questions God, he divides the divine name against itself. He speaks for Sodom. And who is to say that he is speaking not only against God but for God? Bereft of the security of a homeland in location or orthodoxy, he takes it upon himself to pronounce God differently, to insinuate his questions between the manifest God and the event of God.

We do not so much think God's thoughts after God as ask God's questions after God. To question after God, with all the ambiguity of that phrase, seems to me a good watchword for the future of Continental philosophy of religion. It implies neither a detachment from the trace of nature nor a new submission to immediacy or orthodoxy, but a restless, heretical absolution of thinking—"Absolute ab-solution," as Derrida once wrote.[35] This is not only a weird realism (Harman's phrase) but also a queer realism. A realism that can resist in the name of God all the violence done to bodies by the gods of this world. The God in whose name it resists is not a being but a traced God: the negativity of God opening onto the incarnation of the wounded word, which questions us in turn. In Derrida's words, commenting on the poetry of Jabès: "God separated himself from himself in order to let us speak in order to astonish and interrogate us. . . . If God opens the question in God, if he is the very opening of the Question, there can be no simplicity of God."[36] Between the wounded body, the broken tables, and the heretic's ashes, the trace persists only in fragility. The name of God is in question.

Abraham made his way down into the archaeologist's camp. He watched as a band of eager scholars clawed at the amber fossil they had rescued from the earth. They were desperate to unlock the event it held, the truth it promised. But the more they grasped and tried to scrape off the earth that clung to it, the more it seemed to diminish—to dematerialize into the fine mist of contingency, of pure possibility.

No matter. They would not be distracted by the earth that clung to it, by color and gravity. They would intellectually intuit its essence, get down to primaries. Resistance is futile. It had been God's turn to laugh as he revealed his plan to Abraham. Once the amber dissolved, a virulent radioactive isotope would be unleashed. It would be fire and brimstone all over again. That would teach them to respect necessity. The Lord had left him on the hill. "Tell the world what you have seen," he shouted back to Abraham. "They'll believe someone who comes back from the dead!" Abraham thought otherwise. If Sodom were going down, he would not watch from afar. Not again. He felt a pressure on his hand. He looked up from it to find Sarah standing with him. "How . . . ?" he began. She smiled. "In the name of God," she laughed. "Do you think *his* is the only power in the world?"

Notes

1. See John Caputo, *The Weakness of God: A Theology of the Event*. (Bloomington: Indiana University Press, 2006).

2. Quentin Meillassoux, *After Finitude: An Essay on the Necessity of Contingency* (London: Continuum, 2008).
3. Ibid., 10, 14 and 26.
4. Ibid., 54–59.
5. Ibid., 59.
6. Ibid., 64.
7. Ibid., 101–107.
8. For a critique, see Adrian Johnston, "Hume's Revenge: À Dieu, Meillassoux," in *The Speculative Turn: Continental Materialism and Realism*, ed. Levi Bryant, Nick Srnicek, and Graham Harman (Melbourne: re:press, 2011), 104–105.
9. Cf. Ray Brassier, *Nihil Unbound: Enlightenment and Extinction* (Basingstoke: Palgrave Macmillan, 2007), 49–94.
10. Quentin Meillassoux, "Spectral Dilemma," *Collapse* 4 (May 2008): 261–275.
11. See the critique offered by Michael O'Neill Burns, "The Hope of Speculative Materialism," in *After the Postsecular and the Postmodern: New Essays in Continental Philosophy of Religion*, ed. Anthony Paul Smith and Daniel Whistler (Newcastle upon Tyne: Cambridge Scholars, 2010), 316–334.
12. Meillassoux, "Spectral Dilemma," 275.
13. Søren Kierkegaard, *Either/Or Part One* (Princeton, N.J.: Princeton University Press, 1987), 168.
14. Ibid., 167.
15. Ibid., 259.
16. Jacques Derrida, *Without Alibi* (Stanford, Calif.: Stanford University Press, 2002), 71–160.
17. Ibid., 130.
18. Ibid., 130–131.
19. Ibid., 131.
20. Ibid., 133.
21. Ibid.
22. Ibid., 135.
23. Ibid., 147.
24. Ibid., 151.
25. Martin Hägglund, *Radical Atheism: Derrida and the Time of Life* (Stanford, Calif.: Stanford University Press, 2008).
26. Martin Hägglund, "Radical Atheist Materialism: A Critique of Meillassoux," in *The Speculative Turn: Continental Materialism and Realism*, ed. Levi Bryant, Nick Srnicek, and Graham Harman (Melbourne: re:press, 2011), 119.
27. Ibid., 124.
28. Søren Kierkegaard, *Concluding Unscientific Postscript to Philosophical Fragments* (Princeton, N.J.: Princeton University Press, 1992), 314–315.
29. Daniel Whistler, "Language after Philosophy of Nature: Schelling's Geology of Divine Names," in *After the Postsecular and the Postmodern: New Essays in Continental Philosophy of Religion*, ed. Anthony Paul Smith and Daniel Whistler (Newcastle upon Tyne: Cambridge Scholars, 2010), 349.
30. See Graham Harman, *Tool-being: Heidegger and the Metaphysics of Objects* (Peru, Ill.: Open Court, 2002); *Guerrilla Metaphysics: Phenomenology and the Carpentry of Things* (Peru, Ill.: Open Court, 2007); *Towards Speculative Realism: Essays and Lectures* (Ropley, England: Zero Books, 2010).
31. Graham Harman, "On Vicarious Causation" *Collapse* 2 (March 2007): 171–205.

32. Graham Harman, *Circus Philosophicus* (Ropley, England: Zero Books, 2010), 48.
33. Ibid., 49–50.
34. The most substantial theological engagement with object-oriented thought is Adam S. Miller, *Speculative Grace: Bruno Latour and Object-Oriented Theology* (New York: Fordham University Press, 2013). For a further useful brief summary of possible theological engagements with object-oriented philosophy, see Sam Mickey's blog post: http://knowledge-ecology.com/2011/03/27/guest-post-theological-implications-of-object-oriented-philosophy-factishes-imperatives-and-cthulhu/.

There has been other discussion in the blogosphere on the theological implications of this approach. See, for example, Adam Kotsko here: http://itself.wordpress.com/2011/02/08/ooo-a-negative-theology-of-the-object/, and Timothy Morton here: http://ecologywithoutnature.blogspot.com/2011/02/kotsko-on-ooo-and-negative-theology.html.

35. Jacques Derrida, *The Gift of Death* (Chicago: University of Chicago Press, 1995), 73.
36. Jacques Derrida, *Writing and Difference* (London: Routledge, 1978), 67–68.

5 Speculating God

Speculative Realism and Meillassoux's Divine Inexistence

Leon Niemoczynski

Speculating God

The relationship between contemporary Continental philosophy of religion and "the new metaphysics" (twenty-first-century metaphysics in the Continental tradition, otherwise referred to as "the new metaphysics," "the new materialism," "the new realism," or, more controversially, "speculative realism") so far remains largely an unexplored relationship, especially regarding areas of mutual concern, influence, or crossover.[1] Despite new and exciting inroads made by philosophers such as Iain Grant and his articulations of a neo-Platonic–Hegelian Absolute (a perspective not entirely unconducive to the nature theologies of the German idealists), François Laurelle's non-philosophy and surrounding work on "non-theology," or even Bruno Latour's explorations of the social role of "factish gods" (and more recently his dialogues concerning natural religion), little discussion has actually taken place about how the recent turn toward a new metaphysics, with its insistence on various forms of materialism and realism, is able to converse with contemporary Continental philosophy of religion.[2]

Indeed, it is a pressing but also difficult question to ask what directions Continental philosophy of religion might take *in the future*, given this "return" of materialist and realist metaphysics in the twenty-first century. However different and wide-ranging these recent materialist and realist metaphysical perspectives may be, one philosopher in particular may be of especial assistance in exploring Continental philosophy of religion's future, given his concept of "the divine inexistence."[3] That philosopher is Quentin Meillassoux.[4] Situated within the broader perspective of "speculative materialism," Meillassoux is, in this author's judgment, probably one of the more *relevant* touchstones in a conversation about where the future of Continental philosophy of religion might be heading; that is, what it is possible to do in Continental philosophy of religion vis-à-vis the new metaphysics, and to do so with fecundity.[5]

The aim of this essay therefore is simply to parse out what ramifications Meillassoux's theory of the divine inexistence might have for the future of Continental philosophy of religion. Given the parameters of Meillassoux's theory, including belief in creation ex nihilo, a "messianism" with a corresponding Christlike mediator figure who is able to inaugurate the resurrection of the dead, an explicit focus on a forthcoming World of justice after the advent of this Christlike figure, the identification of a God who is not now yet but "may be" in the future, and an ethics of hope tied to the possibility of such a God's arrival, it is natural that the Continental philosopher of religion John Caputo and his own philosophical theology of messianism and of justice, of a God "to come," be introduced as a natural and productive conversation partner.[6] As well, Caputo's own dialogue partner, Richard Kearney, may be brought into the conversation due to comparable ontological features of Meillassoux's God, namely the divine's ontological status as a possibility, or better, as a "virtuality," in likeness to the virtual status of Kearney's own God "who may be."[7] Certainly the immense *constructive potential* behind Meillassoux's theory of the divine inexistence is brought into clear view when compared to the sort of God proposed by Caputo and Kearney—a God "to come," a God who neither is nor is not, but "may be." And while Meillassoux's God does not now "exist" strictly speaking but someday *may* come to exist, in the same vein as Caputo and Kearney we require explanation for the belief in the reality of that nonexistence—the "virtual God"—and *the immanent form of hope* related to it.

The Religious Turn and the Return to Metaphysics

The postmodern "religious turn" of Continental philosophy found in the late twentieth century did not, in general, look favorably upon *metaphysics*.[8] Within Continental philosophy of religion especially, positive metaphysical knowledge was essentially relegated to "onto-theology" and pitted against a more cryptic sort of "fideism" oriented toward a theological *unknown*—a God who was said to be beyond positive metaphysical knowledge but who was also claimed to be revealed through phenomenological religious experience.[9] However, contemporary Continental philosophy of religion, at least within the past half-decade, particularly in France, has felt the mounting pressure of the new metaphysics' critique of its methodological choice of phenomenology for describing religious experience and the divine.[10] Given this critique, one might ask whether the phenomenological God of the recent "religious turn" has indeed fared any better than the God of onto-theology and scholasticism, Caputo's and Kearney's main target.[11] According to Meillassoux, the phenomenological approach to "the postmodern God" is fundamentally "correlationist" and without a true materialist or realist spirit animating it, as Meillassoux's realism sees itself as arriving "after finitude," after the postmodern apophatic context and its corresponding fideism.[12] This is all to say that from the Meillassouxian perspective, speculation about God's *own* reality has been lost to a form of metaphysics pitched in a "human, all-too human" key, where life has been elevated over the sovereignty of reality and the conditions of finite human existence elevated over God's own coming-to-be existence, the ultimate metaphysical "advent" or "event."[13] (We should briefly clarify here that the critique of correlationism is only one move among many in the chess game of Meillassoux's own version of "speculative materialism." He eventually rebuilds a mathematical ontology and *refounds* correlationism only after dismantling other historical versions of it. Still, the critique of the sort of a sort of fideism found in Caputo and Kearney seems to apply.[14])

Following the above speculative materialist critique, then, we may possibly *condemn* the likes of Caputo and Kearney, for they have shied from speculating God and disbanded *any* metaphysics in favor of speculating the ethical, the human-situated and human-centered—placing them dangerously close to an ethical religion of *humanity* that, in seeking to lose orthodoxy, loses contact with the divine altogether. However, it is here that, with qualification, I disagree with such an assessment, for concepts such as *virtuality, power, contingency, weakness,* and *justice* require adumbration indeed—and these are concepts picked up by Caputo and Kearney in both their ethical *and* metaphysical dimensions.[15] One simply requires a key to unlock the bridge between possibility and justice, between the ethical and the metaphysical, and this is possible, I think, by considering the metaphysical God (the divine inexistence) whose power is commensurate with an eternal realm justice, or what Meillassoux calls "the fourth World of justice."[16] However, one must immediately ask whether Meillassoux's call for hope in a future World of justice places his own ethical position in tension with the very "religious turn" in Continental philosophy that he critiques? Is Meillassoux here offering his own fideism in a World beyond, a World possibly understood as a new form of transcendentalism, perhaps even a "transcendental materialism" that is itself too "weak," being founded upon nothing other than hope?[17] What are the conditions surrounding this metaphysical God and the form of hope tied to it?

It should be emphasized that Meillassoux's God is a "coming-to-be" God, a God not of postmodern Continental philosophy of religion but of the new metaphysical realism and materialism, a God captured neither in onto-theological nor strictly ethical (human-centered) discourse but via a speculative metaphysics, a God *virtual* (that is, *nonexistent,* not even as an "actual" possibility), a nonexistent God which is an object of hope that does not properly exist *now* but someday *may be*. This is not to speak of the virtual God's *weakness,* but its *power* as a virtuality, as for some, virtuality may suggest a weakness or "lack" of actuality and concreteness. In fact, however, it is the virtuality of the divine inexistence that signals its power. In hoping for the advent of such a possible God, Meillassoux's ethics has its most secure foundation.

On my view, the debate concerning the divine inexistence and ethics related to it may be clarified (and a much-needed conversation ignited) if we engage Meillassoux's theism of the possible God—the divine inexistence—the virtual God, while we engage simultaneously Caputo's "Messianist weak theology" and Kearney's "dynamatology" or "anatheism." In fact, Meillassoux's theism may be said to have eschatological features that are, for all intents and purposes, what Caputo's thinking of "the to come" indicates, ethically speaking. One could very well say that reading Caputo and Kearney together with Meillassoux may be the translation key that helps Meillassoux's *metaphysics* make even more *ethical sense*.

Absolute Contingency and the Spectral Dilemma

Probably the most astounding claim of Meillassoux's metaphysics is found in his *After Finitude* where he writes that nature is *absolutely contingent*. In his advocating an "acausal" universe we are told, "Everything could actually collapse: from trees to stars, from stars to laws, from physical laws to logical laws; and this not by virtue of some superior law whereby everything is destined to perish, but by virtue of the *absence* of any superior law."[18] The fact that things can be radically otherwise than what they are, due to such absolute contingency, Meillassoux titles "factiality."[19] This absolute contingency means that there is no *reason* that things must be the way they are given a more basic "principle of unreason," the irrationality "nestled in all things" that is "the real possibility of everything's becoming other without reason" *in-itself*.[20] This is the only "eternal principle."[21] In other words, there is no "necessary" causal linkage responsible for the events of the world, nor is there any rational (inferential) explanation for the probability of new events. Each event, being without reason or cause states Meillassoux, should therefore more adequately be referred to as an *advent*.[22] Here "advent" could be understood to be a truly mysterious and miraculous happening produced by absolutely contingent conditions without reason or cause. The religious connotation for Meillassoux here appears to be intentional, as without any prior condition to link created events to, creation is an act ex nihilo. "Every 'miracle' . . . insofar as every radical rupture of the present in relation to the past becomes the manifestation of the absence of any order capable of overseeing the chaotic power of becoming."[23]

The sort of contingency in question here is not chance. Chance requires a totalizable set of outcomes from which a probability can be drawn. But Meillassoux explicitly rejects this. We have no *reason* to assume the likelihood or unlikelihood of a situation given that there is no sum total of possibilities against which we are to measure the certainty of probability occurring *despite the fact that certain events indeed have been regularly occurring*—for example, the fact that the physical laws of the universe occur with the regularity that they do (this is known as the "frequentialist implication").[24] Rather, what we have are *unbounded possibilities,* so there can be no totalization of what is possible. According to Meillassoux's theory of absolute contingency, this is stipulated by the truth of Cantorian transfinite mathematics and Zermelo-Fraenkel (ZF) set theory. As Meillassoux puts it:

> One cannot so totalize the set of possible worlds, for nothing allows one to secure it except the fact that such a totality of possibilities does in fact exist. This cannot be confirmed by experience (no one has ever seen such a totality), nor can it be confirmed by 'pure theory': for since Cantor we know there is no totality of conceivable numbers. The Cantorian transfinite means that for every infinite that exists, there is an even greater infinite, with no limit to this ultimate series of infinitudes.[25]

In other words, "A quantifiable totality of the thinkable is unthinkable."[26]

Logically we are left with a very odd situation. On the one hand, for there to be radical or absolute contingency we must let go of *the principle of sufficient reason* in favor of absolute contingency, the necessity of the principle of unreason: "the absolute necessity of everything's non-necessity."[27] On the other hand, *the law of non-contradiction* must hold in order for there to be alternate states of change, for there to be radical new appearances that are *different* from preceding ones.[28] That is, in order for things to change, something must be able to be *identical to itself* at least in one instant but capable (onto-logically) of becoming something radically else in another instant. This is why Meillassoux introduces a *necessary* characterization of absolute contingency (thus *After Finitude*'s subtitle, "the necessity of contingency"). On the other hand, if, like Hume, we look for a reason *why* anything is the case (or is not the case), Meillassoux states that there is no answer; there is no real explanation other than the advent. Again, we cannot rely on "probabilistic reasoning" (Hume) as that is valid only on the condition of what be "thinkable in terms of numerical totality." Thus Meillassoux abolishes *the principle of sufficient reason* altogether, and we are left with the necessity of contingency and its principle of non-contradiction (understood as the creation of new events, Time): anything is truly possible, and this is the one ultimate ground or principle.[29]

The analysis of facticity begs what Meillassoux titles "figures," or "necessary features of facticity."[30] Here Meillassoux adopts an argument from classical metaphysics which states that if one of two contraries be absolute then the other contrary would not prevail so as to be discriminated. Meillassoux's "absolutely contingent" ground is *itself* therefore necessary because it must serve as the required principle of contrast to contingency. As such, it is the *ultimate* category of existence. Contingency, understood as ground, is also referred to as "hyperchaos" in its absolute nature (in its power to create), or as called elsewhere, the "Surchaos" (also "Surcontingency").[31] This ultimate chaotic ground (an unruly ground that produces novel events—events different than those that "are" now—and does so *without reason*) should, according to Meillassoux, be understood as a reality of "menacing power—capable of destroying both things and worlds, of bringing forth monstrous absurdities, yet also of never doing anything, or of realizing every dream, but also every nightmare.... It is a Time capable of destroying even becoming itself, by bringing forth, perhaps forever, fixity, stasis, and death."[32]

Such a frightening statement does more than assert that there is absolutely no reason for anything to be or remain the way it is. It decidedly says that necessarily everything must be able to be other than it is, including things that now are not. Things that now are not, that do not now "exist," *can* exist in the future. Meillassoux states that *time* is the process whereby anything can arise and come to exist, or cease to exist, at any moment with no reason at all, save "for a contradictory entity," given that time is the determination of any thing's becoming what it is as some self-same thing. Yet, it is to time, to a future world, and the contingent power that is present now in this world, that the *hope* for the appearance of an entity that does not now exist, but someday may, is tied.

If a theory of absolute contingency were not strange enough, Meillassoux then advances an equally shocking thesis. Without the theory of absolute contingency stated in the precise terms that Meillassoux gives us, the theory simply would not be compelling. Meillassoux's thesis is that *we are to believe in God because God does not "now" exist*. In fact, given that God does *not now* exist but someday *may come to exist,* an *ethics of hope* must be tied to this God's future possible appearance, given the injustices of our immanent world.

Typically the question of God's existence is stated as "either God exists, or does not." Both alternatives lead to despair according to Meillassoux, for if God exists then one is left with an irreconcilable problem of evil: how could an existing God permit the injustices of this world to occur? But if God does *not exist* then there is no redemption for those who have suffered and died horrible deaths. This is known as "the spectral dilemma"—or as Meillassoux puts it, "The dilemma is as follows: either to despair of another life for the dead, or to despair of a God who has let such deaths take place."[33] Thus a "spectre" is haunting us, one whose death "we are no longer capable of mourning" as "the passage of time has not sufficiently taken hold in order that one could envisage some kind of pacific relationship between dead and the living."[34] Meillassoux "resolves" the dilemma by adopting a position that is neither religious nor atheist: God does not yet "exist" but *might* exist in the future. With this God's appearance there is hope for a resurrection of the dead and the creation of a World of justice. This God would serve as the advent required to institute a collective justice, the "reparation of an extreme wrong" where "lives are entitled to begin again so as to overcome the atrocious end inflicted upon them."[35]

What remains now is the virtual state of our present reality, which contains the possibility—the "virtual" inexistence—of a God who is still to come as an actual reality, a God of the future who is capable of instituting a world where justice reigns and the injustices of the past are reconciled. Given the advent of this virtual God Meillassoux states an eschatology may find its fulfillment. Meillassoux summarizes: "We must revive the extreme hope of eschatology in order resolutely to act—and right away—in view of an unconditional equality for all people, whose ultimate realization no longer depends on us but on an omnipotent God."[36] This "non-existing" God is what Meillassoux titles "the divine non-existence" (or the divine inexistence), which, interestingly, *also* refers to "the divine character of non-existence," its "power," or, in other words, the *virtual* state that conceals the possibility "of a God yet to come, who will be innocent of the disasters of the world and in whom one could hope for the power to grant to specters something besides death."[37]

Undeconstructibility: Justice, Messianism, and an Ethics of Hope

We are now in a position to ask if Meillassoux's metaphysics of contingency were allowed to invade ethics (perhaps even an ethics demanding law, dare even necessity), could one, to use Caputo's way of putting it, "Have a lawless theory of the law?"[38] In other words, with God being harbored in virtuality as a possibility for the future, how do we speak of a *positive* reality for such a being to govern if this being does not in fact now "exist"? What of divine law for the future? What of justice? Moreover, what of the "immanent hope" tied to such a being, a hope for a future world of justice to come? Meillassoux's spectral dilemma, the choice between a God who permits injustice and there being no God, demands special attention in the sense that we must now question types of deity other than the onto-theological God of necessity and absolute sovereignty.

John Caputo asks, "Is there something 'unconditional' that is nonetheless without 'sovereignty'? Is there something that makes an unconditional claim without laying claim to unconditional force of power . . . that would neither *be* nor be *something*?"[39] While considering what may come to be, it is important to make the distinction between what can be *virtually* or what can be *possibly*—especially with respect to contingency in its own *sovereign* power. As a virtual ground of what "can be," contingency exhibits sovereignty as it does weakness (Caputo having advocated a "weak theology").[40] Specifically, the sovereignty of what "can be" is *noncoercive* because, as a virtual state, it is capable of creating a number of possible futures, where any number of futures "still [may be] strong enough to save us," as Caputo would put it.[41] On the other hand, the sovereignty of this ground is challenged in that, among any number of futures, none are *necessary* in their advent. The virtual ground understood in this way could therefore be considered as a "weak force" (it does not guarantee a reign of justice). On the other hand, as a sovereign and creative power, the ground of contingency "conceals the possibility of a God yet to come."[42] And so a hope for justice is tied to it. This does *not* mean that one can claim that God and a World of justice are part of a prefabricated *telos* awaiting to unfold, and one just "hopes" that God institutes justice sooner rather than later. It also does not mean that God and a World of justice are prefabricated possibilities awaiting actualization (part of a divine plan or a divine Idea awaiting its due reality). Understanding the divine in these ways would not warrant the sort of radical hope that Meillassoux advocates. As the virtual is "not dominated by any pre-constituted set of possibles" anything can happen, and without reason at all.[43] Yet this is the unconditional mark of power as it lays claim to us through its *lack* of necessity, a "weakness." Weakness is the mark of a sovereign unconditional power capable of bringing about a new future in its absolute contingency.

The radical nature of hope under discussion here is made most explicit when we consider how the "virtual" is different from the "possible," and how the virtual is marked by creation ex nihilo and what Meillassoux calls "the advent." The distinction between virtuality and possibility is one of *miraculous* advent where there is a break from physical laws that have bound the world until the point of the advent.[44] As Meillassoux explains, "Surchaos can also give rise to events that do not conform to the physical laws of a world. I call such events *virtualities*. Virtualities can be considered, very precisely, as advents ex nihilo, since they proceed neither from an actually existing world nor from any physical potentiality, nor from some totality of possible world. . . . Virtualities come from a non-totality of possibles, from the untotalizable abyss of the virtualities of Surchaos."[45] The divine inexistence is truly a "miraculous" as its inauguration brings about a radically new world distinct from (though related to) prior worlds and their physical variables and constraints. Human beings may hope for the messianic promise contained in the virtual ground and its lack of totalization; in fact, it is this lack of totalization that justifies our "belief in its efficacy."[46] Again, anything can happen, anything is possible.

Caputo's deconstructive theology affirms this lack of totalization with respect to justice. Deconstructive theology, for Caputo, holds open the possibility of justice based upon an affirmation of something that is itself incapable of being absolutely affirmed or "totalized." Caputo explains: "The misbegotten notion that deconstruction is some kind of intellectual violence, a merely destructive and negative assault on anything still standing, arises from a failure to see what deconstruction affirms, a failure to see that every deconstructive analysis is undertaken *in the name of something,* something affirmatively *un*-deconstructible."⁴⁷ Caputo tells us that without the undeconstructible, deconstruction would be without "impulse."⁴⁸ Likewise, while it is true that there is "no end to deconstruction, no *telos*" it is "not true that there is no point to deconstruction, no spur . . . no thrust."⁴⁹ If the virtual ground renders any possibility as equally likely as any other, then this is not to say that there is no point in hoping for some realization of one possibility (virtuality) over another: namely the advent of an all-powerful being and the arrival of a new World distinct enough from the advent of any prior World (the succession of matter, life, and thought constituting the first, second, and third Worlds respectively) so as to warrant the title "World of justice."⁵⁰ Indeed, hope is all the more significant if contingency is truly absolute.

Deconstruction speaks of a "messianic future," of a future to come, a justice to come, a gift to come.⁵¹ If there is one word that may summarize Caputo's messianism with respect to the justice to come, it is "Come." "Come" could be our prayer when orientating ourselves to the possibility of a God who may come. "Come" as prayer could solicit the messianic in its very structure as "what is to come," given the sovereignty of the virtual, given its power of what "can be." Caputo tells us that "the messianic is the structure of the to come that exposes the contingency and deconstructibility of the present, exposing the alterability of what we like to call in English the 'powers that be.'"⁵² He clarifies the nature of this structure by telling of the promise understood through the lens of deconstruction. Caputo writes, "What right—what a nerve!—does deconstruction have to speak of *justice* (said in a bad temper)" of course.⁵³ Likewise, what nerve, one may ask with Caputo, does speculative philosophy, the "new metaphysics," have to speak of God—of a promise related to a deity who does not now exist? How could justice even be possible? We find a similar structure of query that animates speculating God and speculating justice, both undeconstructible in their very possibility, both being of an undeconstructible nature, both whose arrival is tied to an ethics of hope.

The messianic structure outlined above indicates that justice, too, is of both a weak and a sovereign nature. It "keeps things on the move" while it is "not yet" and "to come." When one prays to God one also prays for justice. An eternal reign of justice requires the power of deity, God, a figure who is capable of resurrecting the dead and reconciling past *injustices,* so that the dead may be properly mourned. Speculation (for Meillassoux thought about the absolute), and deconstruction therefore both seem to serve one and the same goal: to deliver the promise of the "to come," for God but also for justice, by sustaining an "absolute structure of the promise of an absolutely indeterminate."⁵⁴ They both hold open the possibility of justice whose promise is tied to an immanent world connected to the conditions that inaugurate that world's future. Speculation of this ground, therefore, may also be a *speculative hope* for justice.⁵⁵

A speculative hope for justice fits well with Caputo's understanding of "weak theology," for the "weakness" of God references "the to come" as "messianic future"—a future "always-to-come."⁵⁶ The messianic future is an absolute future, "the very structure of the future," which is not sparked by a *determinate* Messiah, that is, by someone who has as a matter of fact not shown up yet, but rather a certain "figure" in the futural sense of a "structure of the to come that exposes the contingency and deconstructibility of the present."⁵⁷ Like Meillassoux's concept of "factiality"—things can be radically otherwise than what they are—Caputo writes that "the messianic future, the unformable figure of the Messiah in deconstruction, has to do with something absolutely unpresentable and unrepresentable that comprises the prestige of the present, the absolutely undeconstructible that breaks the spell of present constructions."⁵⁸ The coming of the Messiah has to do with the very structure of a *messianic time,* "as the time of promise and expectation and opening to the future . . . [a] beyond that is never reached but always pursued."⁵⁹

For Meillassoux, the divine inexistence and the Messiah to come (for him a Christlike mediator figure who actually abolishes his or her own sovereignty once the conditions of justice are met) unfolds a certain ethics of messianism housed within the ontology of contingency, the undeconstructibility of Time. Our hope for this messiah may be understood in terms that could "attract" such a possible future, despite there being no guarantee of her or his arrival. Meillassoux writes, "The most important task for philosophy—its final challenge—is not being, but 'may being.' For the may-be unites within itself the true heart of every ontology (the absoluteness of factual possibility) and the deepest aspirations of ethics (the universal fulfillment of justice). . . . If the fourth world [of justice] can have an effect upon present existence, it can do so *only* in the case of an eschatological subject, moved by the desire for universal justice . . . that is to say one magnetically attracted by the vector of the emancipation to come."⁶⁰ Not only *can* we hope, we *ought* to hope.

Anatheism, Dynamatology, Divinology

Coinciding with Caputo's "weak theology" and a theology of the event (or Meillassouxian "advent"), is Kearney's "anatheism." Our concern here is to develop only the general contours of Kearney's anatheism—a position part of the "religious turn in continental philosophy"—to see how, if at all, his position would be part of the fideism that Meillassoux critiques, where in place of fideism a realism concerning the divine inexistence would be required. On the other hand, it may be possible to read Kearney with Meillassoux (and with Caputo as outlined above) such that Meillassoux's divine inexistence and its corresponding ethics of hope may appear more clearly. I hope to use Kearney's own approach to a God "who may be" as an avenue of closure in the sense that the meaning of "the not yet" can be isolated and clarified with respect to human knowledge of this possibility, in turn saving Kearney and Caput alike from Meillassoux's critique of fideism. For Kearney and Caputo alike, the fact that God "may be" is *not* a matter of human ignorance but is rather part of a determinate ontological structure of indeterminacy.

The indeterminateness of Kearney's virtual God is not epistemological, but ontological. This is most evident in looking at the definition of Kearney's proposed outlook, which he calls "anatheism." In Kearney's own words:

> The *ana* [of "anatheism"] . . . marks a reopening of that space where we are free to choose between faith or nonfaith. . . . It operates *before* as well as *after* the division between theism and atheism, and it makes both possible. . . . Anatheism differs from dogmatic atheism in that it resists absolutist positions *against the divine,* just as it differs from the absolutist positions of dogmatic theism *for* the divine. It is a movement—not a state.[61]

Anatheism relates to Kearney's concept of "the God-who-may-be," outlined in his 2001 book, *The God Who May Be*. Kearney, like Caputo, is not satisfied by the death of God announced by Nietzsche and chooses to go further than simply denying (or affirming) the God of classical onto-theology. Kearny, like Caputo, ties his ethics to an ontology of the possible. For both, "the death of God primarily meant that the absolute center had shifted its residence from transcendence to immanence by means of a metaphysics of *kenosis,* by which the full presence of a transcendent God was transported to the plane of immanence. . . . [We must observe] the undecidable fluctuation of the event that stirs within the name of God."[62] In *The God Who May Be,* Kearney builds on this God of the possible, a God who is yet "to be" after the death of the God of classical onto-theology. If God *was* and then died according to death of God theology, this means that God now is *not.* Therefore, God's inexistence (or possible future existence) cannot be the possibility of human ignorance or error and instead involves a determinate ontological reality: that of the possibility of God (or more deeply, virtuality). This is a God who possibilizes out of the future, and our orientation toward such a God is fundamentally *speculative.*

Kearney's God of the possible—which he calls *posse,* to borrow the sense of that term from Nicholas of Cusa—is "a God who promises to bring life and to bring it more abundantly. A God who even promises to raise the dead . . . emptying deity of its purported power-presence."[63] Like Meillassoux's divinology, which is centered on the divine inexistence and a future kenotic mediating figure who shall empty her- or himself, there is hope for an appearance of the divine from out of the possible understood not as *lack,* but as *promise.* Kearney's anatheism is therefore also a "dynamatology" (deriving from the Greek *dynamis,* meaning potentiality or potency)—a "movement" rather than a "state." In this movement there is the *potential* for justice as much as there is the power of the possible, *posse,* such that a God could resurrect the dead. This is a "logic of the dynamizing possible"—a metaphysics of speculating the power of the possible, or the power of a "to come" that arises from the depths of a virtual world that has slipped "beneath the grid of symbolic and imaginary expression, back into some primordial zero-point of unnameability."[64] Kearney reminds us that what seems *impossible* is only seemingly so, for "once transfigured by God all things are made possible again"—whether a World of justice or the resurrection of the dead. Thus *posse* "keeps us open to hope, in spite of injustice and despair."[65]

My brief discussion of Kearney in this final concluding section has been offered to further illustrate the ethics of hope latent within Meillassoux's own divinology by exploring the various senses of the possible for an ethics centered on justice. Kearney's notion of the God who may be opens up precisely the transformative nature of this hope. Despite Meillassoux's admonition of the religious turn in Continental philosophy and its corresponding fideism (faith in an unknown God who is capable of being described only through some form of phenomenological description), the truth of the matter is that by way of a *metaphysics of contingency* Meillassoux has opened the way also for the possible appearance of a being powerful enough to inaugurate a new World where justice reigns, and where the injustices of the past have been reconciled.

There is much, much more that could be stated regarding this common dynamic of the divine and the possible as shared by Meillassoux, Caputo, and Kearney. Certainly there is *religious* value to a radical metaphysics centered on the necessity of contingency and the possible appearance of a divine being. The question becomes, what shall we then do, those of us who gaze toward a future of justice, but those of us, too, who are without a deity who as of yet has to possibly appear? Before the advent of justice has occurred, Meillassoux offers his readers a hint regarding the inroads of ethical transformation and attraction:

> To love life beyond war, violence and sacrifice—even in a world of war, violence, and sacrifice—that is what is a stake in the ultimate transformation of the eschatological subject.... If it is our task to work towards embracing this last world, then it is the case—as I have already indicated—that this world is posed in way to *hope* [emphasis mine] that there will be a recommencement for terrible deaths [and injustice].[66]

Notes

1. "Speculative realism" is a term that was originally coined by the philosopher Raymond Brassier, author of *Nihil Unbound* (Basingstoke: Palgrave MacMillan, 2007). It was essentially used to describe common elements of realism, materialism, and metaphysics that were discussed at a conference entitled "Speculative Realism," held at the Goldsmiths College, University of London, in April 2007. Earlier, however, the French philosopher Quentin Meillas-

soux used the term "speculative materialism" to describe his own metaphysical position that would later be expounded upon in his *After Finitude* (trans. Ray Brassier [London: Continuum, 2008]). Recently, the term has fanned out to include what is now generally perceived as a certain "spirit" of speculative philosophy that could most generally and simply be described as the "new metaphysics," the "new materialism," or "Continental realism." It is a novel and wide-ranging movement whose exact borders have yet to be determined, as those borders are *fluid*; however, philosophers such as Quentin Meillassoux, Ray Brassier, Iain Hamilton Grant, or even arguably François Laruelle (to name but just a few) could be considered as appropriate figures of reference or at the very least *starting points*. For a more thorough characterization of how this new form of metaphysics can be pitted against more traditional forms of Continental philosophy, see Lee Braver, *A Thing of This World: A History of Continental Anti-Realism* (Evanston, Ill.: Northwestern University Press, 2007), or Leon Niemoczynski, "What Speculative Philosophy Means Today," *Nuori Voima* 5 (2012): 5–9.

2. Iain Hamilton Grant, *Philosophies of Nature after Schelling* (London: Continuum, 2006); François Laruelle, *Future Christ: A Lesson in Heresy* (London: Continuum, 2011); Bruno Latour, *On the Modern Cult of the Factish Gods* (Durham, N.C.: Duke University Press, 2011); and Bruno Latour, "Facing Gaia: A New Enquiry into Natural Religion," Gifford Lectures, University of Edinburgh, February 2013.

3. Quentin Meillassoux, *L'inexistence Divine* (doctorat soutenu sous la direction de Bernard Bourgeois, Paris-1, 1997).

4. Other than *After Finitude*, an excellent introduction to Meillassoux's thinking can be found in "'There is contingent being independent of us, and this contingent being has no reason to be of a subjective nature': Interview with Quentin Meillassoux," in *New Materialism: Interviews and Cartographies*, ed. Iris van der Tuin and Rick Dolphjin (Ann Arbor, Mich.: Open Humanities Press, 2012), 71–81.

5. For Meillassoux's own characterization of the term "speculative materialism," see *After Finitude*, 121. Another characterization can be found in Peter Gratton, "After the Subject: Meillassoux's Ontology of 'What May Be,'" *Pli* 20 (2009): 64.

6. Other than his dissertation, Meillassoux's consideration of the divine inexistence (and associated themes) may be found in articles such as "Immanence of the World Beyond" in *The Grandeur of Reason: Religion, Tradition, and Universalism*, ed. Conor Cunningham and Peter Candler (London: SCM Press, 2010), 444–478, and "Spectral Dilemma," *Collapse* 4 (2008): 261–276. John Caputo's work is certainly immense; however, for purposes of succinctness, brevity, and clarity I will draw on some of his more well known works and one or two lesser known but pointed articles, including *The Weakness of God: A Theology of the Event* (Bloomington: Indiana University Press, 2006), and "Without Sovereignty, without Being: Unconditionality, the Coming God and Derrida's Democracy to Come," *Journal for Cultural and Religious Theory* 4, no. 3 (2003): 9–26. Caputo's *The Insistence of God: A Theology of Perhaps* (Indiana University Press, forthcoming) dialogues explicitly at points with Meillassoux's thinking about religion.

7. Richard Kearney, *The God Who May Be* (Bloomington: Indiana University Press, 2001), also Richard Kearney, *Anatheism: Returning to God after God* (New York: Columbia University Press, 2009).

8. Other than Caputo's own introduction in his edited anthology of *The Religious*, for commentary regarding how the theological turn within postmodern Continental philosophy of religion stands with respect to contemporary speculative philosophy and metaphysics, I would suggest the editors' introduction of "What Is Continental Philosophy of Religion Now?" in *After the Postsecular and the Postmodern: New Essays in Continental Philosophy of Religion*, ed. Anthony Paul Smith and Daniel Whistler (Newcastle upon Tyne: Cambridge Scholars Publishing, 2010), 1–24.

9. In a section titled "Postmodernity and Fideism" Meillassoux writes in "Immanence of the World Beyond," "The end of metaphysics allows a decisive return of religious concern, since, metaphysics having been ended, no one can seriously argue that we can know that God does not exist.... In this way, postmodernity revives, in its own fashion, a fideistic relation between thought and faith, since fideism consists ... in limiting, and indeed annulling, the cognitive claims of reason so as to generate a vacuum in which belief can find its niche." Meillassoux, "Immanence of the World Beyond," 450.

10. See Dominique Janicaud, *Phenomenology Wide Open: After the French Debate* (New York: Fordham University Press, 2010). Janicaud asks explicitly whether phenomenology will cease to be a major influence in Continental thought, and if it will survive among competing new doctrines. See also Dominique Janicaud's *Phenomenology and the Theological Turn* (New York: Fordham University Press, 1997). The major critique of phenomenology made by the new metaphysics can be summarized in one word: "correlationism." Correlationism states that "we cannot access any form of the in-itself, because we are irremediably confined in our relation-to-the-world, without any means to verify whether the reality that is given to us corresponds to reality taken in itself, independently of our subjective link to it"; Meillassoux, "Interview with Quentin Meillassoux," 72. Phenomenology, for the new metaphysics, is always about presentations of phenomenon *to the experiencing human subject,* rather than about a reality *independent of* and *without reference to* that subject.

11. "For clearly it is not God who is dead ... but metaphysics' God, the God of metaphysical theology." John Caputo, "Who Comes after the God of Metaphysics?" in *The Religious* (London: Wiley-Blackwell, 2001). 2. Yet the "God" of the new metaphysics, twenty-first-century speculative philosophy, is indeed a metaphysical Absolute, whether Surchaos as absolute contingency or the Absolute as reality unconditioned. See the absolute as articulated in Meillassoux's *After Finitude* or Grant's *Philosophies of Nature After Schelling.*

12. "Correlationism" is a hallmark concept of the new metaphysics. A correlationist philosophy is any philosophy which holds that reality is inevitably *conditioned* by some form of phenomenal representation of reality, whether through the representation of conscious experience (phenomenology), the activity of signs (semiotics), the existence of text (deconstruction), conscious interpretation of text or experience (hermeneutics), or the analysis of discursive formations (structuralism and poststructuralism and corresponding archaeologies of knowledge and genealogies of morality). In other words, correlationist philosophy asserts that thought and being (reality) are inextricably linked or "co-related" in such a way that access to reality *independent of* any subjective human link to it is impossible or contradictory.

13. Meillassoux, "Immanence of the World Beyond," 460.

14. It is ultimately Meillassoux's thesis that the absolute, reality in-itself, can be understood in terms of its own mathematizable powers or "happenings" (events), which are radically contingent in their nature. For an exceptional explanation of Meillassoux's mathematical philosophy and how it draws from Badiou but also from Cantor see Elie Ayache, *The Blank Swan: The End of Probability* (London: Wiley, 2010), 146 and 153.

15. Kearney's conclusion, "Welcoming Strange Gods," speaks most to this point. See *Anatheism,* 166–182.

16. Meillassoux, "Immanence of the World Beyond," 461.

17. My allusion here is to the "weakness" of God outlined in Caputo's *The Weakness of God.*

18. Meillassoux, *After Finitude,* 53.

19. Ibid., 79.

20. Ibid.

21. Ibid., 54, 62.

22. Meillassoux, "Immanence of the World Beyond," 462.

23. Quentin Meillassoux, "Potentiality and Virtuality," *Collapse* 2 (2007): 74n7.
24. Meillassoux, *After Finitude*, 92.
25. Meillassoux, "Immanence of the World Beyond," 449.
26. Meillassoux, *After Finitude*, 104.
27. Ibid., 62, 84.
28. Ibid., 61. Here, other than Bergsonian intellectual intuition, Meillassoux's commitment to a valorization of contingency in nature follows the Bergsonian commitment to *novel emergence* and *creativity*. See Quentin Meillassoux, "Subtraction and Contraction," *Collapse* 3 (2007): 63–107. For Meillassoux on the law of non-contradiction see "Immanence of the World Beyond," 447.
29. Ibid., 101.
30. For an excellent overview of the logic at work within Meillassoux's argument concerning modal metaphysics, necessity, and contingency, as well as some of its apparent flaws, see Thibaut Giraud and Raphael Milliere, "After Certitude: On Meillassoux's Logical Flaws," unpublished paper, from *Atelier de métaphysique et d'ontologie contemporaines*, Workshop on Contemporary Metaphysics and Ontology at the École Normale Supérieure, http://www.atmoc.fr/resources/Giraud-Milliere-AfterCertitude.pdf. For a discussion of Meillassoux appealing to the "figure" (modal category or logical law) see Quentin Meillassoux, "Time without Becoming," paper presented at the Centre for Research in Modern European Philosophy, Middlesex University, London, United Kingdom, May 8, 2008.
31. Meillassoux, "Immanence of the World Beyond," 446.
32. Ibid., 64.
33. Meillassoux, "Spectral Dilemma," 265.
34. Meillassoux, "Immanence of the World Beyond," 451.
35. Ibid., 453.
36. Ibid., 454.
37. Ibid., 458.
38. John Caputo, *Deconstruction in a Nutshell* (New York: Fordham University Press, 1997), 125.
39. John Caputo, "Without Sovereignty, without Being: Unconditionality, the Coming God and Derrida's Democracy to Come," *Journal for Culture and Religious Theory* 4, no. 3 (August 2003): 9.
40. See Caputo's *The Weakness of God*.
41. Caputo, "Without Sovereignty," 9.
42. Meillassoux, "Immanence of the World Beyond," 458.
43. Meillassoux, "Potentiality and Virtuality," 71–72.
44. Ibid., 71.
45. Meillassoux, "Immanence of the World Beyond," 461.
46. Ibid., 459.
47. Caputo, *Deconstruction in a Nutshell*, 128.
48. Ibid., 131.
49. Ibid.
50. Meillassoux, "Immanence of the World Beyond," 461.
51. Caputo, *Deconstruction in a Nutshell*, 156.
52. Ibid., 162.
53. Ibid., 169.
54. Ibid., 161, and Meillassoux, "Immanence of the World Beyond," 444.
55. Meillassoux, "Immanence of the World Beyond," 472.
56. Caputo, *Deconstruction in a Nutshell*, 162.

57. Ibid., 162.
58. Ibid.
59. Ibid., 163.
60. Meillassoux, "Immanence of the World Beyond," 463.
61. Kearney, *Anatheism*, 7, 16.
62. John Caputo and Gianni Vattimo, *After the Death of God*, ed. Jeff Robbins (New York: Columbia University Press, 2009), 68.
63. Richard Kearney, *The God Who May Be* (Bloomington: Indiana University Press, 2001), 2.
64. Ibid., 7.
65. Ibid., 5.
66. Meillassoux, "Immanence of the World Beyond," 474.

6 Between Deconstruction and Speculation

John D. Caputo and A/Theological Materialism

Katharine Sarah Moody

WHEN RADICAL ORTHODOXY asserts that *"only transcendence . . . 'suspends'"* the material in the sense of "upholding [its] relative worth over-against the void," both John D. Caputo and Slavoj Žižek suspect that matter is not what ultimately matters for John Milbank.[1] Within what Caputo calls "the soft Gnosticism" of "strong" theologies such as Radical Orthodoxy, the spirit is *in* the flesh *but not of* the flesh. Desiring to escape materiality and reach union with God, Milbank's is a theology of *in*-carnation rather than *of carnality*, and Caputo identifies this tendency in Milbank's materialism, which operates within an economy of "bodies without flesh" where "matter does not have the last word."[2] A Radically Orthodox materialism cannot, thereby, fully affirm the material in all its goodness, a "good" that Caputo finds at the heart of fleshy material life and at the heart of the Christian creation narratives and kingdom parables. Similarly, for Žižek, Milbank's theological materialism leads to "standard metaphysics" wherein "material reality isn't everything, there is another, higher spiritual reality." There is a constitutive exception to materiality—a transcendence that grounds it. According to Žižek, therefore, the "true formula of materialism" is not that material reality is (or is not) all there is but that material reality is not-all, is non-all. While there is nothing that does not belong to the material, the field of the material is never an All, never a One; it is lacking, contradictory and conflicted, nontotalized, containing an inherent antagonism that is the possibility of subjectivity, freedom, and revolution.[3]

But when Žižek misreads Caputo's deconstructive theology of the event as a "pure desubstantialized form" of the kind of metaphysical theological materialism proposed by Milbank,[4] he not only forestalls what I feel would be a fruitful dialogue between Caputo and himself, between deconstructive theology and speculative philosophy, between a Derridean "theism" (that rightly passes for atheism)[5] and a Žižekian "atheism" (that passes through the Christian experience),[6] but also precludes the possibility of reading Caputo's Continental philosophy of religion as what might be called an "a/theological materialism." Once Žižek's misreading is made more visible, it enables us to see that Caputo and Žižek are closer in content—if not in tone—than the latter would perhaps like to admit.

I offer a close reading of Caputo's a/theology of the event as a form of ir/religious materialism.[7] I end by suggesting that St. Paul is a mediating figure between Derrida and Žižek, and briefly present the work of Peter Rollins as an example of how a Pauline a/theology might already be being in-carnated by religious collectives. A/theistic practices offer insights into the role that Continental, or more broadly European, philosophy of religion might play in shaping the future of religion in the West. Concrete religious practices might, therefore, come to figure more prominently in the philosophy of religion, raising questions about the relationship of philosophy to ethnographical studies of religion.[8] But, we can also ask, might the Church as an a/theological Pauline community be not only one of the *research sites* of future theo-philosophical reflection, but also a site of the *future practice* of Continental philosophy of religion itself?

Relative Determinacy

In his introduction to an academic roundtable on Žižek and Milbank's *The Monstrosity of Christ,* Gregory Hoskins wonders how "out of place" someone like Derrida, "with his scruples and gentle, civil demeanor," would be among these two "prize fighters." "We can," he writes, "imagine Derrida shoved into the corner to pray and cry while the others duke it out."[9] For despite the apparent differences between Milbank's Radically Orthodox theological materialism and Žižek's Lacanian-Hegelian atheistic materialism, there remains an affinity involving not the *content* of their respective interpretations of Christianity but the *status* each gives to their interpretations, what Derrida calls "interpretations of interpretation," the logics inherent to the interpretations themselves.[10]

Taking Milbank as a paradigm of Radical Orthodoxy, Gavin Hyman distinguishes between three different levels of narratival interpretation within this theological sensibility. There is, firstly, the Christian *narrative,* and then, secondly, Milbank's reading of the Christian narrative, his *metanarrative,* the "story of the end of modernity and secular reason" and "of the futility of liberalism and nihilism."[11] This is a metanarration positing that, since God "includes difference, and yet is unified," the Church as a "participation of the beautiful in the beauty of God" is similarly harmonious and peaceful, a "nonviolent consensus."[12] But, thirdly, there is also what Hyman calls a *meta-metanarration,* the narratival level at which Milbank asserts that *his* is the *only* metanarratival positioning of the Christian narrative that can resist and out-narrate rampant secularism, metaphysical nihilism, an ontology of violence, and a logic of heretical parody.

Milbank's self-narrated omniscience as a "metanarrator"[13] can also be seen in Žižek's atheistic positioning of the Christian narrative. Žižek's is the story of an immanent "Holy Spirit"—the virtual "spiritual substance" or political "cause"[14] of a community of believers that cuts across and is a cut within all particular identities, such that the only true division is that between "those who fight for emancipation and their reactionary opponents; the people and the enemies of the people."[15] This Spirit emerges historically from Jewish and Christian particularity toward the concrete or singular universality of a transcendental materialist theory of subjectivity as negativity, as void, as the Lacanian barred subject of enunciation, such that "the 'subject' itself is *nothing but* the failure of symbolization."[16] First manifest, according to Žižek, in the Jewish stance towards the Law and, following Alain Badiou in this regard, in the albeit mythological truth-event and truth-procedure of Pauline Christianity,[17] the universal and revolutionary collective practices "the hard and arduous work of repeated 'uncoupling'" or unplugging in fidelity to "a universal ethico-political principle"—"the way of Love"—in which "we have to disengage ourselves from the inertia that constrains us to identify with the particular order we were born into."[18] And this "active *work* of love leads to the creation of an *alternative* community"[19] that does not need the institutional Church as a marker of its boundaries. Indeed, Žižek writes, "in my atheism, I am more Christian than Milbank"[20]—no small boast!

In his review of *The Word Made Strange*, Gareth Jones parodies Milbank's metanarration of the Christian narrative, and of the history of Western philosophy and theology, which sets right everything that comes before it:

> In the beginning was God. And God spoke God's Word, Jesus Christ: revelation. The church worshipped the Word, in truth. Then came theologians: they messed everything up, because they persisted in trying to accommodate God's Word to society's words—"the most puerile form of betrayal" (p.1). But fear not: now there is John Milbank, and everything will be fine again. Indeed, it will be better than fine: it will be "really most orthodox and ancient, since the tradition is so rarely re-performed in practice today" (ibid).[21]

I suggest that Žižek's metanarration can be said to run thus:

> In the beginning was the Void. And the Void was a conflict at the heart of matter that disturbed matter into being more-than-being: subjectivity. Then came the ideologues: they smoothed everything out, because they persisted in trying to accommodate the subject of enunciation to the subject of utterances—"to fill out this void."[22] But fear not: now there is Slavoj Žižek, and *nothing* will be "fine" again. Indeed, it will be better than fine: it will be "the Pauline community of believers . . . to be found today in radical political groups, not in churches."[23]

It is these two metanarrations of the Christian narrative that "square off" in *The Monstrosity of Christ* and that lead Caputo to ask:

> What exactly is the compelling need we are under to agree with either one of these positions or to choose between them? ... Why do we need the notion that at the metaphysical base of things there lies either a primordial peace or a primordial violence ... ? Why inscribe either absolute contradiction or absolute peace at the heart of things instead of ambience and ambiguity?[24]

The problem here lies neither in interpreting the Christian narrative nor in making choices between interpretations but, rather, in claiming, as the meta-metanarratival tones of Žižek and Milbank imply, that we can "put to rest our interpretative controversies."[25] For Caputo, there is always the insertion in hermeneutics—the cut, the slash—of undecidability, which Derrida describes as "always a determinate oscillation between possibilities,"[26] between any hermeneutic decision and its possible other(s). So the problem is a question of what Caputo calls the *"relative determinacy"* of our determinations.[27] This is to ask whether there might be determinations that are *more*, and determinations that are *less*, determinate—determinations that are more or less aware that "the particular figures in which our faith and hope and love take shape can always be determined otherwise."[28] Perhaps, then, the difference between Milbank and Žižek, on the one hand, and Caputo, on the other, is that the determinations of Milbank and Žižek are *more* determinate, while Caputo's radical hermeneutics make his own determinations *less* determinate, weaker or more fictional.

But while deconstruction and deconstructive theology do not (cannot) settle (determine) these disputes about determination, it is not the case that Caputo does not determine at all, that he is allergic to determinacy, or that his determinations are somehow *in*determinate, as many critics, including Milbank, have alleged.[29] If there is an undecidability, a disturbing translatability and substitutability, or exemplarism,[30] between determinations, then *"everything* turns on ... determination,"* on determining what we love, the names and traditions that we affirm.[31] So the (Augustinian) questions to ask, for Caputo, I think, are, "What do I love when I love my God?" "What do I love when I love the creation narratives and kingdom parables?" and, increasingly, "What do I love when I love or affirm the incarnation, crucifixion and resurrection?"[32] It is precisely because we love these things, these concepts, these traditions, that "we ask if there is not a promise within that tradition ... that the tradition does not make good on."[33] Hence, Caputo's dual emphasis on both "historical association" with determinate religions and "messianic dissociation" from them,[34] on being "inside/outside" traditions or myths,[35] and on "a/theism."

While the *names* by which we call the event that calls us are *semantically* translatable, the *event* they harbor calls to be translated *pragmatically*. Caputo writes, therefore, that "what matters with the event, is to take a step,"[36] and it is with this evental transformation of individual subjectivity that the slash of undecidability between theist and atheist becomes acute, between acting in the name of God and acting without the name of God, or between acting in the name of God and acting in the name of other names for the event that stirs in the name of God. There is a resultant "working equivalence" between theism and atheism.[37] Caputo may be theistic—but he is not without prayers and tears, and certainly not without doubt, without atheism. He is a/theistic. And this is why radical hermeneutics creates trouble "for both traditional religious faith and modern atheism,"[38] for both Milbank and Žižek.

There exists, then, a slash of undecidabilty between, on the one hand, the theistic determinations of Milbank and, on the other, the atheistic determinations of Badiou and Žižek—an undecidability that Caputo's Continental philosophy of religion and deconstructive a/theology of the event tries to remain with. If it is not possible to exorcise the ghost of undecidability, the specter of other possible determinations, from our hermeneutic decisions, then, Caputo writes, no one "ever really succeeds in getting to one side or the other of this undecidable rift," no one "really 'is' or 'is not' religious, wholly Augustinian or wholly Nietzschean . . . decidably, without doubt."[39] We can add, no one really "is" or "is not" wholly theistic or wholly atheistic, wholly Milbankian or wholly Žižekian. Thus, for Caputo, Žižek's atheism (not because it is atheistic but because it is, unlike Derrida's atheism, *without doubt atheistic*) ends up overdetermining the event and the Spirit (as atheistic), and thereby underestimating them both.[40]

A/Theological Materialism

Žižek mischaracterizes Caputo's theology of the event as a desubstantialized form of theological materialism. But Caputo's a/theism opens the possibility of reading his deconstructive theology not as a *theological* materialism but as an *a/theological* materialism, a materialism that shares much with Žižek's own materialism, even as it differs—since Caputo's materialism, like his theology, is kept "in the weak mode."[41] In it, material reality is marked by an indeterminacy, instability, and undecidability; subjectivity consists in the void, or abyss, of nonidentical identity; and revolution is dependent upon the traumatic risk of human freedom and responsibility.

In *The Weakness of God*, Caputo's metanarration proposes that the Christian narrative posits God as the name of an endlessly translatable event, not as the name of a being nor of Being itself, but as something eventual, something astir in the plane of being, calling being beyond itself. He uses Catherine Keller's *Face of the Deep: A Theology of Becoming* to suggest that creation is not "a movement from non-being to being" but a movement "from being to the good," which goes beyond being to the fullness of life, of being "of a new mind, a new heart," a new subjectivity.[42] When he summarizes Keller's argument—writing, "where the Genesis narratives speak of something, a wild or watery deep, onto-phallo-theology reads 'nothing,' leaving a big erect masculine will to do it all by himself"[43]—is it not possible to hear the Žižekian refrain that there is "no need to resort to myths of creation ex nihilo"?[44] There is, just as for Žižek, no creation from nothing, no primordial Void *before* being and materiality, *before* the already-present barren earth, deep waters, and wind of Genesis 1:2.[45] Instead, the ground of more-than-material life—of, as we shall see, emergent subjectivity, autonomy, and revolution—is a void *within* (rather than *before the genesis of*) the material, a void that Caputo refers to as an "elemental undecidability," "a deep structural mutability and transformability," "an element of irreducible indeterminacy and instability."[46]

For Caputo, this "hypothesis" of ontological ambiguity represents the promise of the possibility of *the* impossible.[47] It is a call *within* the material *for* the more-than-materially possible, for that which is not yet present, for justice beyond the law, hospitality beyond rights, and unconditional love. Ontological undecidability means that *there is a promise within material reality that the event is possible,* and that even our best names for this event—names like God, justice, and love—need to be de-literalized, de-absolutized and de-ontologized, weakened, reduced to the transformative event they harbor: the call to wise-up to that which is other, and to be otherwise. Implications for subjectivity, freedom, and revolution can thereby be drawn from Caputo's materialism, just as they can from Žižek's. The indeterminacy and instability of creation means that, as for Derrida, identity is "different from itself, having an opening or gap within itself," such that, for Caputo, "human beings are inwardly divided, inhabited by an abyss."[48] But, just as for Žižek's theory of subjectivity as negativity, this "cold truth"[49]—which is linked by Caputo to Foucault's "night of truth" and by Žižek to Hegel's "night of the world"—is not a night of despair but, Caputo writes, of "a hope for the freedom to invent something new" since "the 'I' or the 'we' is marked by its capacity to be otherwise." The "abyss that we are" means that "we are not who we are; something different is always possible."[50]

Thus to read Caputo's statement "we do not know who we are, not if we are honest about it"[51] as an affirmation that "'external' material social rituals and/or practices forever fail to reach the subject's innermost kernel, to represent it adequately,"[52] as Žižek might, is to misread an infinite judgment as a negative judgment. While Caputo's negation of the positive judgment ("we know who we are") *might* be read as "we do not know who we are" (i.e., we are a mystery unto ourselves), it should perhaps be read instead—given the opening, gap, division, abyss or negativity of subjectivity—as "we are nothing but our failure to know who we are," or as Žižek puts it, "*nothing but* the failure" of subjectification, of identification with the subject of utterance.[53] For Caputo, the play of *différance* and the void, darkness or abyss at the heart of the human condition—the void of reality and subjectivity *in themselves*—give rise to both "tragic" and "religious," Nietzschean and Kierkegaardian, hermeneutics or construals for coping with this void, with the material and existential flux of human existence.[54] But the event, which, he writes, "cuts across the distinctions among the various confessions, and even across the distinction between the confessional faiths and secular unbelief," is a cut across and a cut within particular names and symbolizations, determinate narratives and hermeneutics, traditions and communities.[55] Perhaps for Caputo, then, subjectivity is *nothing but* this cut or abyss of undecidability—with a/theism, the resultant "slipping back and forth between the two, between Abraham and Zarathustra," theism and atheism, an exemplary example signaling this very negativity.[56]

For Žižek, the fundamental fantasy of an enduring and unified positive subjectivity functions to avoid the void that signals the groundlessness of autonomy. What is avoided is "the abyss of the pure *act*," "the true traumatic cut," the atemporal yet "primordial act of decision" that is the repressed "lost cause" of the "I," "the act of decision by means of which I 'choose myself'—that is, combine this multitude of drives into the unity of my Self."[57] Žižek writes that, when there is "no big Other to provide the ultimate guarantee, the ontological cover for the subject's decision," the illusion of a stable and whole selfhood conceals the utter contingency of current configurations of the self and "the terrifying abyss of the subject's ultimate and *radical* freedom."[58] This truth is monstrous precisely because we, and we alone, are left, as Žižek writes in relation to the double *kenosis* of God at the incarnation and crucifixion, "with the terrible burden of freedom and responsibility for the fate of divine creation, and thus of God himself."[59]

Caputo likewise affirms the excessive monstrosity of the "bottomless obligation"[60] for creation and re-creation that the de-ontologization, weakening or death of God as the big Other places us under, and the risk that human freedom, which can be inhuman, entails. "Žižek is a realist," he writes, "in the sense that he is encouraging us to realize that help is not on the way, that no one is going to save us, save ourselves."[61] That "responsibility is excessive or it is not responsibility," a "surplus" to the law that "leaves no respite, no rest,"[62] has certainly left many critics of deconstruction traumatized. It is a scandal to ethics (since ethics tries to be a law of who I should and should not feel obliged toward), an impossible excess that Derrida calls "an absolute interruption in the regime of the possible"[63] and that is, for Caputo, the madness of the kingdom parables. God's benediction in the biblical narrative, his "good," his "yes" at the moment of creation, suggests to Caputo that being experiences a call to "the infinite task of making good on [God's] 'good,'" of countersigning and signing-on to the risky business of actualizing the kingdom, forgiveness beyond repentance, justice beyond law, hospitality beyond rights, gift beyond economy, and love beyond conditions.[64] For both Žižek and Caputo, then, life remains in the "accusative, put on the spot," shaken out of complacency into revolutionary action.[65]

But Žižek persists in misreading Caputo's theology of the event. "If I may mock it in a very friendly way, the message is, 'Of course God is dead! There is no Grandfather up there. But'—and now I am consciously mocking—'But in this void, from this very absence, Someone, a Voice, is addressing us, an Unconditional Call.'"[66] The claim is, therefore, that, after the death of God *in name*, God remains as a Call that addresses the material, a Call that is a metaphysical exception to the physical and that grounds the material as its constitutive exception.

And yet Caputo, in his weakening of theology, in his reduction of onto-theology to phenomenology, in his a/theism, has sought to take the uncertainties and risks of material life seriously, and to do justice to that which appears to be, he says, "in a good hermeneutic of life, a good account of what our life is like—a centrepiece of it"; namely, "the structure of an unconditional claim" or call, one that is at work within the "concert" of material forces and that is poetically attested to by "the *life-giving transformations*" within the already-present-materiality of the creation narratives.[67] What matters is not, therefore, "whether over and beyond what we might call the hermeneutics of the event, the lived experience of the call and of being on call, there is some entitative cause calling";[68] instead, "the 'matter' that really matters is the risky matter of life,"[69] of responding, of revolution. It is not that, for Caputo, the Messiah has (but Žižek protests) or has not (and Milbank rebukes) turned up, but that "*we* are the messianic generation, in which it is our responsibility to see that he (or she or it) does [turn up], insofar as that impossibility is possible."[70]

So when Caputo writes, "I do not say that God exists but that God insists. I do not say that God is but that God calls. Existence is our responsibility, which is also to say that it is by responding that God exists,"[71] how different, really, is this "God" from Žižek's own notion of the "Holy Spirit" as the spiritual substance of the community of believers, of the revolutionary "fighting collective," which "exists only insofar as subjects act *as if it exists*"?[72] How different is it to speak of God as existing only insofar as subjects respond? This call is, then, a cause that is one in excess of religion and of current configurations of ethics and politics. It is a call that calls for the cause of justice, which is, for both Derrida and Žižek, the justice not of justice-according-to-the-law but of a justice that is described variously as universal, unconditional, and undeconstructible. The call is a cause that is emancipatory not entitative.

We are left, then, to wonder exactly how different Žižek's desubstantialized Christianity or Christian atheism is from Derrida's religion without religion; how far Žižek's Kantian distinction between the "private" God and the "public" universal community of believers[73] is both from Derrida's differentiation between determinate messianisms and the structure of messianicity and from Caputo's language of historical association and messianic dissociation; how close, as Caputo himself notes, Žižek's "spectral materialism"[74] is to Derrida's "spectral messianic."[75] We return to the question with which we began: Why Žižek's atheistic materialism or Milbank's theological materialism? Why a Žižekian atheistic materialism that doesn't need the Church or a Church that needs Milbank's "strong" theological materialism? Why not a less determinate, weak, or a/theological materialism, that can be in-carnated both with and without the carnality of the Church?

Pauline Community

In *The Weakness of God,* Caputo identifies a thinking of the event, subjectivity, and revolution as the point of contact between the New Testament kingdom parables with which his own theology of the event is primarily concerned and Paul's letters to the new communities of faith.[76] Theodore Jennings's *Reading Derrida / Thinking Paul* further demonstrates that the Pauline questions of justice and hospitality also animate Derrida.[77] Perhaps this saint is, therefore, the mediating figure between Derrida and Caputo, on the one hand, and Badiou and Žižek, on the other. Briefly exploring these connections will allow me to conclude by illustrating how an a/theological materialism might already be being in-carnated by religious, or, rather, "ir/religious," collectives.

For Derrida, unconditional hospitality is beyond the law of hospitality-by-rights, beyond the conditions conventionally placed upon hospitality. It is structurally similar to the "no matter whom" and "no matter what" of unconditional love, offered to whoever the guest might be.[78] "Let us say yes," Derrida writes, "*to who or what turns up,* before any determination . . . before any identification" of the one who comes.[79] Paul's Letter to the Romans enjoins his readers to a similar hospitality, to "welcome" (15:7), without "quarrelling over opinions" (14:1), an injunction occasioned by questions regarding whether or not to eat meat. But Jennings wonders whether the real question for Paul is not one of *what* to eat but, rather, as for Derrida, "*how* for goodness' sake should one *eat well*?" This *how* of eating is not about taking in the other, but, Derrida writes, "learning-to-give-the-other-to-eat," "offering infinite hospitality," and giving to and sharing with "the other, the neighbor, the friend";[80] as Paul writes, welcoming one another, "as Christ has welcomed you" (15:7).

For Badiou and Žižek, Paul's letters are an exemplary paradigm of a truth-procedure, the working-out of the consequences of being faithful to the truth-event (of Christ), of the difficult task of creating a universal community of believers in fidelity to the "active *work* of love."[81] For Paul, what is central to the formation and nurturing of concrete collectives is a universal truth-procedure of justice, hospitality, and revolutionary love that "suspends the 'normal' function of one's emotional life" and cuts through all particular identities,[82] enjoining "hatred" of fathers and mothers who stand in Luke 14:26 "for the entire socio-symbolic network,"[83] such that "there is no longer Jew or Greek, slave or free, male or female; all are one in Christ" (Gal 3:28).

But, for Žižek, a Christianity that "draws all the consequences from its basic event" is an atheism, *without doubt*,[84] while Derrida cannot exorcise the specter of a certain "religion," or the trace of a religion without religion—the phenomenological structure of a promise, call, or event—and cannot even say, "*I am* an atheist." So why must this Pauline universal and unconditional love be, as Žižek contends, atheistic? Why must the only forms that the true Pauline community can take be, as he suggests, the revolutionary political party or the psychoanalytic society?[85] If it is to be truly a cut, surely this love must, as Caputo contends, be a cut within both theism and atheism? Must not a truly Pauline community be neither theistic nor atheistic, but a/theistic?

Analysis of the discourse and practice of the emerging church milieu indicates that some of the highly experimental collectives within this loose transnational association are attempting to in-carnate a Derridean-Žižekian a/theology.[86] An identifiable discursive framework that signals the possibility of Church as an a/theological Pauline community, building upon both Derridean theologies and Žižek's atheistic materialism, primarily arises from the accessible publications and magnetic presentations of Peter Rollins, founder of the Ikon collective in Belfast and the one-year church experiment in New York, Ikon NYC. Following Caputo, Rollins distinguishes between the name and the event of God, writing that "it is a happening, an event, that we affirm and respond to, regardless of the ebbs and flows of our abstract theological reflections concerning the source and nature of this happening."[87] Following Žižek, he suggests that the "fundamental antagonism is not located between various distinctions but rather between those who lay all distinctions down and those who hold onto them."[88] Building on both, however, the Pauline community is manifest liturgically for Rollins as a "suspended space"[89] in which the community of believers identifies directly with Christ, who laid down his identity, took the form of a "slave," a "servant," and "made himself nothing" (Phil 2:6–8). He writes, "by having a space in our week where there is 'neither/nor,' where we not only affirm one another in excess of our culturally given identities but expose these identities as contingent, we can more productively engage in exploring how to transform society."[90]

The second half of Rollins's *How (Not) to Speak of God* provides examples of Ikon's gatherings, illustrating the ways in which these theo-philosophical theories are translated into religious practices.[91] While the reproductions cannot fairly represent the mixture of liturgy, ritual, and performance art that forms Ikon's gatherings, they offer insight into the ways the collective itself provides both the narratives, identities, structures, and boundaries to be transgressed and the opening through which this transgression might take place. The notion of "transformance art"—"anarchic experiments" in performance art that are designed to "open up the possibility of a theodramatic event" in order to effect radical subjective transformation[92]—has reached wide audiences through events at

Greenbelt Arts Festival in the UK since 2003; workshops such as 2008's Minnekon, run in conjunction with Solomon's Porch in Minneapolis; Rollins's Insurrection Tour of the United States in 2010; and his 2011 online Dis-Courses Seminar Series about courses—such as Atheism for Lent: Giving up God for Lent and The Omega Course: Exiting Christianity in 12 Weeks—that are designed to send participants "off-course." Fusions and juxtapositions of prose and beat poetry; songs and ambient soundscapes; liturgy and ritual; prayer, meditation, reflection, and discussion; art installations and theater pieces, all refract "historical associations" with Christianity through points of "messianic dissociation," and enable those gathered to explore a horizon against which a transformative event of alterity might occur.

Such rituals of transformative suspended space can be better performed by the Church if the Church recognizes its properly a/theological nature, if it enacts what Žižek calls the "properly *ethical* monstrosity" of striking or shooting at oneself, of "renouncing what is most precious to oneself."[93] In fidelity to the universal Christ event of unconditional justice, hospitality and love, the Church sacrifices even that which is most precious to this community—its act of decision in relation to which it knows itself *to be* the Church; in other words, in fidelity to the endlessly translatable event, it enacts a betrayal of its fidelity to Christ and becomes an a/theological collective, marked by an indeterminacy, instability, and undecidability. Such a collective is not the rarefied Church of Radical Orthodoxy, the one "perfect community," both remembered and hoped for;[94] rather, it is *nothing but* its failure to know whether *it* or the atheistic fighting collective is where the Spirit or cause of justice is being actualized, such that it must in every moment say "yes" to the traumatic risk of freedom and responsibility, countersigning through revolutionary response whenever and wherever the "good" of life is emergent within material reality.

Notes

1. John Milbank, Catherine Pickstock, and Graham Ward, eds., *Radical Orthodoxy: A New Theology* (London: Routledge, 1999), 3; my emphasis. For their respective responses to John Milbank's "The Double Glory, or Paradox versus Dialectics," in Slavoj Žižek and John Milbank, *The Monstrosity of Christ: Paradox or Dialectic?* (Cambridge, Mass.: MIT, 2009), see John D. Caputo, Review of *The Monstrosity of Christ: Paradox or Dialectic?* in *Notre Dame Philosophical Reviews* (2009.09.33), available from http://ndpr.nd.edu/review.cfm?id=17605, and Slavoj Žižek, "Dialectical Clarity versus the Misty Conceit of Paradox," in Žižek and Milbank, *The Monstrosity of Christ*, 234–306.

2. See John D. Caputo, "'Bodies without Flesh': The Soft Gnosticism of Incarnational Theology," in *Intensities: Philosophy, Religion and the Affirmation of Life*, ed. Steven Shakespeare and Katharine Sarah Moody (Aldershot: Ashgate, 2012), 79–94; and Caputo, Review of *The Monstrosity of Christ*.

3. Slavoj Žižek, "The Fear of Four Words: A Modest Plea for the Hegelian Reading of Christianity," in Žižek and Milbank, *The Monstrosity of Christ*, 95.
4. Žižek, "Dialectical Clarity," 256.
5. See Jacques Derrida, *Circumfession*, in Geoffrey Bennington and Jacques Derrida, *Jacques Derrida* (Chicago: University of Chicago Press, 1993[1999]), 154–155.
6. See Slavoj Žižek, *The Puppet and the Dwarf: The Perverse Core of Christianity* (Cambridge, Mass.: MIT Press, 2003), 6.
7. In a recent response to Martin Häglund's *Radical Atheism*, Caputo summarizes that Häglund "wants to redescribe deconstruction as a logic of materialism—which I do not simply reject—but at the cost of a certain religion, which I certainly reject"; John D. Caputo, "The Return of Anti-Religion: From Radical Atheism to Radical Theology," *Journal for Cultural and Religious Theory* 11, no.2 (Spring 2011): 49. While welcoming his presentation of deconstruction as a materialism and, in particular, his defense of Derrida against stereotypes that Caputo sees circulating among speculative materialists and realists, Häglund's atheistic deconstruction excludes what Caputo calls Derrida's "religious materialism" (33). I use the phrase "ir/religious materialism" to signal the materialism of a Derridean religion without religion.
8. My own research occupies a position at the intersection of European philosophy, philosophical theologies, and the empirical study of religion. See further, Katharine Sarah Moody, *Radical Theology and Emerging Christianity: Deconstruction, Materialism and Religious Practices* (Aldershot: Ashgate, forthcoming 2014).
9. Gregory Hoskins, "Introduction to the Academic Roundtable," *Expositions* 4, nos.1 & 2 (2010): 87.
10. Jacques Derrida, *Writing and Difference*, trans. Alan Bass (London: Routledge, 1978 [1997]), 292.
11. Gavin Hyman, *The Predicament of Postmodern Theology: Radical Orthodoxy or Nihilist Textualism?* (Louisville, Ky.: Westminster John Knox Press, 2001), 86.
12. John Milbank, *Theology and Social Theory: Beyond Secular Reason* (Oxford: Blackwell, 1990 [2006]), 438 and 434; and John Milbank, "The End of Dialogue," in *Christian Uniqueness Reconsidered: The Myth of a Pluralistic Theology of Religions*, ed. Gavin D'Costa (Maryknoll, N.Y.: Orbis Books, 1990), 189.
13. Hyman, *The Predicament of Postmodern Theology*, 79.
14. Žižek, "The Fear of Four Words," 74 and 60.
15. Slavoj Žižek, *First as Tragedy, Then as Farce* (London: Verso, 2009), 45.
16. Slavoj Žižek, "Class Struggle or Postmodernism?: Yes, Please!" in Judith Butler, Ernesto Laclau, and Slavoj Žižek, *Contingency, Hegemony, Universality: Contemporary Dialogues on the Left* (London: Verso, 2000), 120. See further Adrian Johnston, *Žižek's Ontology: A Transcendental Materialist Theory of Subjectivity* (Evanston, Ill.: Northwestern University Press, 2008).
17. See Alain Badiou, *Saint Paul: The Foundation of Universalism*, trans. Ray Brassier (Stanford, Calif.: Stanford University Press, 2003).
18. Slavoj Žižek, *The Fragile Absolute—or, Why Is the Christian Legacy Worth Fighting For?* (London: Verso, 2000 [2001]), 128; Slavoj Žižek, *The Parallax View* (Cambridge, Mass.: MIT Press, 2006 [2009]), 10 and 35; and Žižek, *The Fragile Absolute*, 128–129.
19. Žižek, *The Fragile Absolute*, 129–130.
20. Žižek, "Dialectical Clarity," 248.
21. Gareth Jones, "Editor's Choice," *Reviews in Religion and Theology* 4, no. 2 (1997): 6, quoting John Milbank, *The Word Made Strange: Theology, Language, Culture* (Oxford: Blackwell, 1997), 1.

22. Slavoj Žižek, *The Metastases of Enjoyment: Six Essays on Woman and Causality* (London: Verso, 1994), 144.
23. Žižek, "Dialectical Clarity," 287.
24. Caputo, Review of *The Monstrosity of Christ*.
25. John D. Caputo, *The Prayers and Tears of Jacques Derrida: Religion without Religion* (Bloomington: Indiana University Press, 1997), 34.
26. Jacques Derrida, *Limited Inc.*, ed. Gerald Graff, trans. Samuel Weber (Evanston, Ill.: Northwestern University Press, 1988), 148.
27. John D. Caputo, "What Do I Love When I Love My God? Deconstruction and Radical Orthodoxy," in *Questioning God*, ed. John D. Caputo, Mark Dooley, and Michael J. Scanlon, (Bloomington: Indiana University Press, 2001), 313.
28. Caputo, "What Do I Love When I Love My God?" 311.
29. For this criticism see, for example, Milbank's forward to James K. A. Smith's *Introducing Radical Orthodoxy: Mapping a Post-Secular Theology* (Grand Rapids, Mich.: Baker Academic, 2004), where he states that "Derrida in truth ultimately denigrates the particular" (18). Also, Kevin Hart highlights what he calls Derrida and Caputo's "religious abstractionism," James K. A. Smith asserts their "allergy to the scandal of particularity," Shane Cudney suggests that they "'formalize' or bracket out religion," Ronald A. Kuipers emphasizes their "ambivalent, if not allergic, relationship with determinate, concrete human communities," and Graham Ward asserts that the resultant religion without religion is "bloodless and incorporeal"; Kevin Hart, "Without," in *Cross and Khôra: Deconstruction and Christianity in the Work of John D. Caputo*, ed. Marko Zlomislić and Neal DeRoo (Eugene, Ore.: Pickwick Publications, 2010), 102; Smith, *Introducing Radical Orthodoxy*, 116; Shane Cudney, "'Religion without Religion': Caputo, Derrida, and the Violence of Particularity," in *Religion with/out Religion: The Prayers and Tears of John D. Caputo*, ed. James H. Olthuis (New York: Routlegde, 2002), 41; Ronald A. Kuipers, "Dangerous Safety, Safe Danger: The Threat of Deconstruction to the Threat of Determinable Faith," in Olthuis, *Religion with/out Religion*, 23; and Graham Ward, Review of John D. Caputo's *The Prayers and Tears of Jacques Derrida*, in *Modern Theology* 15 (1999): 507.
30. On exemplarism, see Jacques Derrida, *On the Name*, ed. Thomas Dutoit, trans. David Wood, John P. Leavey Jr., and Ian McLeod (Stanford, Calif.: Stanford University Press, 1995), 76, and 142–143n14.
31. Caputo, "What Do I Love When I Love My God?" 291; my emphasis.
32. On incarnation, crucifixion, and resurrection, see especially Caputo, "'Bodies without Flesh.'"
33. Caputo, "What Do I Love When I Love My God?" 305.
34. Caputo, "What Do I Love When I Love My God?" 303–304.
35. John D. Caputo, *Demythologizing Heidegger* (Bloomington: Indiana University Press, 1993), 186.
36. John D. Caputo, *The Weakness of God: A Theology of the Event* (Bloomington: Indiana University Press, 2006), 298.
37. Caputo, *The Weakness of God*, 274.
38. John D. Caputo, "Atheism, A/theology, and the Postmodern Condition," in *The Cambridge Companion to Atheism*, ed. Michael Martin (Cambridge: Cambridge University Press, 2007), 279.
39. John D. Caputo, *Radical Hermeneutics: Repetition, Deconstruction and the Hermeneutic Project* (Bloomington: Indiana University Press, 1987), 287–288.
40. Milbank performs a similar overdetermination, but in an "opposite" direction, implying a Christian exclusivism, since *only immersion in the Christian tradition* can form individuals and communities in the ways necessary for correct cultural discernment. Of course,

Žižek couples his atheistic triumphalism with his own form of Christian triumphalism: *only Christianity* is "the religion of a God who dies" and, he says, a Christianity that "draws all the consequences from its basic event" is an *atheism*. Žižek, "Dialectical Clarity," 287; and Slavoj Žižek, *Living in the End Times* (London: Verso, 2010), 401n50.

41. John D. Caputo, "From Radical Hermeneutics to the Weakness of God: John D. Caputo in Dialogue with Mark Dooley," in Zlomislić and DeRoo, *Cross and Khôra*, 335.

42. Caputo, *The Weakness of God*, 67 and 206.

43. Ibid., 65.

44. Johnston, *Žižek's Ontology*, 194.

45. See Catherine Keller, *Face of the Deep: A Theology of Becoming* (London: Routledge, 2003).

46. Caputo, *The Weakness of God*, 74 and 64.

47. For his use of the language of hypothesis, see Caputo, *The Prayers and Tears of Jacques Derrida*, 63 and 339; and Caputo, *The Weakness of God*, 268.

48. Jacques Derrida, "Villanova Roundtable: A Conversation with Jacques Derrida," in John D, Caputo, *Deconstruction in a Nutshell: A Conversation with Jacques Derrida* (New York: Fordham University Press, 1997 [2006]), 14; and John D. Caputo, "On Not Knowing Who We Are: Madness, Hermeneutics, and the Night of Truth in Foucault," in *More Radical Hermeneutics: On Not Knowing Who We Are* (Bloomington: Indiana University Press, 2000), 24.

49. Caputo, *Radical Hermeneutics*, 273.

50. Caputo, "On Not Knowing Who We Are," 30, 36, and 35.

51. Ibid., 36.

52. Žižek, "Class Struggle or Postmodernism?" 119.

53. Ibid., 120.

54. Caputo, *Radical Hermeneutics*, 278–288.

55. Caputo, *The Weakness of God*, 4.

56. Caputo, *Radical Hermeneutics*, 288.

57. Žižek, *The Fragile Absolute*, 78 and 73; and Slavoj Žižek, *The Indivisible Remainder: An Essay on Schelling and Related Matters* (London: Verso, 1996), 95 and 33–34.

58. Slavoj Žižek, "Da Capo Senza Fine" in Butler, Laclau and Žižek, *Contingency, Homogeny, Universality*, 258.

59. Žižek, "The Fear of Four Words," 25.

60. John D. Caputo, "Hoping in Hope, Hoping against Hope," in Olthuis, *Religion with/out Religion*, 123.

61. Caputo, Review of *The Monstrosity of Christ*. See also Caputo, *The Weakness of God*, 43.

62. Jacques Derrida, "'Eating Well,' or the Calculation of the Subject," trans. Peter Connor and Avital Ronell, in Jacques Derrida, *Points . . . : Interviews 1974–1994*, trans. Peggy Kamuf (Stanford, Calif.: Stanford University Press, 1995), 286.

63. Derrida, *On the Name*, 43.

64. Caputo, *The Weakness of God*, 128.

65. Ibid., 97.

66. Slavoj Žižek, "Whither the 'Death of God': A Continuing Currency?" Panel with Thomas Altizer at the American Academy of Religion, Montreal, Quebec (November 8, 2009), http://vimeo.com/12744096. I have capitalized several words where one could imagine Žižek's own capitalizations might occur.

67. Caputo, "From Radical Hermeneutics to the Weakness of God," 335; and Caputo, *The Weakness of God*, 59 and 62.

68. Caputo, *The Weakness of God*, 40. Elsewhere, Caputo states explicitly, "I am not making ontic, ontological, me-ontological or hyper-ontological claims about a hyper-being or hyper-

person called God. (I am running out of ways to explain this.)"; "The Return of Anti-Religion," 43.

69. Caputo, Review of *The Monstrosity of Christ*.

70. Caputo, "The Return of Anti-Religion," 36.

71. John D. Caputo, "The Insistence and Existence of God: A Response to DeRoo," in Zlomslić and DeRoo, *Cross and Khôra*, 322.

72. Žižek, *The Puppet and The Dwarf*, 130; and Žižek, "The Fear of Four Words," 60.

73. See, for example, Žižek, "Dialectical Clarity," 295.

74. Žižek, "The Fear of Four Words," 92.

75. Caputo, Review of *The Monstrosity of Christ*. Elsewhere, Caputo writes, "when Žižek leaves off abusing postmodern theories he often serves up excellent postmodern goods"; John D. Caputo, "Spectral Hermeneutics," in John D. Caputo and Gianni Vattimo, *After the Death of God*, ed. Jeffrey W. Robbins (New York: Columbia University Press, 2007), 48.

76. He writes, "subjects are constituted, galvanized, and radicalized by the event that overtakes them, a point on which Kierkegaard and the New Testament, on the one hand, and Badiou and Žižek, on the other hand, are agreed, the middle term between them being St. Paul," Caputo, *The Weakness of God*, 139.

77. Theodore W. Jennings Jr., *Reading Derrida / Thinking Paul: On Justice* (Stanford, Calif.: Stanford University Press, 2006).

78. Derrida, *On the Name*, 73.

79. Jacques Derrida, *Of Hospitality*, trans. Rachel Bowlby (Stanford, Calif.: Stanford University Press, 2000), 77.

80. Derrida, "'Eating Well,'" 282 and 279.

81. Žižek, *The Fragile Absolute*, 129–130. While it can be argued that Badiou's reading of Paul plays an important role in the development of Žižek's own reading of Christianity and its materialist potential, there remain, of course, important differences between these philosophers. Žižek is critical of Badiou's interpretation of Paul on the Law, as well as of his claim that Lacanian psychoanalysis is not able to furnish "the foundation of a new political practice"; Slavoj Žižek, *The Ticklish Subject: The Absent Centre of Political Ontology* (London: Verso, 1999 [2008]), xxvi. See further, Moody, *Radical Theology and Emerging Christianity*.

82. Žižek, *The Puppet and The Dwarf*, 112–113.

83. Žižek, *The Fragile Absolute*, 121.

84. Žižek, *Living in the End Times*, 401n50.

85. Žižek, *The Fragile Absolute*, 160.

86. For an introduction to emerging Christianity, see my "'I Hate Your Church; What I Want Is My Kingdom': Emerging Spiritualities in the UK Emerging Church Milieu," *Expository Times* 121, no.10 (July 2010): 495–503.

87. Peter Rollins, *The Fidelity of Betrayal: Towards a Church beyond Belief* (Brewster, Mass.: Paraclete Press, 2008), 141.

88. Peter Rollins, "An Economy of Nobodies and Nothings" (February 1, 2010), http://peterrollins.net/blog/?p=889.

89. Peter Rollins, "The Worldly Theology of Emerging Christianity," in *Church in the Present Tense: A Candid Look at What's Emerging*, ed. Kevin Corcoran (Grand Rapids, Mich.: Brazos Press, 2011), 26.

90. Rollins, "The Worldly Theology of Emerging Christianity," 27.

91. Peter Rollins, *How (Not) to Speak of God* (London: SPCK), 73–137.

92. Ikon, "About," http://ikonbelfast.wordpress.com/about/. The term "transformance art" stems from a review of Rollins's work and has been adopted by Rollins, Ikon, and other collectives; Rollins, *The Fidelity of Betrayal*, 195.

93. Žižek, *The Fragile Absolute*, 153 and 157.

94. John Milbank, "Postmodern Critical Augustinianism: A Short Summa in Forty-Two Responses to Unasked Questions," in *The Postmodern God: A Theological Reader*, ed. Graham Ward (Oxford: Blackwell, 1997), 272.

Part II
Liberation

7 The Future of Liberation

Philip Goodchild

A Parable

Finally Socrates drank the hemlock, died, and the movie ended.

"The thing I don't get," said one viewer, "is why he chose to drink the poison."

"I'm not surprised you don't get it," said her companion. "When I get a thing it is usually a pack of popcorn, or a hangover, or a girl. What is this thing you don't get?"

"That's just it. I don't know," she replied.

"Then how do you know you've not got it?" he said. "What's the matter with you?"

So together they continued to stare at the blank screen in the hope that it might show them what was the matter. But neither turned to each other, nor did they make the slightest move to leave and venture out into the sunlight.

A Diagnosis

A case could be made that philosophy is the safeguard of human freedom. For if our environmental, economic, and cultural worlds are determined primarily by *how* we think, and only subsequently by *what* we think, then all power passes through thought, and thinking otherwise is the essence of liberation. Thus liberation would be conceived as liberation from oppression, injustice, ignorance, and illusion. If liberation from *oppression* may be conceived as the freedom to access and employ physical, social, and educational resources required for human flourishing without fear of external appropriation or restriction, then such liberation may be conceived, in turn, as dependent on liberation from *injustice*, as freedom of political representation to ensure that the cries of body and soul are heard and interests are met. Political liberation, in turn, is dependent on liberation from *ignorance and delusion*, so that one speaks, struggles, and acts in one's own interests and against one's own oppression. Liberation from delusion, in turn, requires the liberation of *truth* so that it may germinate and grow in its own proper elements of reason, attention, and insight. So is philosophy to be regarded as the source of liberation?

Three distinctive features of our current era may call the work of liberation by thought into question. First there is the collision between economy and ecology: the immense global transformation of human life and production in the twentieth century, under the guidance of reason, has reached fundamental limits set by ecological, economic, and energy crises that are only just beginning to manifest themselves.[1] Once overall growth is no longer possible, wealth is only to be obtained at the expense of others. The predatory nature of our collective quest for material wealth starts to manifest itself—perhaps present before and throughout modernity, but formerly justified in the name of progress—once economic contraction is met with the transfer of wealth to the elite few alongside expulsion from productive society of the many. Disaster capitalism extends dispossession just as it intensifies the opportunity for neoliberal market reform in the name of recovery.[2] In short, in the surpassing of ecology by economy we see an illusory quest for the infinite; it leaves many outside the social production of value and recognition, those who count for nothing. Since they have nothing to offer, their demands are unreasonable.

A second distinctive feature of our era is the financialization of culture, securitization of debt, and invention and proliferation of trading in derivatives. Those who profit from speculation can make money by shorting the markets just as easily as by investing: there is a disengagement of economic power from the production of wealth. What this amounts to is the "end of politics": political decisions have to serve the interests of financial capital first, rather than the interests of the people, for without financial stability there is no economy for the people.[3] In disaster capitalism, elected governments are blackmailed into transferring wealth from the majority to the wealthy elite simply in order to preserve a temporary stability. Then social control is most effective when it operates through debt—an obligation to the wealthy elite. Indeed, when the wealthy become largely disengaged from dependence on the poor, the poor lose all privileged access to economic power, to political power, and even to truth. One has no experience of the essence of capitalist power if one is excluded from capitalism: one merely observes its masks and tools.

This brings me to a third distinctive feature of our era: an eclipse of truth. This is more than the predominance of the chatter of lies, propaganda, and interested opinion in public discourse. More fundamentally, the management of information has replaced understanding. For understanding concerns intrinsic relations such as limits, conditions, proportions, interdependence, continuity, the interrelation of means and ends, and judgments of significance or decisiveness, whereas in the management of information extrinsic relations govern the exercise of thought. This eclipse of truth involves the end of philosophy once prophesied by Martin Heidegger in the rise of positivist science: once we know the facts of history, culture, and religion, we will possess all requisite knowledge—requisite, that is, for the pursuit of our interests. Once philosophy is reduced to a weapon of reason in the battle of ideas, such battles are mere shadowboxing, for under the rule of the particular, positions are decided by prior commitments and interests. Then if competing interests cannot be negotiated via reason, their relative distribution can be settled more economically. Over a decade ago, therefore, I posed the question of the pricing of thought: of its determination by a symbolic economy of innovation and prestige directly convertible into material wealth.[4] The prophecy of the end of philosophy is fulfilled when reason is situated directly within the marketplace, demanding payment for its services, promising career advantages for those it teaches, while demonstrating with hard evidence the economic or cultural impact of its research: presentation takes over from interior reasoning. The danger, here, is that reason itself becomes unreflective and unthinking, reproducing established habits, presuppositions, concepts, grammatical structures, and evaluations, pausing to reflect on its inner constitution only in order to manage reason more efficiently and profitably—replacing the liberal arts with marketing courses, and philosophy with sophistry. Freedom degenerates into the liberty to assert, exploit, neglect, and destroy.

These three characteristics of our age are each expressed in material, social, and epistemic practices. The end of modernity, in the surpassing of ecological finitude by economic growth, discloses *our illusory quest for the infinite;* the end of politics, in the emergence of a society disciplined by debt, discloses *our illusory quest for disengagement;* the end of philosophy, in the substitution of appearances for intrinsic reasons, discloses *our illusory substitution of the extrinsic for the intrinsic.* These are our three habitual illusions: infinitude, disengagement, substitution.

In the face of such illusions, one might expect a revived philosophy to safeguard human freedom. For if our environmental, economic, and cultural worlds are determined primarily by *how* we think, and only subsequently by *what* we think and do, then all power passes through thought, and thinking otherwise is the essence of liberation. Yet here lies the pivotal dilemma: how might we think otherwise, how might we seek to liberate thought, without engaging in a quest for infinitude, for disengagement, or for substitution?

The foundational myth of philosophical liberation is given in Plato's allegory of the cave: a prisoner, whose vision has been restricted to moving shadows on the wall, escapes his chains, flees the cave, and finally sees objects themselves in direct sunlight. The time has come to consider seriously whether this escape from constraint, detachment from others, and fulfillment in vision does not embody precisely the practices of infinitude, disengagement, and substitution from which we need liberation. For if we seek a truth independent of any thinker or occasion, do we not embark on an infinite quest for that which no actual, living thinking can attain? If we seek a universal form of truth that can concern anyone or anything, do we not seek to think in a way that is disengaged? If we take any particular proposition as embodying a universal truth, do we not substitute an extrinsic statement for an intrinsic character?[5] Are we ourselves enchained by the way in which our attention is fixed to the screen of ideas? Do we need liberation from the quest for liberation in the Western tradition?

In the allegory, the illusion of moving shadows derives from the fact that the prisoners were chained and could not move, and the fire in whose light the shadows are projected is itself concealed behind a wall, leading to a transposition in which the two-dimensional and colorless shadows seem real, while the concealed servants carrying the shapes seem imaginary. Then perhaps the task of liberation is to break the chains of fixed attention, move around the cave and touch its walls, discover the fire as the source of projection, greet the servants and share their labor in bearing shapes. It is by moving the mind, discovering its limits, forming new alliances, and overthrowing illusions and appearances that truth comes to germinate in the soul. Such liberation would compel our attention back to finitude, engagement, and the intrinsic. In doing so, the truth of its transformation is proven by the encounter with a third dimension and with color that is made visible as soon as the mind is able to move. The task of philosophy becomes liberation through moving the mind, using it as an organ of groping experimentation and discovery.

The prisoners in Plato's cave were immobilized such that their sole activity was vision of shadowy images. It is not merely in our mass-media society that we are immobilized by the spectacles presented to us: in a similar vein, the entire history of Western thought has been dominated by a habitual theoretical attitude in which matters are presented as forms, as ideas, or as Heidegger put it, "the outward appearances in which beings as such show themselves."[6] The content of thought has taken precedence over its own activity: "everything is only as it is known."[7] According to Plato's explication of the Socratic principle, "virtue is knowledge," a virtuous life is possible only through knowledge. This is the theoretical attitude that underlies metaphysics, science, propaganda, and common sense alike, and it is precisely the Platonism that Nietzsche sought to reverse with his "revaluation of all values."[8] Now when Kierkegaard posed the Socratic question ethically, "can virtue be learned?"[9] the task was no longer one of theoretical vision but one of inward appropriation. Here we have another reversal of Platonism, even if one that is also an appropriation. Instead of the essence of virtue being conceived in terms of truth, the essence of truth is conceived in terms of virtue. It is the enactment of thinking and how it relates to its content that are set free from the theoretical model.[10]

An Experiment

Let me propose a way of thinking otherwise: to practice philosophy as a spiritual exercise. We may practice thought as an experiment, where the aim is to discern what is possible, not what is the case; we may undertake thought as an ordeal, where the aim is to produce a transformation, not a conclusion; we may exercise thought as a performance, where the aim is to encounter, not expound. This proposal is not a proposition whose truth is to be tested; it is a task to be undertaken, a trial by ordeal, the significance of which may be given by the new thoughts that actually occur.

Immediately, the projection of the content of thought is switched off. There is nothing to see, nothing to think, nothing to hear but the breath or the heart. As in meditation, let us attune an elementary thought to the rhythm of breathing. Thinking becomes a habitual, repetitive activity: it constrains the flow of perceptual stimulation into one thought, and discharges that thought freely. Thinking breathes like a lung: it requires fresh stimulation for new energy, while releasing in a single motion the thought that is spent. Too much spent thought becomes toxic, and a thought that aims to feed on the waste of its imagination will decay, while only an open, attentive mind can grow. The first distinction such a thought makes, then, is between the nutritious and the toxic, and as it turns from the toxic toward the nutritious, it reads the signs, follows the gradients, and discovers a purpose.[11] Yet the irony here is that thought always turns from the known to the unknown: it moves with purpose, yet this purpose is never given.

Such an elementary thought alone can only meet its waste, so let us turn from this initial thought to a multitude of breathing cells of thought.[12] At first, such thinking appears to be a chaotic dissipation of energy, a primal delirium that perpetually turns from any consistent behavior, where each thought turns from itself to another. In biological life, by contrast, matters are different: the product of one organic molecular reaction may catalyze another, just as one thought leads to another; yet, in rare cases, the product of the second may catalyze the first. Where products normally inhibit their own reactions, now they become conditions for amplification. An intuition of Stuart Kauffman is "that life is based on some form of collective autocatalysis, in which molecules in a set catalyze one another's formation."[13] Rare though such catalytic closure might be, its effects are disproportionate: complex life forms can emerge in metastable states far from equilibrium. Could an analogous process operate in thought? Is it perhaps only those groups of thoughts that attain a mutually catalytic closure that impose themselves upon consciousness, with all the force and necessity of reason? Can we regard reason as a local synthetic operation, where each living thought is a habit, a working activity, a bonding of impressions?

If so, then delirium is interrupted by purposeful direction, for no one knows in advance what processes a product of thought may catalyze. Each thought may have a potential role in a future context where it gives rise to others, but no one knows where this might be: the discovery of such a relation is the disclosure of an objective field of possibilities. Once discovered, what counts is not the content of a thought but its capacity to generate others. Then to think is to experiment with new juxtapositions of thoughts; if such thoughts catalyze and bring life to each other, then an objective possibility has been crystallized. Once discovered, such objective possibilities become a memory, a judgment, a habit, and a disposition to be reactivated whenever the context demands. Thinking builds an architecture of such habits and dispositions as a growing set of objective possibilities. Each stimulus to thinking then results in the expression of a complex characteristic response. Yet we should notice that only the enacted process of thinking is energized, actual, and conscious; the objective possibility or disposition remains virtual, while the product of thought, the conclusion, no longer thinks, and may have limited power for stimulating thought. Conclusions can prove toxic, while virtual dispositions can nourish thinking.

All this indicates the need to intensify the conversion of thought: if the products of our thinking may prove toxic, then perhaps we should shift our attention to the process of thought. For in addition to finding thoughts nutritious or toxic, we may also find potential allies. No thinking process is an end in itself; further meanings and significance emerge from reactions, alliances, and syntheses of thought. Each thought may be incorporated into a wider body. Paradoxically, these bonds require a certain freedom of attention. Most processes passing through the brain regulate physiological functions such as breathing, digestion, hormone production, and the immune system, for example, or else the habits of daily life. Such dispositions provide a stable, fixed response to given stimuli: the world is perceived as nutritious or dangerous. There is little scope for such dispositions to experiment directly with new alliances. And yet if there is a small section of the brain given over to experimental delirium, the prefrontal lobes where the attention may wander and thoughts float freely, then this organ may be capable of adapting the entire organism to purposeful activity that it discerns by making and mirroring alliances without. Analogously, the dispositions and habits of thinking of an entire society can remain relatively stable, yet if there are experimenters in thought, then it is possible that they may discover new adaptations that profoundly affect the entire body politic. It is only through indeterminate behavior and the dismantling of habits that attention discovers what is significant; it is only through lack of purpose that purposes are formed. Yet what is most significant here is the capacity of thought to pay attention, to seek its heart's desire beyond itself. To be reasonable, in this sense, is not to assert a view but to be attentive.

Each complex thought, while primarily responding to signs of nutrients or toxins, has a limited objective indeterminacy through which it may shift attention to divine objective possibilities. Instead of attending to the product of another thought, it is possible to attend to the process: one thought mirrors another, shares in its work, resonates with its rhythm, and undergoes its ordeal. We are no longer in the realm of the nutritious or toxic, good or bad, but in the realm of compatibility or incompatibility, pertinence or irrelevance. Emergent relations may begin with mutual attention, a dyadic process, like the meeting of the gaze between infant and parent. Yet this attunement may then form the basis for a common mind: the same external focus can be selected for joint attention, so that a common experience is undergone, where one is aware of the other's awareness of the focus, and of sharing awareness.[14] Yet such joint attention is far less significant and profound than a resonance, a common thinking, occurring in the construction of shared dispositions. Not merely to see the same world as another, but to see it through similar eyes as another—this is the task of reason. It is a question of mutual adaptation and attunement, using mirror neurons to reproduce the experience of others.[15] As described by Maurice Merleau-Ponty, "It is as if the other person's intentions inhabited my body and mine his."[16] It requires the emission of signs, flexibility, trust, and openness—the attentive listener builds a disposition in their own thought that corresponds to another's through intuition. Yet once the focus of such dispositions becomes the other's awareness of an object, and each responds primarily to each other's awareness, then a fresh class of dispositions emerge based on trust or suspicion.

A Task of Thinking

What seems to emerge from this experiment is a different conception of reason, one founded less on common notions and more on common motions and emotions. The only common experience of the prisoners in the cave was what appeared on the screen of rational thought. Yet as soon as these thought-prisoners are permitted to speak with each other, to laugh, tease, make love, or fall out with each other, then common experience becomes much richer as an effect of mutual attention. To feel the force of your thinking it is not sufficient for me to propose which abstract reasons have nourished it. Instead, it is necessary for me to share the work of your thinking, including its habits, its fears, and its delights. I even have to intuit objective possibilities, further alliances and applications. Reason itself becomes an ethos, a disposition, or habit.

What liberation does such an experimental thought discover? A first ethical response is simply attending to the nutritious and avoiding the toxic. Such a gradient provides the stimulus and environment in which all further ethical levels may emerge. Another level of ethical behavior involves adaptation to one's place and role in a wider system of collaboration. In a well-functioning society, the dispositions that enhance the stability of society include such cardinal virtues as courage, justice, temperance, and prudence, while the institutions of a stable society are such as to evoke these virtues. A moderate dose of nutrients and a moderate dose of poisons facilitate the greater nourishment of the common good. Yet a further level of ethical engagement is introduced beyond the desire for the individual good or for the common good, when sympathy itself becomes an explicit aim: the soul enriches itself and others by learning and sharing its dispositions and objective possibilities. Such enrichment can come only through attention to the processes and dispositions of others, via virtues formerly called "theological": faith, hope, and love.[17] Human wealth is no longer simply a matter of having individual goods, nor a matter of dwelling in a good society. It becomes a matter of possessing a wealthy soul alongside rich relationships.[18] A soul may be wealthy in depth in its capacity to form rich relationships with similar souls; it may also be wealthy in breadth in adapting to diverse relations and circumstances. In either case, only through our dispositions and habits are we most closely united. Such union is undergoing for a duration another's experience, sharing in joint attention the joys and sorrows of nutrients and toxins.

Already we see potential conflicts between levels of ethics: sympathy may conflict with prudence, while both sympathy and courage may expose the mind to danger or poison. Such ethical conflict raises the possibility of internal self-division, which, in turn, may limit closeness to others: if proximity is established through agreement, internal conflict must eventually manifest in external conflict.[19] The path of liberation does not run straight. Could it not be the case that the habits of reason celebrated in society involve a fragmented attention? Do all our writings and conference papers speak past each other? For every time we seek the unlimited we switch off our attention to let our own thoughts run; every time we disengage from a concrete situation in the name of reason we become deaf to concrete claims and demands; every time we find an agreement or enter a contract we substitute an extrinsic relation for the intrinsic mutual catalysis of thought.[20]

The need for a philosophical liberation of thought remains acute. Yet any such liberation can be undertaken only as an ordeal. For in disengaging from pathological habits of thinking, one loses attunement to a wider social whole and its nutrition; in thinking otherwise, one becomes invisible, incomprehensible, and impoverished. To practice philosophy is to drink poison. Philosophy itself, then, is a further ethical response in conflict with all the preceding: the philosopher is a traitor who breaks the chains of the cave, deliberately choosing isolation, guilt, shame, and occasionally persecution. We are no longer in the ethical realm of the nutritious or toxic, nor in the ethical realm of compatibility or incompatibility, but in one of fight or flight. Nevertheless, how else are we to remove those toxic external conditions? For all the dispositions and institutions through which we are united may be deeply ambivalent, nutritious in some respects and toxic in others. Each thought has its domain of pertinence beyond which it becomes dangerous and false. For what we see is determined by how we direct attention, and the direction of attention is shaped by habits, dispositions, institutions, and beliefs. Once dispositions extend beyond their domain of pertinence, imagination suffocates attention, and illusions are projected into the void. Of course, it is in the nature of a thought to express itself, to proclaim its force, and to extend itself through imagination out over the void. Each thought is used to exert force: each opinion and intention seeks its "place in the sun";[21] it seeks to assert its right, in a tone of contention; its judgments are also condemnations of other possible thoughts. While there may be a time for thought to exert force, make judgments, and condemn evils, this is not the activity by which thought will be emancipated from its own chains. When judgments condemn possible thoughts, they condemn the shadow of thinking and not the substance: the characteristic of force is that it turns anyone who is subjected to it into a thing—it kills, it removes the life.[22] Even when it is simply a matter of the encounter between one thought and another, force is pitiless to its victim while intoxicating for those who benefit from its power.[23] Then philosophy has to break all alliances with common sense. As Simone Weil once wrote: "Truth—Among men (except in the supreme forms of saintliness and of genius?) that which gives the impression of being true is almost necessarily false, and that which is true almost necessarily gives the impression of being false."[24]

An ethical philosophy must pursue its vocation in secret. The unity it seeks is no longer that of agreement, but that of the pertinence of a process of thinking to its external conditions. Its liberative potential, by contrast, lies in the objective possibilities it discerns: an ethical philosophy is completed by a philosophy of religion understood as awakening intuition and insight. To liberate truth we need germs or prophecies that act on the soul. Let me illustrate these proposals with some apocalyptic remarks of relevance to a politics of thought. In place of syllogisms and syntheses, such a philosophy has three fundamental habits of thinking by which it enacts its process and releases its power.

First, there is the transposition of extrinsic and intrinsic, the chiasmic inversion, whereby a habitual movement of thought is halted and a new one is awaited. Philosophy begins with critique. Such a transposition of thought is a sharp intake of breath, an increase in intensity, a moment of apocalyptic expectancy. Let me offer one imprudent example, taken from Nietzsche's *Ecce Homo*, "Why I am a Destiny":

> I was the first to *discover* the truth, in that I was the first to sense—*smell*—the lie as lie. . . . With all that I am necessarily a man of fatality. For when truth steps into battle with the lie of millennia we shall have convulsions, an earthquake spasm, a transposition of valley and mountain such as has never been dreamed of. The concept politics has become completely absorbed into a war of spirits, all the power-structures of the old society have been blown into the air—they one and all reposed on the lie: there will be wars such as there have never been on earth. Only after me will there be *grand politics* on earth.[25]

Grand politics is conceived here as a war of spirits: one of the stranger transpositions of valley and mountain enacted here is to wrest politics from its foundations in material interests so as to suspend it from the sky of a cosmic battle of spirits, of perspectives of evaluation; the intrinsic replaces the extrinsic. Materialism and idealism alike are inverted: instead of seeing things in terms of their participation in reality or the good, one sees things in terms of their evaluations of what is real or good. Such an apocalyptic statement appeals to no ground or evidence: one cannot really ask whether it is true or relevant, for it claims that all previous foundations were lies. It is only meaningful if it discloses something—a spirit, a way of seeing, a perspective of evaluation.

Second, there is a profound engagement, the mutual catalysis of differing dispositions. Perceiving one thought in light of another, while the second in turn sheds light on the first, crystallizes an insight. Philosophy proceeds by creation. Such a crystallization is an explosive outbreath, a release of potential, a moment of apocalyptic revelation. Let me offer another imprudent example, taken from a fragment penned by Søren Kierkegaard, in response to the revolutionary events of 1848, in which he interprets the collapse of political authority in terms of the Christian doctrine of atonement, in turn implying a reinterpretation of atonement as the work of political martyrs:[26]

> Until now, tyrants (in the form of emperors, kings, popes, Jesuits, generals, diplomats) have been able to rule and govern the world at a crucial moment, but from the time the fourth estate[27] is established—when it has had time to establish itself in such a way that it is properly understood—it will become manifest that only martyrs are able to rule the world at a crucial moment. That is, no human being will any longer be able to rule the generation at such a moment; only the divine can do it, assisted by those unconditionally obedient to him, those who are also willing to suffer, but they are indeed the martyrs. In an older order, when the crucial moment was past, an orderly secular government took over, but from the moment the fourth estate is established, it will be seen that even when the crisis is over, the governing cannot be done *secularly*.[28]

Here is a strange and unrealistic prophecy of the overcoming of force, not by reason or by consensus, but by sacrifice; politics becomes theological, based on respect for martyrs, while piety becomes political, a means of ruling the attention of the masses.

Third, there is a moment of trembling where we rediscover our finitude and limitations. When it is noticed that an insight has a bearing on one's heart and life, then a catastrophic shock is released that resonates throughout attentive thinking. After such quakes, the chains are momentarily broken: habitual dispositions may never be the same again. Of course, the same chains are likely to be rebuilt unless one entrusts oneself to the oncoming wave. So philosophy awakens on credit. Such quaking is an apocalyptic transformation of thinking, fracturing existing paths of thought and throwing up fresh juxtapositions and possibilities. Let me offer one example of an insight that might occasionally make one tremble, taken from Weil, who in her imprudent project of "decreation of the self" sought to dismantle the architecture of habits and dispositions of thinking: "To love truth signifies to endure the void and consequently, to accept death. Truth is on the side of death. To love truth with all one's soul is something which cannot be done without a wrenching."[29]

I do not wish to suggest that any of these three apocalyptic statements should be regarded as true. On the contrary, they are manifestly false in nearly all circumstances. As Weil once remarked about Christian doctrine, the nature of such spiritual truths is that by affirming them one destroys them, because they are not true on the level on which they are affirmed.[30] They have to be enacted according to their nature and level, not affirmed or represented.[31] How, then, are we to fulfill the ethical task of philosophy, and raise thought to its appropriate level? How are we to think according to that which matters, which has most significance, which is decisive? Chiasm, crystal, and quake: these are the three syllogisms of an apocalyptic logic. The clue is to be found in contradiction or apparent falsehood: strangely, only contradiction is the criterion of reality, for there is no contradiction in what is imaginary.[32] We live inside products of the imagination, whether individually or collectively, until we run up against resistance from reality itself. We are trapped in a cave of illusion until we feel ourselves up against some solid resistance in the dark. Only the body in its resistance to our desire and imagination grounds us in reality. Such resistance, whether in affliction or in the failure of desire, presents the opportunity to wait and look up. As Weil puts it, "Evil is the shadow of good. All real good, possessing solidity and thickness, projects evil. Only imaginary good does not project it."[33]

The problem in reading such apocalyptic statements lies in hearing their prophetic character. They remain fragments, riddles, or dreadful chances until they are composed into a fresh context where their sense becomes pertinent. For this, philosophy has to move beyond experiment, beyond ordeal, to become performance. And today, in your own reading, perhaps these prophecies have become true.

Notes

1. New Economics Foundation, *Growth Isn't Possible* (London: New Economics Foundation, 2010).
2. Naomi Klein, *The Shock Doctrine* (London: Penguin, 2008).
3. David Rothkopf, *Superclass: How the Rich Ruined our World* (London: Abacus, 2009).
4. Philip Goodchild, "Money, Gift and Sacrifice: 13 Brief Episodes in the Pricing of Thought," *Angelaki* 4, no. 3 (1999): 25–39; also Goodchild, *Capitalism and Religion: The Price of Piety* (London: Routledge, 2002).
5. For a development of these points, see Philip Goodchild, "Truth and Utopia," *Telos* 134 (Spring 2006): 64–82.

6. Heidegger, "The End of Philosophy and the Task of Thinking," in *Basic Writings*, rev. and expanded ed., ed. David Farrell Krell (London: Routledge, 1993), 444.

7. Heidegger, *The Phenomenology of Religious Life*, trans. Matthias Fritsch and Jennifer Anna Gosetti-Ferencei (Bloomington: Indiana University Press, 2004), 27.

8. Thomas H. Brobjer, "Critical Aspects of Nietzsche's Relation to Politics and Democracy," in *Nietzsche, Power and Politics*, ed. Hermann W. Siemens and Vasti Roodt (Berlin: De Gruyter, 2008), 205–230.

9. Søren Kierkegaard, *Philosophical Fragments*, trans. Howard V. Hong and Edna H. Hong (Princeton, N.J.: Princeton University Press, 1985), 9.

10. Søren Kierkegaard, *Concluding Unscientific Fragments*, trans. David F. Swenson and Walter Lowrie (Princeton, NJ: Princeton, 1968), 181; see also Heidegger, *The Phenomenology of Religious Life*, 43.

11. Stuart Kauffmann points out that when a single-celled organism follows a sign such as a glucose gradient, its activity is now invested with meaning and purpose, and an "ought" emerges from an "is." Kauffmann, *Reinventing the Sacred* (New York: Basic Book, 2010), 87.

12. "The desert hour when the dromedary becomes a thousand dromedaries snickering in the sky." Gilles Deleuze and Félix Guattari, *A Thousand Plateaus* (London: Athlone Press, 1988), 38.

13. Kauffmann, *Reinventing the Sacred*, 55.

14. Eleonore Stump emphasizes how recent psychological studies may show that triadic attention to a common object may emerge from dyadic attention. See Stump, *Wandering in Darkness* (Oxford: Oxford University Press, 2010), 114–115.

15. For the role of mirror neurons, see Giacomo Rizzolatti and Corrado Sinigaglia, *Mirrors in the Brain—How Our Minds Share Actions and Emotions*, trans. Frances Anderson (Oxford: Oxford University Press, 2008).

16. Maurice Merleau-Ponty, *Phenomenology of Perception*, trans. Colin Smith (London: Routledge, 2002), 215.

17. For an account of the Thomist theological virtues interpreted in terms of joint attention, see Andrew Pinsent, "The Gifts and Fruits of the Holy Spirit," in *The Oxford Handbook to Thomas Aquinas*, ed. Brian Davies and Eleonore Stump (Oxford: Oxford University Press, forthcoming).

18. In this respect, a wealthy society is rich in institutions that lend stability and resilience to relationships, in turn enabling trust, openness, and attentiveness, and so facilitating rich relationships.

19. Stump points out that internal integration is necessary for closeness, and that while desires for lesser goods may divide, desires for spiritual goods bring integration since spiritual goods can be shared. Yet, contrary to her Thomist emphasis on unity, the conflicts of the ethical life suggest that the most integrated soul may also be the most isolated. See especially Stump, *Wandering in Darkness*, 125–127.

20. As Martin Buber put it, "But there seems to cling to *thought* something of the life of monologue to which communication takes a second, secondary place. Thought seems to arise in monologue." Buber, *Between Man and Man*, trans. Ronald Gregor-Smith (London: Routledge, 2002), 30.

21. Levinas draws on Pascal's expression: "Ethics as First Philosophy," in *The Levinas Reader*, ed. Seán Hand (Oxford: Blackwell, 1989), 82.

22. See Simone Weil, *The Notebooks of Simone Weil*, trans. Arthur Wills (London: Routledge & Kegan Paul, 1956), 183.

23. Ibid., 191.

24. Ibid., 121.

25. Friedrich Nietzsche, *Ecce Homo*, trans. R. J. Hollingdale (Harmondsworth, England: Penguin, 1979), 126–127.

26. The apocalyptic structure of Kierkegaard's thinking has been elucidated, in parallel to that of Karl Marx, by Jacob Taubes in *Occidental Eschatology*, trans. David Ratmoko (Stanford, Calif.: Stanford University Press, 2009).

27. Here meaning the masses, not Burke's notion of the press.

28. Søren Kierkegaard, Supplement to "Two Ethical-Religious Essays," in *Without Authority*, ed, Howard V. Hong and Edna H. Hong (Princeton, N.J.: Princeton University Press, 1997), 214.

29. Weil, *Notebooks*, 160–161.

30. Ibid., 63.

31. As Weil says, one experiences evil by refusing to accomplish it, but one experiences good only by accomplishing it: error is to be represented but not enacted, while truth is to be enacted but not represented. Weil, *Notebooks*, 269.

32. Simone Weil, *Gravity and Grace*, trans. Emma Crauford and Mario von der Ruhr (Abingdon, UK: Routledge Classics, 2002), 98.

33. Weil, *Gravity and Grace*, 102.

8 Monetized Philosophy and Theological Money

Uneasy Linkages and the Future of a Discourse

Devin Singh

Claims about the future involve perceptions of the present and discourses about the past. This is especially so in the case of money. As a peculiar social technology that indexes value and regulates relations of credit and debt, it reflects and shapes expectations and, hence, projects a future. In consideration of the course this monetary future might take in the West, theology and the philosophy of religion are necessary resources with which to engage. As genealogies of modernity and capitalism have laid bare, theological and religiously inflected philosophical discourses have been determinative for the Western sociopolitical imaginary.[1] Money has likewise been determinative. It follows that the relationship of these codeterminants of modernity must be elaborated, that this past be unearthed. As we will see, the relevance of theology/philosophy stems not (or not only) from the need to render ethical judgments about the nature and consequences of monetary economy. The necessity emerges from a co-implication of money with these discourses, such that their pasts, presents, and futures are intimately connected.

Reflecting on the long-standing interaction between philosophy and money, I argue that core aspects of Christian theological doctrine are influenced by monetary economy, and that emerging Christian theopolitical vision shapes how money is conceived and deployed. The legacy bequeathed to modernity is one of an uneasy conceptual proximity between Jesus and money, and the secular permutations of this relationship have enduring implications for political and economic spheres. On one hand, early ideas of the Son of God as lord over an economy of redemption and as a form of payment bear marks of a monetized imaginary. On the other, subsequent shifts from Christian imperial and pastoral power to modern techniques of governmentality retain the traces of this fundamental linkage between Christology and money. The future of money and the future of theology and the philosophy of religion are intimately connected, therefore, and analysis must proceed from the acknowledgement of this history of mutual conditioning.

This chapter begins with exploration of the peculiar nexus of money, philosophy, and political modes of sovereignty. Early Greek reflection on money betrays anxieties about money's apparent ties to philosophy, as well as the ways money facilitates hierarchical modes of authority and bureaucratic complexity. Such assumptions, I suggest, shape emerging Christological doctrine, influencing the conceptualization both of the Son as lord and of the manner in which redemption is effected. This complex of theological and political ideas, this theo-political imaginary, in turn inflects monetary economy and its administration with a theological valence. Theological and philosophical attempts to grapple with money's present dominance must also reckon with a historical legacy of mutual implication of the practice of monetary economy and central Christian ideas. I conclude by situating Philip Goodchild's work within this exploration, suggesting further avenues of research.

Money, Philosophy, and Sovereignty

The advent of money was significant for the Greek philosophical imaginary. The possibility of this link was broached years ago by Marc Shell in a groundbreaking study, and has been further elaborated more recently by scholars such as Richard Seaford and Leslie Kurke.[2] Not only does money appear to correlate with new abstract concepts and forms of transcendental thought, but philosophical discourse evinces an anxiety about its own proximity to money. For instance, Shell analyzes an early fragment from Heraclitus, which exhibits both a horror and a fascination with money as a material artifact that engenders universal exchangeability: "All things are an equal exchange for fire and fire for all things, as goods are for gold and gold for goods."[3] Shell claims that "the fragment defines a kind of exchange (or metaphor) that did not exist in the world much before the time of Heraclitus."[4] Heraclitus wrote at a time of much upheaval and transition in Greek society, not the least of which included wider circulation of a new social technology: coinage. In Shell's estimation, the fragment hints at transformations in the ways thought could be expressed that correlate to the new relationships between and among people and objects facilitated by money.

Shell devotes careful analysis to the interplay of several sets of metaphors in the fragment and examines how they are set off from one another, claiming that the type of conceptual exchange Heraclitus sets up reflects not barter but money. Heraclitus splits the transaction into two distinct moments of exchange, implying the need for a mediating third category. Some unspoken object or principle grounds the relation between the two apparently disparate strophes. Furthermore, that gold is juxtaposed to goods indicates that it is not functioning as merely another commodity, but stands for something that is universally exchangeable. Goods are not simply being swapped, as in barter, but commodities are being converted first into gold, the medium of exchange, and then gold changed into commodities.

Heraclitus's monetized exchange of gold and goods is linked via simile to fire's relation to "all things." The image invokes the elemental notion of a fundamental essence of cosmic reality. Fire can be set into relation with all aspects of reality since it is a component of their existence. Previous interpreters have been stumped by apparent lack of parallel here, for fire, as a core constituent of reality in this ancient worldview, must also belong to the category of "all things." It simultaneously stands in exchange relation to the group and can be counted as part of it. Yet gold, as we have seen, is juxtaposed with goods and at first blush does not partake of this category. Shell solves the dilemma by recalling the slippage between commodity and token inherent in money. Money, at least in many of its manifestations in history, is both a material object and potential commodity, on one hand, and a sign or token of value aiding in commodity exchange, on the other. Gold is both a commodity, or good, and the means of exchange, just as fire is both an element of reality and the transfer point or nexus for the coming into being of all things. "Gold is thus both a good and a nongood, as fire is both a thing and an exchange for all things."[5]

Furthermore, in my view, the collocation of gold and fire evinces anxiety and ironic protest on the part of Heraclitus concerning money. Writing approximately a century after the advent of coinage and its gradual permeation of Greek exchange relations, Heraclitus offers commentary on the impact felt throughout the world as he knew it. Fire is a core constituent of all things, and is also their unmaking, as a corrosive, consumptive force. It spreads and destroys, putting itself in the place of, exchanging itself with, the things with which it comes into contact. Gold, or money, was coming to infiltrate various aspects of economic and broader civic life. Richard Seaford claims that the emergence at this time of Greek tragedy as a dramatic form was linked in part to the effects of money seen in political arrangements, most notably tyranny, a connection to be shortly discussed.[6] It may be that here Heraclitus's metaphorization, a novel structure upon which, claims Shell, money's influence is felt, expresses its own dismay at money's spread, like fire, consuming other notions of value and good.[7]

Heraclitus, and the type of thinking his metaphorization represents, that of flux and continual (ex)change, is one of Plato's targets. Shell claims that, in response,

Plato makes *ousia* into a substantive concept that, he hopes, will lift the philosopher out of the mire of economic exchange. What Plato dislikes in Heraclitus's philosophy is a lack of a concept of metaphysical stillness and of a concept of justice above the supposedly escapable movements of commodities. . . . Although he was as much the enemy of money and the monied classes as was Plato, Heraclitus internalized the money form into his thought differently, focusing on metaphorization and symbolization themselves. If Plato studies the metaphor of still Being, Heraclitus studies the activity of metaphorization itself.[8]

To Shell, philosophy's opposition to money serves as a crucial architectonic structuring principle for the *Republic*. Plato's persistent concern is to set true philosophy apart from thinking influenced by the love of money: hence his critique of sophistry. Yet, as Shell points out, aside from the bankrupt theorizing of the sophists, even Socratic notions of hypothecation—to wager and draw interest on an initial (truth) claim—bear monetary marks, as Plato was well aware. Turning from visible things to the realm of the Idea reflected Plato's attempt to rise above the play of material referents and immanent notions of value seen in monetary economy. Arguably, however, even the realm of fixed transcendence retains traces of the capacity seen in money for universal exchangeability, a ground of stable value to moderate divergent local manifestations. Shell thus suggests that, from their inception, Western philosophy and money apparently occupy positions of mimetic rivalry and mutual influence. While it is impossible to resolve the question of origins—whether money made possible new philosophical capacities or if advances in thinking facilitated the development of this revolutionary economic instrument—evidence of co-emergence and mutual conditioning exists.[9] The possibility follows that Christian theology, so indebted to Greek philosophy, inherits this anxiety about some originary proximity to and homology with money.

Such concerns persist in philosophy, as seen, for instance, in the more recent charge by Simon Critchley and Tom McCarthy that Derrida's deconstruction serves as a "cipher for capital."[10] Their critique emerges as something of an aside within an analysis of Joyce's *Finnegans Wake*, in which they review the play of monetary metaphor in the text. Examining and arguably succumbing to what they see as Joyce's monetary-literary jouissance, they remark that money functions as a transcendental excess that both grounds and disrupts economy. As such it exhibits a structure similar to grammatology, which seeks to map and undo the possibilities for semiotic meaning in the text: "Money is a kind of deconstruction, opening the totality of the proper's economy, but is not the reverse of this proposition also plausible, namely that deconstruction is a kind of money?"[11]

Space precludes a full consideration of their position, and indeed as a passing remark their claim is so truncated that it resists analysis. I will simply in turn make two passing observations. The first is that the same type of anxiety glimpsed at the advent of Western philosophy creeps up here, manifested in the need to distance "true" philosophy from monetary economy. The implication is that associating an interlocutor's views with money serves as a self-explanatory critique. The second is that, ironically, their hasty rhetorical reversal evinces its own monetized logic, for the exchange between "money is deconstruction" and "deconstruction is money" appears to "turn on a dime," so to speak. The transaction is neither justified nor qualified, but takes place on its own accord as if a universal equivalent governs the encounter. Heraclitian metaphorical structure appears at work, and monetary force, like fire, elides and consumes difference in their text, as money cascades into deconstruction, deconstruction into money, and money, much too swiftly, into capital.

Early Greek philosophy's diatribe against money not only deals with its conceptual closeness, but also addresses money's role in problematic political arrangements. As Shell observes, Plato's condemnation of sophistry parallels his critique of the tyrant, for whom "wage-earning is . . . [the] substitute for philosophy," and his preference for the philosopher-king.[12] The tyrant's connection to money is epitomized in the myth of Gyges, as told by both Plato and Herodotus. Gyges is a usurper turned tyrant whose ring of power enables him invisibly to spy on his subjects. His kingdom lives in terror of the panopticon that simply is his presence. According to Herodotus, coinage was first invented in Lydia, and Gyges is associated with this region. His ring, a *symbolon,* shares lexical associations with coins, and the first coins were possibly, like rings, tokens given in pledge of some bond related to debt. The ring evokes resonances with treasure, wealth, and monetary power. There is something about Gyges's possession of wealth that enables him to exert control at a distance, from the shadows as it were, and to ensure that the tendrils of his power extend everywhere.

The foil to Gyges, claims Shell, is Deioces the Mede, who in Herodotus is the purported founder of imperial bureaucracy. Deioces as king remains invisible in the metaphorical sense of being hidden within the mazes and concentric rings of his castle. Of him and his walled city Herodotus writes: "And when all was built, it was Deioces first who established the rule that no one should come into the presence of the king, but all should be dealt with by the means of messengers; that the king should be seen by no man."[13] Both Gyges and Deioces are depicted as tyrants, and their tyranny is facilitated by their inapproachability. The king exists as sovereign, as figurehead, as seat and symbol of authority, but the management, administration, and day-to-day dirty work of running the kingdom is actually taken on by others. Yet such bureaucratic mechanisms are extensions of sovereign power. A central anxiety then, expressed figuratively as invisibility in Gyges and literalized in Deioces, is the inaccessibility of the sovereign. Money and wealth are recognized as integral to this dynamic, as they facilitate the construction and proliferation of bureaucracy.[14] Money aids the ability to exert influence at a distance while remaining hidden, as exchanges no longer require face-to-face transactions or idiosyncratic determinations of value as in barter haggling. Such tyranny is also facilitated by money through disrupting traditional links of communal reciprocity, enabling emerging leaders to command submission outside the ritualized bonds of mutual obligation.

Such monetized political arrangements had their theological analogues. Richard Seaford observes the changes that occurred in Greek religious thought during the period of increased monetization. Just as tyrants could rule from the shadows and direct outcomes at a distance through money, and just as they disrupted communal patterns of reciprocity, gods could be construed likewise. This is glimpsed in Xenophanes's new form of monotheism and critique of Greek pluralism and its anthropomorphic deities:

> Xenophanes lived during the high tide of tyranny, and I would suggest that his concept of deity is influenced by the experience of tyranny. The tyrant, in contrast to the Homeric leader, is to some extent freed from the principle of reciprocity by his control of money. The invisible but ubiquitous power of money was in the sixth century a strange and radical novelty, which is reflected, I suggest, in numerous aspects of sixth-century philosophy, including Xenophanes' strange and radically new notion of a single nonanthropomorphic deity staying in the same place while nevertheless agitating all things by the thought of his mind and (probably) needing nothing.[15]

The ongoing interplay between historical modes of political rule and theological models is nothing new. What is noteworthy here is the interaction of money with Greek political and philosophical (and, by extension, theological) thought. Philosophical discourse displays marked animosity toward the money form, and Greek tragedians lament its corrosive effect on political life. Furthermore, and somewhat counterintuitively, money may indirectly facilitate new models of power and efficacy—such as monarchy or imperial centralization—that later come to be valorized in political practice and its supporting ideologies (and theologies). Xenophanes was hailed by the Christian fathers as an early example of monotheistic faithfulness. If indeed his thought exhibits the impact of monetization on forms of rule and if monotheism itself might be correlated to political monarchy and the money form, another source of Christianity's vexed relations to monetary economy might here be glimpsed.

In contemporary economic analysis, so-called heterodox monetary theory, drawing on historical and sociological studies of money's nature, function, and deployment, confirms many of these early Greek concerns.[16] As sociologist Geoffrey Ingham argues, transhistorical studies reveal money to be a tool of sovereignty, used in conjunction with other means of regulation and control of space.[17] The precise historical origins of money are obscure, but what appears as a consistent historical theme is money's employment by territorial power. Money is minted and set into circulation by such power and is efficacious only because of its creation and guarantee by state authority structures. Such tokens are mobilized and valorized by the declaration that such are the primary media through which subjects can render tribute or taxes to the power.[18] Failure to pay taxes, or attempts to render false tribute through counterfeiting, lead the state structure to manifest its "legitimate" violence. The state thus polices the circuits of this central sign, regulating its use and deployment.

Therefore money, like law, is tied to conquest and struggle, and serves to reinforce particular power arrangements.[19] Just as law, as Foucault notes, manifests the political extension of war, money, deployed as the privileged signifier for economic activity, codifies hegemonic relationships.[20] A principal means by which the victor declares reign over a conquered territory is through the enforcement of new monetary signs, ones bearing the mark of the new power.[21] Numismatic historians note that the monetization of ancient Greece and the Roman Empire took place primarily through militarization.[22] State powers send out money tokens into new lands via military presence, reclaiming such tokens through enforced taxation. Money is not a neutral medium of exchange but a loaded symbol, charged with power and implicated in authority structures that render it effective through modes of violence and discipline. Money is therefore implicated in a constellation of power arrangements that presuppose sovereign rule and bureaucratic management of a space. Money contributes to and disperses a particular political vision of sovereignty, as a tool that is legitimated by its issuing authority and that in turn legitimates such authority as the one facilitating economic exchange.

Christology and the Greco-Roman Imaginary

It was Rome that came to instantiate many of these Greek anxieties, establishing a stable, territorially unified currency and a centralized empire, managed with unprecedented bureaucracy.[23] Hellenistic monarchies served as an important transition to this comparatively monolithic monetary economy. The Roman Empire, beginning with Augustus, realized (ideologically, if not in practice) the inaccessible ruler, masked in bureaucracy and military might. The Roman economy dramatically increased the monetization of the region, disseminating monetary habits. The imperial image was circulated on coinage, further shoring up the ideological matrix of sovereign reign and governance.[24] Sovereign representation, monetization, bureaucratic management—these are key elements of the Greco-Roman context in which Christian theology developed.

Therefore Giorgio Agamben's recent archaeology of the patristic notion of *oikonomia* is at once dazzling, necessary, and yet insufficient.[25] It is important for it maps the ways in which formative ideas of God correlate to the Greco-Roman political context. Examining the tension between ideas of political sovereignty and reign, on one hand, and engaged governance, on the other, Agamben explores the manner in which emerging Christian ideas of the godhead appear to relate. In short, the Father designates the site of sovereign authority while the Son indicates the place of bureaucratic administration. What Agamben neglects is the critical role that monetization and economy proper play in conceptions of sovereignty and administration. Drawing this out would provide a linkage to the monetary language used to describe the identity and work of the incarnate Son.

As Agamben explains, *oikonomia* becomes crucial in patristic texts as a method of reconciling the Father's relationship to the Son, making sense of the possibility of this duality (to which, of course, later is added the Spirit), of how God could be transcendent, reigning in heaven, as well as immanent, and embodied on earth. *Oikonomia* comes to denote this very relationship between Father and Son, as well as the process of incarnation and redemption. God is not simply sovereign king, transcendent and impassible. God is, in the Son, immanent and directly overseeing the redemption of creation. God manages such redemption, and this management reflects something about the inner nature of God as well.

What is significant about this development in patristic thought, says Agamben, is the reconciliation of two previously disparate strands of theopolitical thought. In Gnostic perspective, for instance, God, the One, is utterly transcendent and uninvolved with creation. Interaction with creation falls to the demiurge, since the originary ground and source of Being would not be sullied through interaction with the base materiality of the world. This parallels aspects of Greco-Roman political thought, in which the sovereign reigns as figurehead, as seat and center of power, while governance of a territory falls to bureaucratic administration. As Agamben notes, the old adage "the king reigns but does not govern" relates to this traditional separation between the sovereign and his bureaucracy. The novel Christian development seeks to unite these two distinct elements in one center, in the singular being of God, managed through the *oikonomia* of Trinitarian differentiation. Now God is posited as both sovereign lord *and* manager or overseer of his kingdom and its subjects. Two branches of authority combine in one being. The Father marks out the seat of sovereign reign and power, while to the Son falls the designation of manager and overseer of redeeming creation.

The Son, therefore, legitimates by association the structures of bureaucratic administration. As Tertullian argues, just as it is acceptable for monarchs to have attendants who execute their judgments, it should be acceptable for God the Father, who has angelic emissaries, also to have a Son whose existence does not threaten divine monarchy.[26] Bureaucratic management presupposes a money system, and the Son as lord of a redemptive economy becomes an authorizer of such symbolic mediation. Similarly, Eusebius claims that God's timing of the incarnation correlated to the acme of Roman imperial power, manifested in territorial consolidation and efficient infrastructure.[27] Underlying such possibilities of sovereign representation and efficient bureaucratic administration is money as a tool of governance. Eusebius's claim is that God waited for proper social, political, and epistemological preparation before becoming manifest. Part of such preparation, I suggest, involved monetization. Agamben's study, profound as it is, just scratches the surface of the interpenetration of political and economic concepts and theological doctrine. The foregoing exploration of money in the Greek context makes clear that including analysis of this social technology provides an important augmentation to Agamben's study.

It is in such a context—understanding money as an extension of sovereignty and a foundation to bureaucratic governance, and seeing the Son as the central arm of the Father's kingdom and administrative overseer of redemption—that we should consider the litany of monetary tropes applied to Christ. As redeemer, ransom, payment of debt, treasure, gold coin, chief steward, the connections abound.[28] Money crosses the divide between the space of the sovereign and its field of power. Money literally brings the image of the ruler into the context of its dominion. Money *incarnates* sovereignty, and shapes a pattern of life accordingly. The movement of the Son parallels this, as the image of the Father, the token and representative of the Father's account and kingdom, enters the space of the Father's rule, that is, creation, and effects a particular outcome, altering evaluations and transforming (exchange) relations.

It should therefore come as no surprise when the Christian emperor Justinian II, in an unprecedented display of theopolitical economy, merges the icon of Christ with imperial coinage.[29] Simultaneously Christ is currency, the material coin circulating in the empire, and *Rex Regnantium,* Lord of those who rule, as the coin's inscription reads. Ideas of Christ as lord of economy and as currency, percolating for centuries in the Christian theopolitical imaginary, here coalesce. This merger is symptomatic of more fundamental linkages between Christology and money, and it is efficacious in materially instantiating such a vision and legitimating corresponding forms of dominion. Any genealogy of modernity and capitalism in the West, with their extension and secularization of early ideas of theopolitical rule and bureaucratic administration, needs to tell the tale of money's uneasy relationship to Christ.[30] The vexed and ambivalent history of Christian discourse about money may highlight the tensions of this close linkage.

The Future of a Discourse

To the extent that theological and philosophical reflection on money and economy today begins from a position of simple opposition or dichotomy between divine or spiritual economy and that of money, this originary linkage is again suppressed. Such sentiments crop up continually in attempts to pit theologically informed analyses of economy *against* capitalism, for instance. What does it mean for theological social critique of money and political economy if fundamental building blocks of theological discourse are linked with monetary economy? Where is the ground on which to stand, from which to issue a critique of the dynamics and abuses of the monetary system? What does it mean that Christian discourse, so often a language of power in Western history, may serve to legitimate certain types of governmental administration through money? For if Christ is the chief economist and steward, as well as the precious currency of salvific exchange, does this not serve to ground at a distance various secular models of governmental administration and control through money and its cousins: statistics, census, surveillance—in short, biopolitics and governmentality?[31]

From such a perspective one could criticize Philip Goodchild's recent engagement with money and capitalism for the ways it fails to reckon with this preexisting enmeshing of money and philosophy/theology.[32] Goodchild accepts without interrogation the biblical image of Jesus and money existing in "starkest opposition," as "God and wealth are set into competition."[33] Yet, how might such scriptural fears of conflation actually betray a conceptual proximity? For the scriptural texts are much more complex, as Jesus and the kingdom are favorably compared with lost coins and treasure, and faithful discipleship is likened to shrewd financial stewardship, for instance. Additionally, as noted above, early Church thought continually drew on language of economy and money to articulate redemption and the Son's status as payment. The push-pull of monetary influence in Greek philosophy can be glimpsed here as well. It could be that the persistent need to set Jesus apart from money emerges from a threatening proximity. Without such a critical perspective, Goodchild approaches monetary economy with the "pure" lens of the philosophy of religion, and theological concepts are employed as if they stand outside the purview of money. Money and theology are brought together as disparate fields requiring conceptual mediation, with religious concepts speaking the word of discipline to economy.

Goodchild's title—*Theology of Money*—is partially ironic. By it he does not mean to construct a theology analyzing money, and indeed engages very little with theology in his text. Rather, he critiques the ways money resembles and invokes the transcendental and eschatological yearnings of religious piety and discourse.[34] There is a theology of money operative that he seeks to unmask and undo. Yet, it may be that his inquiry is not ironic enough, for while money can be an object of religious devotion and shape capacity for subjective judgment just like "religion proper," theology itself needs to be assessed for its monetary logic. Perhaps money is theological not simply because of these thematic resonances but due to a common history and conceptual heritage. In this sense then, we might ask, giving in to Heraclitus, Critchley, and McCarthy's metaphorization, how might money not only be theological but theology be monetary? Shouldn't we elaborate not only the theology of money but also the money of theology?

At least in terms of money's development and deployment in the West, ties to fundamental aspects of the Christian theological tradition should be considered. *It is not simply a question of money being worshipped, idolized, or pursued with* religious zeal. It is rather one of monetary and theological economies commingling and legitimating particular forms of sovereign reign and bureaucratic governance. It is such an ideological and institutional context that needs to be assessed for the ways it shapes subjectivity. While it is important to address the manner in which money relates to personal identity, decision, will, and desire, for instance, so also monetary sovereignty in relation to sociopolitical institutions, disciplinary technologies, and communal identity calls for consideration. As the above exploration has suggested, money must be analyzed in relation to such wider political forms of sovereignty and the theopolitical visions that nourish them.

Singling out Goodchild in this regard is somewhat unfair, however, since to this point few if any theological or philosophical engagements with money have considered this legacy of mutual implication. Indeed, there is an ambivalence in Goodchild's text, for he recognizes the intermeshing of metaphysics and money, citing money as a key component in the construction of Truth in Western thought.[35] For him, however, this influence appears as primarily a modern phenomenon, as the ubiquity of money through global capitalism undergirds popular perceptions of value and forms an alternative conceptual edifice for considering the realm of ultimate concern. Religion, then, offers a place of conceptual reserve from which this tyranny of money can be critiqued and transformed. To be sure, he maintains, the critique must remain immanent and not be subject to old dualisms, since capital will always fill the space between.[36] Yet, we must ask whether in fact this space for agonistic critique, however immanent, actually exists. While I hope that it does, a greater amount of work remains in order to delineate what it might look like.

Nevertheless, Goodchild's engagements with capitalism do well to explore the similarities and disjunctures between economic and religious attitudes and mentalities. He devotes important attention to superstructural elements of money, the ways, for instance, that it influences individual consciousness, dictates choice, and structures desire. Goodchild also offers a fascinating exploration of the relations between metaphysics and credit, the ways forms of representation reflect differing assumptions about ontology, which have analogues in the social relation of credit. In this regard he is expanding and pushing forward the ancient Greek philosophical concerns about money and philosophy, linking analytical thought with the category of credit and debt in new and imaginative ways. With a more nuanced attunement to the preexisting connections between money, theology, and the philosophy of religion, the route charted by Goodchild promises fruitful assessments of money as a powerful structuring principle of present reality.

The futures of the philosophy of religion and of theology are tied to the futures of money, capital, and sovereignty, for better or for worse. It is Goodchild's inspired observation that "the 'true nature' of money is revealed only progressively through history, and since history has yet to end, we cannot yet be sure what money will have been."[37] The same can be said about theoretical reflection itself, as "the owl of Minerva begins its flight only at the onset of dusk."[38] As we seek to assess our current situation, to unearth persistent sources of domination (whether conceptual or social) and chart hopeful routes forward, continued self-reflexivity, contextual awareness, and interrogation of inherited conceptual tropes are required. Achieving liberation from structures and systems that orient reality problematically first requires acknowledgement of how deeply enmeshed we actually are. It also calls for clarity about the complicit history of the tools we would use to try to free ourselves.

Notes

1. I refer to the post-Schmittian sensitivities to the theological residues in modernity, taken up variously by Agamben, Asad, and Taylor, to name a few. See, e.g., Carl Schmitt, *Political Theology: Four Chapters on the Concept of Sovereignty*, trans. George Schwab (Chicago: University of Chicago Press, 2005); Giorgio Agamben, *Il Regno e la Gloria: Per una genealogia teologica dell'economia e del governo* (Vicenza: Neri Pozza, 2007); Talal Asad, *Formations of the Secular: Christianity, Islam, Modernity* (Stanford, Calif.: Stanford University Press, 2003); Charles Taylor, *A Secular Age* (Cambridge, Mass.: Belknap Press of Harvard University Press, 2007).

2. Marc Shell, *The Economy of Literature* (Baltimore: Johns Hopkins University Press, 1978); Richard Seaford, *Money and the Early Greek Mind: Homer, Philosophy, Tragedy* (Cambridge: Cambridge University Press, 2004); Leslie Kurke, *Coins, Bodies, Games, and Gold: The Politics of Meaning in Archaic Greece* (Princeton, N.J.: Princeton University Press, 1999).

3. Frag. 90 in Heraclitus, *Heraclitus, the Cosmic Fragments*, trans. G. S. Kirk (Cambridge: Cambridge University Press, 1952), 345, cited in Shell, *The Economy of Literature*, 51–62.

4. Shell, *The Economy of Literature*, 52.

5. Ibid., 54–55.

6. See, e.g., Richard Seaford, "Tragic Tyranny," in *Popular Tyranny: Sovereignty and Its Discontents in Ancient Greece*, ed. Kathryn A. Morgan (Austin: University of Texas Press, 2003). Cf. Richard Seaford, "Tragic Money," *Journal of Hellenic Studies* 118 (1998), 119–139.

7. Heraclitus's negative view of money is hinted at in Fragment 125: "May you have plenty of wealth, you men of Ephesus, in order that you may be punished for your evil ways." Cited in Shell, *The Economy of Literature*, 51n115.

8. Ibid., 50–51.

9. See also David M. Schaps, *The Invention of Coinage and the Monetization of Ancient Greece* (Ann Arbor: University of Michigan Press, 2004). Money as an abstract concept can be traced further back to ancient Near Eastern civilizations. See Michael Hudson, "The Archaeology of Money: Debt Versus Barter Theories of Money's Origins," in *Credit and State Theories of Money: The Contributions of A. Mitchell Innes*, ed. L. Randall Wray (Northhampton, Mass.: Edward Elgar, 2004). Yet coinage first appears in Greece, materially instantiating the "abstract money of account" developed earlier and making its presence felt within conceptual (and incidentally prosaic and poetic) discourse.

10. Simon Critchley and Tom McCarthy, "Of Chrematology: Joyce and Money," in *Theology and the Political: The New Debate*, ed. Creston Davis, John Milbank, and Slavoj Žižek (Durham, N.C.: Duke University Press, 2005), 191.

11. Ibid.

12. Shell, *The Economy of Literature*, 25. Cf. P. N. Ure, *The Origin of Tyranny* (Cambridge: Cambridge University Press, 1922).

13. Herodotus, *Histories* 1.99, cited in Shell, *The Economy of Literature*, 18.

14. This is confirmed by Max Weber, that great theorist of bureaucratic mechanisms, who notes that the structural organization and reification manifested within bureaucracy presuppose a monetary economy. See Max Weber, *Economy and Society: An Outline of Interpretive Sociology* (Berkeley: University of California Press, 1978).

15. Seaford, "Tragic Tyranny," 100.

16. The term "heterodox" seeks to contest the hegemonic "orthodoxy" of neoclassical economic theories, which regard money as a commodity that functions neutrally as a medium of exchange. While this umbrella term encompasses many divergent perspectives that have as common opponent this orthodoxy, I am drawing primarily on what is termed chartalism and a state-centered analysis of money. See, e.g., L. Randall Wray, ed., *Credit and State Theories of Money: The Contributions of A. Mitchell Innes* (Northampton, Mass.: Edward Elgar, 2004). For a helpful survey see, Philip Arestis and Malcolm C. Sawyer, eds., *A Handbook of Alternative Monetary Economics* (Northampton, Mass.: Edward Elgar, 2006). For a classic, orthodox statement on the evolution from barter to money economies see Michael Latzer and Stefan W. Schmitz, eds., *Carl Menger and the Evolution of Payments Systems: From Barter to Electronic Money* (Northampton, Mass.: Edward Elgar, 2002), 25–107.

17. Geoffrey K. Ingham, *The Nature of Money* (Cambridge: Polity, 2004).

18. See also L. Randall Wray, *Understanding Modern Money: The Key to Full Employment and Price Stability* (Northampton, Mass.: Edward Elgar, 1998).

19. Consider the opening lines to G. F. Knapp's monumental and influential study *The State Theory of Money*: "Money is a creature of law. A theory of money must therefore deal with legal history." See Georg Friedrich Knapp, *The State Theory of Money*, ed. H. M. Lucas and James Bonar, abridged ed. (London: Macmillan, 1924), 1.

20. For Foucault's linkage between politics, law, and war, see Michel Foucault, *Society Must Be Defended: Lectures at the Collège de France, 1975–76*, ed. Mauro Bertani, et al. (New York: Picador, 2003).

21. For one of many examples from the modern colonial context see C. A. Gregory, "Cowries and Conquest: Towards a Subalternate Quality Theory of Money," *Comparative Studies in Society and History* 38, no. 2 (April 1996): 195–217.

22. See, for instance, Kenneth W. Harl, *Coinage in the Roman Economy, 300 BC to AD 700* (Baltimore: Johns Hopkins University Press, 1996).

23. This is not to deny diverse provincial coinage and varying degrees of monetization throughout the empire. Yet Roman government administration was highly monetized, and the image dispersed from the imperial center was one of economic unification, in which coinage played a crucial role. See Richard Duncan-Jones, *Money and Government in the Roman Empire* (Cambridge: Cambridge University Press, 1994).

24. Andrew Wallace-Hadrill, "Image and Authority in the Coinage of Augustus," *Journal of Roman Studies* 76 (1986): 68–87; S. R. F. Price, *Rituals and Power: The Roman Imperial Cult in Asia Minor* (New York: Cambridge University Press, 1984).

25. Agamben, *Il Regno e la Gloria*. Citations are from the French translation, Giorgio Agamben, *Le Règne et la Gloire: Pour une généalogie théologique de l'économie et du gouvernement*, trans. Joël Gayraud and Martin Rueff (Paris: Seuil, 2008). Cf. Giorgio Agamben, *"What Is an Apparatus?" And Other Essays*, trans. David Kishik and Stefan Pedatella (Stanford, Calif.: Stanford University Press, 2009).

26. Tertullian, *Against Praxeas*, 3, cited in Agamben, *Le Règne et la Gloire*, 76–77. Agamben refers to this passage as "quasi-Kafkaesque." For Agamben's reflections on angels as bureau-

crats see Giorgio Agamben, *Die Beamten des Himmels: Über Engel*, trans. Andreas Hiepko (Berlin: Verlag der Weltreligionen im Insel Verlag, 2007).

27. Eusebius, *Demonstration of the Gospel*, 3.7.

28. Early ransom theory, as in Gregory of Nyssa, can be seen in this light as both an economic transaction and a divine sovereign conquest of death and the devil. See Gregory of Nyssa, *An Address on Religious Instruction*, 20–26, in Edward R. Hardy, *Christology of the Later Fathers*, Library of Christian Classics (Philadelphia: Westminster Press, 1954).

29. I am here using "economy" in multiple senses: the adeptness and acumen of *realpolitik*, the management of emperor-subject relations, and the administration of monetary economy itself. The definitive work on the Justinian Christ coin remains James Douglas Breckenridge, *The Numismatic Iconography of Justinian II (685–695, 705–711 AD)*, Numismatic Notes and Monographs 144 (New York: American Numismatic Society, 1959). Cf. Marcell Restle, *Kunst und byzantinische Münzprägung von Justinian I. bis zum Bilderstreit* (Athens: Verlag der "Byzantinisch-neugriechischen Jahrbücher," 1964); Hans Belting, *Likeness and Presence: A History of the Image before the Era of Art* (Chicago: University of Chicago Press, 1994); Marie-José Mondzain, *Image, Icon, Economy: The Byzantine Origins of the Contemporary Imaginary* (Stanford, Calif.: Stanford University Press, 2005).

30. One provocative exploration along somewhat different lines is Gil Anidjar, "Christians and Money (the Economic Enemy)," *Ethical Perspectives: Journal of the European Ethics Network* 12, no. 4 (2005): 497–519.

31. Thus to Foucault's now classic genealogy of pastoral power and state governmentality we must add money's relationship to theology as an important layer of consideration. See Michel Foucault, *Security, Territory, Population: Lectures at the Collège de France, 1977–1978*, ed. Michel Senellart and Arnold I. Davidson (New York: Palgrave Macmillan, 2007); Michel Foucault, *The Birth of Biopolitics: Lectures at the Collège de France, 1978–79*, ed. Michel Senellart (New York: Palgrave Macmillan, 2008). Obviously the question of the secularization of theology into political philosophy and policy is vexed and complex, and must be approached with nuance. I am not suggesting a direct one-to-one correspondence but setting out one possible lens through which the scope of influence might be considered.

32. Philip Goodchild, *Theology of Money* (Durham N.C.: Duke University Press, 2009); Philip Goodchild, "Capital and Kingdom: An Eschatological Ontology," in *Theology and the Political: The New Debate*, ed. Creston Davis, John Milbank, and Slavoj Žižek (Durham, N.C.: Duke University Press, 2005).

33. Goodchild, *Theology of Money*, 3, 6, 201, 202.

34. Ibid., 218ff and passim.

35. Ibid., 207–210.

36. Goodchild, "Capital and Kingdom: An Eschatological Ontology," 130.

37. Ibid., 136.

38. Georg W. F. Hegel, *Elements of the Philosophy of Right*, ed. Allen W. Wood, trans. Hugh Barr Nisbet (New York: Cambridge University Press, 1991), 23.

9 "Between Justice and My Mother"

Reflections on and between Levinas and Žižek

Gavin Hyman

IN 1957, ALBERT Camus received the Nobel Prize for Literature. As Camus travelled to Stockholm to receive the award, the editor of *Le Monde,* Hubert Beuve-Méry, said that he was convinced that Camus would say something stupid, and, in his own mind, he was proved right.[1] Having received the Nobel Prize, Camus said, "I believe in justice, but I will defend my mother before I will defend justice," subsequently converted by the press into "between justice and my mother, I choose my mother."[2] The statement became notorious and gave rise to much puzzlement, debate, and hostility. Part of the reason for this lies in the statement's inherent ambiguity and its susceptibility to widely heterogeneous interpretation. Michael Wood, for instance, has pointed out that "if Camus means—or if what he said turns out to mean—that as far as he is concerned genuine justice must always give way to private life, we can understand his personal dilemma, but we can hardly applaud his formulation, since no colonist or privateer or free-market liberal ever said anything different."[3] On the other hand, Camus's recent biographer Alain Vircondelet sees in the statement an articulation of an "ultimate truth,"[4] and Wood himself also says that "it suggests both a loyalty to what's human and a flight from politics."[5] Furthermore, it may perhaps be viewed as a radically anti-Kantian gesture. Kant famously warned against the dangerous lure presented by "sympathy and warmhearted fellow-feeling";[6] in this context, sympathy for one's mother threatens to obscure one's duty to the universal moral law and is thus also an enemy to the realization of universal justice. Perhaps Camus's statement is to be understood as an unequivocal rejection of this uncompromising Kantian stance.

The dilemma raised by Camus's statement is one that has become increasingly pertinent to recent debates in Continental philosophy of religion. Over the last few decades, Continental philosophy has witnessed a pendulum swing from a reification of particularity to a revivification of universals. In ethical and political terms, this has been manifested in the transition from the dominance of Emmanuel Levinas's thinking on the unconditional call that the particular Face issues to us, to the recent prominence of Slavoj Žižek's trenchant call for the recovery of political universals. At issue here is a conflict between the sovereignty of particularity on the one hand and of universality on the other. Camus's formulation of his dilemma crystallizes what is here at stake. And although he "resolves" the dilemma in the way that he does, the very fact of his raising it bears witness to the difficulty and complexity that any such resolution involves. How is one to negotiate the inevitable tension between defending justice and defending my mother? While there may be occasions where the requirements of the two imperatives coincide, it is not difficult to see that there will be occasions where they come into direct conflict. Furthermore, to confront this dilemma is also to confront the question of precisely what is signified by the command to love one's neighbor as oneself. Does the commandment enjoin me to put aside all self-interest in favor of the universal claim of (all) my neighbors? Or does it enjoin me to love my particular neighbor against a background formed by the universal multitude?[7]

I want to suggest that in negotiating this dilemma, we must do so in a way that is attentive to—and does not seek prematurely to dissolve—the tension by which it is constituted, namely, the conflict experienced in my being susceptible to the universal call of justice *and* the particular claim of my mother. Indeed, I want to suggest this conflict may in some sense be understood to *constitute* the ethical and political. As Terry Eagleton has observed:

> There is a tension at the heart of ethical thought between the universal and the particular. Moral behaviour is a material affair, bound up with the needs and desires of mortal animals, part of their expressive or symbolic communication and so ineluctably local; but it is also supposed to stretch beyond this specificity into some more universal domain. . . . Like language, ethics is both grandly general and irreducibly specific.[8]

Thus, the ethical and political are experienced by us as a susceptibility *both* to the universal call of justice *and* to the particular claim of my mother. This tension between the universal and the particular is a productive and creative one with which we should tarry, and any premature attempt to dissolve it will ultimately result in the dissolution of both the ethical and the political. Clearly, the tension cannot be allowed to induce a paralyzing stasis, but any "resolution" of the tension can come about only in singular ethical and political judgments that must repeatedly be made anew.

To make these claims is, therefore, to register a protest against the approaches of both Emmanuel Levinas and Slavoj Žižek. For both, ultimately and a priori, resolve the tension between the universal and the particular by elevating one over the other. Levinas ultimately prioritizes the particular call of the Face, while Žižek ultimately valorizes the universal call to justice for the nameless Third. In what follows, I want to show the problems inherent to these premature resolutions. It should be acknowledged, of course, that both thinkers do recognize and are sensitive to a certain necessary equivocation between the universal and the particular in the domains of the ethical and political. But however much this may be so, for both thinkers, such equivocation is not irreducible but, rather, penultimate.[9] Both believe that such equivocation must, finally, be resolved, and it is precisely these resolutions that I find to be problematic. But I also want to show how the deficiencies of each may be "corrected" by the insights of the other, thereby indirectly confirming the ethical and political necessity of *both* the particular *and* the universal, albeit in such a way that the preeminence of one over the other cannot be prejudged.

Let us turn first to the thought of Emmanuel Levinas. As is well known, for Levinas, the ethical is located in the subject's primordial experience of subjection, a call of responsibility toward the singular other, the Face, which operates unilaterally and unconditionally, irrespective of the other's disposition toward me and irrespective of the existence of any third party. Furthermore, this call of responsibility is "absolute"; it is without limit. As Levinas puts it, there is "no longer any limit or measure for this responsibility, which 'in the memory of man' has never been contracted, and is found to be at the mercy of the freedom and the fate, unverifiable by me, of the other man. It is to catch sight of an extreme passivity."[10] It is, of course, the case, according to Levinas's phenomenological description, that others are equally placed under the same absolute and infinite responsibility as I am. But this is of no relevance to the infinite responsibility under which I am placed: "the subject affected by the other cannot think that the affection is reciprocal."[11] The fact that others are responsible for and to me is in no way a precondition or justification for my own responsibility toward them; this would be to relapse into a conception of ethics as idolatry, wherein autonomous subjects rationally decide to make a contract to be responsible for each other. On the contrary, the responsibility of others toward me is of no concern or relevance here:

> The knot of subjectivity consists in going to the other without concerning oneself with his movement toward me. Or, more exactly, it consists in approaching in such a way that, over and beyond all the reciprocal relations that do not fail to get set up between me and the neighbor, I have always taken one step

more toward him—which is possible only if this step is responsibility. In the responsibility which we have for one another, I have always one more response to give, I have to answer for this very responsibility.[12]

But, as numerous commentators have pointed out, such a model seems to give rise to *both* a suicidal self-abnegation *and* a megalomaniacal self-inflation. For in fulfilling our responsibility to the other in an absolute way, that is to say, without limit, it seems that this can only end ultimately in our own self-negation, in a sacrifice of oneself for the other. This might be understood as in some sense a reinscription of the Kantian diremption between love of self and love of other; the affirmation of one is always at the expense of the other, so that absolute responsibility for the other seems to compromise one's own right to exist. This is made explicit when Levinas asks, in a much quoted passage:

> What is an individual, a solitary individual, if not a tree that grows without regard for everything it suppresses and breaks, grabbing all the nourishment, air and sun, a being that is fully justified in its nature and its being? What is an individual, if not a usurper? What is signified by the advent of conscience, and even the first spark of spirit, if not the discovery of corpses beside me and my horror of existing by assassination?[13]

Thus, my very existence, my very being, is at the expense of the other, and my own response to this can only be the sacrifice of myself to the other. It would therefore appear that Levinas has sundered the enigma that lies at the heart of the commandment to love my neighbor as myself. Interpreting the commandment not as embodying an enigma but as an impossibility, Levinas "overcomes" this impossibility by sacrificing the self to the other. On Levinas's own grounds, it is difficult to see how this could lead logically to anything other than a suicidal self-negation.[14]

But we may well wonder whether such pathological self-denial does not tip over only too easily into its opposite. Is not a phenomenological structure that is constituted by an absolute opposition between the other on one side and the self on the other far too self-centered? Is this nihilistic self-denial not produced in response to a situation in which the self is affirmed and inflated as that which *alone* is answerable to and responsible for the other? Indeed, as Slavoj Žižek has suggested, Levinas makes the subject a privileged and centered site which is itself responsible for all others.[15] In spite of all the talk of absolute responsibility and self-denial that we have been expressing, there appears to be here an inflation of the subject, which is constituted by its being called to responsibility for all that which is not itself. The individual ethical subject is seen to bear the weight of the whole world. As Terry Eagleton has commented with regard to Levinas here, "Universality means being responsible for anyone, not, *per impossible*, for everyone at the same time. To assume that it does, even while insisting on its impossibility, betrays a certain hubris of the infinite, however apologetic and self-castigating in tone."[16] Thus, in its burden of responsibility for all, the ethical subject sees itself as alone carrying the burden of ethical responsibility in a way that betokens a remarkable self-promotion.

Furthermore, when Eagleton talks here of a "hubris of the infinite," we begin to get a sense that the human subject is here being expected to assume divine responsibilities. Indeed, we might say that this inflation of the self in Levinas's thought is such that it commends a degree of human responsibility that is, in reality, only appropriate to and realizable by God. The particularity, finitude, and limitations of human beings seem to drop from view, and humanity is being expected to love as God loves, namely, indiscriminately, and to exercise responsibility as God exercises it, namely, absolutely on behalf of all, and without reserve. As David Wood has commented: "Levinas is confusing the fact that there are no a priori limits to my ethical exposure to the other, the powerful grain of truth here, with the claim of infinite obligation or responsibility. . . . I am not a divine being."[17] Thus the absolute responsibility demanded by Levinas is, in effect, a demand that we cease to be finite and situated and that we exercise that responsibility as God is believed to do.

But how has it come about that an ethic of suicidal abnegation has turned into one of human hubris? How are we to understand this assumption of divine responsibility? One way of understanding it, I suggest, is to see it as an effect of Levinas's valorization of the particular over the universal, and to see this, in turn, as an effect of the immanentist and perhaps nihilistic aspects of Levinas's work. At first sight, this may appear to be a counterintuitive observation, for is Levinas not the thinker, who, above so many others, emphasizes otherness and transcendence, particularly in his insistence on the heteronomy of the other and the transcendence to which the face gestures? While these elements are undoubtedly there, they do nonetheless flow alongside an undeniably immanentist or atheistic stream. This aspect of Levinas's work is well brought out by John D. Caputo, when he suggests that Levinas's thought comes very close to being a "death of God theology." He says that, for Levinas, "our being turned to God (*à-Dieu*) is our being returned to the neighbor, and that is all the God there is. God commands but God does not exist. About the separate and supreme being of classical theology, Levinas (the most theological resource of postmodern thinkers) is no less than Nietzsche (their most antitheological resource) an atheist."[18] If this is so, if, for Levinas, "our being turned to God (*à-Dieu*) is our being returned to the neighbor, and that is all the God there is," then we can see why the subject feels impelled to assume divine responsibilities. We must take on the full responsibility for the neighbor, for there is no other God who will do it for us. It is thus the death of the universal that impels us unequivocally to elevate the domain of the particular. The subject thereby assumes the divine task of absolute responsibility for the other.

At the same time, however, because the subject is finite and contingent, just like the other for which it is responsible, a certain rivalry is installed such that one can be affirmed only at the expense of the other, a rivalry that is well expressed in Levinas's imagery of the individual as a usurping tree.[19] If the subject is to exercise absolute responsibility for the other, as a finite contingent being, this can ultimately be done only by means of the negation of the self. This, I suggest, is how we should understand the co-presence of the subject's hubris and self-negation in Levinas's thought. The hubristic ambition, which is consequent upon the death of the universal, can be realized by a particular subject only by means of its own self-negation. Not only are the self-promotion and self-negation undesirable in themselves, but taken together, they result in an extreme fragmentation and, ultimately, a dissolution of the subject. These outcomes are, I suggest, consequent upon a denial of the necessary ethical and political interplay between the domains of the universal, the particular, and the singular. Specifically, in this instance, it results from an a priori subordination of the domain of the universal.

It is precisely here that we can see Žižek as enacting a "correction" of Levinas, in his insistence on the necessary role of the Third "that grounds justice in the domain of *universality* proper." Žižek wants to rehabilitate the domain of universality not as a secondary supplement, but as an integral part of the primordial phenomenological encounter. As Žižek puts it:

> The Third is a formal-transcendental fact; it is not that, while, in our empirical lives, the Third is irreducible, we should maintain a kind of regulative Idea the full grounding of ethics in the relation to the Other's Face. Such a grounding is not only empirically impossible, it is a priori impossible, since the limitation of our capacity to relate to Others' faces is the mark of our very finitude. In other words, the limitation of our ethical relation of responsibility toward the Other's face which necessitates the rise of the Third (the domain of regulations) is a positive condition of ethics, not simply its secondary supplement.[20]

So it is the emergence of the Third that reminds me that I am one among others, that there is a wider context in which my call of responsibility takes place. The domain of the Third thus in a sense "relativizes" or "limits" my responsibility for the Other by acknowledging my finitude and limitations as one among others. In this sense, then, we can see how Žižek's rehabilitation of the domain of the universal can serve to correct some of the problems we identified in Levinas's thought. By invoking the universal domain of the Third as both an empirical and an a priori principle, Žižek wishes to show how the kind of absolute responsibility advocated by Levinas is strictly impossible. The invocation of the domain of the universal, of the Third, has the effect of contextualizing the subject as a finite contingent being. The subject is not alone, Godlike, in its responsibility toward the other. On the contrary, that obligation or responsibility arises out of a context wherein I am one finite being among others. The invocation of the domain of the universal has the effect of affirming my finitude and contingency and thus qualifying the extent of my responsibility accordingly.

But in making this correction, Žižek thereby installs another problem. Rather than "supplementing" Levinas's primordial account of the encounter between the particular and the singular by insisting on the simultaneous necessity of the domain of the universal, Žižek wants to insist on the phenomenological *priority* of this universal. In particular, we should give priority to the Law, understood as an external and universal intervention that intervenes and guards against the "lure" of the face:

> In contrast to love, justice begins when I remember the faceless many left in shadow in this privileging of the One. Justice and love are thus structurally incompatible: justice, not love, must be blind; it must disregard the privileged One whom I "really understand." What this means is that the Third is not secondary: it is always-already here, and the primordial ethical obligation is toward this Third who is *not* here in the face-to-face relationship, the one in shadow, like the absent child of a love-couple.[21]

Thus, for Žižek, "the true ethical step is the one *beyond* the face of the other, the one of *suspending* the hold of the face, the one of choosing *against* the face, for the *third*. This coldness *is* justice at its most elementary."[22] So the particularity of the face in front of me is a lure that must be resisted because it is in danger of blurring the universal gesture of justice that would focus on the faceless Thirds that are thereby relegated to the background. That this move embodies a critique of Levinas's prioritizing of particularity in favor of the universality of justice is made explicit when Žižek goes on to say, "it is only such a shift of focus onto the third that *uproots* justice, liberating it from the contingent umbilical link that renders it 'embedded' in a particular situation. In other words, it is only such a shift onto the Third that grounds justice in the dimension of *universality* proper."[23]

That this moves in the direction of violence is obvious and, indeed, is scarcely denied by Žižek. An unequivocal renunciation of violence as such can only lead to passivity and what has been described as the "fakery of liberalism."[24] In his response to the question posed to him by John Milbank, namely, "wherein lies the good for Žižek?" he replies that it is in love—not, he stresses "in sentimental love, but in love on account of which, as Kierkegaard put it with his matchless radicality, I am ready to kill my neighbor."[25] What we have here is an obvious echo of Kant's universalism, as was evoked at the outset of our discussion. What Kant characterizes as "warmhearted fellow feeling" and Žižek describes as "sentimental love" should be regarded as a temptation to be resisted. It is a temptation to be resisted because it threatens to interfere with my resolve to be ready to kill my neighbor—in the name of justice, in the name of the universal.

But is this commitment to revolutionary violence not a symptom of an undue elevating of the domain of the universal over the domains of the particular and the singular? In asking this question, we are led also to ask two further and related questions. First, why is it that in "correcting" Levinas's neglect of the domain of the universal, Žižek thereby asserts the unequivocal sovereignty of the universal over the domains of the particular and the singular, a sovereignty that results in the kind of revolutionary violence we have here been amplifying? Secondly, how are we to explain the fact that Žižek's assertion of the universal appears to be prompted by the same atheism or nihilism that we saw to be the underlying feature of Levinas's contrary subordination of the universal? In other words, if Levinas's atheism led him to turn away from the universal, how is it that Žižek's atheism leads him back to it? Both of these questions can, I suggest, be addressed by means of a common answer and, in particular, by turning to Žižek's explicit espousal of nihilism.

As with much else in Žižek's thought, his espousal of nihilism would appear to be counterintuitive, not least when set beside his simultaneous espousal of materialism. But, as Žižek himself explains, his understanding of materialism stands in marked contrast to most standard understandings, not least in that he understands nihilism to be the true formula of materialism: "Materialism has nothing to do with the assertion of the inert density of matter; it is, on the contrary, a position which accepts the ultimate void of reality—the consequence of its central thesis on the primordial multiplicity is that there is no 'substantial reality,' that the only substance of the multiplicity is void."[26] Žižek's ontological *materialism* is therefore also an ontological *nihilism*, a materialism that asserts that there is ultimately only the void. This is, of course, a distinctive type of materialism, one that is refracted through his "parallax" lens, which means also that it is a materialism shot through with equivocation and incommensurability.

This in turn means, among other things, that there is an equivocation between necessity and contingency, but it is an equivocation that arises out of an ultimate prioritizing of the contingent. This can be seen, for instance, when Žižek says, in relation to dialectics, that "a process of formally inevitable unfolding must prevail," but this means that

> the conceptually determined "formally inevitable unfolding" is not there from the very beginning of the process, it gradually "prevails," and this "prevailing" is the (in itself contingent) process by means of which the conceptual necessity (I am almost tempted to say: in an autopoietic way) forms itself out of the initial contingency. In other words, there is no preexisting necessity that directs the dialectical process, since this necessity is precisely what arises through this process, i.e. what this process is about. . . . Yes, there is a necessity, but this necessity is *retroactive,* it arises as the (*contingent*) self-sublation of contingency.[27]

What we see here, then, is that the equivocation between necessity and contingency ultimately gives way to the ultimate prioritizing of contingency. So too ethical equivocation is weakened by the bracketing or suspension of one of the three domains of the ethical triad, paradoxically because it is the very domain that is ontologically privileged. Thus, Žižek's ontological privileging of the contingent, the finite, and the immanent means that that very domain, the domain of particularity, can, in a sense and in ethical terms, be allowed to take care of itself.

What does it mean to say this? Because the contingent, the particular, is all there really is, there is a sense in which the universal has to be *produced*, as an ethical task. Practical attention thus gets shifted to the task of inaugurating *singular* instantiations of the *universal*. This means in turn that the ethical/political imperative gets shifted away from the particular neighbor to the nameless multitude, the universal third. This leads Žižek to prioritize the political over the ethical; the call of the neighbor who is close at hand serves only as a stumbling block to the realization of universal justice, a universal justice that can be instantiated only through the enactment of revolutionary violence. Whereas the task of instantiating universal justice might properly be thought to be a divine one, in Žižek's explicitly atheistic materialism, there is no God to undertake it for us. It must therefore be assumed in its entirety by humanity itself; humanity must bring about the instantiation of the universal.

So for Žižek, there is a sense in which this "elevation" of the universal is necessary precisely because of the "death" of the universal. In other words, it is because God is dead that humans must assume God's role for themselves. On Žižek's atheistic reading of Christianity, "we get a God who abandons [his] transcendent position and throws himself into his own creation, fully engaging himself in it up to dying, so that we, humans, are left with no higher Power watching over us, just with the terrible burden of freedom and responsibility for the fate of divine creation, and thus of God himself."[28]

But is not Žižek's assumption of divine responsibility as worrying as that assumed by Levinas? As the human threatens to become God and as the universal threatens to become violent, is this not the point at which Levinas's salutary warnings should again be heeded? Indeed, this is what has been suggested by Regina Schwarz, who has rightly pointed out that this commitment to an inflated universalism with its necessarily violent outcome is one that Žižek shares with Alain Badiou. For Schwarz, the elements in their thought that tend toward violent totalitarianism should not be taken lightly and should not lie uncontested. She has said that

> Badiou, seeing Paul as exemplary in his community building by conversion, is willing to run the attendant risks of totalitarianism and fundamentalism. Levinas, fearing totality with its connotations of intolerance and fascism, would be faithful to Revelation without any attempt to convert others. . . . In Badiou, being faithful to the Truth-Event requires speaking that truth, organizing it politically—only then is it universal. For Levinas, the universal truth

of revelation issues in a completely different regard for the other: he is not the object of persuasion, he is the one for whom I am responsible.[29]

So the Face of the Other, far from appearing as a dangerous lure to be resisted, instead comes to us as a necessary corrective at precisely the point at which I might be most tempted (out of a "love of justice") to kill my neighbor. Thus, for Schwarz, Levinas's thought has the decisive advantage that in it, "he embraces an ethics that goes beyond politics—not an alternative to politics, but an ethics he believes works when politics fails, and so an ethics that politics must answer to."[30] So for Schwarz, Levinas's undercutting of the logic of universalism, is done with good reason: in order to outflank the totalitarianism and violence that always comes in its wake.

Unlike Schwarz, however, I am not suggesting that we should unequivocally make a judgment *for* Levinas and *against* Žižek. For there may well be times when we are called upon to "suspend" the claim of the Face of the Other in the interests of justice and of the domain of universality. There may well be occasions, as Žižek claims, when, *in extremis*, I should indeed be ready to kill my neighbor. Put less dramatically, there may well be times when it is judged right to put the demands of justice before the demands of my immediate neighbor. Furthermore, Žižek is right to warn us of the ways in which Levinas's perpetual subordination of the political to the ethical can serve to usher in the "fakery of liberalism" and to make him an unwitting accomplice of the political status quo, of the current regime of global capital. But having said this, we must equally acknowledge that there may also be times when we are called upon to "suspend" the claims of universal justice in favor of the neighbor who stands before me in his nakedness and vulnerability. There may well be occasions when I should indeed defend my mother before defending justice. So too, and as Schwarz points out, Levinas is right to warn us of the ways in which the political lies logically and structurally in close proximity to the "said," to ontology, to the attempt to compare the incomparable. As such, it is always prone to a violent totalitarianism in which the Face of my particular neighbor falls from view.

There is therefore a sense in which the ethical and political require *both* Levinas and Žižek. And yet, the positions of Levinas and Žižek cannot be mediated; they are incapable of synthesis. As we have seen, their phenomenological accounts of the ethical and political, of the call of the neighbor and the call of justice, are strictly incompatible. There can be no question, therefore, of formulating a middle way "compromise" between them, of developing a systematic unified account that would somehow "incorporate" the insights of each. In the absence of any such mediation, our only way forward will be to tarry with both Levinas and Žižek in a way that acknowledges rather than resolves the incommensurability between them. Indeed, I am suggesting that the ethical and political are preserved precisely through this tarrying with incommensurability, through a perpetual labor of negotiation between the demands of the universal and those of the particular. When one of these domains is a priori privileged and the labor of negotiation is thereby overcome, the results, I suggest, are ultimately fatal for the ethical and political.

But how is this tension best preserved? How are we to avoid any a priori prioritizing of either the universal or the particular? In the cases of both Levinas and Žižek, I have suggested that their respective failures to sustain this tension and their concomitant a priori privileging of the universal or the particular was impelled by the death of God, even though the implications of that death are for each of them strikingly different. This difference may be explained by the fact that they each assume different aspects of the divine responsibility. When God is conceived as the infinite, noncontingent, nonexistent Other, he may be thought to pursue both aspects simultaneously, albeit not necessarily within the domain of creaturely time.[31] But when finite, contingent beings assume these duties for themselves, they necessarily have to choose between them and thereby elevate either the demands of the universal or the demands of the particular. The difference between them, though emerging out of the common context of the death of God, may be understood in these terms. Thus, whereas for Levinas, the subject is constituted by the call of responsibility for every singular other that appears before it, so that the subject takes on a divine responsibility for all, for Žižek, the subject takes on divine responsibility for the universal task of instantiating justice. So Levinas takes on the divine task of responsibility for the salvation of each singular face while Žižek takes on the divine task of ushering in the City of God here on earth. But both are impelled to assume or commend these tasks in the wake of the death of the God who might otherwise be trusted to enact them simultaneously, and who would teach the folly of attempting such tasks within the conditions of finitude. It seems that if human finitude is properly to be respected, this demands that the tension between the universal and the particular be left unresolved.

In which case, could it perhaps be said that this tension and this interplay would best be perpetuated through the invocation of a God who himself demands such an interplay in creaturely time? This is indeed the direction in which my analysis has been heading. At the same time, however, it is important to caution against such an invocation of God as some kind of easy panacea. Indeed, a perennial temptation is for God to be invoked in such a way as to smooth over and mend this tension rather than to perpetuate it, thus inducing an easy complacency rather than the labor of negotiation and judgment. If we should beware of assuming divine responsibilities for ourselves, we should simultaneously beware of leaving such responsibilities to God. Here too there is a necessary tension that must constantly be negotiated. Such judgments can be made only by finite human beings in specific instances, which are inseparable from the singular circumstances of the contexts in which they are made. They must therefore be made without the comfort and security of knowing that either the universal or the particular is to be a priori privileged, without the guarantee of a God's-eye view. Without such comfort and security, each decision is the taking of a risk in which one cannot know in advance whether it will turn out to have been justified. Such decisions as risks are therefore taken in faith and hope and in the recognition that they will be open and answerable to a retrospective judgment that, we might wish to say, can only be divine.

In conclusion, then, my suggestion is that we should understand the respective premature resolutions of Levinas and Žižek as being symptoms of the death of God. In the wake of this death, the human subject seems impelled to take on divine responsibilities. In the process, human finitude is in danger of being forgotten, and the ethical and political are themselves in danger of self-destructing. In which case, perhaps human finitude will best be respected, the universal-particular-singular tension will best be preserved, and the ethical and political will thereby best be perpetuated, within the context of the death of the death of God. So perhaps what Levinas and Žižek indirectly confirm is the continuing need of Continental philosophy for God, even if this is to open up further questions as to what this might ultimately mean.[32]

Notes

1. Michael Wood, "Losing the Light," *London Review of Books* 32, no. 16 (2010): 15.
2. Alain Vircondelet, *Albert Camus: fils d'Alger* (Paris: Fayard, 2010), 337, 339.
3. Wood, "Losing the Light," 15.
4. Vircondelet, *Albert Camus*, 337.
5. Wood, "Losing the Light," 15.
6. Immanuel Kant, *Critique of Practical Reason*, trans. Lewis White Beck (New York: Liberal Arts Press, 1956), 123.
7. For extended discussions of these questions, see Slavoj Žižek, Eric L. Santner, and Kenneth Reinhard, *The Neighbor: Three Inquiries in Political Theology* (Chicago: University of Chicago Press, 2005).
8. Terry Eagleton, *Trouble with Strangers: A Study of Ethics* (Oxford: Wiley-Blackwell, 2009), 111.
9. Gillian Rose has made this point with respect to Levinas. She identifies various ways in which Levinas acknowledges such equivocation, but ultimately sees this equivocation as something to be overcome. See *The Broken Middle: Out of our Ancient Society* (Oxford: Blackwell, 1992), 261–263.
10. Emmanuel Levinas, *Otherwise Than Being or Beyond Essence*, trans. Alphonso Lingis (The Hague: Martinus Nijhoff, 1981), 47.
11. Ibid., 84.
12. Ibid., 47.
13. Emmanuel Levinas, *Difficult Freedom: Essays on Judaism*, trans. Sean Hand (Baltimore: Johns Hopkins University Press, 1990), 100, quoted by Žižek in Žižek, Santner, and Reinhard, *The Neighbor*, 150.

14. For Levinas, there is, admittedly, more equivocation on this question than this statement would suggest. Nonetheless, like Gillian Rose (see note 9), I regard this equivocation as being penultimate rather than irreducible. I address this point in more detail in chapter 1 of my forthcoming book (see note 32).

15. See Žižek in *The Neighbor*, 155.

16. Eagleton, *Trouble with Strangers*, 258.

17. David Wood, *The Step Back: Ethics and Politics after Deconstruction* (Albany: SUNY Press, 2005), 145, 146.

18. John D. Caputo, "Atheism, A/Theology and the Postmodern Condition," in *The Cambridge Companion to Atheism*, ed. Michael Martin (Cambridge: Cambridge University Press, 2006), 273–274.

19. As Rowan Williams has observed, when we are confronted with a juxtaposition between subjects who are alike precisely in their finite contingency, then "the shadow of rivalry is never wholly absent." See *Lost Icons: Reflections on Cultural Bereavement* (Edinburgh: T & T Clark, 2000), 180.

20. Žižek in *The Neighbor*, 184.

21. Ibid., 182.

22. Ibid., 183.

23. Ibid., 183–184.

24. Regina Mara Schwarz, "Revelation and Revolution," in *Theology and the Political: The New Debate*, ed. Creston Davis, John Milbank and Slavoj Žižek (Durham, N.C.: Duke University Press, 2005), 106, in the course of expounding Badiou's critique of Levinas.

25. Žižek in Slavoj Žižek and John Milbank, *The Monstrosity of Christ: Paradox or Dialectic?* (Cambridge, Mass.: MIT Press, 2009), 254.

26. Ibid., 97. For a full explication of this, see 95–97.

27. Ibid., 246.

28. Ibid., 25.

29. Schwarz, "Revelation and Revolution," 106.

30. Ibid., 118–119.

31. To speak of God as the "nonexistent" Other is not necessarily to embrace an atheistic ontology. We can conceive of how Thomas Aquinas and Jean-Luc Marion might speak similarly, and Rowan Williams too invokes this term in *Lost Icons*, 180.

32. Some of the themes in this essay are given more extended treatment in my book, *Traversing the Middle: Ethics, Politics, Religion* (Eugene, Ore.: Cascade Books, 2013).

10 *Verbis Indisciplinatis*

Joseph Ballan

WHICHEVER CONTINENT, REAL or imagined, it is aligned with, philosophy of religion in the United States occupies a somewhat uneasy position alongside other disciplines and institutional arrangements. Scholars who work on or within Asian philosophical traditions find themselves facing much the same predicament as those who locate themselves somewhere within the vaguely post-phenomenological landscape called "Continental philosophy of religion." To what disciplinary genus does this species of scholarship—which has also become a recognizable *style* of scholarship—belong? To philosophy? To religious studies? To theology? Perhaps to none of these options? In what follows, I would like to think about what this strange and perhaps uncomfortable distance from other modes of knowledge production might make possible. What kind of thought might be available precisely because of this lack of a proper home? To begin posing the question about what connects philosophy of religion to empirical approaches like sociology and anthropology, and to humanistic approaches like history and literary studies, what differentiates philosophy of religion from them, and what those connections and differentiations demand and entail for responsive and responsible scholarship, I appeal to Jacques Rancière's concept of theoretical *in*-discipline.[1] Before articulating exactly what indisciplinarity might mean, however, I shall sketch part of the background against which Rancière's idea of indisciplinarity emerges, in order to suggest how it might be a fruitful challenge for scholars of religion to take up.

Interdisciplinarity

The thought that philosophers of religions should talk to other scholars of religion is far from controversial; who in today's academic climate would come out *against* interdisciplinarity (at least in public)? Indeed, for the past fifty or so years "interdisciplinary" has functioned as a kind of synonym for "respectful," "open," "relevant," such that there exists today a whole ethics—if not a dogmatics—of interdisciplinarity. In a series of lectures delivered in 1967, Louis Althusser called interdisciplinarity a contemporary academic *dogma* and a *myth*; its devotees look to it as to a "miracle cure"; its practices are "magical" acts; the roundtable in particular is an academic "mass."[2] The interdisciplinary thereby becomes, like religion itself,[3] a privileged example of an ideology in need of critique, and discussing it gives Althusser the chance to articulate his own conception of philosophy.

An old image has philosophy as the "science of sciences," without content of its own, but operating at a kind of distance, if not from a height, in relation to the sciences and in relation to other fields of human inquiry and activity such as art and literature, performing a work of abstraction and synthesis that its distance makes possible. Althusser gladly embraces this height of philosophy, which is not without its comedy: "philosophy? The discourse of theoretical impotence on the real work of others (scientific, artistic, political, etc., practice)" (*SPS*, 77). But while philosophy can and must speak of anything and, indeed, of everything! including, Althusser notes, of religion (*SPS*, 108), only its relationship to *science* makes it philosophy as such, because philosophy's task is above all to make separations (*SPS*, 75) and in particular to make separations between what belongs to ideology and what belongs to science (*SPS*, 83). Philosophy is not a science, because it has no real object of its own, nor should it take as its models the investigations pursued by the hard, empirical sciences, but philosophy's own internal resources let it distinguish the scientific from the ideological. So much is this the case that this work of separation and division is said to be the "primary function of philosophy."

Interdisciplinarity furnishes Althusser with a contemporary example by which he can establish a dividing line between ideology and its other. Instead of building out of the philosopher's comically impotent relationship to all the objects of science, art, and politics a conception of the philosopher as quintessential interdisciplinarian, Althusser insists on a definitive difference between philosophy and other disciplines, and it is this distance that permits it to perform the work of demystification, to enunciate what is *really* happening in so-called interdisciplinary encounters. Collaboration between *scientists* with different kinds of training does not count as an instance of interdisciplinarity, because scientific problems themselves necessitate such meetings (think of chemists, pharmacologists, and oncologists working together on the development of a cancer treatment). Now contrast this example with that of the roundtable of those who work in the human sciences. In this latter scenario, Althusser thinks, we have an illustration of interdisciplinarity qua ideology, an ideology that one can express in the following formula, given by Althusser: "when one does not know what the world does not know, it suffices to assemble all the ignorant: science will emerge from an assembly of the ignorant" (*SPS*, 97). A double ignorance, then: first the ignorance of the linguist about what is properly the purview of the literary historian, for instance, but second, the ignorance constitutive of ideology as such, the fact that *something else* is really at work in one's statements than that about which one thinks one is speaking. Althusser grants that educational ideologies are particularly difficult for those subject to them to recognize (*SPS*, 95), whence the *practical* importance of philosophy to other fields of intellectual inquiry. The ideology that dwells "silently" (*SPS*, 97) in the minds of the practitioners of what we in this time and place call the social sciences and the humanities is so insidious because these scholars think that they are actually *advancing* the cause of knowledge. The philosopher's intervention is to point out the merging of science and ideology in this domain (*SPS*, 99), first identifying and then pulling apart these two elements, thereby revealing to the ignorant their compounded ignorance.

Knowledge for Ignoramuses

Now it was precisely this kind of philosophical pedagogy, this hypothesized relationship between knowledge and ignorance, or more specifically between those who know and those who do not, that led Jacques Rancière to break so violently with Althusser, his erstwhile master, in a series of texts published in the early 1970s. Althusser's committed Marxism cannot mask his no less militant commitment to an epistemological hierarchy that maps rather neatly onto a hierarchy of kinds of people. Althusser's strategy is but a more subtle one than Plato's for separating the philosophers, the ones whose business it is to know, from the ignoramuses (including the proletarians, as Rancière has shown, but also in the case I was just discussing, the humanists and social scientists). To put it bluntly, and in terms of the Althusserian theme I have just discussed, "in the end, the science/ideology distinction will have had no other function than that of justifying ... the eminent dignity of the bearers of knowledge."[4] At this point in Rancière's intellectual itinerary, he does not want to abandon the Marxist vocabulary of ideology, but he relocates it; no longer the opposite of science, ideology is the "very space in which scientific knowledges are inscribed,"[5] which is to say, the bourgeois university system, thus a very particular institutional configuration or division of knowledges, but also of people. Where Althusser was willing to differentiate between philosophically correct cooperation among scientists and philosophically specious interdisciplinary activity among humanists and social scientists, Rancière detects a different kind of problem with this whole manner of dividing up kinds of knowledge. Althusserian philosophical practice simply justifies the (bourgeois) order of things, privileging a not very progressive existing institutional hierarchy.

After his public falling-out with Althusser, Rancière abandoned his open polemic with his former teacher, but he has consistently attempted to put into practice a form of thought that would avoid the same, tacitly political, privileging of philosophy that proved to be so problematic in Althusser. Rancière is thus in continuity with a Feuerbachian-Marxist tradition of antiphilosophy that attacks not so much the content of particular philosophical doctrines as a "particular mode of being" characteristic of contemporary philosophers.[6] Jean-Luc Nancy has rightly observed that "[Rancière] wants to be anything but a philosopher."[7] Yet for Rancière it is not a matter of turning from the speculations of philosophy, the metaphysical temptations that Althusser could not resist, to the empirical study of concrete historical situations. His critique of the sociological theory of Pierre Bourdieu is no less devastating than his earlier attack on Althusser. His book *The Philosopher and His Poor* traces a connection between concepts of philosophical knowledge and concepts of social division that philosophy and sociology share. Bourdieu's sociological accounts of class divisions are shown to be a kind of perverse double of the Platonic myth accounting for the existence of and relations between different *kinds* of people, most basically those whose business is to know and those whose business it is to work with their hands.[8] The criticism leveled at Bourdieu is but another version of the one aimed at Althusser. Turning Bourdieu's definition of sociology (as the bringing to light of what is concealed in everyday knowledge about the social) against him, Rancière discerns in Bourdieu's sociology a parallel to what I just called the second level of ignorance in the functioning of the contemporary ideology of interdisciplinarity, namely the ignorance constitutive of ideology as such, the fact that *something else* is really at work in one's statements than that about which the ignorant one thinks he is speaking. Bachelard famously quipped that there is no science but of the hidden,[9] and Bourdieu takes his cue from this epistemological principle in his effort to go behind appearances to the hidden dimension obscured by "immediate experience," "spontaneous sociology," and "ordinary language."[10] What results from this excavation is that "something else" that for Bourdieu only social science, and for Althusser only philosophy, can discern.

Undisciplined Words

After his withering critiques of investigators of the logic of the "something else" of which certain kinds of people are fated to be constitutively ignorant, of philosophers from Plato to Althusser, and of sociologists from Marx to Bourdieu, what practice of thought remains available to Rancière? Recently, albeit without reference to Althusser, Rancière has taken up the question of disciplines and their relationships to each other that we were discussing a moment ago. Without engaging directly with the Althusserian theses on interdisciplinarity, Rancière works to develop what he calls a practice of "in-disciplinary" thought, a practice that tries to evade the divisions of intellectual labor that Rancière has criticized since his early work on Althusser. He describes his method as "indisciplinary" because, for him, it is "not only a matter of going beside the disciplines but of breaking them." The problem, he says, is to "escape the division between disciplines," to take up "the question of the distribution of territories, which is always a way of deciding who is qualified to speak about what."[11] The criticism of interdisciplinarity in the name of philosophy is just as much a way of effecting this kind of decision, of putting to a work a distribution of capacities, as is the dogma of the interdisciplinarian. No longer a Marxist, however, Rancière does not couch his critique of the current state of the disciplines in the same language with which he criticized Althusser. But he *does* continue to frame the problem in terms of struggle. Disciplinary boundaries, he writes, are "weapons in a dispute."[12] Indisciplinary thought tries to lay bare this reality, which philosophy and sociology tend to cover over. And disciplinary boundaries are weapons in a dispute because they always seek to delineate a territory; they are boundaries in just this sense of determining what and who is in and what and who is out. Michel Serres often makes a similar point,[13] but in place of what we might call the pacifist epistemology of Serres, which denies that all knowledge generation need be combative, Rancière insists on the unavoidably polemical nature of the action by which these boundaries are established, contested, and broken.

What is more, and what demands the practice of indisciplinary thought, rather than the simple cooperation between practitioners of already existing academic methods, that is, rather than simple multidisciplinarity, is not that historians and sociologists are in the thrall of an ideology of which they are unaware. Instead, it is the fact that the received lines of division between history and literature, between philosophy and sociology, along with the more general division between the descriptive and prescriptive, are ultimately arbitrary (or at least contingent, nonnecessary). At bottom, when any discipline, including philosophy, seeks to establish its boundaries, to identify its proper object, and to set itself apart from the others, it ultimately appeals to the strategy of narrative, of storytelling. For each discipline, there exists, at minimum, a founding myth, if not a myth of the overthrow of the founders, or a story that recounts a sequence of such mutinies. The very notion of "polemical reason" that, following Bachelard, Bourdieu privileges over "architectonic reason"[14] is a perfect example of such a narrative. Historical epistemology in the tradition of Bachelard is ultimately a story about how scientific progress is accomplished as a series of narratable ruptures or epistemological breaks.[15] Yet, because Rancière is not interested in playing the game of demystification, this thesis about the narrative constitution of academic knowledges does not, by itself, disqualify these disciplines as methods that give access to a truth; rather, this thesis, which is the most basic gesture of what he calls a "poetics of knowledges," means to claim that the disciplines "must borrow their presentations of objects, their procedures for interaction and their forms of argument from language and common thought. A poetics of discourse is first a discourse which reinscribes the force of descriptions and arguments in the equality of common language and the common capacity to invent objects, stories, and arguments. In this sense, [a poetics of knowledges] can be called a method of equality."[16]

Circulations

Finally, then, what promise might this method of equality, this practice of indisciplinary thought, this poetics of knowledge, hold for scholars of religion? Rancière's name is not often associated with the "return to religion" in contemporary European philosophy.[17] For reasons that should become clear by the end of this section, it is hard to conceive of a return of religion (or a return to religion, it matters little) on Rancière's terms that would not also be, in some sense, a return of mastery and inequality. In introducing Rancière in this context, I do not mean to suggest that his writings offer a model that scholars of religion could simply transfer to their own domain; rather, and first of all, it prompts us to begin to do the more basic work of interrogating the self-evidence of our current division of intellectual labor, the association of certain ways of being—and certain ways of believing and practicing faith—with certain forms of knowledge. Why is it a given, for example, that the study of the role of religion in everyday life, of what sometimes gets called "material religion," properly belongs to sociology or anthropology, that it cannot attain the dignity of a philosophical problematic? The response typically made to this kind of problem—by sociologists, anthropologists, and others—is to effect a simple positivist reversal, whereby the empirical "low" becomes privileged in relation to the conceptual "high," humiliating philosophical speculation by the fascination of allegedly self-evident ethnographic "facts." The example of Rancière invites us to refuse such an easy solution to the problem of disciplines and their patterns of delineating what is sensible and what is intelligible, and to whom. To simply shift the focus of thought from abstract speculation to concrete practices is but one other way of confirming, albeit "beneath the seeming honesty of a good methodological principle . . . the division between those whose lot is production and struggle, and those whose lot is discourse."[18] As his critique of Bourdieu makes clear, the epistemological presuppositions underlying the social sciences are not necessarily more democratic than those of the philosopher who reflects on the justice of the social order while holding himself apart from the din of everyday life. Practicing indisciplinarity is a matter not of simply reversing the position of Althusser on interdisciplinarity by saying that philosophers and anthropologists should talk to each other, but rather of undermining the principle according to which Althusser tried to keep them apart. To put it more positively, indisciplinarity in our context is about inventing new ways of presenting and re-presenting, which is to say narrating, knowledge about religion that dissent from the established ways of dividing up kinds of human activities and modes of existence in the same strokes by which kinds of knowledge are divided and kept safe from contaminating each other.

Insofar as this fictional or aesthetic dimension is constitutive of it,[19] indisciplinary scholarship requires a specifically literary practice because of this *dissensus* that it puts to work. Scholarship is political, somewhat surprisingly, insofar as it is literary, that is, insofar as it is governed by the principle of democratic "literarity," a condition whose political possibilities have been discovered only recently, in what Rancière calls the "aesthetic regime" of artistic practices.[20] "Literature," which is a category that has existed for only a few hundred years, is defined by Rancière as being "involved in this partition of the visible and the sayable [characteristic of politics], in this intertwining of being, doing and saying that frames a polemical common world,"[21] but the condition of possibility of this art of partition, this art of using words, is literarity. Literarity is essentially everything that Plato is worried about when he develops his critique of writing in the *Phaedrus*, to wit, "the radical democracy of the letter that anyone can grab hold of."[22] Literature differs from older forms of writing in that it does not lay down rules for how certain people, objects, and topics should be presented. As a practice of knowledge production that is literary in this sense, indisciplinary scholarship not only has the quality of *a-disciplinarité* strictly speaking, that is, non-disciplinarity, the state of lacking disciplinarity or disciplinary principles; it is also a practice of using words in an undisciplined way, a practice of *verbis indisciplinatis*.[23]

Thus, in *La nuit des prolétaires*, a book that Rancière describes as belonging neither to history nor to philosophy properly speaking, in which he puts the indisciplinary principle to work by blurring the lines between history, philosophy, and sociology, and which is also possibly the best book available on the Saint-Simonian utopian religion of work and technology, he reports that he took Virginia Woolf's *The Waves* as his model for writing the history of the appropriation of philosophical, literary, and theological language by manual laborers in nineteenth-century France.[24] Woolf's most experimental novel follows the interconnected lives of a group of friends by interweaving their interior soliloquies, without additional narrative structure. It handles its themes of being-together and being-apart by means of its very narrative form, influencing Rancière's singular work of labor history by means of this formal feature. An unstable, even undecidable, position that Rancière takes in this book with respect to the political effect of the many socialist religions that were created in early 1830s France is a result of this particular literary influence, and it is exemplary for the manner in which it is deployed: not as a theory about religion and politics, nor as a standard Marxist "criticism of heaven," but, especially insofar as it weighs the effects of the *Pantheismusstreit* on these debates, as a philosophically and even theologically subtle story about the conflict between a variety of different actors from different segments of society, over the means by which a common world might be reimagined, reorganized, reinvented, a story in which definitions of God and religious community were very much at stake. The discussion and debate of theological ideas by working-class intellectuals of this time and place is not notable for its conformity to a certain ideal of "working-class thought," responsive and responsible to the miserable conditions of laborers.

Rancière's radical idea is that the thoughts of these plebeians are not reducible to an identity determined by the way they spend their hours and use their hands at work, but are instead the result of a refusal to be identified by these works and days. As an effort to write labor history as a story about "an exchange of arguments and fantasies . . . passions and frenzy," *Nuits* does not give itself the task of recovering the authentic voice of the proletarian philosopher, perhaps as a counterweight to his contemporaries (say, Hegel), but restores a voice inasmuch as it attests to an "impossible quest."[25] Among Rancière's commentators, Oliver Davis appears to be the only one to have recognized that this book amounts to a contestation of the way in which critical theory of religion is so often practiced. "If the role of religious mysticism in working-class thought had seemed suspect to a Marxist and socialist historical tradition which sought to explain protest in predominantly material terms (working conditions, class consciousness, trade practices and so forth), then Rancière," writes Davis, "puts a strong case for seeking to try harder to understand the personally transformative and politically transgressive role which an encounter with such 'improper science' had in the lives of some of those touched by it."[26] In the context of this history, the ideas produced by the many utopian religions of the time were so many forms of impossibility, so many impossible ways of de-realizing the common world as found by both the bourgeois "apostles" of Saint-Simon and the proletarians attracted to their message.

So Rancière never falls back on the old Marxist criticism of religion as false consciousness, but nor does he follow Walter Benjamin in looking to theological images or forms of reasoning for assistance in articulating the struggle for emancipation. If he talks about religion, he declines to give special weight to words from the religious archive *as such*. That they belong to a certain history of sacralized, desacralized, and resacralized things does not imply that they require special handling. When it comes to theological tropes, it is a matter not of explicating the usage of concepts whose valence comes from their place in a religious past, but of thinking what Rancière in an interview calls a "circulation between theological meaning and empirical meaning."[27] The method of equality inquires into these kinds of circulations, these ways of reimagining the borderlines between the real and the unreal that make possible a questioning of the established distribution of roles and territories.

One finds this method deployed in the exemplary indisciplinary gesture of Rancière's essay on "The Surface of Design," which breaks with the accepted principles for dividing up intellectual labor among literary critics, art historians, and philosophers. In this piece, he audaciously posits the existence of an idea of "symbol" or "type" that would be common to the industrial designer Peter Behrens and the poet whose name is virtually synonymous with "art for art's sake," Stéphane Mallarmé. Not only does this essay convincingly call into question received wisdom about the absolute opposition between functionalism and noninstrumental abstraction in the modernist period, it gives itself to think the configuration of a surface common to spirituality or ideality and materiality, thus a circulation between sense and sense, that is, a circulation between sensible material givens and the spiritual (if not theological) *sens* that seeks to determine it and make it serve a certain role within a common world. "Mallarmé's types," writes Rancière, are "a substitute for the sacraments of religion . . . the consecration of human artifice and human imagining as such,"²⁸ a form of elevation without sacrifice. Without saying as much, Behrens, inspired as he is by the neo-Gothic Arts and Crafts movement represented by John Ruskin, William Morris, and the like, would be involved in a similar project of furnishing contemporary society with a "spiritual unity" that it lacks.²⁹

Another recent deployment of an analysis of circulations between the theological and the empirical is a fascinating account of the return of logics of incarnation that traverse the worlds of contemporary art and continental European philosophy alike, incarnation being a form of circulation between word(s) and presence. The title of a spring 2008 conference at the University of Chicago, dedicated to unpacking the implications of this new hope, is representative of this phenomenon: "the return to presence," that is, the new interest among artists and among theorists of art and culture in "forms of immediacy, intensity, encounter, contact, the Real, excess, event, birth, suddenness, in a word, whatever breaks through (shatters, overwhelms, exceeds . . .) the hermeneutic enterprise."³⁰ As it aims to circumvent not only hermeneutics, but any positive relation between sensibility and intelligibility, Rancière might describe this trend as it applies to specifically visual art and culture, a trend characterizing not so much artistic practice as theorization about art, in the following way: "this is what is demanded by the contemporary celebration of the image or its nostalgic evocation: an immanent transcendence, a glorious essence of the image guaranteed by the very mode of its material production,"³¹ in other words, a new form of incarnation, a new relation between spirit and flesh that evades the detour of the letter (and with it, perhaps, the egalitarian principle of literarity).

This desire for a pure power of incarnation that circumvents any relation between words and life (letter and spirit), but is instead deployed by the image's sheer materiality, or depending on you talk to, alterity, implies a vision of community. Specifically, it implies, in Ranciere's terms, a vision of *ethical* community, as opposed to *political* community; as opposed to the latter, ethical community "revokes every project of collective emancipation,"³² dedicating itself to strengthening existing "social bonds." Ethical community is to political community as consensus is to dissensus. The recent theoretical penchant for pure, excessive, incommensurable alterity or materiality implies a subjection of the common to some absolute force that both overwhelms it and encloses it in a new circle of the Whole or the totality. By associating incarnation with ethical as against political community, even making his argument depend on this association, Rancière seems to imply that this latter-day reappearance of the theological in the world of art is a matter of consensus rather than dissensus. In this context, he does not consider how it might be the case that, as Philip Goodchild puts it, "religious experience . . . is a break with consensual reality and a consensual state of consciousness; it is exceptional."[33] Nor does Rancière consider how liturgies and other religious practices might stage a different common world, a different way of partitioning the sensible order than what one gets in the world of work, a sphere in which one's identity is bound up with one's occupation. That is to say, he does not consider how religious practices have the capacity to define and redefine specific distributions of the sensible.[34] The method of equality would, then, benefit from being exposed to, which is to say complicated by, distributions and partitions of the sensible whose forms of symbolization (taking symbol here in the sense of the "Surface of Design" essay discussed above: as an "abstract element shared by the thing, the form, and its idea"[35]) and sense-making derive from theological and religious figures and forms.

In addition to opening a new set of questions that Rancière's own deployments of the method of equality have yet to pose in greater detail, an indisciplinary approach to religions might escape the institutional-epistemological-disciplinary demand that one align with either the empirical or the speculative,[36] thereby enabling an investigation of the ways in which forms of theological meaning have, in different places and times, contributed to specific formations of common sense, making earthly life "waver in appearance"[37] in different ways and to different degrees, establishing (and transforming) relationships between empirical sensibility and theological intelligibility. An indisciplinary practice of knowledge about forms of piety and religious community would situate itself in the unstable place between these two forms of sense.

Notes

1. Jacques Attali calls for a similar mode of theory, which he also distinguishes from "multidisciplinary" work. *Noise: The Political Economy of Music*, trans. Brian Massumi (Minneapolis: University of Minnesota Press, 1985), 5.

2. *Philosophy and the Spontaneous Philosophy of the Scientists and Other Essays*, trans. Ben Brewster, ed. Gregory Elliott (New York: Verso, 1990), 78, 97. Hereafter referred to in text as SPS.

3. Louis Althusser, *Lenin and Philosophy*, trans. Ben Brewster (New York: Monthly Review Press, 2001), 120–126.
4. Louis Althusser, *La leçon d'Althusser* (Paris: Gallimard, 1974), 258.
5. Ibid., 254.
6. Daniel Brudney, *Marx's Attempt to Leave Philosophy* (Cambridge, Mass.: Harvard University Press, 1998), 7.
7. Jean-Luc Nancy, "Jacques Rancière and Metaphysics," in *Jacques Rancière: History, Politics, Aesthetics*, ed. Gabriel Rockhill (Durham, N.C.: Duke University Press, 2009), 85.
8. Jacques Rancière, *The Philosopher and His Poor*, trans. John Drury, Corinne Oster, and Andrew Parker (Stanford, Calif.: Stanford University Press, 2003), 170.
9. See Pierre Bourdieu, *Sociology in Question*, trans. Richard Nice (London: Sage, 1993), 10.
10. See, e.g., Pierre Bourdieu, *The Craft of Sociology*, ed. Beata Kreis, trans. Richard Nice (New York: de Gruyter, 1991), 14, 17, 22.
11. "Jacques Rancière and Indisciplinarity: An Interview," trans. Gregory Elliott, *Art and Research* 2, no. 1 (2008): 2–3.
12. Jacques Rancière, "Thinking between Disciplines," *Parrhesia* 1 (2006): 9.
13. E.g., Michel Serres, *Conversations on Science, Culture, and Time*, trans. Roxanne Lapidus (Ann Arbor: University of Michigan Press, 1995), 37–38.
14. Bourdieu, *The Craft of Sociology*, 27.
15. See Gaston Bachelard, *La philosophie du non* (Paris: Presses Universitaires de France, 1988).
16. Rancière, "Thinking between Disciplines," 11–12.
17. Although Agamben gives a brief theological reading of the basic principles of his political philosophy in *The Time That Remains*, trans. Patricia Dailey (Stanford, Calif.: Stanford University Press, 2005), 57–58. I also try to put Rancière's idea of a distribution of the sensible to work in "The Prophethood of Work and the Gospels of *The Souls of Black Folk*," *Political Theology* 13, no. 1 (2013): 60–75.
18. Jacques Rancière, *Les scènes du peuple: Les révoltes logiques, 1975–1985* (Lyon: Horlieu, 2003), 29–30.
19. For a discussion of how this principle of fiction is not a claim about the inaccessibility of the truth of the real, but is instead the principle that this truth is accessible only through a certain "interpenetration of the logic of facts and the logic of stories," see Jacques Rancière, *The Politics of Aesthetics*, trans. Gabriel Rockhill (New York: Continuum, 2004), 38–39.
20. This is not the context to explain what is meant by "aesthetic regime." For a good overview of the argument behind this concept, see *Aesthetics and Its Discontents*, trans. Steven Corcoran (Malden, Mass.: Polity Press, 2009), 17–44.
21. Jacques Rancière, "The Politics of Literature," *SubStance* 33, no. 1 (2004): 10.
22. Jacques Rancière, *The Politics of Literature*, trans. Julie Rose (Malden, Mass.: Polity Press, 2011), 13.
23. On this term, see Michel de Montaigne's very different usage of it in his essay *On Prayers* in *Essais* I.56. *The Complete Essays*, ed. and trans. M. A. Screech (New York: Penguin Books, 2003), 361.
24. Davide Panagia and Jacques Rancière, "Dissenting Words: A Conversation with Jacques Rancière," *Diacritics* 30, no. 2 (2000): 121.
25. Rancière, *Les scènes du peuple*, 21, 30.
26. Oliver Davis, *Jacques Rancière* (Malden, Mass.: Polity, 2010), 57.
27. Jacques Rancière, "Aesthetics against Incarnation: An Interview by Anne Marie Oliver," *Critical Inquiry* 35, no. 1 (2008): 175.

28. Jacques Rancière, *The Future of the Image*, trans. Gregory Elliott (New York: Verso, 2007), 97.

29. Ibid., 100.

30. "The Return to Presence," http://german.uchicago.edu/05_events/events_archive.html, accessed August 19, 2011; no longer available. An example of this kind of position is elaborated in Hans Ulrich Gumbrecht, *The Production of Presence: What Meaning Cannot Convey* (Stanford, Calif.: Stanford University Press, 2004).

31. Rancière, *The Future of the Image*, 9.

32. Rancière, *Aesthetics and Its Discontents*, 21.

33. Philip Goodchild, *Capitalism and Religion: The Price of Piety* (New York: Routledge, 2003), 194.

34. The categories of "*partage du sensible*," the concept whereby Rancière operates a link between aesthetics and politics, are "appearance, play, work"; *Aesthetics and Its Discontents*, 31.

35. Rancière, *The Future of the Image*, 102.

36. In an interview, Rancière nicely summarizes the principle about knowledge production that we have been investigating in this paper: "The prescriptive and descriptive are always interlaced in such a way that they constitute landscapes of the possible (the one who describes reconfigures the possibles of a world; the one who prescribes presupposes a certain state of the world that is itself made up of sedimented prescriptions). The configuration of these landscapes is always, in the last instance, a poem: an expression in common language of the common resources of thought." "Jacques Rancière et a-disciplinarité," in *Et tant pis pour les gens fatigués: Entretiens* (Paris: Editions Amsterdam, 2009), 477.

37. *La nuit des prolétaires: Archives du rêve ouvrier* (Paris: Librairie Arthème Fayard, 1981), 31.

11 Overwhelming Abundance and Everyday Liturgical Practices

For a Less Excessive Phenomenology of Religious Experience

Christina M. Gschwandtner

A LOGIC OF SUPERABUNDANCE describing experience at the limit. Excessively saturated phenomena to which we are devoted with total and kenotic abandon. Absolute and utter immediacy—the very Life of God in our self-affecting passion. Limitless desire for the undeconstructible impossible. Abnegation. Liminality. The Immemorial. The Unhoped for. Contemporary phenomenology of religion exalts in the absolute, the excessive, the radical, and the extreme. The experiences it depicts always balance on the very edge of the abyss, on the very line of liminality, on the razor blade of the most extreme paradox.

Until fairly recently phenomenology barred any talk of the divine or faith from its investigations. Husserl was quite clear that any notion of transcendence must be radically excluded from phenomenology and that therefore religion would lie outside phenomenological endeavors and cannot be examined by phenomenology.[1] Heidegger, especially in his early thought, also drew a radical distinction between phenomenology and theology.[2] There is an "absolute difference" between the two and, in fact, theology is much more like geometry or chemistry than it is like philosophy. Theology is a regional or ontic science, while phenomenology is more fundamental and ontological. While phenomenology examines the experience of *Dasein* as such, theology can examine only the much more limited and regional experience of a particular expression of faith. Much French phenomenology, from Sartre onward, was rigorously atheistic or at the very least agnostic. Dominique Janicaud reiterated this conviction in regard to what he perceived as a troubling "theological turn" in recent French phenomenology.[3] He argues that several contemporary thinkers, especially Emmanuel Levinas, Jean-Luc Marion, and Michel Henry have subverted phenomenology by reintroducing metaphysical questions and abandoning rigorous phenomenological method by engaging in a "maximalist" phenomenology. Instead, he suggests, phenomenology should focus on "every-day phenomena" and the more immediate data of human experience.[4]

Contemporary Phenomenologies of Religious Experience

Several contemporary thinkers have responded to these "atheistic" tendencies in phenomenology and instead attempted to develop phenomenological treatments of the divine or of religious experience. Jean-Yves Lacoste challenges Heidegger's radical distinctions between the two fields and argues that human being-before-God, although optional and voluntary, is a valid phenomenological experience and in fact one that goes much deeper and shows something more fundamental about human experience than Heidegger's analyses of anxiety, care, and being-toward-death do.[5] Jean-Louis Chrétien has provided careful phenomenological depictions of many kinds of religious moments and activities, such as those of prayer, of the call, of promise, of beauty.[6] Michel Henry has argued more radically that Christianity provides the only truly phenomenological account of the total immanence of human fleshly experience and gives the only genuine access to reality.[7] Probably the most well-known thinker is Jean-Luc Marion, who has developed the notion of the saturated phenomenon for describing a phenomenon of revelation, which is an experience of the divine that is so radical and excessive that it blinds us entirely in its abundant self-givenness and that we cannot grasp or comprehend it.[8]

Almost all of these contemporary proposals are characterized by very excessive language. Let me briefly focus on a couple of examples in more detail, beginning with Marion's notion of the saturated phenomenon. First of all, Marion repeatedly tells us that he is looking for a new "first" or "last philosophy" (the two end up meaning the same thing for him). This would be a phenomenology ordered by an absolute principle, one that is completely pure, concerned with the most abundantly given.[9] This most purely given is the saturated phenomenon. A saturated phenomenon is a phenomenon that is utterly excessive and gives itself entirely on its own account. We experience it as completely overwhelming, as something that we cannot control or contain. It is so brilliant and bedazzling that it blinds us and makes it impossible to express it in a concept: "The excess of intuition overcomes, submerges, exceeds—in short, saturates—the measure of each and every concept" (*IE*, 159). At one point Marion describes its impact as like that of an explosion that hits a screen. The event itself cannot be seen, but its radical impact can be measured. The saturated phenomenon of revelation is saturated to the second degree, a paradox of paradoxes that transcends all horizons and any parameters in which its phenomenality could possibly be measured (i.e., it is beyond quantity, quality, relation, and modality). It gives too much, is too brilliant, one can have no relation with it, and so forth. Marion introduces its possibility by saying: "Saturation passes beyond itself, exceeds the very concept of maximum, and finally gives its phenomenon without remainder or reserve" (*BG,* 241). In a more recent text he makes the very impossibility of God a foundation for thinking divine possibility.[10] While this might be very appropriate for talking about the divine, similar excess seems to characterize all religious experience. Even the devoted gives him- or herself "par excellence" (*BG,* 323). In fact, *adonné* itself is an extreme term: it means that I am utterly "devoted" to the saturated phenomenon, completely "given over" to it, "addicted" to it, obsessed with it. It seems that religious experience is like being on drugs. Marion himself reinforces this perception: "The excess of intuition is accomplished in the form of stupor, or even of the terror that the incomprehensibility resulting from excess imposes on us" (*IE,* 161). He uses similarly extreme language in his account of eros, where love is repeatedly compared to a declaration of war and the lover expected to abandon him- or herself entirely to the beloved in utterly sacrificial devotion.[11]

Michel Henry is maybe even more extreme than Marion. He insists that the "Truth of Christianity" (which he consistently capitalizes), is absolutely different from the "truth of the world" and differs from it in its very essence (*IT,* 23; Henry italicizes this insight in the text for extra emphasis). While biology shows us absolutely nothing of life, Christianity alone gives us access to Life as such. This Life is the absolute divine self-revelation to which we have access as we realize our own self-affection flowing from this divine Life.[12] This is what Henry calls being a "son of God": being directly and immediately rooted in the divine absolute Life and experiencing that very life in one's own most immediate joys and sufferings.[13] Henry stresses this immediacy: there is no separation at all between myself and my flesh; joy and suffering are experienced directly, and no phenomenological distinction can be made between the phenomenon and its phenomenality. This pathos that I experience in my flesh is the absolute life of God. No authentication for this experience of the divine is necessary: "Only one who has entered into that absolute truth can, illuminated by it, hear what is said in the Gospel, which is nothing other than that absolute Truth that, revealing itself to itself, reveals itself to that person" (*IT,* 10). Throughout Henry's work the starkest distinctions are drawn between the Life, Truth, and Passion of Christianity, which are all essentially equated with the divine Life, and the unreal, false, lying, and manipulative truth and life of the world, represented by Galileo and technology. Despite the important criticisms of technology articulated throughout Henry's writings, this seems just a bit too black and white.

John D. Caputo, although quite critical of Marion and Henry, is equally radical in his writings. He constantly stresses the impossible and the undeconstructible or, more recently, the absolute event. In fact, it seems that almost everything is impossible: forgiveness, the gift, hospitality, the event, justice, democracy, love and so forth.[14] Deconstruction, we are told is "the affirmation of the impossible, of the coming of the event . . . of the hyper-real."[15] This event is "an event that is unforeseeable, unimaginable, uncontainable, undeconstructible."[16] Caputo's language is throughout drenched in superlatives. Religion is "that notion of life at the limit of the possible, on the verge of the impossible."[17] Faith is similarly impossible: "By faith I mean the feeling that wells up in us when we take our measure against some immeasurable immensity, like the feeling that stirs within us when we stand at the ocean's edge at midnight, alone."[18] Faith is consistently associated with limitless passion, inordinate desire for we know not what, excessive undecidability:

> Everything turns on keeping the gap between the name and the event open, on keeping the tension between them strong and alive, and thereby to be transported by that tension into the passion of life. The passion of life, the passion of desire, the passion of prayer, is fueled by revving up this tension to the breaking point. Undecidability fires passion to the limit, feeding the flames of faith in the unknown God by the very fluctuation of names. It is when I truly do not know what I desire that desire is fired white-hot. It is when I truly do not know if there is anyone to pray to that I find myself praying like mad. [WG, 298]

Yet, is the passion devoted to prayer really as disproportionately related to the emptying of its content and the undecidability of its addressee as Caputo suggests? Why would *not* knowing even whether there is anyone to pray to make me *more* committed to doing so? The "poetics of the kingdom" is put in particularly extreme terms:

> Unlike logic, it is a discourse with pathos, with a passion and a desire, with an imaginative sweep and a flare, touched by a bit of madness, hence more of an a-logic or even a patho-logic, one that is, however, not sick but healing and salvific. A poetics of the impossible describes the dynamics of a desire beyond desire for the kingdom, a desire beyond reason and beyond what is reasonably possible, a desire to know what we cannot know, or to love what we dare not love, like a beggar in love with a princess, whose desire is not extinguished by the impossible but fired by it. For our hearts are burning with a desire to go where we cannot go, to the impossible, praying and weeping for what eye has not seen nor ear heard, hoping against hope. [WG, 104]

While in Marion we at least encounter something (even if it is entirely excessive and certainly not a "thing"), in Caputo the empty desire itself appears to conjure all the excess up on its own.

Even Paul Ricoeur, who is usually much more balanced, speaks of religious language and experience in extreme terms. In analyzing biblical language he points especially to its use of paradox and hyperbole: "Paradoxes and hyperboles dissuade hearers in some way from forming a coherent project of their lives and from making their existence into a continuous whole."[19] Religious language challenges and disorients us precisely by its excessive nature:

> In the same way that the proverb (submitted to the law of paradox and hyperbole) only reorients by first disorienting, the parable (submitted to what I call the law of extravagance) *makes the extraordinary break forth in the ordinary*. Indeed, there is no parable that does not introduce into the very structure of the plot an implausible characteristic, something insolent, disproportionate; that is, something scandalous. Thus it is the contrast between the realism of the story and the extravagance of the denouement that gives rise to the kind of drift by means of which the plot and its point are suddenly carried off toward the Wholly Other. [FS, 229; emphasis mine]

For Ricoeur, this leads to a reorientation of our lives.[20] Repeatedly, he contrasts what he calls the "logic of the world," which is a logic of equivalence, with religious logic or the logic of Jesus, which is a logic of "superabundance." This excessive logic is particularly evident in Jesus' sayings and parables:

> And this pattern is that of a sort of excess of response in relation to the response that is normally expected. Yet, each response gives more than that asked by ordinary prudence. The right cheek? The other one also! The coat? The cloak as well! One mile? One mile more! Not just this, but even that! It is this *giving more* that appears to me to constitute the point of these extreme commands. And beyond this giving more is manifested the same logic of Jesus that can be found in his parables, proverbs, and eschatological sayings. This logic of generosity clashes head on with the logic of equivalence that orders our everyday exchanges, our commerce, and our penal law. [FS, 281; emphasis his]

The main characteristic of the logic of faith is precisely its excessive and extreme nature.

Contemporary phenomenology of religion, then, almost always operates at an excessive and radical level and appears to disregard more mundane religious experience. These (and other) thinkers focus exclusively on religious experience in its most excessive and extraordinary register. They are about ecstasy, mystical experience, radical transfiguration.[21] All are, so to speak, mountaintop encounters. Ordinary humans rarely seem capable of experiencing them. If examples of concrete figures are given, they tend to be the great mystics: Teresa of Avila, John of the Cross, Joan of Arc, the original disciples, or most prominently Christ himself.[22] Indeed, the contemporary conversation seems to think religious experience almost exclusively in the singular. The Mystic. The Ascetic. The Saint. The Fool for Christ. The Lover. Apparently, religious experience is only for outstanding individuals who are alone in their dark night of terror or bathed in the dazzling sunshine of bliss. This is not to say, of course, that such experiences do not happen or have no validity. But the problem is precisely the fact that all religious experience here seems to be thought in terms of such excessive, extraordinary, and usually individual instances, instances that are rare, even for the great mystics, and that are notoriously difficult to confirm or document. And how would it be possible to analyze such excessive experiences phenomenologically? Such phenomena are essentially not testable or repeatable and possibly not even particularly representative of genuine spiritual life. By their very nature such experiences are rarely communicable.[23] Surely such events do happen; we have too many accounts of them to doubt their existence entirely. Yet, they are unusual and certainly are not the average religious experience. And, in fact, such excessive encounters are played down by the very people who undergo them. Teresa of Avila and John of the Cross both emphasized that levitation or visions of demons or the divine are not proof of high spirituality or particular holiness.[24] The saints consistently exhorted their followers and communities not to strive for such experiences, but instead to be faithful to the practices of prayer and sacramental participation in their communities and those provided by their ecclesial structures and practices. Similarly, the desert monastics warned others of imitation of extreme feats of asceticism merely for the sake of excess.[25] While these extreme experiences do and did take place (and certainly do deserve some sort of phenomenological recognition), they are not the norm for the believer or for the life of faith more generally. Richard Kearney puts it well: "We're not all desperate Desert Fathers waiting for Godot as the apocalyptic dusk descends! It need not be that angst-ridden or melodramatic. The world is a place of light and dark: we always have a little bit of both."[26] Without dismissing the possibility of such phenomena (or making any sort of judgment about their source), I would submit that these are not the best places to look for a phenomenological analysis of religious experience.

At the same time, this emphasis on mystical excess has led to a kind of "quietism" in Continental philosophy of religion. Rarely do any of these thinkers engage social or political issues.[27] Marion especially has been repeatedly criticized for paying no attention to ethical or political questions,[28] but a similar claim could be made about most of these thinkers: social or political concerns do not usually appear on the horizon in their descriptions of religious experience.[29] It is not immediately obvious, of course, that a description of religious experience must necessarily have political implications. Yet, religion has had and continues to have tremendous social and political import in both positive and negative ways. It is hence troubling that the emphasis on excess and bedazzlement comes much closer to describing the experiences of religious fundamentalisms than it does to depicting more benign (and more common) experiences of faith.[30] Does not the blind and radical faith of the suicide bomber fit the description of a saturated phenomenon much better than the volunteer serving in a soup kitchen or helping in an inner-city after-school program? The concrete works of justice and mercy that are by many measures the most salutary effects of religious faith seem, in fact, the most removed from the description of abundance and liminality provided by these thinkers. Something is awry when a phenomenology of religious experience provides a better description of religious extremism than of the social action that flowed out of the faith of Mother Theresa, Dorothy Day, or Martin Luther King Jr.[31]

How, then, might we "tone down" the excess in the phenomenology of religious experience? How might we include more common and more "average" religious experiences? How might we, as Kearney proposes, return to the "everyday" and the "littlest things"?[32] I suggest that we do so by articulating a phenomenology of liturgical experience rather than one of individual mystical transfiguration. Lacoste has already begun to go in that direction with his analysis of human being-before-God, which he does indeed name "liturgical" being. Yet, he is quite clear that he is not really talking about ecclesial liturgy, but instead of more general being-before-God. And although the emphasis on "more general" being is salutary, his examples are indeed again limit-experiences and individual experiences of excess: the ascetic, the pilgrim, the fool for Christ, who are engaged in all-night vigils and other acts of radical abnegation.[33] Something similar is true of Chrétien. Although he stresses the communal and bodily experiences of faith much more than the other thinkers,[34] still he tends to speak of excessive and unusual experiences or at least focuses on their most excessive and special characteristics.[35] It is precisely his avowed intent to show "the extraordinary in the ordinary."[36] His beautiful phenomenological analyses go a long way toward demonstrating that phenomenological analysis of religious experience is possible and meaningful. But ultimately these experiences are still on some level about abundance and excess. Let us turn instead to liturgy.[37]

Toward a Phenomenology of Liturgical Practices

Phenomenology is the study of experience.[38] And liturgy is most fundamentally experiential. Liturgy happens as an event in which the whole gathered community participates. The word itself means "work of the people."[39] Liturgy lends itself to phenomenological analysis because it provides a plethora of experiences. It has noetic aspects: it can be observed, felt, imagined, even judged. And it abounds in noematic content: liturgy involves the whole body and all of the senses by providing things to see, to touch, to hear, to taste, to smell. It is not passive: the body stands, moves, bows, kneels, prostrates, crosses itself, and moves forward for participation in the Eucharist. And although there are indeed liturgical texts, these texts become liturgy only when they are chanted and sung and practiced, when we become fully involved in them. Liturgy takes place in space and time. It is not an other-worldly experience, but it happens in the here and now, even while remembering the past (*anamnesis*) and anticipating the future (*eschaton*).[40] The way it arranges space and time is deliberate, and these arrangements can be observed, depicted, and analyzed. It matters where and when one stands, sits, or kneels. The narthex, the nave, the sanctuary, or the altar have particular significance and meaning, and the liturgy moves around and through them in ways that are concretely exercised and meaningful. All these things can be observed and experienced: liturgy provides plenty to intuit.

Second, liturgy is cyclical and follows established patterns. Thus it provides naturally the back-and-forth between intuition and intention explicated by Husserlian phenomenology. The longer we participate in liturgy, the more we expect its regular patterns to reoccur. Plenty is given to intuition, but contra Marion, intention is also fully present.[41] Liturgy is not so overwhelming that it completely sweeps us away. Rather, we come to liturgy with expectations, and these expectations are disappointed or confirmed. We are not always and entirely blind. Meaning emerges precisely through this cycle of repetition. Much study has been done (mostly through sociology and anthropology of religion) about how ritual and symbol are meaningful.[42] Thus, for example, we form concepts about what the Eucharist means and how it functions. Every time we approach the chalice, these expectations are filled with intuitive meaning or rendered inadequate and therefore rejected or reformed. We "intend" how the priest will move, what will be said, and how we are to respond. We prepare for liturgy by going to confession, by praying and fasting. Because we do so over and over, we begin to recognize, to know what it means, and to perceive its "signification." In fact, this may be why many Roman Catholics or Eastern Orthodox who have not attended church in years will still cross themselves almost automatically when they enter a church and will have a pretty good idea of what to do and what to expect from a service. This is also why liturgical cycles matter, why we celebrate the same feasts over and over again, and have several periods of fasting every year. Their meaning emerges precisely through their recurring nature.

Third, liturgy is communal. One's personal experience can be validated or indeed criticized by the experience of the community. Liturgy cannot be celebrated on one's own.[43] Thus, signification of the liturgical experience arises through communication about it, whether in terms of homily, catechesis, or indeed informal communal conversation. We can evaluate whether liturgies are life-giving or death-dealing by the experience they communicate and foster. This is an absolutely fundamental point. What makes individual mystical experience or even an analysis of prayer so problematic phenomenologically is its unique and often unrepeatable nature. What renders thinkers like Janicaud so uncomfortable with Marion's and Henry's accounts is to some extent precisely this extremely individualized aspect of their examples.[44] How do we confirm what Joan of Arc or Teresa of Avila experienced?[45] We do approach spiritual experience and even prayer with certain expectations based on our prior participation in the traditions and actions of particular communities.[46] Thus experience can be verified by comparing it to that of others and especially by experiencing it together.[47]

Fourth, liturgical practices allow for, indeed require, hermeneutics and discernment. Both Marion and Henry have been quite critical of hermeneutics and reluctant to acknowledge its importance in analyzing phenomena of religious experience. Marion now admits that hermeneutics might be at work in the historical event, possibly even in the face of the other.[48] But in general he is quite dismissive about it and criticizes the fact that theologians find it more interesting than phenomenology.[49] Henry categorically rejects the hermeneutic exercise for phenomenology.[50] True phenomenology of the flesh is one of utter immediacy and requires no hermeneutics whatsoever. It is completely self-authenticating. Hermeneutics would imply interpretive distance and judgment. Thus it would deny the very project Henry proposes, namely a phenomenality of concrete experience. Yet, interpretation is absolutely central to phenomenological experience and to ascertaining its meaning. And do not religious practices especially require hermeneutic interpretation and judgment?[51] How do we know that we speak authentically of the divine? How do we know that some forms of worship are better than others? How do we criticize our own sense of revelation? How do we interpret what the scriptures say? And liturgy is by its very nature hermeneutic. It arises out of a rich tradition that rejects certain types of worship or certain activities as inappropriate or inauthentic. This can of course lead to the kind of hardening of liturgy that believes that any kind of change is impossible or evil. Yet, it also assumes a continual cycle between the tradition and today's experience. Liturgy opens a world, in Ricoeur's terms, and invites us to inhabit this world.[52] We confirm its validity or truth by our continual and cyclical engagement within it, expecting certain things or insights and rejecting others.

Finally, liturgical experience is closely linked to action, and this action is taken to be meaningful beyond its immediate performance. Liturgy itself is already practiced, it is neither a passive experience nor is it solely based on texts. Yet, even more importantly, liturgy is supposed to have an effect on its participants and on the world. Many liturgies end with a call to action and an admonition to transform the world in accordance with the insights gained within the liturgy. Liturgical space and time are to transfigure "ordinary" space and time. Liturgy hence has profound social and political implications, even when it does not always make these explicit.[53] Liturgy flows from the deep conviction that liturgical actions both represent and shape the world, encapsulated in Kavanagh's oft-repeated claim that liturgy is "doing the world as it was supposed to be done."[54] Liturgy claims to be transforming the world into its eschatological reality, hence in some ways making the eschaton present already today.[55] And indeed many religious activities with social and political implications are closely connected to liturgical space and time.⁵⁶ Sometimes this link between liturgy and political action can seem quite tenuous or the liturgical justification for certain kinds of social actions unconvincing, but that does not detract from the fact that almost any religiously motivated activism either flows out of liturgical practices or that such practices are employed to motivate believers toward concrete actions.

Of course, a phenomenological analysis of liturgy necessarily abstracts to some extent from the experience. It observes and reduces the experience and attempts to validate it and to reach its meaning. It thus does not make judgments about whether God is indeed encountered in the liturgy or whether the liturgy does indeed transform the earth into the eschaton, although it can surely analyze the behavior of the ecclesial community in this regard. Any claims about existence "out there" are set aside or "put in parenthesis" by phenomenological reduction. Thus, phenomenology does not attempt to "prove" anything, certainly not God's existence and ultimately not even whether liturgy is meaningful and something in which we should participate.⁵⁷ Phenomenology is descriptive not prescriptive.

Yet, surely the close phenomenological study of liturgical experience is useful. Phenomenological analysis can give us some real insight into what religious believers do and what meaning they derive from it—and for such study hermeneutics is absolutely necessary. And close phenomenological and hermeneutic study may indeed arrive at a deeper and fuller account than what can be articulated by the average attendee at a worship service and may thus serve to illuminate liturgical practice itself. Such a richer account does not invalidate the experience but shows its meaning (it may even give some access to its "essence" in the Husserlian sense). At the same time such phenomenological analysis may enable the phenomenologist to appreciate and begin to understand the meaning of religious experiences and practices in a manner that deals with the actual experiences of religious communities instead of the rare and radical raptures of isolated individuals.

Theophany as an Example of Liturgical Practice

Let me take one particular example, a sliver from the Eastern Orthodox service of Theophany and attempt a brief phenomenological analysis.⁵⁸ Theophany is a celebration of Christ's baptism and in parishes on the new calendar coincides with the Western feast of Epiphany (which the East celebrates together with nativity, i.e., Christmas).⁵⁹ Theophany is also called the "Great Blessing of Waters" as big vats of water are blessed on that day, and Orthodox Christians take the holy water home to their houses. How might we discern the meaning of this event phenomenologically? When believers enter the church and throughout the elaborate and extensive ceremony, they experience many phenomena involving all of the senses: seeing (water, candles, icons, priest and altar servers in colorful vestments performing many different activities), hearing (singing, chanting, reading of scripture and prayers), smelling (incense and candles), tasting (water, wine, bread), and touching (icons, water, Gospel, hands of the priest). These are complex phenomena that are experienced within a larger context. Even the moment of the blessing of the waters provides plenty to intuit: the water is censed, candles and the cross are dipped into it, the priest breathes on it, and multiple prayers are read over it. It involves many activities by the whole congregation that alternate between standing and kneeling and finally include coming forward to drink the water and to be sprinkled with it.

These various sensory experiences can be confirmed through other people's experience and the fact that this service is repeated every year at the same time and in the same fashion. Intentions are fulfilled (or falsified) again and again. Believers come already with such intentions or expectations. This is a special day (one of the most important feasts) and they know what will happen. The transformation of ordinary water into holy water is anticipated. And indeed this "holiness" of the water is not a "scientific" but a phenomenological claim. It is the communal experience that confirms that the water becomes holy. It does so by the way the water is treated, carried carefully, drunk, saved for illness, sprinkled on other items for purification. The experience of the service is meaningful precisely in the communal response to what is performed. The water is regarded, treated, and experienced as holy. And this is a decidedly communal experience. The people pray and experience together.[60] In fact, in some traditionally Orthodox countries this particular holiday extends into a village or community celebration and is often held outside.[61]

But there is more: Can we "reduce" the experience and find its essential meaning? What signification might we attribute to the liturgical experience of Theophany? I would suggest that it has eminently social and political implications: its larger meaning is the sacredness of all of creation, which today can no longer be thought separately from the environmental destruction wreaked on this creation.[62] It is *water* that is blessed, not just people. The liturgical texts convey this meaning. All of creation participates in the liturgy, not merely the humans who are present in it (Jordan is consistently personified in the liturgical texts). And in the past the holy water was similarly sprinkled on animals and fields (this still happens in predominantly Orthodox countries). Certainly material objects, such as the icons and people's houses, are blessed with it. Theophany signifies the sacrality of space and time, the transformation of the merely material into a higher materiality that is sacred and holy, although it does not erase materiality itself. As Christ's baptism signifies the divine hallowing of all flesh, so the waters of Theophany make holy the material world, including (but not limited to) human and animal flesh.[63] And this, I would submit, has meaning that goes beyond the event in church. In a world in which water sources are increasingly polluted, aquifers are being depleted, weather patterns are shifting, bringing hurricanes to some places and droughts to others, this liturgy has phenomenological meaning beyond its place. It gives a different hermeneutic reading of our relationship to the natural world, one that hallows and sanctifies instead of exploiting and destroying; one that is just and merciful instead of oppressive of the poor and destructive of the planet. This liturgy provides an alternative to the secular liturgy of consumerism and pollution, of economic systems that desacralize and destroy. While there is surely something excessive and saturated also in these experiences, they provide a sacramentality of the mundane and worldly that may invite and embrace the secular and ordinary into its experience instead of escaping from it or rejecting it.

Notes

1. See especially §46–51 in *Ideas I*.
2. As developed in his article "Phenomenology and Theology," reprinted in *The Religious*, ed. John D. Caputo (Oxford: Blackwell, 2002), 49–66.
3. Translated by Bernard G. Prusak in Dominique Janicaud, et al., *Phenomenology and the "Theological Turn": The French Debate* (New York: Fordham University Press, 2000), 1–103.
4. See especially the final chapter, "Reorientation," of ibid., 86–103.
5. Jean-Yves Lacoste, *Experience and the Absolute* (New York: Fordham University Press, 2004), and *La phénoménalité de Dieu: Neuf études* (Paris: Cerf, 2008).
6. Jean-Louis Chrétien, *The Unforgettable and the Unhoped For,* trans. Jeffrey Bloechl (New York: Fordham University Press, 2002); *Hand to Hand: Listening to the Work of Art,* trans. Stephen E. Lewis (New York: Fordham University Press, 2003); *The Call and the Response,* trans. Anne A. Davenport (New York: Fordham University Press, 2004); *The Ark of Speech,* trans. Andrew Brown (London: Routledge, 2004).Chrétien has published many other books that have not yet been translated and include phenomenological analyses of promise, of sleep, of love, of beauty, and especially of the human voice.
7. Michel Henry, *I Am the Truth: Toward a Philosophy of Christianity,* trans. Susan Emanuel (Stanford, Calif.: Stanford University Press, 2003), hereafter cited as *IT*; *Incarnation: Une philosophie de la chair* (Paris: Seuil, 2000); *Words of Christ* (Grand Rapids, Mich.: William B. Eerdmans, 2012).
8. Jean-Luc Marion, *The Visible and the Revealed* (New York: Fordham University Press, 2009), which includes several of the essays elucidating the saturated phenomenon. See also *Being Given: Toward a Phenomenology of Givenness* (Stanford, Calif.: Stanford University Press, 2002), henceforth cited as *BG*, and *In Excess: Studies in Saturated Phenomena* (New York: Fordham, 2002), henceforth cited as *IE*, as well as his most recent works *Cértitudes négatives* (Paris: Grasset, 2010) and *Le croire pour le voir* (Paris: Parole et Silence, 2010).
9. "In all cases, the formula 'as much reduction, so much givenness' plays as last principle: not only the last one to be found, but above all the principle stating that the last—the seeming, in its supposed metaphysical fragility—is finally always equal to the single and unique first—to the appearing, the unique screen open to receive all manifestations, all truths, all realities. The last becomes first, the principle is defined as last principle, and thus phenomenology would only retake the title of 'first philosophy' in inverting it—'last philosophy'" (*In Excess*, 26–27). I

criticize this strong emphasis on purity in my article "Praise—Pure and Personal?" in *Phenomenology of Prayer*, ed. Bruce Ellis Benson and Norman Wirzba (New York: Fordham University Press, 2005).

10. Jean-Luc Marion, "The Impossible for Man—God," in *Transcendence and Beyond*, ed. John D. Caputo (Bloomington: Indiana University Press, 2005), reworked as ch. 2 of *Cértitudes négatives*.

11. I analyze this combative language about love in my article "Love as a Declaration of War?" in *Love's Wisdom*, ed. Bruce Ellis Benson and Norman Wirzba (Bloomington: Indiana University Press, 2009).

12. "The phenomenological analysis of life has shown that life's givenness to self in the transcendental 'me' is founded in absolute Life's givenness to self and is only possible through it. If absolute Life's self-givenness is God's self-revelation, then the latter is implicated in the life of the transcendental 'me,' which is only self-revealed in this absolute Life's self-revelation—that of God himself" (*IT*, 174).

13. "When 'man' is understood in his condition of Son generated in the original Ipseity of absolute Life, there is also a prior state of affairs. It is no longer programming but rather predestination—*the radical and essential pre-destination by virtue of which, through his condition of Son, a person is destined to be this living person generated in absolute Life's self-generation, living only from it, able to accomplish his own essence only in the essence of this absolute Life*" (*IT*, 184–185; emphasis his).

14. Of course, it's not simply impossible, it's impossible in a very complicated way where the impossibility of the impossible makes possible the possibility of the impossible.

15. John D. Caputo, *What Would Jesus Deconstruct? The Good News of Postmodernism for the Church* (Grand Rapids, Mich.: Baker Academic, 2007), 78.

16. John D. Caputo, The *Weakness of God: A Theology of the Event* (Bloomington: Indiana University Press, 2006), 123, henceforth cited as *WG*.

17. John D. Caputo, *On Religion* (London: Routledge, 2001), 11.

18. John D. Caputo, *Philosophy and Theology* (Nashville: Abingdon Press, 2006), 68.

19. Paul Ricoeur, *Figuring the Sacred: Religion, Narrative, and Imagination*, ed. Mark Wallace, trans. David Pellauer (Minneapolis: Fortress Press, 1995), 229, henceforth cited as *FS*.

20. "Parables, paradoxes, hyperboles, and extreme commandments all *dis*orient only in order to *re*orient us" (*FS*, 281).

21. In fact, Marion's example for the phenomenon of revelation is precisely the transfiguration (*Being Given*, 234–247). His example for the radical encounter with the saturated phenomenon is Caravaggio's painting of the calling of St. Matthew (also the image on the cover of the English translation). See *Being Given*, 283–287.

22. See, for example, Marion's analysis of the disciples' encounter with the resurrected Christ on the way to Emmaus. Henry mentions Joan of Arc's voices as an example for the immediacy of the divine word that requires no interpretation (*Words of Christ*, 132). Chrétien repeatedly refers to St. John of the Cross (*Unforgettable*, 76–77). In another context he analyzes the visions of St. Francis, St. Bonaventure, and several other saints (*Hand to Hand*, 38–44).

23. Kierkegaard's account of Abraham's struggle is the quintessential example of this. If he cannot even communicate the divine call to sacrifice Isaac to his wife Sarah, how does he know it really comes from God? How can he test this call? (See the final section of *Fear and Trembling*.) Symeon the New Theologian's poetry constitutes an interesting attempt to communicate ecstatic experiences. Like many other mystics, Symeon was very suspect to most of his contemporaries (and not only the ecclesial hierarchy). The poetry itself is evidence for Symeon's difficulty in expressing his encounters in prayer.

24. Teresa warns her nuns frequently not to put any stake in excessive experiences. Her *Interior Castle* (and many portions of her other works) is a guide to prayer that tries to establish patterns for religious experience that would make it possible to teach and evaluate it. The most famous imagery is probably that of the stages of watering and growing a garden. See, for example, chapters 11–16 of her *Life* for one outline of the stages of prayer (the one that employs the irrigation imagery) and chapter 17 for warnings about the dangerous effects of imagination and faulty memory. The works abound in similar admonitions. *The Collected Works of Teresa of Avila*, 3 vols., trans. Kieran Kavanaugh (Washington, D.C.: ICS Publications, 1987). These warnings of excessive experiences are frequent also in other religious traditions. Many rabbinic stories, for example, refuse extreme revelatory experiences in favor of interpretation of the already received word.

25. There are many stories of this sort in the *Apothegmata* (Sayings) of the desert fathers. To give just one example: Abba Anthony is sent into the city to see a doctor who helps the sick, to show him that this humble doctor without greater spiritual experiences is equal to him in holiness. *The Book of the Elders: Sayings of the Desert Fathers. The Systematic Collection*, trans. John Wortley (Collegeville, Minn.: Liturgical Press, 2012), 310.

26. Richard Kearney, *After God: Richard Kearney and the Religious Turn in Continental Philosophy*, ed. John Panteleimon Manoussakis (New York: Fordham University Press, 2006), 378.

27. In fact, in some ways the "theological turn" can be interpreted as precisely a turn away from the more politically engaged French philosophy of the sixties.

28. See, for example, several of the essays in Kevin Hart's edited volume *Counter-Experiences: Reading Jean-Luc Marion* (Notre Dame: Notre Dame University Press, 2007), especially the essays in part 4.

29. On this point John Caputo's work is an important exception. See especially the final chapter of his *What Would Jesus Deconstruct?* It is not always entirely clear, however, how his depictions of religion as blind faith in the impossible are directly connected to his calls for serving the poor and outcast of society.

30. It does suggest, however, that some of these descriptions might actually be useful for understanding the phenomenality of extreme expressions of religion, although they have to date not been employed in that way. Most of the thinkers tend to stick with entirely "positive" and benign religious examples in their work, but their insights may well prove valuable for making sense of the excessive emotion and even violence religion at times evokes.

31. While at first glance these also seem extreme examples, their faith was expressed not in mystical bedazzlement but in concrete work for the oppressed, poor, ill, and suffering.

32. Kearney calls this a "micro-eschatology." See his *The God Who May Be: A Hermeneutics of Religion* (Bloomington: Indiana University Press, 2001), his introductory essay in *After God*, and his most recent *Anatheism: Returning to God after God* (New York: Columbia University Press, 2010).

33. See, for example, ch. 5 "Existence as Vigil," as well as his analysis of the night (§55), or abnegation (§59), of asceticism and dispossession (§64), and of the "holy fool" (§§66–67). Abnegation is a central term in his analysis, which he defines as follows: "Abnegation must be understood, then, as a radical form of making oneself available, and as sanction for the liturgical dismantling of the 'subject'" (*Experience and the Absolute*, 162). Lacoste's language also has a tendency to fall into excess and superlatives. To give just one example: "Ascetic extravagation is not significant because it exceeds what everyone is strictly bound to do if they wish to lead a life that pleases God: it is significant because it pushes to the limit a logic that is already present, even if no more than discreetly implicit, as soon as man is willing to encounter the Absolute and the Absolute alone 'suffices' for him. We do not need the ascetics' extravagation for liturgical disappropriation to be thinkable, nor do we need them for it to be part of our

experience. They do, however, provide us with the best mirror in which to perceive what is ultimately at stake in this experience—that, in order to exist face-to-face with God, man may dress in clothing closely resembling the lunatic's" (178–179).

34. In fact, Chrétien is frequently critical of Henry's focus on utter immediacy in his analysis of the flesh. See, for example, *Unforgettable*, 69, 127, and the chapter "Body and Touch" in *Call and Response*.

35. This is particularly evident in his examinations of the "absolute immemorial," the "unforgettable" and the "unhoped for." For example: "Just as the immemorial—as my absolute past, my past which cannot be rendered present and which for me, for the one who writes or speaks here, never could be present—does not include the time of my historical life, so the immemorial has for me something excessive about it, an excess that founds me, that sends me and destines me, and is known to me only obliquely, in the excess of being" (*Unforgettable*, 16); "Forgetting is the measure of the excess of the Good over us" (38). Later he speaks of the "excess of the promise" (74, 77) and of the excess of the unforgettable (90).

36. "It is this *excess* of the encounter with things, other, world, and God that is at the center of the project of which this book is a part: this encounter requires, most imperatively, our response, and yet seems at the same time to prohibit it. Different figures of this excess have been tackled in successive works" (*Unforgettable*, 121; emphasis his).

37. By liturgy here I mean the ecclesial practices of faith: what happens in church (or temple or synagogue or other places of worship) when believers gather together on a daily or weekly basis. I do not presume to judge here whether this must be "high" or "low" liturgy. And while my concrete examples will be taken primarily from my own tradition, Eastern Orthodoxy, certainly even the most "unliturgical" Protestant services still display certain patterns of worship, although so-called high liturgy might lend itself more easily to this sort of analysis. And of course even liturgy can be "excessive" experience. Yet regular participation in liturgical practice is considerably more mundane and rarely characterized by momentous spiritual encounters. It is this more ordinary and everyday experience that I seek to examine here.

38. Phenomenology, as articulated by Husserl, is about a careful study of conscious experience in order to recognize its meaning and validity. As such, it guards against psychologism and scienticism, two emphases Husserl always tried to avoid. Phenomenology is thus not merely a study of mental or emotive experiences of consciousness that the analyst might call forth and interpret in terms of subconscious urges and desires. Here indeed religious phenomena might quickly (though unsatisfactorily) be explained in terms of needs and desires in the caricatures of religion provided by Feuerbach and Freud. Rather, phenomenology attempts to analyze experience on a higher or deeper level through phenomenological and eidetic reduction to essence and meaning. The phenomenon will truly be given if we can set aside all our preoccupations with its existence "out there" and focus instead on how it presents itself to consciousness in repeated experience. By experiencing the phenomenon over and over again, its essence can be constituted and confirmed through the experience of others. Phenomena thus emerge through the constant interplay of intuition and intention, which were never separated for Husserl. Intentionality designates precisely the way in which we approach the world already within certain contexts of meaning that are continually confirmed and challenged through experience. Phenomena are also, however, experienced in various modes, and how one approaches them is significant. Whether I perceive a phenomenon or imagine it or judge it or dream it makes an important difference in how the phenomenon is constituted and what meaning or signification is drawn from it. Heidegger enriches this project by contributing phenomenological analyses of moods and our experience in the world, our facticity and being-toward-death as fundamental orienters for experience. For both Husserl and Heidegger, and indeed for most thinkers following them, phenomenology is not a system or a theory, but a method: a method for carefully analyzing experience and revealing its meaning and valid-

ity. For Husserl, this validity is still understood primarily in scientific terms; from Heidegger onward it moves increasingly away from such scientific conceptions of verification and instead thinks itself more a type of revelation of the inner truth of experience.

39. It is not possible to include a full review of the rich field of liturgical studies here. For good introductions from a variety of traditions see: Alexander Schmemann, *For the Life of the World: Sacraments and Orthodoxy* (Crestwood, N.Y.: St. Vladimir's Seminary Press, 1973), and *Introduction to Liturgical Theology* (Crestwood, N.Y.: St. Vladimir's Seminary Press, 1986); Aidan Kavanagh, *On Liturgical Theology* (New York: Pueblo, 1984); David Fagerberg, *Theologia Prima: What Is Liturgical Theology?* (Chicago: Hillenbrand, 2004); Kevin Irwin, *Context and Text: Method in Liturgical Theology* (Collegeville, Minn.: Liturgical Press, 1994); Graham Hughes, *Worship as Meaning: A Liturgical Theology for Late Modernity* (Cambridge: Cambridge University Press, 2003); Gordon Lathrop, *Holy Things: A Liturgical Theology* (Minneapolis, Minn.: Fortress Press, 1993), *Holy People: A Liturgical Ecclesiology* (Minneapolis, Minn.: Fortress Press, 1999) and *Holy Ground: A Liturgical Ecology* (Minneapolis, Minn.: Fortress Press, 2003). The foremost Jewish liturgical scholar is Lawrence A. Hoffman. See especially his *Beyond the Text: A Holistic Approach to Liturgy* (Bloomington: Indiana University Press, 1987).

40. Of course it does believe itself to participate in a world beyond this one. But both the anamnetic (remembering past events, e.g., in a feast that celebrates them) and eschatological (entering the future "kingdom" and making it present in the celebration) dimensions of the liturgy occur in the *here and now*.

41. He is certainly right that intention cannot grasp or control the divine, yet intention does seem to play a much more important function in religious practices than he is willing to admit.

42. See especially Mircea Eliade's work. For a more philosophical treatment, see Paul Ricoeur's early writings on *The Symbolism of Evil*. Many liturgical scholars also focus on the importance of symbolism and ritual in worship. See, for example, David Powers, *Unsearchable Riches: The Symbolic Nature of Liturgy* (New York: Pueblo, 1984), and Gail Ramshaw-Schmidt, *Reviving Sacred Speech: The Meaning of Liturgical Language* (Akron, Ohio: OSL Publications, 2000).

43. Although Roman Catholic priests used to be allowed to "say Mass" on their own, that practice has been discouraged since Vatican II (and "concelebration" encouraged). The Orthodox church forbids celebration of the liturgy when the priest is the only one present. A Protestant service without congregation would be similarly unthinkable.

44. This would go a long way in helping Marion respond to the accusation (articulated most explicitly by Jean Benoist) that there is "nothing to see" in religious experience. See Marion's attempt to respond to this in *Visible and Revealed*, 122–124.

45. To some extent the injunction by Teresa's confessors for her to write down her experiences was precisely to make it possible to share them in some way. They were to be verified as authentic through their communicability and through their fitting into a certain accepted pattern.

46. This may be why Christian mystics tend to have revelations of Christ or Mary and Hindus or Buddhists generally do not, even when they have a very similar spiritual experience, e.g., in meditation. There are quite a few interesting sociological (and even neurological) studies comparing religious experiences of different religious traditions. One particularly well-known study compared the neurological responses and brainwave patterns of Catholic nuns during the prayer with that of Buddhist monks during meditation.

47. It might be interesting to investigate further to what extent some of Husserl's late work on community might be helpful here.

48. See his concessions in this respect especially in ch. 5 of *In Excess* (123–127).

49. See especially his early article "Christian Philosophy: Hermeneutic or Heuristic?" (*Visible and Revealed*, ch. 4). Similar comments appear repeatedly in his work. (See, for example, *In Excess*, 29.) A recent treatment of Marion's phenomenology stresses this lack of hermeneutics in particular: Shane Mackinlay, *Interpreting Excess: Jean-Luc Marion, Saturated Phenomena and Hermeneutics* (New York: Fordham University Press, 2010).

50. See especially *I Am the Truth*, 1–11 and (for a particularly dismissive comment) 225. *Words of Christ* argues even more strongly that the words of Christ are completely self-authenticating and require no interpretation whatsoever. I have criticized this dismissal of hermeneutics in my "Can We Hear the Voice of God? Michel Henry and the *Words of Christ*," in *Words of Life: New Theological Turns in French Phenomenology*, ed. Bruce Ellis Benson and Norman Wirzba (New York: Fordham University Press, 2010), 147–157.

51. Richard Kearney makes this point particularly convincingly. He argues that hermeneutic judgment and ethical discernment is absolutely necessary for identifying the "(w)holy other" (whether divine or demonic) and for guiding appropriate religious practices (whether "extending a cup of cold water" to the "least of these" or violence and terror in the name of religion). See especially his *The God Who May Be*, 76. Similar comments pervade his treatment in *Strangers, Gods and Monsters: Interpreting Otherness* (London: Routledge, 2003), and *Anatheism*.

52. Ricoeur develops this idea about the "world of the text" and its possibilities especially in regard to scriptural texts. See especially the early chapters (for example, "Philosophy and Religious Language" or "Manifestation and Proclamation") of *Figuring the Sacred* and the chapter on biblical interpretation (ch. 4) in *From Text to Action*. Yet, this also seems an excellent description of what happens in liturgy.

53. Bruce Morrill is the one to explicate this the most fully in his *Anamnesis as Dangerous Memory: Political and Liturgical Theology in Dialogue* (Collegeville, Minn.: Liturgical Press, 2000). There is extensive discussion of the social and political implications of liturgy in contemporary liturgical scholarship.

54. He makes this statement repeatedly in his *On Liturgical Theology*, and it becomes a guiding principle for the introduction to liturgical theology by his student David Fagerberg in his *Theologia Prima: What Is Liturgical Theology?*

55. According to liturgical scholar Alexander Schmemann this is the fundamental point of liturgy: it helps us to enter the kingdom here and now (see especially his *Life of the World* for a succinct statement of this, but most of his works make this fundamental argument).

56. This extends even to explicitly political action (again, in both positive and negative ways): many of the marches of the civil rights era began in churches and included rousing sermons and hymns; much of the activism in East Germany before the fall of the Iron Curtain was organized in churches or even took place there; several African tree-planting projects include religious ceremonies (this is also true of the tree-planting projects in Israel on the holiday of *Tu B'Sh'vat*). More negatively, historically the calls for the crusades were made in the context of religious ceremonies, and such ceremonies blessed the outgoing armies and "sanctified" their violence. Today, religiously precipitated violence in the Middle East and other Islamic countries often follows Friday prayer services. (That is not to say, of course, that Islam necessarily incites violence, but merely to give an example of the link between political action and liturgical experience.)

57. Here Marion's distinction between phenomenology's examination of the "possibility" of religious experience (leaving considerations regarding its "actuality" or "effectivity" or "truth" to theology) seems appropriate. See the extended footnote 90 in *Being Given* (367) in this regard.

58. The liturgical texts for the feast can be found in *The Festal Menaion*, trans. Kallistos Ware and Mother Mary (South Canaan, Penn.: St. Tikhon's Seminary Press, 1998), 295–387.

59. Some Orthodox countries (and immigrant parishes in the West) have not accepted the Gregorian calendar and still operate on the Julian one. They are thus thirteen days behind the "new" calendar. The feast of Theophany is a very early feast of which we have evidence going back to the fourth century. The tradition of blessing water is significantly later. See the introduction to the feast in *Menaion*, 55–59.

60. In fact, there is a canon that forbids private prayer during a service, since it is meant to be *communal* worship.

61. The rubrics call for a blessing of waters that takes place inside the church (over water that has been brought into the church) and another blessing outside over a flowing water source, such as a river or stream.

62. Almost all Orthodox scholars who write on environmental issues point to the importance of Theophany. For the fullest collection of Orthodox essays on environmental issues, see Bruce Foltz and John Chryssavgis, eds., *Toward an Ecology of Transfiguration: Orthodox Christian Perspectives on Environment, Nature and Creation* (New York: Fordham University Press, 2013). For an essay specifically on the ethical environmental implications of Theophany, see Vigen Guroian, "Ecological Ethics: An Ecclesial Event," in his *Ethics after Christendom: Toward an Ecclesial Christian Ethic* (Grand Rapids, Mich.: William B. Eerdmans, 1994), 155–174.

63. Or maybe recognize their inherent holiness. There is some controversy over whether the water hallows the material or whether it recognizes and makes obvious that the material is *already* holy.

12   Countercurrents
Theology and the Future of Continental Philosophy of Religion
Noëlle Vahanian

The general theme of this current volume is that of the future of Continental philosophy of religion. One could focus on established or more recently introduced authorial paradigms—for instance and to name but a few, Derrida, Deleuze, Caputo, Malabou, Goodchild, Westphal, Laruelle, and so on—and assess their legacy, debate their future, or perhaps even establish a vanguard. But in the vanguard or not, these contemporary thinkers and their followers attest to the recent so-called return to religion of Continental phenomenological thought. Cast in this way, the volume's theme could suggest not merely that faith and religious thought have regained ascendency over reason and scientific dogmatism, but more problematically, that this dichotomous relationship is not only one that is perpetual, it is, as it were, ontological, a fait accompli. This latter assumption is one that I reject and condemn. To be upfront at the outset about some of the main points to follow: I will say first, that the artificial separation between theology and philosophy is untenable in a postmodern world; second, that when philosophy turns to religion this only makes evident how language is theological and thought is animated by a theological desire to no end (note: theological desire is not to be conflated with a messianic hope); and finally, that the future of Continental philosophy of religion is most certainly not theology as it is proclaimed in most of today's seminaries.

The Question: What Is the Future of Continental Philosophy of Religion?

Jean-Jacques Rousseau won an essay contest with his thesis that art and civilization corrupt rather than improve humankind. His point was simple, but countercurrent: man is naturally good, and it is by his institutions alone that he becomes evil. The price of knowledge is impiety, that of the printing press—a vain desire for posterity, and that of civilization—dependence and frailty. The refutation of his argument is worthy of the most sophisticated smear campaigns. Indeed, who has not heard of the noble savage? And yet, Rousseau never coined the concept. His evaluation of the human situation is more properly expressed in the rhetorical question that he poses: "Why is man alone subject to becoming an imbecile?"[1]—and that he no less rhetorically or prosaically answers along the lines of Oedipus. That is, man is born an innocent child, and in old age, he loses all that his freedom from instinct, "his *perfectibility* has enabled him to acquire."[2] But Rousseau's solution is most certainly not a return to an imaginary state of nature, whether idyllic or chaotic. Instead, he calls for the transformation of man's original goodness into a social goodness. The individual should espouse the aims of a general will. Beginning to think is what turns man upon himself, and in so doing, it engenders egocentrism—here Oedipus thought his intellect could overcome fate, when it only fulfills it. The way out of this tragic egocentrism is through a radical reformation of personal identity, such that individual happiness is forsaken for morality and the general good. And this point is still countercurrent today. Whether you think Rousseau prefigures Nietzsche's critique of knowledge as the art of deception, or Freud's theory of the instincts as the ineluctable origin of conflict and disappointment between the individual and society, or Camus's absurdist response to the intellectual malady that is thinking, what appears in common with these thinkers is a fated human condition where the only types of solutions call for a deep psychological transformation: a change of ego-ideals. Of course, the proposed avenues for reconciling man with himself clearly differ. Rousseau's individual must become a concrete universal. Camus's absurd hero must remain an individual out of spite.

But let these remarks on Rousseau mark the beginning *in medias res* of this essay on the future of Continental philosophy of religion. I cannot compete with those whose posterity is not in question. I cannot pretend to think on a par with those whose ideas I borrow, misread, and, most assuredly, distort. However, I can aspire to give an answer that, in a profound sense, is as countercurrent as was Rousseau's. As for the fatalistic gloss on the human condition that I mentioned, one could also argue that it stems from a failure of the imagination. After all, this would not be inconsistent with Rousseau's own views of our intellectual faculties. Otherwise put, it is up to us to rethink and reshape the contours of reality. As Camus admonished, "one must imagine Sisyphus happy."[3] There is no reason *why* life. Should there be a reason, then surely, it would not be worth it. I'd much rather love for no reason at all. That love is the sacrifice to redeem humanity. All the reasons bring me back to myself: puny, inconsequential, and an imbecile in the end. If there is no reason, if there is no plan, then there is no limit. One must think to the limit.

Part 1. The Future of a Philosophy of the Future

Feuerbach is another one of those thinkers who felt that philosophy should offer a program for living where man would be reconciled with himself. He proposed that the task of the modern era was the dissolution of theology into anthropology. First came Protestantism, and its reclaiming of the humanity of God; then came speculative philosophy, and its dissolution of God into mind. But, marshaled Feuerbach, the full realization and humanization of God would not be complete without the full realization of speculative philosophy, a realization that should correspond, in his words, to "the negation without contradiction of this philosophy."[4] Only this complete humanization of God would usher in a new world of human solidarity, where the individual's heart and his reason could be in the same place, because that place would be wholly human, such that man's sociality would finally be understood as inseparable from his corporeality and sensuality. There is no God but in man and among men; theism is the very repudiation of this anthropology, as in theism, man projects his true essence onto God only to alienate himself from his true nature. Thus, atheism is theology dissolved into anthropology, and philosophy is a middle term in this process of dissolution. Philosophy is a necessary term, but only its negation fulfills its purpose. The philosopher of the future ought to desire not to be a philosopher. Thus man and his world are the true essence of Christianity. And the humanization of God is both the death of God at the hands of man—the Nietzschean nihilistic thread—and the incarnation of God in man—the Christological-secular thread, such that Thomas J. J. Altizer might pronounce: this is Christian atheism. The most profound nihilistic vision is also at once the greatest revolutionary power of Christianity. There is no absolute future, no new world, without God bleeding to death into his creation, without this ultimate sacrifice. And this is such a powerful revolution that it simultaneously impels its own reversal. That is, the philosophy of the future, when philosophy is dead apart from its realization in the full man; the completion of the humanization of God is the new world devoid of future; or what is the same now, an always already old world, in which the new is so impossible as to be incredible.

Perhaps this reversal of Christianity is evident in Rousseau's own conception of the social contract and its need for a civil religion. Rousseau loathed skepticism, materialism, and atheism; yet, he foresaw that Christianity's future lay elsewhere. The true Christian, according to Rousseau, would make it in this world only if everyone else were equally and authentically a Christian; otherwise, Christianity would only make slaves of its followers. But, Rousseau's secular alternative to religious faith: the civil profession of faith—"the articles of which it belongs to the sovereign to establish, not exactly as dogmas of religion, but as sentiments of sociability, without which it is impossible to be a good citizen or a faithful subject"—simply brackets out the spiritual and introspective nature of religious faith on account of its impracticality for this world by calling for a different sort of sacrifice, one that civilization already and silently requires, the sacrifice of the individual as individual.[5] If it were not for the French Revolution, Rousseau's solution might have inspired Freud's own way of reckoning with his dilemma that the religious illusion may be detrimental to the welfare of civilization, but that it may be hard to replace people's motivation for obedience with a rational reason when they are "ruled by their passions and instinctual demands."[6] It is not that Rousseau's political philosophy humanizes God in an enfranchising way. In fact, many would argue that Rousseau abides to a classical dualistic metaphysic, where the spiritual and the material do not meet. But, if Feuerbach pointed out that modern philosophy had transformed God into mind only to pit mind against body, when Rousseau excludes religion from civil society, this is precisely because he's turned body into spirit—only the mind can will to be civic. The heart is elsewhere, already divine.

Between Rousseau, Feuerbach, and Freud, we see an outline of two prongs of the modern age: secularity, as the realization of the Christian worldview on the one hand, and on the other, secularism, as the retrograde movement of dogmatism against obscurantism. Both have many contemporary versions, from Mark C. Taylor's a/theology to Gianni Vattimo's and John Caputo's weak concepts of God and from Daniel Dennett and Richard Dawkins to Christopher Hitchins's fundamentalist atheisms. Yet, this picture leaves another one untouched, the one according to which religion "as usual" is alive and well, and of which some of the most egregious or indomitable manifestations have prompted all sorts of questions concerning the so-called return of religion. While the religious turn of philosophy or phenomenology can be seen as precipitated by those timely political concerns, another way to put it might be that philosophy as phenomenological reduction is bereft of the task assigned to it, at least by Feuerbach. The exclusion of God as a "highly-mediated" experience from the purview of Husserlian phenomenology is the case in point. Furthermore, such a philosophy of exclusion not merely thrusts the religious to its outer side, but, like Rousseau, it inevitably runs the risk of relegating the religious to utmost privacy—spiritual otherworldliness. In this sense, secularism returns God to himself, and in so doing, reverses secularization.

A completed return to religion of philosophy in this sense means that the humanization of God is complete, and completed thanks to philosophy grappling once again with God, the name of God, and the being of God, but in the vernacular of this age. In this case, the time for philosophy proper is over. There is no future. When evangelicals are reading Caputo—this is a new age, and anything beyond it is impossible.

Or, religion "as usual" is the remainder that proves the historical thesis of secularization false, because philosophy cannot and can never totally humanize God—whether it bleeds God or dispenses with him altogether. In which case, either there is no future for philosophy proper, since it fails perforce, or there is an endless future for philosophy proper, since it fails perforce.

Let me summarize my main points in this analysis of the future of philosophy of religion thus far. First, the major premise is that the task of philosophy is the completion of the humanization of God. Here are the different interpretations:

a. This humanization is not complete; therefore, there is a future for philosophy, which future is the end of philosophy.
b. This humanization is complete; therefore, there is no future for philosophy, save that this realization impels its own reversal, which means that there is a future for philosophy.
c. This humanization cannot be completed; therefore, there both is and is not a future for philosophy: it is an endless, purposeless future; the future of a Sisyphean feat.

But these are historical futures beholden to the ghost of eschatology one way or another. Instead, I propose that we consider the question concerning the future of continental philosophy of religion from the standpoint of the experiment in thinking that is philosophical inquiry.

If what religion as usual provides, besides all that can be explained away—namely, it is a moralizing force, an ideological tool, it serves a psychological need, an evolutionary purpose, it offers a communal experience—if besides all these clichés, religion is an affirmation of faith—of a passion for life, or of the state of being ultimately concerned, as Tillich would say, philosophy is fundamentally a symptom of faith. In that sense, astonishment, or wonder, or awe might be better understood as modes of faith. Boredom, ennui, lackadaisicalness, and nausea are modes of unfaith. But both faith and unfaith, the mode of the real and important, and the mode of the phony and trivial, are modes of thinking. In astonishment, or wonder, or awe, such thinking to the limit is a thinking that—for a moment, and in that moment—does not disappoint: faith does not disappoint or else it is not faith, or else there is no such faith.[7] In boredom, in trivial pursuits, in disgust or aversion, thinking is stumped, powerless, without life; thinking sees its limit, and in unfaith, it cannot transcend it.

The complete humanization of God is thus the moment when faith and unfaith coincide, when thinking to the limit meets its limitations, when openness to the future is blindness to the future. And, this is another explanation for the current state of contemporary philosophy of religion.

Or, thinking is theological, and philosophical inquiry does not fail in its blindness, and by definition philosophy—not this or that philosophy, not modern or postmodern or post-postmodern philosophy—philosophy as an activity of ultimate concern cannot and can never ultimately fail in its openness. That is, philosophy will kill God, it will relativize truth, and most important, it will reveal to man that he is a trope. In that sense, the humanization of God is how the human being, fully human, passionately engaged and ultimately concerned, profoundly thoughtful from the depths of her womb, realizes her bottomless-ness, that this bottomless-ness is the infinite dwelling within: a two-faced God who lures you only to confound you and confounds you only to lure you. The humanization of God could then signify the captivating enterprise of desiring a thinking that does not disappoint and of thinking a desire to no end.

Part 2. Thinking to the Limit

> "If," writes Aristotle, "he who sees perceives that he sees, and he who hears, that he hears, and he who walks, that he walks, and in the case of all other activities similarly there is something which perceives that we are active, so that if we perceive, we perceive that we perceive, and if we think, that we think; and if to perceive that we perceive or think is to perceive that we exist (. . .); and if perceiving that one lives is in itself one of the things that are pleasant . . . : if this be true, as his own being is desirable for each man, so, or almost so, is that of his friend. Now his being was seen to be desirable because he perceived his own goodness [his good life], and such perception is pleasant in itself. He needs, therefore, to be conscious of the existence of his friend as well, and this will be realized in their living together and sharing in discussion and thought."[8]

Given that experience is the limit of existence since existence is perception or thought, what then is the thinking such that he who thinks, perceives that he thinks, perceives that he perceives that he thinks, and perceives—not that his world, but—that his life is more than his will and his representation?

In *The Metaphysics*, Aristotle explains how we begin our quest for knowledge—for speculative theoretical knowledge—out of curiosity. Following our inclinations, we step into the realm of philosophy—we decipher our world, interpret our aspirations, explain our actions and our reactions, describe our feelings; we eat, sleep, work, play, think well—that is, given our abilities, considering our options. Curiosity, then, is not only a product of need. It may be born of a sense of awe: in our curiosity we marvel at the world; we praise our world.

But, what is the value of philosophy once the philosopher's eyes are gouged—once the philosopher understands that, noble or vulgar, extraordinary or ordinary, all things amount to nothing outside the text? That initial praise of our world is revealed as a subjective judgment in disguise: we did not know any better, we were impressed—impressed by ourselves. We were impressed because we were impressionable, not by anything impressive in and of itself—not by anything outside the text.[9]

Now, it would seem that the only end that is pursued as an end in itself cannot be attained through the actions that fulfill the function of a human being—

that happiness is pursued through actions that are proper to the human being, but that this happiness appears more as a subterfuge to incite us to become fully human, namely, bottomless, gouged, and in the service of mere life. If that is the case, the best we can do is settle for the mild discontents of civilization—as Freud would have it.[10] The thinker, the philosophic type, would settle for the comfort of his acquired scholarly lenses and language. There is a certain value that accompanies the act of putting thoughts into words—of expressing, of becoming proficient and articulate. There is at least a performative value—sometimes virtuosity.

Still, mastery is not synonymous with happiness. Marx, Nietzsche, and Freud also all concur to the extent that mastery devalues more than nature; it devalues human nature along with human culture. Alienation has less to do with the growing divide between man and nature than it does with the objectification of the human. (For Marx, as soon as language ceases to be a tool, and lends itself to abstractions, those who own the means of production then appropriate it: this is how historical materialism is born. For Nietzsche, mastery, today, is the art of chewing the cud—of being as cowlike as possible, as predictable and inert as possible). Mastery is a form of suffocation; it is a form of death. Imagine, for instance, what mastery means for a philosopher who knows that he is bottomless and ignorant. Mastery, in his case, is like finding yourself in a room with no exit, and bracketing out the possibility of an exit even though you cannot help but think that insofar as there had to be a way into the room, there should also be a way out of it. Given such a scenario, is it any wonder that some have sought to relegitimate some appeal to an outside authority, whether the politically sovereign or the theologically transcendent.[11]

Only a subject knows an object—finding yourself in a room without an exit is finding yourself as an object; it is recognizing that your origination is not original, that you are the room, and all those in the room, but that you are not yourself, you are not your own. In this room without an exit, where speculative talk of the exit is an insult to the quest for truth, the greatest moment of consciousness, of lucidity, does not seem to invigorate the spirit. Lucidity, in the name of truth, seems to prohibit, now, more than speculation or contemplation; it aborts intellectual action. In the sense that existence is consciousness, the good life, the life that is worth living, life that is invaluable, is the activity of the soul that is the best and most complete realization of the best and most complete virtue—namely, "whatever . . . it be that is thought to rule and lead us by nature, and to have cognizance of what is noble and divine."[12] In the sense that existence is consciousness, the thinking that goes to the limit of its function is, to be sure, the thinking that is cognizant of alterity, yet, it is also the thinking that arouses the breath of life (the activity of the soul). It is that thinking that awakens the spirit, and awakening the spirit it contemplates the gift of existence—that kind of life that is consciousness. And in that moment, life is divine—but it is not over, not yet complete.

Thinking, in itself, seems to be a doing or an acting, wherein the deed is nothing besides the doing. And so, that I can conceive of something that than which nothing greater can be conceived does not make it so. This does not mean that my thinking does not affect anything else besides my thoughts; it means that there is a difference between intending to think and thinking with intent. In the former case, nothing comes out of the thinking besides thoughts. In the latter, those who think the thoughts own the means of production, not because they think the thoughts, but because others make it possible for them to go on thinking rather than tilling. In a room without an exit, aware that there is no exit, there is no intent to think without intent. I intend to think to the limit—for the moment of lucidity. Under the guise of a call, of a duty to the other, I think with intent to think to the limit, which means, however, that I do not think only insofar as I am human, or only insofar as I can think. It means that thinking is theological; it means that I want to run into the walls of my room, because, in that collision, I am alive and I know it, and life is real. It means that when I think to the limit, I am thrust against a wall, and in that collision, I am forced to recognize life—that it is more than me, more than human, and in that strange sense, more than mortal. Thinking is theological, because it holds the promise of the other. Albeit this promise is a virtue—as such, it is effective without being actual, it remains a promise, it is never not a promise. I don't simply think to the limit to realize my ignorance; before I think with a sense of duty, with intent, I think, because that activity is the promise of the other, and that promise is good. That promise makes life worth living, and living worth completing. I do not mean a form of messianism. This is not hope deferred—such hope, we know, makes the heart sick. I—singularity or singular illusion—I—breathing to be and exhaling not to—I make and break the promise.

Answer to the Question: There is no future to Continental philosophy of religion, unless thinking is theological.

There is no place for theology in the philosophy of religion, let alone in the academic study of religion. Nor should there be, because after all, what passes for theology gives itself over to either obscurantism or triumphalism. Stuck in a room with no exit, thinking the same all over again, my point is simple, but countercurrent. The thinking that is theological—theological thinking—provides a real future to Continental philosophy of religion.

Notes

1. Jean-Jacques Rousseau, "Discourse on the Origin of Inequality," in *The Basic Political Writings*, trans. Donald A. Cress (Indianapolis: Hackett, 1987), 45.
2. Ibid.

3. Albert Camus, *The Myth of Sisyphus*, trans. Justin O'Brien (New York: Vintage International, 1991), 123.

4. Ludwig Feuerbach, *Principles of the Philosophy of the Future*, trans. Manfred Vogel (Indianapolis: Hackett, 1986), paragraphs 20, 31.

5. Jean-Jacques Rousseau, "On the Social Contract," in *The Basic Political Writings*, trans. Donald A. Cress (Indianapolis: Hackett, 1987), bk. 4, ch. 8, 226.

6. Sigmund Freud, *The Future of an Illusion*, trans. James Strachey (New York: W. W. Norton, 1961), 58.

7. For a developed approach to theological thinking as a thinking that does not disappoint see Charles E. Winquist, *Desiring Theology* (Chicago: Chicago University Press, 1995).

8. Aristotle, *Nicomachean Ethics*, in *The Basic Works of Aristotle*, ed. Richard McKeon, trans. W. D. Ross (New York: Random House, 1941) bk. 9, ch. 9, 1089–1090.

9. This is the epistemological crisis that postmodern deconstruction confronts us with, and perhaps it is also the reason for the urgency with which many within contemporary philosophy have "turned to" theology. In this sense, I can appreciate Janicaud's critique because the theological turn manifest in contemporary phenomenology is an effort to shield oneself from the wound of postmodernism. In other words, it is the very opposite of "thinking to the limit" that I am describing here as the proper nature of theological thinking.

10. See Sigmund Freud, *Civilization and Its Discontents*, trans. James Strachey (New York: W. W. Norton, 1989).

11. For instance, see Carl Schmitt, *Political Theology*, trans. George Schwab (Cambridge, Mass.: MIT Press, 1986). Or, more current, the radical orthodox theologians who make the seemingly contradictory argument that true democracy is not possible apart from some transcendent authority.

12. Aristotle, *Nicomachean Ethics*, bk. 10, 1177a (NE ed. H. Rackham: bk. 10, 1177a).

Part III
Plasticity

13 The Future of Derrida

Time between Epigenesis and Epigenetics

Catherine Malabou

THE TITLE OF my chapter, "The Future of Derrida," was John D. Caputo's idea. In suggesting such a title, a beautiful one indeed, Caputo has made clear that, for him, my intellectual journey—starting with Hegel, going on with Heidegger, and then turning, in a move that might have appeared as a rupture, toward neurology and neuroplasticity—was not an estrangement from deconstruction but on the contrary a way of bringing it forward in trying to adapt it to the political as well as scientific and philosophical realities of the twenty-first century. Caputo knows that everything I have written since *The Future of Hegel* was originally oriented toward the possibility of affirming the future of Derrida.

Clayton Crockett, who has been a friendly and demanding reader of my work during the last ten years, recently presented, in his stunning book, *Radical Political Theology*, a strikingly accurate and promising political elaboration of the concept of plasticity. This concept, in his view, should help us to lay foundations for a new materialism and define the future of deconstruction as an orientation toward an immanent, rather than transcendent, form of freedom.

In this chapter, I recapitulate some of the important moments of my philosophical trajectory. My leading thread here is time. First, I claim that "Time" seems to have gradually disappeared, as a concept, from our philosophical horizon. First displaced by Heidegger, who proposes in the end to subordinate it to the gift, "*es gibt Zeit*," and then disrupted by Derrida, who proposes to substitute, as he says in "Faith and Knowledge," "the opening to the coming of the other" for temporality, time has eventually vanished. According to Derrida, time would always refer to a horizon of expectation, to the possibility of anticipation, and, in that sense, to presence. To free the future from time and temporality: such is the final and most important gesture of deconstruction. Liberated from time, the future is what appears in Derrida to be the locus of faith, of, according to a now famous definition, "the messianic, or messianicity without messianism." I quote from "Faith and Knowledge":

> The messianic, or messianicity without messianism. This would be the opening to the future or to the coming of the other as the advent of justice, but without horizon of expectation and without prophetic prefiguration. The coming of the other can only emerge as a singular event when no anticipation sees it coming, when the other and death ... can come as a surprise at any moment.[1]

Time as such has been dissolved into messianity. The future has become the defeat of the future understood as what we can expect. The disenchantment of anticipation.

Second, I argue that messianity, even thought of as a messianicity *without* messianism, is perhaps not the most accurate form of future for deconstruction, as it just paralyzes its dynamics in appearing, as Derrida puts it, as undeconstructible, as "what remains irreducible to any deconstruction."[2] I state that undeconstructibility cannot be the future of deconstruction, and consequently also that messianity cannot be the future of Derrida. I am thus postulating the existence of both a frontier and a fork between two deconstructive paths toward the future, the one that is explicitly developed by Derrida, and a more secret one, which perhaps works behind his back and resists messianity. In order to make them both visible, I will present two possible readings of Kant, the one developed by Derrida in "Faith and Knowledge," and a second one, based on a passage of the first *Critique*. Both readings develop different answers to the same issue. This Kantian mediation will allow me to reaffirm in the end the necessity of elaborating a dialectical and nonmessianic notion of time.

In *Being and Time*, as we know, Heidegger declares that authentic temporality, as opposed to the vulgar, metaphysical—that is, traditional—notion of time, orients itself primarily toward the future and is not governed by the sovereignty of present and of presence. Such a sovereignty finds its most accomplished expression in Hegel's concept of time. "Hegel's concept of time presents the most radical way in which the vulgar understanding of time has been given form conceptually."[3] Dialectics wouldn't have been able to renew the traditional vision of time understood as a mere succession of nows and would, for that reason, only be a paraphrase of Aristotle's notion of time developed in *Physics* IV. A time that is never oriented toward the future and remains understood as a momentarily and finite expression of the absolute's eternity or *parousia*.

In his 1930 course on the *Phenomenology of Spirit*, Heidegger states: "Undoubtedly [Hegel] occasionally speaks about the having been, but never about the future. This silence fits with the fact that (for him) the past is itself the decisive character of time, and for a good reason: time is both passing and what passes; it has always passed away."[4] Further: "Hegel's explanation of the genuine concept of Being, . . . is nothing less than a farewell to time on the road to spirit, which is eternal."⁵

The concept of plasticity, which I first discovered in the preface of the *Phenomenology of Spirit*, helped me to elaborate a strategy that, I hoped, would be able to counter Heidegger's argument according to which Hegel had remained blind to the future, that is, to the essential dimension of ecstatic temporality. Plasticity is used as a concept in the preface to characterize the speculative relationship between the subject and its predicates or accidents. The subject, Hegel says, is neither polymorph nor flexible nor rigid, but plastic. It means that it does not tolerate any kind of accident, change, or deformation, that it does not resist accident either, but holds itself somewhere in between total malleability and absolute rigidity to what happens. Plasticity has the double meaning of what is susceptible to receive form, like clay or marble, and also to be able to bestow form, to give form, as we can hear in the expressions of plastic arts or plastic surgery. Plasticity also characterizes what is about to explode, as we can hear in the French *"plasticage,"* which is another name for bombing. I argued that plasticity might then be considered as temporality itself understood as the relationship of the subject to what is coming, to the accident, the future, and the sudden explosion of the unexpected. Plasticity characterizes the subject's temporal mode of being in relation to events that both give form to it and are formed by it. Plasticity was for me thus able to allow us to displace the locus of time in Hegel, to show that it is not restricted to the exposition of temporality in his *Philosophy of Nature* but spread out everywhere as the very ticking of the absolute.

It became possible then for me to set the stage for a confrontation between Hegel and his posterity. That being done, I abandoned these issues for a while and undertook my relatively long excursion through the neurosciences and my exploration of neural plasticity. This exploration was motivated by two contradictory movements. The first one was the desire to pursue the elaboration of plastic time and to confer a new dimension to it. The second, which was more obscure and which I didn't immediately perceive, was a feeling of failure regarding precisely my elaboration of plasticity as temporality.

I gradually realized that, as I said to start with, time, as a concept, had purely and simply disappeared from the Continental philosophical scene and had become a ghostly notion. Consequently, my modest attempt at elaborating the notion of a temporal plasticity was useless when set against a philosopher who, in the end, admits that time is after all perhaps not the problem. *Sein und Zeit*, as we know, is not Heidegger's last word on time. In his later works, Heidegger discovers that time, as well as the identity of time and being, is perhaps not ontologically as originary as he had thought it to be in the first place. Time, understood as the ecstatic temporality primarily oriented toward the future, as the very structure of *Dasein*'s existence, is itself derived from a more originary instance,

Ereignis, that is first of all the opening of the gift. Considering the priority of gift over being, sentences like "time is" or "being is time" are inappropriate. "To think Being explicitly requires us to relinquish Being as the ground of beings in favor of the giving... that is, in favor of the It gives.... Being *is* not. It gives Being as the unconcealing."[6] Further: "Time *is* not. There is, It gives time."[7]

These affirmations render the determination of the relationship to the future as a relation between a subject and its accidents impossible. As Heidegger says, the "It" in "It gives" is not a subject, "a *hypokeimenon* in relation to the *symbebekos*, the accident."[8] Plasticity appears then to be deprived of any strength and any use. As time becomes a derived and secondary issue, it is less possible than ever to regard it as both the formative and explosive mode of being of the subject. "The It," declares Heidegger, "names a presence of absence." Time is henceforth absent, as if it had deserted philosophy.

This issue of time's withdrawal has been clearly radicalized by Derrida. In "Différance," published in *Margins of Philosophy*, he already declared that time and space had to be more accurately replaced by "temporalization and spatialization," even by the word *différance* itself, to the extent that they undoubtedly conveyed a metaphysical reminiscence of presence. In his later works, like in *Given Time* for example, Derrida also comes back to the issue of gift as being more originary than that of time. Gift is understood as the pure opening to the utterly other, or the "absolute *arrivant*." To that extent, there is no time any longer, time is out of joint, or out of date. Temporality now appears as the promise, the possible coming of the event without anticipation or prefiguration. And messianity accounts for the future understood as this undeniable and undeconstructible possibility.

It is clear, for Derrida, that we cannot call "time" such a possibility. He also refuses, for the same reason, the idea of plasticity. Plasticity is too closely linked with presence and subjectivity, too structured a horizon of expectation. Plasticity and Hegelian temporality in general would not be able to account for the event. In his beautiful preface to *The Future of Hegel*, "A Time for Farewells," Derrida writes: "This event can or may come from . . . behind me, as if it came in my back, from behind my back, without ever presenting itself in front of me, in, so to say, the face of my face. . . . The coming of an event which . . . will never present itself."[9] To this extent, such a coming necessarily exceeds the plastic structure of what is coming. Was it to say, then, that Derrida and I had two different futures?

It is true that I momentarily came to that conclusion. Again, my journey through neuroscience was certainly a way to distance myself from what appeared to be, in my opinion, an unacceptable redefinition of time. Messianity, I thought, was open to criticism for two main reasons: first, it implied a stasis of deconstruction, due to the emergence of the indeconstructible; second, it made it impossible to articulate any concept of anticipation, of a formation of the future as well as of material encounters (I didn't see, and still don't, why the event cannot "present itself in front of me"). What, then about the front, the frontal, the war front, the face-to-face encounter with the enemy or the friend or the lover? Don't they belong to the realm of authentic events?

Exploring the neurological concept of plasticity was for me a way to look for a new systematic question of time opposing messianity. By a systematic question of time, I mean both a thought that takes time as its object and a thought of what time may be when it is considered from within a system. A systematic temporality is a temporality that does not proceed from the opening of an outside, a temporality that is not assimilable to transcendence. On that point, the Hegelian system and what I discovered about the nervous system obviously converged: plasticity, in Hegel as in neurosciences, is precisely the name of the dynamism of events as well of the mode of being and meaning of the future in a world deprived of transcendence, breaches, or holes.

Turning toward the functioning of a biological system; entering, if I may say so, the realm of sheer materiality, helped me to reconsider the possibility of a return to dialectics and of a reaffirmation of temporal plasticity. I won't at present exposit here what neuroplasticity is but will insist very briefly on two of its main characteristics. First, by neural plasticity, scientists designate the formation of neural connections during embryonic life and after birth in the young child. The growth in mass of the brain coincides with the extension of axons and dendrites and with the formation of synapses. This first plasticity characterizes the neural genesis. This genesis is subject to strict genetic determinism.

Second, plasticity means a different kind of shaping: the modification of neural connections by means of the modulation of synaptic efficacy as well as the formation of new connections along with the disappearance of others. One of the most striking recent discoveries about the brain precisely concerns the strong influence of environment, experience, education, and learning on the shapes of the connections. When the connections are frequently solicited, in playing piano regularly for example, they increase in size and volume (it is LTP, long-term potentialization). On the contrary, when certain connections are not solicited, they decrease, and scientists talk about synaptic long-term depression (LTD). Plasticity acts thus like a sculptor, and we can speak of a plastic art of and in the brain. Here, we can see that this art is not determined and appears on the contrary as culturally oriented.

The two meanings of plasticity can then be interpreted as two interlocutors of a dialogue between determinism and freedom. This dialogue can also be interpreted as a dialectical relationship between genetics and epigenetics. Epigenetics is a science that has known a dramatic development since the second half of the twentieth century The name "epigenesis" comes from the Greek: επί: over, above, and *genesis:* movement, development. Epigenetics, as a science, studies nongenetic changes or modifications, that is, changes that do not alter the DNA sequence. Originally, epigenetics takes care of all mechanisms that control gene expression, the translation or transcription from DNA into proteins via RNA, and makes possible the passage from genotype to phenotype, that is, from the genome to the individual physical structure and appearance of each living being.

By extension, epigenetics studies also the changes that are due, as is the case in the brain, to experience or education. Nongenetic changes include these kinds of modifications, caused by cultural influences. In a sense, plasticity and epigenetics may be regarded as identical or synonymous. Because of its plasticity and the epigenetic character of an important part of its development, the brain is not a mere biological organ. It can also be considered a historical organ. It seems that a critical space between biology and history is opening today. This space might precisely be that of time.

Let's now come back to Derrida. For him, the opening to the coming of the other marks out the locus of faith. As we know, he understands this faith as the contemporary version of Kant's "rational faith," developed in *Religion within the Limits of Reason Alone*. And this is the reason why I am now turning to Kant. In this book, Kant sets out a gap between the "simple cult of religion" and "reflective faith." This reflective faith, says Derrida, "is not essentially dependent on any historical revelation and so accords itself to the rationality of pure practical reason."[10] It is interpreted as a belief in what Derrida calls the absolutely other possibility. The opening to the coming of the other coincides with the undeniable possibility that everything could have been otherwise, that history could have happened otherwise. That an absolutely other possibility could have guided time and that other events could have occurred that would have constituted another tradition. The utterly other can always come as a manifestation of this other possibility. Faith is faith in the future understood as the other origin. It is also, in its own way, an economy of determinism and freedom. Freedom appears in Derrida as the shadow of the undeniable possibility that doubles history as its imaginary reflection. "The gap between the opening of the possibility . . . and the determinate necessity of this or that [event] will always remain irreducible." As the space without space of "the most originary possibility."[11]

As I said, I was never totally convinced by this definition of the future and this messianic interpretation of Kantian reflective or rational faith. If Derrida is right, the future appears as the other possibility. We are then allowed to produce the future of deconstruction as another possibility than one of messianism. We can try to render visible the imaginary doubling or shadow of Derrida's future, which is perhaps repressed by the explicit one.

I recently discovered the possibility of another reading of Kant that might help to orient the future of deconstruction differently. My attention was recently drawn by an enigmatic expression that appears in the first *Critique*, more precisely in §27 of the Transcendental Deduction; Kant coins a surprising expression: "Epigenesis of Reason." Of course, such an "epigenesis" for me immediately resonated with "epigenetics." Let me briefly retrace the context in which Kant makes use of this expression. In §27, Kant explains that the logical categories of judgment, as well as the laws of our understanding and all the rational structure of our knowledge in general, form a transcendental apparatus that is given prior to any empirical experience. How can we understand that the transcendental does not proceed from experience? Does it mean that it is innate or given by God? No, says Kant. The transcendental is a priori but it is not innate. Again, how can we understand this difficult point? Kant answers: we have to admit the existence of an epigenesis of reason.

Kant uses the term "epigenesis" in its original sense, that of a biological theory that opposes preformation. Epigenesis and preformation, as we know, are two ways of describing and seeking to explain the development of individual organic form. Does every individual start from a material that is unformed, and the form emerges only gradually, over time? This is epigenesis. Or does the individual start in some already preformed, or predelineated, or predetermined way? This is of course preformation.

Kant is very clear on this point: there is an epigenesis of reason, which means that there is an epigenesis of the a priori. In §27 of the *Critique of Pure Reason*: our knowledge is not "all derived from experience. The pure intuitions of receptivity and the pure concepts of understanding are elements in knowledge, and both are found in us *a priori*."[12] If this is the case, Kant goes on, how can "we account for a necessary agreement of experience with the concepts of its objects?" This agreement cannot be preformed, otherwise "the categories [would be] subjective dispositions of thought, implanted in us from the first moment of our existence, and so ordered by our Creator that there employment is in complete harmony with the law of nature in accordance with which experience proceeds—a kind of preformation—system of pure reason." If this agreement was preformed, our concepts and judgments would lose all necessity: "the concept of cause, for instance, which expresses the necessity of an event under a presupposed condition, would be false if it rested only on an arbitrary subjective necessity, implanted in us, of connecting certain empirical representations according to the rule of causal relation."

We cannot accept this preformed notion of the transcendental, which deprives it of any necessity. We have to admit on the contrary that reason itself is the creative power of the transcendental: "There remains, therefore, only the second supposition—a system, as it were, of the epigenesis of pure reason." There exists a kind of development of the transcendental, as if reason was a self-formative power, as if it was able, in a certain sense, to form itself, to form its categories. And we see that Kant uses a biological metaphor to describe this strange formation of the transcendental.

We can then differentiate between Derrida's interpretation of the Kantian rational faith and the conception of time that emerges from the idea of an epigenetic rationality. Both refer to the origin as well as to the utmost possibility. In

Derrida, this utmost possibility appears to be cut off from the power of reason. It is rational—rational faith—but reason is not seen as the creative power of the object of its faith. Rational faith is faith in the possibility that an utterly other instance than reason might secretly be at work in reason. The other possibility is alien to reason, the other of reason in reason. Reason has no agency on it. An epigenesis of reason on the contrary supposes that there cannot be any other origin than reason. The a priori is neither a gift from God nor a result of experience. It does not come from outside. It is formed—otherwise it would be given; but formed by itself. In that sense, reason appears to be the power of fashioning its own possibility. Understood from this perspective, the future coincides with the self-shaping of reason.

If reason is creative and self-formative, we are then allowed to say that the transcendental itself is plastic, and that there must be a kind of experience within the realm of the a priori. Plasticity of the transcendental: Kant would have at the same time strongly contested this expression. But not Hegel. We might even consider that Hegel's philosophy as a whole is an attempt at reinterpreting, re-elaborating and radicalizing the idea of an epigenesis of reason in assimilating it to a fashionability of truth. The transcendental, all our a priori concepts or categories, are malleable and transformable, both determined and open to transformation. Categories and rational principles of knowledge as well as moral rules are plastic, movable, moldable, deconstructible instances. Accordingly, time would not be the opening of a messianic horizon but the immanent development of the transcendental.

If we consider the system as Hegel describes it, we see that a system is nothing static but a development, an *Entwicklung*. This development is structured by a dialectical relationship between what appears as a determined movement, that of the "immanent deduction of the real," and a free process of culture, open to accidents as well as to the plastic formative virtues of education and history. Understood on the model of the relationship between genetics and epigenetics, a material temporality could help us to articulate a new relationship between nature and freedom.

Plasticity of the transcendental can then be understood in two ways: both historically: truth is nothing outside its genealogical constitution; and biologically: we have to take into account the natural character of the creative power of our reason. Again, it is clear that Kant was perfectly aware of the biological meaning of his metaphor. The in-between space between history and biology is the space in which we live today, in the neurobiological age. Which means that the frontier between history and biology, between historical genesis and biological epigenesis tends to erase itself, thus opening the issue of a new kind of truth that amounts to a new kind of ethics.

To claim that the transcendental is fashionable does not amount to the emergence of a new skepticism. The dialectically radicalized epigeneticist position that I have just espoused means that we are responsible for the formation of our rational productions, beliefs, and values and we know that all of them are deconstructible. We have to know how to inhabit the space that opens between nature and history, which is the new space for deconstruction. We are responsible for this invention, because nobody else than us will tell or teach us how to become the subjects of our time.

According to Derrida, the alterity of the other, the foundation itself of ethics, would always have to take place on the outside. The encounter with the other, the response to the moral injunction, would always have to occur outside. But where there is no outside, where the transcendental can only proceed from itself, who is the other and how can we wait for its coming?

What could an absolute *arrivant* be when there is no outside, no "elsewhere"? And particularly no outside of and no elsewhere from deconstruction? Again, the motive of the undeconstructible is not acceptable. It is too easy and too immediate. It arbitrarily both limits deconstruction and marks its sovereignty. In that sense, it cannot open its future. I believe—and this is my faith—that nothing is undeconstructible. To insist on the transcendental's plasticity amounts to insisting on its deconstructibility.

In his book, Clayton Crockett asks, "If plasticity can be seen as the wake of deconstruction, is this a dialectical movement, a shift in the strategy to save the modern Western . . . subject? Or an explosion in thinking, a subversion of what even deconstruction saves (justice, the Name of God)?"[13] I am of course not able to answer this question. What I know is that, between salvation and shift, the future of Derrida does not belong either to Derrida or to me but depends on its self-formative destiny.

Notes

1. Jacques Derrida, "Faith and Knowledge: The Two Sources of 'Religion' at the Limits of Reason Alone," trans. Samuel Weber, in *Acts of Religion,* ed. Gil Anidjar (London: Routledge, 2002), 56.

2. Quoted from Jacques Derrida, *Specters of Marx,* in Clayton Crockett, *Radical Political Theology: Religion and Politics after Liberalism* (New York: Columbia University Press, 2011), 146.

3. Martin Heidegger, *Being and Time,* trans. Joan Stambaugh (Albany: SUNY Press, 1996), 390.

4. Martin Heidegger, *Hegel's Phenomenology of Spirit,* trans. Parvis Emad and Kenneth Maly (Bloomington: Indiana University Press, 1988), 82.

5. Ibid., 147.

6. Martin Heidegger, *On Time and Being,* trans. Joan Stambaugh (Chicago: University of Chicago Press, 2002), 6.

7. Ibid., 18.

8. Ibid.

9. Jacques Derrida, "A Time for Farewells," in Catherine Malabou, *The Future of Hegel: Plasticity, Temporality and Dialectic* (London: Routledge, 2004), 32.
10. Derrida, "Faith and Knowledge," 21.
11. Ibid., 93.
12. See Immanuel Kant, *Critique of Pure Reason,* trans. Norman Kemp Smith (New York: St. Martin's Press, 1965), 173–175.
13. Crockett, *Radical Political Theology,* 152.

14   On Reading—Catherine Malabou

Randall Johnson

> So, more than a substance, plastic is the very idea of its infinite transformation; as its everyday name indicates, it is the ubiquity made visible. And it is this, in fact, which makes it a miraculous substance....
>
> —Roland Barthes, *Mythologies*

For the most part, it seems that we approach reading as if it were neutral in all valences of any consequence: language or other sign indicators on the screen or page are touched, usually by vision, and then processed by the synaptic workings of the brain for the purpose of transfer of information. And often all of this happens without awareness, even at times the very choice of what we read. Here, there is *pure*—and isn't this *the* ideological word par excellence that slips its way into speculative idealisms, scientific empiricisms, and even materialisms of the real—form of sedimented functioning with its somehow contained contents to be critically apprehended and assessed, if not dismissed. It is because of the illusory imaginary of this structure of an already forgotten *assumed* neutrality of reading in its broadest senses that we function so smoothly in the shared symbolic, cultural world, that we keep to our place of produced and producing consumption, that we remain flexible in the diminished sense of forgotten or disavowed resistance, that we continue to fit in. Indeed, at times reading mindlessly is both necessary and useful for survival. But this reading, which abdicates its own plastic potential, is clearly not neutral in the sense that Barthes opens for us in his lectures of 1978: "I define the Neutral as that which outplays the paradigm, or rather I call Neutral everything that baffles the paradigm."[1] To read mindfully with this Neutral is to reclaim the nuances of resistance by noticing the contradictions that persist in any effort to keep form fully separate from content and hence, in some obscure and mystical manner, pure.[2] Barthes continues: "My definition of the Neutral remains structural. By which I mean that, for me, the Neutral doesn't refer to 'impressions' of grayness, of 'neutrality,' of indifference. The Neutral—

my Neutral—can refer to intense, strong, unprecedented states. 'To outplay the paradigm' is an ardent, burning activity."[3] To read as an ardent, burning activity is one way truly to put our brains to work.

To claim this Neutral as mine—in what perhaps seems to be an inverted if not perverted phenomenological reduction—requires a deliberate calling forth of bio-graphic, perhaps even bio-logic, particularity so that *the I is both its material and its materializing,* so that by mental effort what we attempt to keep bracketed is not particularity itself but the usual and, as we said, at times necessary automaticity of the functioning of any one of our determinate particularities. To assume that we can fully bracket particulars is to be blind to the manner in which such particulars continue to determine thought itself: whatever mistakes itself to be within this Neutral as specified by Barthes is then at risk of allowing the paradigm (and we will retain this now almost archaic sounding word in its undifferentiated broad sense) to remain fully at play by not recognizing the preconscious automaticity of its particulars that continue to function in its assumed neutrality. To recognize, acknowledge, and bring to awareness our determinate particularities, while making an effort to hold in abeyance as much as possible any automaticity of their functioning by which the paradigm persists in the real, opens the path for singular universal truths to show themselves. This is a logic of phenomena that grasps its very materiality. This epoché is the practice of a phenomenology that does not disavow or disown its inherent power of critique but brings this capacity to bear in apprehending its being instituted, its own subjectivation by whatever paradigm, as well as its capacity to institute, to create, to re-form. This is the ethos of a creaturely praxis of care. To know the plasticity of the play of particulars is to reawaken the opening, however slight, for resistances and is to reclaim the potential to outplay the paradigm. To allow oneself proximally to be baffled by reading may begin the process of thawing the icy, opaque paradigms frozen into one's own particularities. This is to know the bone in the spirit. Malabou knows this.

Psychic Mimesis Reflects Mirror Neurons

As any reader of Derrida will have instantly recognized, there is presumptive allusion in the mimesis of the very title given to this brief effort to think on a specific theme by referencing a singular philosopher by her name and by employing the dash as that which punctuates the holding of the two in anticipatory separation.[4] We can up the ante of such presumption not only by raising the spectral retro-activity of psychic mimesis but also by mentioning the discovery within the last two decades of the mirror neuron system, which has so excited neuroscience researchers and those who put such empirical findings into the play of thoughtful speculations, including both the researchers themselves and the occasional philosopher who is not afraid of, daunted by, or dismissive of what science finds. In a review article, Rizzolatti and Craighero describe that mirror neurons are a class of visuomotor neurons first discovered in monkeys that have been demonstrated to be associated with action understanding.[5] They summarize the neurophysiologic evidence, based predominantly on MRI studies, which supports the existence of the mirror neuron system in humans and suggests that in addition to action understanding, this system also plays a role in imitation learning in our species. As they state in the abstract to the article, having an understanding of action is essential for survival and for social organization, and possessing a capacity to learn by imitation, perhaps shared only with apes, is in their words the "faculty" that is "at the basis of human culture." They conclude with a theory of language evolution from gestural movements and the possible link of such evolution with the mirror neuron system, which has also been demonstrated to include audiovisual as well as visuomotor neurons. The authors use the word "speculative" to describe this theory regarding the association of mirror neurons with language acquisition.

We can only fantasize about what use Lacan would have made of such research when describing the mirror stage of development and about how he might have incorporated such empirical findings into his thoughts regarding the unconscious being structured like a language, which perhaps we can now speculate may even imply that the unconscious is primordially structured like a gesture. At the least, these findings may create openings in how we understand both pre-discursive motor memory and its essentially communicative nature as well as how we conceptualize affective resonances outside of spoken language. But one can get lost in the reflections of mirror images, and the shine of things may become all the more alluring in the formation of specular representations, so we will cease fantasy for now, except to add that perhaps these empirical findings remind us that the brain in its materializing is always already outside itself as much as it is inside itself in the time of its happening. Or, to shorten the formulation into an aphorism of phenomenological materialism: the brain re-*minds* us. However, an auto-graphics becoming aphoristic risks an untimely return to mindlessness.

Hegel Teaches Malabou How to Train Us to Read

In what in some ways is a surprise ending, the penultimate chapter of *The Future of Hegel* is an auto-graphics on reading as an *act* of plasticity, which in the "Conclusion" is folded back onto the text itself in a more directly material biographics; as Malabou phrases it: "Having become experienced through the speculative ordeal of a shared speech, the reader is from now on able to *respond* to the reading. Hence it is now this reader who can finally speak in her own voice."[6] In glancing back through this text to reclaim the never original first reading, one finds in its very introduction a foreshadowing that helps to explain why there is an already arrived sense to this surprise at the end: "Reading Hegel amounts to finding oneself in two times at once: the process that unfolds is both retrospective and prospective. In the present time in which reading takes place, the reader is drawn to a double expectation: waiting for what is to come (according to a linear and representational thinking), while presupposing that the outcome has already arrived (by virtue of the teleological ruse)."[7] In this epoch at the dusk of writing *as it will have been* and at my own age past the midday of life, I find that I must read Hegel at dawn, both for an adequate rest and rejuvenation of the brain as the organ of reading and for the more immediate memory of any dream of a future. Particular subjects vary in their circadian openness to reading as an ardent, burning activity before its inevitable fall into forgetful mindlessness, and for me the time for the most plastic illiteracy coincides with what, despite our astrological knowledge, we continue to call sunrise.[8] Malabou states: "The speculative proposition checks our confidence in 'knowing how to read,' thus training the reader in an illiteracy of the second power which will make the reader write what he or she reads."[9] The diminished neutrality of some assumed pure form of reading transforms itself into an act worthy of Barthes's Neutral. In this is an instance of the always already mediated immediacy of the deflagration that is the co-incident manifesting of plasticity: to receive form *and* to produce form.

To evoke the particulars of circadian rhythms is to remind us of the circular foldings of our creaturely reformations. While there are singular universal truths that can evidently be shared, such truths must continue to be brought forth by ongoing originating. To remember the power inherent in illiteracy may help re-awaken within us this capacity to read with vital passion. And yet, there is an inevitable evanescence of absolute knowledge in closing any one of Hegel's texts: this is the mourning of writing in the very act of reading. Close to the closure of *Plasticity at the Dusk of Writing* as we begin to mourn writing itself, in what is now less of a surprise for us readers of *The Future of Hegel*, Malabou returns to this ardent, burning act: "*The plastic reading of a text is the reading that seeks to reveal the form left in the text through the withdrawing of presence, that is, through its own deconstruction.*"[10] To re-read this form is already its transformation. It is my contention that there is a necessary and singular auto-graphics—understood in its slight gap of difference from the particularity of bio-graphics—for material phenomenology to apprehend a nonspurious infinite (of singular universals) by not fleeing its very particular finiteness.[11] This is the re-version of the epoché that we attempt to call forth in a more plastic practice of reduction and is the manner in which I read the directly prescriptive proposition on how to read her that Malabou writes in the "Afterword" to this text on plasticity:

> The book must be read as a narrative, written by a fictitious subject, whose reality is of no importance. I am just trying to show how a being, in its fragile and finite mutability, can experience the materiality of existence and transform its ontological meaning. The impossibility of fleeing means first of all the

impossibility of fleeing oneself. It is within the very frame of this impossibility that I propose a philosophical change of perspective that focuses on closure as its principal object.¹²

This is an opening to closure that re-forms the beyond of messianic transcendence into a material immanence *that can change*.¹³

Reading the Science of the Brain Reminds Us of Belief

To get at such material immanence from the perspective of science, Malabou reads neurology. Science at times is misunderstood, both from within and without, as the belief in and search for causation that is calculably specified, objectively repeatable, and affectively neutral. In its continuing effort to make *what is* intelligible, science is no longer trapped in some allure of causal hierarchies as it seemed to be in the days of mechanistic determinism. However, its experimental methodology does seem to assume that truth is adequation in the repeatability of measurable dimensions and that such truth is independent of whatever particular passions motivate the individual scientist in such pursuit of rendering intelligible. As we know, radically empirical philosophies revealed that elements of belief are inherent in the reification of thinking into the categories of cause and effect long before the mitigation of such causal allure in the aim of the practices of science. If, as some thinkers suggest, quantum physics has arrived at a point in its empiricism at which it is impossible *not* to ask itself questions that were formerly called metaphysical, then perhaps it is possible that in a congruent manner current cognitive neuroscience is at that empirical point at which it becomes necessary to ask itself questions that would formerly have been dismissed as spiritual, that is, questions of mind. Malabou's reading of neuroscience with its increasing language of plasticity *is* the future of Hegel. In the last section of the conclusion of this eponymous text, titled "To see (what is) coming," she states:

> It is not by chance that the notion of plasticity today operates in the domain of cell biology and neurobiology. For example, the "plasticity" of the nervous system or the immune system means their ability to tolerate modifications, transformations of their particular components which affect their structural closure, or modifications and transformations caused by perturbations from the environment. Thus, the possibility of a closed system to welcome new phenomena, all the while transforming itself, is what appears as plasticity.¹⁴

In *What Should We Do with Our Brain?*, she thinks through the findings of current neuroscience and critiques the ideology that remains embedded in the explanatory constructs of this research.¹⁵ In many ways, both in neuroscience and in the human sciences, "explanation" is the euphemism for the retention of the allure of causation—as if on its last page science can get to its empirical and measurable version of absolute knowledge.¹⁶ While Malabou in her reading of the extent to which the disciplines of neuroscience have given up their hard reductionisms is more generous than I am, she deliberately chooses not to enter the reductionist/anti-reductionist debate and suggests that it is no longer a particularly pragmatic use of our brain power. What she does with such readings is *to make use of the findings of science for thinking* rather than to remain in contentious debates over value or methodology. Again going back to the future of Hegel, Malabou sets the path for her own thinking:

> Thus it is Hegel who will have discovered before its discovery the plastic materiality of being: that free energy, whether organic or synthetic, which circulates throughout in each and every life. From now on the philosopher lives in the tension created by the existence of pure "possibility" inherent in such an energy, and bears the responsibility of protecting and preserving the rudimentary being of subjectivity: its fragile and finite kernel.[17]

This is using our brains for thinking toward a creaturely praxis of care. We must keep in mind, however, that *pure* may be the philosophical word that most belies its underlying and often forgotten ideologies, especially regarding any political possibilities for the newly forming mediated networks of the *socius*.

To resume the presumptions of my own reading: the spectral form that thus far still seems to persist in the background of her writing—perhaps in some portion of the un-thought that we all inevitably carry in our own determinate particularities—is that of *pure* reason. Malabou in several instances uses the expression "reasonable materialism," and my concern is that the un-reformed form that persists is that of some *pure* intelligibility. While Malabou reclaims for us the materialism that is Hegel's dialectic, there are points in his thinking at which Hegel is not materialist enough—and this has nothing to do with those oscillating, aleatory points of absolute knowledge that are transforming themselves in much of current conceptual thought into singular universals. In *Philosophy of Mind*, Hegel gives prescient readings of both sensibility and affectivity that are materialist, but at multiple points in this speculative ordeal he calls for a sublation that uncharacteristically wishes to be complete, perhaps by vanishing its very mediation, so that in some manner the body and its emotions are *fully mastered* to make way for reason *in some assumed purity*. These points in the speculations constitute an antimaterialist hierarchy of valuation.[18] Such phallic mastering always seems to disavow its matrixial[19] originating and risks renouncing its singular materialisms by not relinquishing its hopes for a *purely* universal idealism. Perhaps the prevalence of this very disavowal has allowed philosophy to fool itself into thinking for so long that it is purely secular. This is one future of Hegel that invites a *phenomenological* materialism to remind us that in addition to a thinking brain of reason we are also a sensing/sensed body always already in the midst of affects.[20] This constitutes a call for a praxis of care that proceeds not only with intelligibility but also with sensibility and affectivity by valuing in an equal manner not only the psyche of its materializing brain but also the affective, phenomenal body of its finite and particular bio-logic in all expressions of its full organology in concert with others.[21] This would be a materialism that claims its very *impurity* in deflagrations that elude measure and that exceed truth as adequation. In addition to its reading science, this philosophy would also practice plastic readings of religions to critique and make use of their findings[22]—findings of praxes that are in some last instances experienced and articulated as beliefs[23]—in order to *think* the ongoing reformations of *how to live*. Reading Malabou materially re-*minds* us how to live.

Notes

1. Roland Barthes, *The Neutral* (New York: Columbia University Press, 2005), 6.
2. "Mindfulness" is intended to be heard in its Hegelian materiality and not as a reference to any New Age spiritualisms that have diluted the meaning of this word to the point of rendering it neutral in the diminished sense.
3. Barthes, *The Neutral*, 7.
4. The titular mimesis is to Jacques Derrida's text, *On Touching—Jean-Luc Nancy* (Stanford, Calif.: Stanford University Press, 2005), at least in its trans-gesture from the French *virgule* in the original publication in 2000, *Le toucher, Jean-Luc Nancy*, to the Anglicized dash. That such mimesis is an act of presumption requires no further explanation, except to imagine that perhaps the specific and highly suggestive arena of neuroscience research summarized in the text that follows anticipates this superficial sarcasm (which constitutes indirect if not unfair critique by irony): *my mirror neurons made me do it*. The exaggeration of humor may help us notice the at times disguised allure of causality at work in the discourse of neuroscience. A truly material plasticity already knows that mimesis makes neurons happen as much as neurons make mimesis manifest. This is a dialectic that must not stop at any assumption of final sublation.
5. Giacomo Rizzolatti and Laila Craighero, "The Mirror-Neuron System," *Annual Review of Neuroscience* 27 (2004): 169–192. The direct quote from the abstract is from 169.
6. Catherine Malabou, *The Future of Hegel: Plasticity, Temporality and Dialectic* (New York: Routledge, 2005), 185.
7. Ibid., 17.
8. This intrusion of perhaps overly distracting bio-graphics about my own reading is partly in response to what seems to be a cryptically allusive last sentence, constituting its own paragraph and hence standing alone for emphasis, that Malabou writes at the closure of *The Future of Hegel*: "The philosophy of Hegel invites us to enter into the serenity and the peril of the Sunday of life" (193). In one of those lines of flight provoked by reading with Barthes's Neutral close to my heart, I was reminded of "Sunday Morning" by Wallace Stevens and found the poem on re-reading to be freshly revelatory during this era of the rethinking of the secular/religious divide. Perhaps the beauty of a singular poem—or even any good writing in general—persists because of its plasticity as much as its form. This raises the question for philosophy of how to think aesthetics by reintroducing into its realm this now intensified concept of plasticity, which it first borrowed from art and its techné, with renewed emphasis on the ongoingness of its transformations.
9. Malabou, *The Future of Hegel*, 182.
10. Catherine Malabou, *Plasticity at the Dusk of Writing* (New York: Columbia University Press, 2010), 52, author's emphasis.

11. In an unpublished essay "Skin-of-Body-Flesh-of-World," I began an initial effort to think this difference between auto-graphics and bio-graphics in the writing of phenomenology:

> The effort to write lived experiences of the "I"—whatever name one proudly or hesitantly gives the "I," that aspect of being human which is intertwined with the expressions of language—to capture this reflexive, moving "I" *is* autobiographical. But this is a peculiar autobiography which is not attempting to give a historical, narrative account of its particular life in the meanings of its particular happenings. In contrast, the attempt of this autobiography is to say the happening itself towards a writing of the logic of phenomena. To be more direct, there is an isomorphism between autobiography and phenomenology. And the inevitable torsion is the (dare I say) irreducible hiatus, gap, dehiscence between the "I" in the immediacy of its living experiencing, in some ways an "I" crossed out, and the "I" thinking about/writing about its lived experiences, in some ways an "I" hypostasized. For this to be an autobiographical phenomenology which we can stomach, we must recall and let speak the body which is there, with its needs, including that for food, and its expressions, including the gurglings of digestion.

As we will see, Hegel does notice such gurglings, in spite of his wish, perhaps, to be rid of such intimate materiality of bodiliness.

12. Ibid., 81–82.

13. In a dialogue with Noëlle Vahanian in *Journal for Cultural and Religious Theory* (http://www.jcrt.org/archives/09.1/Malabou.pdf), Malabou's response to a question about the relationship of the individual to the public realm may help further clarify what for her is included in such closure:

> I don't believe in transcendence at all. I don't believe in something like the absolute Other, or in any kind of transcendence or openness to the other. So in this sense, as a Hegelian, I am quite convinced with Žižek that we're living in some kind of closed organizational structure, and that society is the main closed structure. But at the same time, this structure is plastic. So it means that inside of it, we have all kinds of possibilities to wiggle and escape from the rigidity of the structure. What happens in the brain is the paradigm to figure out what happens in society as such. We are living in a neuronic social organization. And I'm not the only one to say it. The neuronic has become the paradigm to think what the social is, to think society and social relationships. So it is clearly a closed organization; if by closed we understand without transcendence, without any exit to the absolute Other. But, at the same time, this closed structure is not contrary to freedom or any kind of personal achievements or resistance. So I think that in such a structure, all individuals have their part to play [10].

Toward the end of the dialogue, Malabou comments further about determinism and materialism:

> I believe in determinism to a certain extent because I believe that the structure is given once and for all. And when you read Marx you know that determinism is inescapable. But, I believe in dialectics, and it's true to me that Hegel was right to say that freedom was always a struggle between determinism and its opposite. There's no pure freedom and no pure determinism; they're always sort of a negative transformation of both of their mutual relations. And that's what plasticity's about [13].

While this demonstrated lack of purity within Malabou's thinking of plasticity may undermine the presumptions of my reading to come, it does seem that this lack remains within the realm of reason in its very determined freedom. That for which I will contend is a reclamation of the impurity of feeling bodies—the auto-affectivity of the sensed sensible and its necessarily reflexive (making of and undoing of) sentience.

14. Malabou, *The Future of Hegel*, 192–193.

15. Catherine Malabou, *What Should We Do with Our Brain?* (New York: Fordham University Press, 2008).

16. Isabelle Stengers, in *Cosmopolitics I* (Minneapolis: University of Minnesota Press, 2010), offers a brief critique of the neurosciences in their leap from the experimental findings regarding neurons, as what she calls "agents," to a postulated (or at least assumed as possible) knowledge of what she calls "state," that is, the workings of the brain as an entire organ. She states: "Although connected agents are mute about their contribution to this production [that is, 'mental production'], reference to the 'state' postulates that if all agents and their connections could be described at a given instant, they would provide the explanation of what we describe in terms of thought and feeling at that instant" (94). And here I will repeat my concern that "explanation" is a code word for the retention of the allure of cause within the myth of a somehow final and absolute empirical knowledge. In what for her is an uncharacteristically strong critique, if not outright dismissal, Stengers goes on: "I don't believe that there has been any concept to this day that has been so misused, that has involved such disastrous blends of intuitive pseudo-evidence and an operation of disqualification, as the concept of a 'state'" (95). For the most part, I remain convinced that an ongoing resistance to the reductionisms that continue to inhere in the neuro-cognitive sciences is still needed and that critical readings of these assumptions of "state," as Stengers calls it, remain productive.

Indeed, if there were time it would be interesting to discuss the review article on mirror neurons keeping in mind Stengers's critique of "state." When scientific writing is as well thought out and carefully presented as it is in this article, the need for such careful reading to notice the subtle residues of such an allure of (one-way) causality is perhaps even greater. In the midst of perusing the authors' summary of the study that reaches the conclusion that audiovisual mirror neurons exist, I was surprised to read the following sentence, having anticipated that it would refer to the number of monkey brains that had been studied: "Out of 33 studied neurons, 29 showed auditory selectivity for one of the two hand actions" (cited above, 173). And later, even more amusing for me: "One neuron showed a more pronounced response in the hidden condition than in full vision" (174). My politics remains for this singular neuron without a leap to the assumed "state" of brain! However, a politics that remains in the singular risks forgoing an ethos of care in the plural.

17. Malabou, *The Future of Hegel*, 193.

18. Close to the conclusion of the beginning subsection on anthropology in *Philosophy of Mind* (Oxford: Oxford University Press, 2007), as we have progressed from the natural soul to the actual soul, Hegel states: "The soul, when its bodiliness has been thoroughly trained and made its own, becomes an *individual* subject for itself; and bodiliness is thus the *externality* as a predicate, in which the subject is related only to itself. This externality represents not itself, but the soul, of which it is the *sign*" (136). We will allow this wish for a *thoroughly trained body* to be exemplary of such hoped-for purity (of intelligible reason) by sacrifice of the feeling body. In the *Zuzatz* to the last paragraph of his anthropology, Hegel does admit that such sublation cannot be complete, that there is an organic, material remainder that must be expelled:

> The soul's pervasion of its bodiliness considered in the two previous Paragraphs is not *absolute,* does not completely sublate the difference of soul and body. On the contrary, the nature of the logical Idea, developing everything from itself, requires that this difference still be given its due. Something of bodiliness remains, therefore, purely organic and consequently withdrawn from the power of the soul, so that the soul's pervasion of its body is only one side of the body. The soul, when it comes to feel this limitation of its power, reflects itself into itself and expels bodiliness form itself as something *alien* to it. By this *reflection-into-self* the mind completes its liberation from the form of *being,* gives itself the form of *essence* and becomes the *I* [140–141].

In ruseful teleological anticipation, the Absolute Mind perhaps should not forget to remember this originarily violent expulsion of its intimate body become extimate alien and should allow for some strategic rehabilitation by retroactive un-training of its affective bodiliness. While the body is often not easy to love, the alien is all too easy to hate. Affects do happen and cannot be sublated (philosophically) in any manner other than pathologic and, indeed, are difficult enough to sublimate (psychoanalytically) in the pragmatics of survival.

Perhaps from this Hegelian *purely organic bodily remainder* and the anxiety it makes happen, we could trace forward to Freudian-Kleinian paranoia and projective identification and to Lacanian foreclosure as paths that in many ways are constitutive of the Other. This will serve as a reminder that there is an inaugural and necessary dissensus in any praxis of care in the plural.

19. "Matrixial" is a psychoanalytic concept developed in the writings of Bracha Ettinger that addresses a way of understanding pre-Oedipal development in a manner distinct from the paradigm of phallic mastery. A number of her essays have been collected in the text *The Matrixial Borderspace* (Minneapolis: University of Minnesota Press, 2006).

20. On the chance that it is not as self-evident as it seems to me, my effort to think a phenomenological materialism has its roots primarily in a sustained reading of Merleau-Ponty *as* a materialist, who perhaps already knew Hegel to be also. His *hyperdialectic* of the flesh is for me more an *aesthesiology* (that is, a logic of aesthesis that gives equal priority to sensibility and affectivity along with intelligibility) than an *ontology*. Merleau-Ponty is a thinker who, as Malabou, is neither afraid of nor dismissive of science and who makes such good use of its findings (at the finite time of his work) for thinking the flesh in all its transformative plasticity.

21. It will be a good use of our brains to read, alongside Malabou, Bernard Stiegler's work, especially the call for a general organology of a system of care that reclaims its long-term future from the midst of the regime of capitalism that has subjectivated our psyches into short-term consumerists. See *Taking Care of Youth and the Generations* (Stanford, Calif.: Stanford University Press, 2010) and *For a New Critique of Political Economy* (Malden, Mass.: Polity Press, 2010).

22. In "Plasticity and the Future of Philosophy and Theology," an article coauthored with Clayton Crocket (*Political Theology* 11, no. 1 [2010], http://www.politicaltheology.com/PT/index), Malabou's concept of plasticity is employed to critique the deconstruction of Christianity in the works of Jacques Derrida and Jean-Luc Nancy. The authors write: "A task in which a radical philosophy and a radical theology can collaborate is to create a new brain for our species, based upon a shared insight into the plasticity of form, both material and immaterial. This is an urgent political, or perhaps even a post-political task" (32). As we have phrased it, this would be a praxis of care for *how to live*.

23. If a praxis of care is to be concretely determined and immanent (in its closure, as Malabou might say) rather than always deferred in teleological anticipation of the to-come (in spite of this being a perhaps less objectionable way to name a form of transcendence), then there may be a need for belief in some manner of reconciliation, both in the singular and in the plural. We will read again with vital passion Hegel's words on *belief* so understood: "Belief—at once this immediate unity as the relationship of these different determinations—has, in *devotion*, in the implicit or explicit *cult*, passed over into the process of sublating the contrast up to spiritual liberation, the process of *verifying* that initial certainty by this mediation, and of gaining the concrete determination of this certainty, names the reconciliation, the actuality of the spirit" (*Philosophy of Mind*, 258). The plastic relation between believing and thinking (the findings of the praxis of such belief) must remain in question, must remain (hyper)dialectical.

15 Necessity as Virtue

On Religious Materialism from Feuerbach to Žižek

Jeffrey W. Robbins

> It makes a tremendous emotional and practical difference to one whether one accept the universe in the drab discolored way of stoic resignation to necessity, or with the passionate happiness of Christian saints.
> —William James

In his "Circumscription of the Topic" from *The Varieties of Religious Experience*, William James famously defined the religious sentiment as making "*easy and felicitous what in any case is necessary.*"[1] To James, it was this total and joyous acceptance of the universe that stood out as the most distinguishing characteristic of religious experience. Far from the dour or legalizing portrait of religion, James insisted it was by religious people's genuine good cheer that religion separates itself from both stoicism and bare morality. "More than a difference of doctrine," James insists; "rather [it is] a difference of emotional mood that parts them." Contrast, for instance, the tone in the manner of acceptance of the universe from Marcus Aurelius and Job: from Aurelius, "If gods care not for me or my children, here is a reason for it"; and from Job, "Though he slay me, yet will I trust him!" Whereas Aurelius braces himself for a life lived in harmony with eternal reason, Job's struggle is one full of passionate intensity as he tries to reconcile himself to his love and trust for God with the fact of his unrelenting suffering. As James writes, "the difference of emotional atmosphere is like that between an arctic climate and the tropics, though the outcome in the way of accepting actual conditions uncomplainingly may seem in abstract terms to be much the same."[2]

James's thesis, and even more the richness and array of examples by which James brought this thesis to life, made an enduring contribution to the academic study of religion, not to mention the burgeoning field of psychology. It might also still help to explain at least one path open for the future of Continental philosophy of religion, specifically with regard to the significance of Slavoj Žižek, the self-described "ethical monster" who has resolved himself to do "what is to be done" with a "cold and cruel passion," and thereby has effectively rendered bare life and brute reality as joy and freedom. By his atheistic materialist theology, he has taken particular pleasure in the articulation of the perverse irony that lies at the core of Christianity. But along the way, he not only has rehabilitated a strict death-of-God theology and the classical materialist critique of religion, but also has made the case for the enduring, positive, even revolutionary legacy of Christianity—one that could be dispensed with only at our peril. Which brings me to my thesis of this chapter—which is, namely, that there is a new materialism in religion, one that accepts the classical materialist critique of religion, but employs this critique not in order to dispense with religion, but as an embrace of its revolutionary potential. Put otherwise, the new materialism in religion turns the materialist critique of religion as a form of false consciousness into a possible virtue. Through and beyond what was once a revolutionary critique of religion, the new materialism is now marked by an enthusiastic embrace, turning necessity into a virtue, and thereby offering one way forward for the future of philosophy of religion.

* * *

Before turning to Žižek's radical recasting of the classical materialist critique of religion, a word must first be said about a new materialism that is emerging in the field of religious studies and helping to chart a path forward for the future of Continental philosophy of religion. This new materialism is examined most thoroughly and thoughtfully by Manuel Vásquez in his book *More Than Belief: A Materialist Theory of Religion*. As Vásquez explains at the outset of the book, he is endeavoring to explore the "materialist turn" in religious studies that has always stood at the margins of the discipline. More specifically, he aims to "show how there have always been insurgent materialist countercurrents within religious studies and philosophy that have short-circuited the temptation towards idealism, subjectivism, essentialism, and transcendence in religious studies."[3] The great advantage of attending to this insurgent materialist genealogy is that it both deprovincializes the study of religion by better historicizing and contextualizing it, and also decolonizes religious studies methodologies by challenging "the privileging of the written texts and beliefs by dominant, hegemonic cultures [that] has led to a marginalization of other ways of knowing, other sources of knowledge."[4]

This approach results in Vásquez detailing the post-Cartesian materialist lineage of Hobbes, Leibniz, Spinoza, and Nietzsche, each of whom struggles against the Cartesian dualistic split between the mind and body in his own way. With Spinoza, for instance, his metaphysical monism provides an early form of a nonreductive materialism wherein the mind and body are not conceived as separate and distinct substances, but rather as "the multiple attributes of a single substance—God—who informs the entire universe."[5] With this materialist understanding, Vásquez continues, "Spinoza breaks the primacy of representation in Cartesianism. Knowledge does not entail recovering correct images from the mind. Rather the task is to explain how the mind and ideas are constituted by a confluence of material—biological and sociocultural—processes."[6] This is nonreductive because it does not merely reverse Descartes; the mind is not merely a reflex of bodily processes. Rather, it is dialectical, the result of a complex interplay. What Nietzsche provides to this insurgent materialist countercurrent is a more praxis-oriented approach. While Vásquez worries that Spinoza overplays necessity and determination, Nietzsche emphasizes contingency and chance. As Vásquez puts it, Nietzsche "shares Spinoza's monism and materialism, but he rejects the appeals to necessity, rationality, and order."[7]

From this lineage, Vásquez goes on to articulate a materialist phenomenology of religion, one that provides an embodied form of knowledge that takes social practice, evolutionary theory, and neuroscience seriously. This phenomenology of embodiment, as he calls it, holds social constructionism in check, and helps move the broader field of religious studies from its prevailing textual approach to more concentration on practice and emplacement. In this way he shows that religions are more than merely texts to be interpreted or decoded, and that practices and institutions are not merely the externalizations of interiorized beliefs.

At the same time, and this is what is most significant for our present purposes, while he accepts a naturalistic approach to the study of religion that limits itself to the immanent frame—that is to say, as a scholar of religion, he does not appeal to supernatural or supra-historical forces or beings—he is equally committed to providing a nonreductive theory of religion. He writes that "immanence for me is a way to restore the full materiality of our being-in-the-world."[8] At the same time, it must not be used to "disqualify the religious practitioners' appeals to the supernatural as nothing more than delusions, false consciousness, maladaptive habits, pathologies, or even more benignly, social constructs."[9] This is consistent with his new materialist approach because if nothing else the scholar of religion must acknowledge "that the practitioners' appeal to the supernatural, god(s), the sacred, or the holy have powerful material consequences for how they build their identities, narratives, and environments."[10]

As will be shown in the pages that follow, while Vásquez provides an alternative genealogy to the lineage I lay out below and effectively recasts the study of religion away from its heavily text-based approach, the materialist theory of religion he articulates ultimately joins with mine not only by his insistence that religion is more than belief, but also by his demonstration of how the employment of a materialist critique in religion need not eventuate in the repudiation of religion. On the contrary, in Vásquez's words, it is by this new materialism that religion might be seen "as the open-ended productive of the discursive and non-discursive practices of embodied individuals who exist in particular times and spaces."[11] To that, I will add that it is by this new materialism that religion might also be recognized, if not revisioned, as a revolutionizing practice. It is to that latter point that this chapter now turns.

* * *

The classical materialist critique of religion begins with Ludwig Feuerbach. By his description of God as a human projection Feuerbach accepts, while simultaneously going beyond, Friedrich Schleiermacher's definition of the subjective essence of religion as feeling. In a manner reminiscent of—or better, inspired by—the post-Kantian dialectics of Hegel, Feuerbach is not content with the ready-made definition of religion as a feeling of absolute dependency lodged in a precognitive state of human consciousness. Just as there is a subjective essence to religion, so too is there an objective essence. Not only is the religious subject born out of the infinitude of the power of feeling, but by its objectification of that feeling, religion becomes more than a feeling. It becomes ontological. It becomes material.

So Feuerbach stands to Schleiermacher as Hegel does to Kant. While Schleiermacher accomplishes a Copernican revolution in religious thought by reorienting theology from God to humanity, Feuerbach goes a step further wherein even the precognitive realm of human consciousness reserved for the religious is revealed as an afterthought. That is to say, religion is a historical construct, a product of the human mind that simultaneously explains humanity to itself and alienates humanity from itself.[12] While this unfolding dialectic is recognizably Hegelian, what must not be lost is that it was also an attempt at a materialist reversal of Hegelian idealism.[13] As such, Feuerbach gave preference to naturalism over Hegel's emphasis on humanity as the bearer of reason, and in contrast to Hegel's speculative abstractions, Feuerbach's new philosophy concerned "itself with the embodied human individual and its concrete feelings and needs."[14] From this prototypical materialist critique of religion we get the by-now familiar conclusion. Namely, once God is revealed as a human projection, religion as alienation, and theology as anthropology writ large, the revelation of religion to itself exposes the religious denial or rejection of all things human, which is shown most clearly by the Christian despising of the world. This becomes the template for the hermeneutics of suspicion wherein it is a very short step from Feuerbach to Marx, Nietzsche, and Freud.[15]

But to advance this materialist critique of religion, we must go one step further with Marx and beyond Feuerbach. It is not enough to see religion as a form of ideology, a superstructural tool obscuring the material bases of social, economic, and political reality. Nor is it sufficient to identify and explain the self-alienating aspects of religion. In Marx's terminology, "The chief defect of all hitherto existing materialism—that of Feuerbach included," is its lingering privileging of the "theoretical attitude" over "revolutionary," or "practical-critical" activity.[16] In short, to make this materialist critique complete, it must not be "a question of theory but a *practical* question."[17] For all Feuerbach's efforts at embedding his religious analysis in concrete feelings and needs, for his employment and reversal of the Hegelian dialectic that shows religion as a historical and cultural product and the idea of God as a human creation, Marx will ultimately conclude that Feuerbach "does not see that the 'religious sentiment' is itself a *social product,* and that the abstract individual whom he analyzes belongs in reality to a particular form of society."[18] Put otherwise, Feuerbach remains an essentialist whose religious critique relies upon a naturalized notion of what he terms "species consciousness." Or, to put it in the terms of Vásquez, Feuerbach's theory of religion is still a subjectivist theory of religion, one that still sees religion as an internal matter of personal belief and private conscience. As such, Feuerbach was not so much a materialist as he was a proto-materialist.

What he misses as a proto-materialist, or as a result of his insufficiently materialist theory of religion, is the complex interplay, and the creative and constant interaction, between the internal and the external, a truly embodied theory of knowledge that knows along with the social constructionist that reality is always mediated by our practices and cognitive categories. It is for this that Marx reserves what is perhaps his harshest thesis on Feuerbach when he writes, "The human essence, therefore, can with him [Feuerbach] be comprehended only as 'genus,' as an internal, dumb generality which merely *naturally* unites the many individuals."[19] By criticizing Feuerbach's treatment of humanity as an "internal, dumb generality," Marx is concerned with Feuerbach's treatment of the human in static terms, as if we consisted of an unchanging essence. Further, that this "dumb generality" "naturally unites" all of humanity leaves the impression of a mechanical determinism, as if human beings and communities are simply made by history and cannot also be the makers of history.

Contrast this accusation of Feuerbach's treatment of humanity as "internal, dumb generality" with the sense of pathos from Marx's most well-known, and perhaps most widely misinterpreted, passage on religion:

> *Religious* distress is at the same time the *expression* of real distress and the *protest* against real distress. Religion is the sigh of the oppressed creature, the heart of a heartless world, just as it is the spirit of a spiritless situation. It is the *opium* of the people.
>
> The abolition of religion as the *illusory* happiness of the people is required for their *real* happiness. The demand to give up the illusions about its condition is the *demand to give up a condition which needs illusions.*[20]

With Marx's critique of religion, the distress and the protest against the distress are very real, even if its expression is misplaced and/or confused. As Marx sees it, people turn to the opium of religion only because they so desperately need the happiness it provides, albeit an illusory happiness. And this too must be heard: religion gives the oppressed voice; it provides the heart and spirit where otherwise there would be neither. In other words, religion is not the problem, only its symptom. Marx holds no special animus toward religion. Rid the world of religion and we will still find ourselves plagued with war, violence, dehumanization, exploitation, and injustice. Rid the world of religion without altering the material conditions of society and something else would no sooner take its place.[21]

But further, the problem with Feuerbach's construal of religion, and this is the mistake made by many later Marxists as well, is that it is a crude materialism that treats human history and cultural production in terms of mechanical determination, a reductive dichotomy wherein reality is conceived strictly in terms of "a determining base and a determined superstructure": such a crude materialism portrays individuals as simply *reacting* to the physical demands of survival, and all forms of cultural production as merely epiphenomenal, "the phantom and inverted reflection of economic production, which determines all human expressions with an iron grip."[22] Marx, on the other hand, sees human activity as consisting of the potential for a truly revolutionizing practice. As he writes in his *Theses on Feuerbach*, "The materialist doctrine that men are products of circumstances and upbringing, and that therefore, changed men are products of other circumstances and changed upbringing, forgets it is men who change circumstances and that it is essential to educate the educator himself. The coincidence of the changing circumstances and of human activity can be conceived and rationally understood only as revolutionizing practice." It is precisely this insurgent materialist countercurrent that the new materialism aims to thematize, lift up, and enact.

What Feuerbach and Marx (and Freud) share in common, and what thus defines the first wave of the materialist critique of religion, is the critique of religion as a form of false consciousness. With Feuerbach we find this in its most basic articulation by his analysis of God as a human projection. The problem is that by projecting what is best and most desirable about humanity onto God, we render the internal external and thus become alienated from ourselves. Who among us, after all, can measure up to the perfection of God? Yet God is precisely the sum of our very own parts. If we could only recognize ourselves in our self-made creation of God, then we might learn to love this life and this world, here and now.

Marx is in basic agreement with this psychosocial interpretation of religion, but his analysis goes further precisely because it is not content with providing an interpretation of already existing religious ideas and concepts. By getting at the material conditions that lie as the basis or cause of the allure of religion in the first place, the critique of religion may now not simply expose religion as a form of false consciousness, but help to establish the possibility for altering those very conditions that are in need of the illusory happiness religion provides. In short, Feuerbach's theology-turned-anthropology becomes the basis for Marx's political action. Likewise with Freud, by getting beyond the boilerplate reading of Freud's critique of religion as a search for a father figure who will not disappoint (a critique, mind you, that might very well be simultaneously reductive and condescending, but nevertheless true insofar as it goes), we can not only appreciate the nuance of his crafting of an argument against religion in *The Future of an Illusion,* but also recognize it as a real call to arms. Religion has become a crutch that actually impairs humanity's development and moral maturity. It must be rejected not because it is false, but because it is lazy, an evasion of our own moral responsibility.

But along the way in this developing materialist critique of religion, there are certain untested claims and false choices. This is shown most clearly by Žižek, who takes issue with the first premise upon which the classical materialist critique of religion is based, and in the end, comes to a very different assessment of the role that religion may play for a new materialism.[23] No longer must the materialist rendering of religion be articulated in the language of critique alone. In fact, with the new materialism, religion might become a source of empowerment and political mobilization. It is in this way that Freud's either/or choice with regard to the future of religion and the prospect for human advancement is revealed as a false one. The question is not whether we keep religion and thereby preserve the status quo, or alternatively, do away with religion and thereby provide the motivation finally to lift ourselves out of the muck wherein reason and experience might once and for all prevail. This is a false choice on both fronts. On the one hand, it treats religion as static and uniform, violating the original basis for the materialist critique of religion that begins with Hegel's locating of religion *within* history. What if, on the contrary, religion had the capacity to subvert the status quo? In what ways has religion in fact functioned as a source of change? On the other, while "the criticism of religion is the premise of all other criticism," getting rid of the crutch of religion provides no guarantee that reason and experience will take its place. In this way, Freud's extreme confidence in the ultimate triumph of science is revealed as a faith.[24] When Freud writes in the concluding chapter to *The Future of an Illusion* that "in the long run nothing can withstand reason and experience, and the contradiction which religion offers to both is all too palpable," and that eventually "purified religious ideas . . . will also lose their hold on human interest,"[25] this sentiment is becoming increasingly difficult to sustain. As an expression of the secularist hypothesis, it has proven to be yesterday's incorrect vision of the future.

What we have promised with Žižek is a materialist theology with the political capability to reverse the dominant power structure. This revolutionary potential is found not by ridding the world of religion, *but by thinking religion otherwise*. For instance, the meaning of the incarnation is not exhausted by the judicial-penal logic of atonement. That God became human promises so much more than merely the forgiveness of sins. Put otherwise, the Christian concept of the incarnation is not so much soteriological as it is material. As Žižek explains it:

> Incarnation is the birth of Christ, and after his death, there is neither Father nor Son but "only" the Holy Spirit, the spiritual substance of the religious community. Only in this sense is the Holy Spirit the "synthesis" of Father and Son, of Substance and Subject: Christ stands for the gap of negativity, for subjective singularity, and in the Holy Spirit the substance is "reborn" as the virtual community of singular subjects, persisting only in and through their activity.[26]

What the incarnation teaches is not only that God becomes human, but that God becomes in and of the world, and thereby, theology is rendered not simply anthropological (à la Feuerbach), but political. To borrow the phrase from Giorgio Agamben, with Christ's promise of the Holy Spirit, he is instituting and authorizing the church as a "coming community."[27]

By his becoming human, the death of God in Christ was inevitable. And really thinking what it means that God was made human lays bare the radical materialist base of Christian theology. "When people imagine all kinds of deeper meanings because they 'are frightened of four words: He was made Man,'" Žižek writes, channeling while simultaneously radicalizing his religious muse, G. K. Chesterton:

> What really frightens them is that they will lose the transcendent God guaranteeing the meaning of the universe, God as the hidden Master pulling the strings—instead of this, we get a God who abandons this transcendent position and throws himself into his own creation, fully engaging himself in it up to dying, so that we, humans, are left with no higher Power watching over us, just with the terrible burden of freedom and responsibility for the fate of divine creation, and thus of God himself.[28]

This is the new materialist recasting of the standard materialist critique of religion. Echoing Feuerbach's original interpretation of God as a human projection, Žižek writes, "It is not just that God gives birth to—creates—man, it is also not merely that only through and in man, God becomes fully God; much more radically, it is man himself who gives birth to God. God is nothing outside of man . . . and in this abyss, the very difference between God and man is annihilated-obliterated."[29] Echoing Nietzsche's proclamation of the death of God, Žižek writes, "The point of Incarnation is that one cannot become God—not because God dwells in a transcendent Beyond, but because God is dead, so the whole idea of approaching a transcendent God becomes irrelevant."[30] Just as with Feuerbach, Marx, and Freud, Žižek uses religion as a means to an end. But in so doing, he does not also dream of dispensing with religion. While religion might be a form of false consciousness, as Žižek makes clear, there is no consciousness that is not at least in some sense invented, or projected. Furthermore, and this is where Žižek's Hegelian logic is decisive, while religion is self-alienating, "the notion of 'self-alienation' . . . is more paradoxical than it may appear." As Žižek explains, "The paradox is thus that there is no Self that precedes the Spirit's 'self-alienation': the very process of alienation creates/generates the 'self' from which the Spirit is alienated and to which it then returns."[31]

It is here where Žižek's most significant analysis on religion is found—specifically in what he terms the "fetishist disavowal of belief": "never a case of simply believing—one has to believe in belief itself."[32] This structure of fetishist disavowal works not only with regard to religious belief, but with all aspects of human civilization. The very same things Freud rightly identifies and analyzes as the privations that lead to the alienation and discontentment with civilization Žižek lauds for "the efficiency of the symbolic fiction" and "the way this fiction structures our experience of reality."[33]

So too with religion: what separates the new materialist understanding of religion from both fundamentalism and cynicism alike is its appreciation of this disavowal. "A fundamentalist does not believe," Žižek insists, "he *knows* directly."[34] Likewise with the cynic who uncritically accepts the fundamentalist presupposition that "religious statements are quasi-empirical statements of direct knowledge." For both, according to Žižek's analysis, there is "the loss of the ability to believe in the proper sense of the term," because what remains "unthinkable for them is the 'absurd' act of *decision* which installs every authentic belief, a decision which cannot be grounded in the chain of 'reasons,' in positive knowledge."[35] In this way, the new materialist understanding of religion can be described as a form of "sincere hypocrisy," or of "lying sincerely."[36] By pretending to believe, by living as if we believe, we not so much are gambling on the promise of eternity, the win-win proposition by which Pascal's wager is described in order to demonstrate the rationality of belief. Instead, by going through the motions, by practicing the religious rituals prescribed for us by another, we do not somehow arrive at a more authentic belief; on the contrary, we get rid of, or over, our belief, acquiring the necessary distance, curing us of its overproximity, and thereby, recognizing religious *belief* as such.[37]

This more ironic (which is not to be confused with cynicism) understanding of the nature of religious belief is illustrated most vividly by the Tibetan prayer wheel:[38] with the prayer wheel, a prayer is first written down—literally inscribed and thus made material. It is then placed in a rotating drum—thus made external and becoming mechanical. The rotating drum is then spun automatically. In this way, it is the wheel that is doing the praying. Religious ritual is revealed as a material practice, and religious belief is shown to be exterior.[39] In short, and returning to what we termed the untested claims and false choices offered by the classical materialist critique of religion, to the extent that this critique of religion consolidated around the shared notion that religion is a form of false consciousness, what Žižek has effectively done is turned that critique into a possible virtue. From the perspective of the new materialism, religion is not only privileged as the premise of all criticism, but also it is religion that unveils the proper structure of disavowal best. Yes, religion is a form of false consciousness; *but all consciousness is a form of false consciousness*. Strip ourselves of all illusions and false assurances and what is laid bare is not our innermost, authentic self, but a pure void utterly bereft of the protection that transcendence guarantees.

Therefore, while Žižek is a materialist through and through, it is a new materialism that does not repudiate, but instead radicalizes, religion, by taking God's act of revelation without reservation as an act of absolute kenosis "after which transcendence has now arrived in the heart of the material world completely devoid of the protection that transcendence guarantees."[40]

The point of this new materialist critique is not that it finally exposes the illusory nature of religion, an illusion that conceals a deeper truth. "Rather," as John Milbank writes of Žižek, "it is a fiction necessary to human civil existence. The only collective house which humans can and must inhabit is a pretend one."[41]

Not only does it not offer us the guarantee of a God who is watching over us or of good triumphing over evil, but even more radically, we cannot even be sure of our efforts at distinguishing between right or wrong, friend or foe—all to the point that we are left utterly abandoned, a world without the guarantee of God that is nevertheless—and on this point, without irony—the promise of religion.

By this materialist theory of religion that sees religion as more than belief, we can get over the obsession with belief—in Žižek's terms, even get rid of our belief by its externalization and materialization—and thus get on with the business of religion, which at least by this conception, should be about the business of revolutionizing the world.

Notes

    1. William James, *The Varieties of Religious Experience: A Study in Human Nature* (New York: Modern Library, 2002), 59; italics his.
    2. Ibid., 49.
    3. Manuel A. Vásquez, *More than Belief: A Materialist Theory of Religion* (New York: Oxford University Press, 2011), 4.
    4. Ibid., 3.
    5. Ibid., 44.
    6. Ibid., 47.
    7. Ibid., 52.
    8. Ibid., 323.
    9. Ibid., 5.
    10. Ibid.

11. Ibid., 8.

12. Ludwig Feuerbach, *The Essence of Christianity*, trans. George Eliot (Amherst: Prometheus Books, 1989), xxi; emphasis his.

13. As one prominent scholar puts it, Feuerbach "aimed at nothing less than the overthrow of Hegelianism," an overthrow that is simultaneously the true and full "realization" of Hegel's speculative thought in "Feuerbach's own materialism and atheism." In Van A. Harvey, *Feuerbach and the Interpretation of Religion* (Cambridge: Cambridge University Press, 1995), 136.

Or in the words of Frederick Engels in a review from 1888 expressing the "debt of honor" he and Marx owed to Feuerbach as having more influence on their thinking than any other post-Hegelian philosopher: "Then came Feuerbach's *Essence of Christianity*. With one blow it pulverized the contradiction in that without circumlocutions it placed materialism on the throne again. Nature exists independently of all philosophy. . . . Nothing exists outside nature and man, and the higher beings our religious fantasies have created are only the fantastic reflection of our own essence. The spell was broken; the "system" was exploded and cast aside, and the contradiction, shown to exist only in our imagination, was dissolved. . . . Enthusiasm was general; we all became at once Feuerbachians." Frederick Engels, *Ludwig Feuerbach and the End of Classical German Philosophy*, trans. Progress Publishers ([Moscow]: Progress Publishers, 1946), http://www.marxists.org/archive/marx/works/1886/ludwig-feuerbach/ch01.htm.

14. Harvey, *Feuerbach and the Interpretation of Religion*, 136.

15. For instance, as Marx would famously assert, "The criticism of religion is the premise of all criticism." Here, like Feuerbach before him, Marx is signaling the employment of religious critique as a means to an end. Likewise, in the famous introduction to his "Contribution to the Critique of Hegel's Philosophy of Right," Marx provides the perfect summation to Feuerbach's notion of religion as self-alienation when he writes, "The basis of irreligious criticism is: *Man makes religion,* religion does not make man. In other words, religion is the self-consciousness and self-feeling of man who has either not yet found himself or has already lost himself again." Though Marx would make frequent use of theological imagery in his political economy, for the most part this imagery was merely illustrative. Nevertheless, by attending to how religion functioned ideologically in service of a repressive economic order, he demonstrates how knowledge of religion is a form of self-knowledge—or, more accurately, how religion is a form of false-consciousness, and thus the need for a materialist critique of religion as the premise of all ideological critique. See "Contribution to the Critique of Hegel's Philosophy of Religion," in Karl Marx and Friedrich Engels, *On Religion* (Atlanta: Scholars Press, 1964), 41.

16. See "Theses on Feuerbach," in Marx and Engels, *On Religion*, 69.

17. Ibid.; emphasis his.

18. Ibid., 71.

19. Ibid.; emphasis his.

20. From Marx, "Contribution to the Critique of Hegel's Philosophy of Right," in Marx and Engels, *On Religion*, 42.

21. We find the same qualified critique of religion from Freud. Like Feuerbach and Marx before him, Freud did not believe religious ideas come from God, but the reverse. Based on his psychoanalytic theory and its application to the life of culture, it seemed clear to Freud that God was a human projection—or more technically, an infantile neurosis. So the question becomes: if religious beliefs are so obviously false—or more minimally, if there is so little scientific or rational basis for belief—whence the power and enduring appeal of religion? The power and enduring appeal of all religions, Daniel Pals answers for us,

> lies not in the truth of their teachings about a god or a savior, their claims about miracles or a chosen people, or their hopes of a life after death. These doctrines are empty because they lie beyond any chance of proof. The concepts of psychoanalytic science,

> however, are very different. And they show in ever so interesting ways that the real power of religions is to be found beyond their doctrines, in the deep psychological needs they fill and the unconscious emotions they express.

Daniel L. Pals, *Eight Theories of Religion*, 2nd ed. (New York: Oxford University Press, 2006), 75.

With this we have another ingredient to the materialistic critique of religion—namely, the power of religion is independent of its truth and is to be found beyond its doctrines. The power of religion is instead lodged in the psychological need it fulfills. Religion endures because human beings have willed it so, wishing beyond wishing it true. Religion is powered by the energy of desire.

From this point, Freud arrives at his thesis—namely, that religion is a wish fulfillment. Technically speaking, as an illusion—that is to say, something that is "insusceptible to proof" and therefore, "no one can be compelled to think them true, to believe in them"—religious ideas fulfill "the oldest, strongest, and most urgent wishes of mankind. The secret of their strength lies in the strength of those wishes." Freud, *The Future of an Illusion*, 40, 38. Therefore, because religion cannot be proven one way or another, because it is not a matter of truth, it becomes a question of whether it is a positive or negative force in society, whether we are better off with it and retaining the status quo, or without it and making an attempt to improve the lot of human civilization and existence. "Religion has clearly performed great services for human civilization. It has contributed much towards the taming of asocial instincts," Freud explains. "But not enough," he finally concludes. In Freud, *The Future of an Illusion*, 47.

22. Vásquez, *More than Belief*, 240.

23. If the materialist critique of religion begins with Feuerbach's attempt at a materialist reversal of Hegel that "aimed at nothing less than the overthrow of Hegelianism," then Žižek's return to, and rehabilitation of, Hegel in the wake of an entire series of postmodern detractors would seem an odd choice for his self-described materialist theology. But as Žižek insists, Feuerbach's attempts at a materialist reversal of Hegel was not so much a repudiation of Hegel as it was a "fantasy formation" reckoning not with Hegel himself but with the "ridiculous image of Hegel as the absurd 'Absolute Idealist' who 'pretended to know everything.'" So in Žižek's championing of Hegel we are returning to the materialist basis for the eventual materialist critique of religion, and in so doing, we find our own basis for the new materialism.

24. See *Anatomy of an Epidemic*.

25. Freud, *The Future of an Illusion*, 69.

26. Slavoj Žižek, *The Monstrosity of Christ: Paradox or Dialectic?* ed. Creston Davis (Cambridge, Mass.: MIT Press, 2009), 33.

27. See Giorgio Agamben, *The Coming Community* (Minneapolis: University of Minnesota Press, 1993).

28. Žižek, *The Monstrosity of Christ*, 25.

29. Ibid., 33.

30. Ibid., 31.

31. Ibid., 71.

32. Slavoj Žižek, *The Parallax View* (Cambridge, Mass.: MIT Press, 2006), 353. Perhaps this is explained best in the anecdote Žižek is fond of telling of the Nobel Prize–winning physicist Niels Bohr: once when a guest visited Bohr at his home, the guest expressed surprise that there was a horseshoe hanging above the door. This was a popular practice thought to bring good luck, but a superstition the guest thought hardly befitting a world-renowned expert in quantum mechanics. When the guest announced his disbelief in the efficacy of the horseshoe, Bohr retorted: "I don't believe in it either; I have it there because I was told that it works even if one doesn't believe in it!" "What this paradox makes clear," Žižek explains, "is the way a belief is a reflexive attitude: it is never a case of simply believing—one has to believe in belief itself."

33. To take one case in point, when it comes to the intimate relationship with our neighbors, a kind of forced intimacy that might easily feel stifling and breed contempt, Žižek writes: "We behave *as if* we do not know that they also smell bad, secrete excrement, and so on—a minimum of idealization, of fetishizing disavowal, is the basis of our coexistence." Ibid., 347.

34. Ibid., 348.

35. Ibid.

36. Ibid., 353. It is an indirect form of belief that at one point Žižek summarizes as "Alcoholics Anonymous meets Pascal: 'Fake it until you make it.'"

37. Echoing Feuerbach's original interpretation of God as a human projection, Žižek writes, "It is not just that God gives birth to—creates—man, it is also not merely that only through and in man, God becomes fully God; much more radically, it is man himself who gives birth to God. God is nothing outside of man . . . and in this abyss, the very difference between God and man is annihilated-obliterated." Echoing Nietzsche's proclamation of the death of God, Žižek writes, "The point of Incarnation is that one cannot become God—not because God dwells in a transcendent Beyond, but because God is dead, so the whole idea of approaching a transcendent God becomes irrelevant." Ibid.

38. See Slavoj Žižek, *The Sublime Object of Ideology* (New York: Verso, 1989), 34.

39. This ritual is no different from the canned laughter on television sitcoms. As Žižek observes, the idea here is that the canned laughter is not, as commonly thought, a prompt to get the viewer to laugh, but actually laughs in the viewer's place. TV laughs for us. Even what we regard as perhaps our most spontaneous and natural emotion is mechanized and exteriorized.

40. Žižek, *The Monstrosity of Christ*, 18.

41. Ibid., 179. Milbank then goes on to explain how this theory of religion relies on Žižek's "Hegelian modification of Marxism": "Religion is not so much, as for Marx, a meta-illusion which disguises the necessary illusions of the State and the commodity as, rather, a primary necessary human illusion which allows human subjectivity to come into being at all, and then further permits the necessary illusions of the State and market to be realized."

16   Plasticity in the Contemporary Islamic Subject

John Thibdeau

I DO NOT BEGIN from the premise that religion, as a set of beliefs, thoughts, or symbols, is an independently individuated entity of its own. By this I mean that religion is individuated as a phenomenon through human behavior and thought. This is intended to imply that the study of religions must think about religions as arising through, or possibly existing in, human behaviors. In this sense, religion does not exist independently of a human subject with causal or agentive powers in the world. Seeing religion as something in-itself fails to capture this aspect of it and consequently fails to capture the full depth of the phenomenon. So in thinking about religion as a way of engaging with the world, it seems plausible to turn to the more fundamental questions about the nature of the self and its relationship to the world. I approach such questions with the goal of understanding how particular modes of thought and behavior come to be acquired and transmitted in ways that shape both individual behavior and community practices and customs.

In much of Western academic discourse and literature the subject is assumed to possess universal capacities and desires that drive its actions. Such assumptions are grounded in a model of the subject as an individuated consciousness that operates through autonomous, rational decision-making processes. Furthermore, since the Enlightenment these notions of subjectivity have for the most part remained unquestioned in political, legal, and academic discourse—leading to the privileging of a particular type of subjectivity that is characterized by its interiority and rational capacities and tendency toward self-empowerment.

In *Politics of Piety,* Saba Mahmood problematizes these assumptions through her work with the women's mosque movement in Egypt.[1] She does this by highlighting two crucial aspects of subjectivity that are often left out of the model of the modern subject. The first feature is that the subject's desires are culturally constructed, not innate and universal. The second aspect is that the subject's actions are given form through the individual intentions and volitions that drive those actions, and that this form can both reveal certain aspects of religious beliefs and religious traditions and promote change from within the tradition.

Additionally, through a study of cassette sermon listening in Egypt, also part of the *da'wa* movement that Mahmood studies, Charles Hirschkind in his book *The Ethical Soundscape: Cassette Sermons and the Islamic Counterpublic*, is able to demonstrate the importance of perception and gesture as crucial components of subjectivity.[2] He also shows how the cultivation of affective-volitional dispositions can occur at the nonconscious level as well as the conscious level that Mahmood primarily engages. Of particular interest with respect to Hirschkind's work is the interrelation of subject and environment, or more broadly self and other, that blurs these ordinarily distinct boundaries and helps to show that the landscape *is* what the people do, how they live, and how they reason about and perceive the world. Given this relationship to the world, it becomes important to look at how acting subjects within a particular sociopolitical context produce traditions themselves and how those traditions operate within the structures of power to give form to their subjects.

Drawing on the work of the philosopher Catharine Malabou, I will argue that these features of subjectivity, rather than illustrating entirely distinct types of subjects, actually demonstrate the plasticity of the subject. Such a theory of the plastic subject can accommodate these different models within a single framework that can provide an alternative way of conceptualizing the subject and its patterns of thought and behavior, thereby enabling us to better understand religion as it relates to human experience.

The concept of plasticity that I will be using here is excavated by Catharine Malabou from the work of Hegel in her book *The Future of Hegel: Plasticity, Temporality and Dialectic*,[3] and it is subsequently combined with the phenomena of neural plasticity in her book *What Should We Do with Our Brain?*[4] In the general sense plasticity refers to the capacity to give form, as in "plastic surgeon" or "plastic arts," as well as the capacity to be formed.[5] Thus, in arguing for a plastic subject I am saying that a theory of the subject must be able to account for the culturally constructed aspects of subjectivity in addition to the self-directed aspects and that the nature of the plastic subject is such that it necessarily possesses these capacities.

In looking at Malabou's work on Hegel, we see plasticity being used to describe the process by which the spirit becomes individuated, as well as the nature of that individuated spirit. In Hegel, the spirit has the power of self-determination, which means that it possesses the power to give form; but, since it is forming itself, it must also have the capacity to receive form. For Malabou, this is the fundamental process of subject formation in Hegel's work and more generally demonstrates how plasticity can be used to conceptualize this formative process.[6]

However, plasticity is not merely a philosophical concept. It is also a term that describes the development of a variety of brain processes. And, since every subject has a brain, it is worth considering that subjects might display some of the same characteristics as their brain. Malabou explores the connection of the philosophical concept with the neural phenomena in her book *What Should We Do with Our Brain?* Here she makes reference to three forms of plasticity that occur in the brain and central nervous system: developmental, modulation, and reparative plasticity. The first refers to the development and growth of the brain through the establishment and strengthening of neural connections as dictated by genetic factors, as well as the subsequent formation and alteration of the brain through environmental interaction. For Malabou:

> The genesis of the brain, through the two phases of establishing connections and their maturation under the influence of surroundings, thus makes evident a certain plasticity in the execution of the genetic program. In both cases, the brain appears at once as something that gets formed—progressively sculpted, stabilized, and divided into different regions—and as something formative: little by little, to the extent that the volume of connections grows, the identity of an individual begins to outline itself.[7]

This process has been well established in neuroscientific literature for quite a while, but many argued that this plastic period was limited to the child's brain. However, more recent research demonstrates that these processes are active through adult life, a claim that drastically extends the theoretical and practical application of the study of plasticity.

The second is *modulation plasticity*, which is associated with the processes of memory and learning; it demonstrates how certain synapses in the brain can become more effective and that they have the power to form networks and connections on their own. Certain experiences activate certain neurons, and the repeated activation of a neuron causes it to increase in size and efficiency. Furthermore, when particular neurons are activated simultaneously, they connect to form various networks. It is this process that allows for forms of associative memory, whereby certain stimuli can give rise to unforeseen responses (thoughts, feelings, actions). She goes on to say:

> The fact that synapses can see their efficacy reinforced or weakened as a function of experience thus allows us to assert that, even if all human brains resemble each other with respect to their anatomy, no two brains are identical with respect to their history. . . . Repetition and habit play a considerable role, and this reveals that the response of a nervous circuit is never fixed. Plasticity thus adds the functions of artist and instructor in freedom and autonomy to its role as sculptor.[8]

A particular example of this phenomenon can be seen in the case of adult stem cells: "nonspecialized cells found in specialized tissues. They renew themselves, and most of them specialize, in order to produce all the types of cells in their tissue of origin that normally die."[9] However, in addition to taking the form of their tissue of origin, these cells can also change themselves into other types of specialized cells. Malabou calls this process *transdifferentiation,* and it is this capacity that she refers to as stem-cell plasticity. This open-ended notion of plasticity is extended to apply to the general "ability to change one's destiny, inflect one's trajectory, to navigate differently, to reform one's form."[10] Therefore, just as the stem cells and neurons are able to form themselves and establish new connections in order to maintain the individual, so too is the subject able to give itself form and establish new social relationships.

The third dimension of plasticity explored by Malabou is *reparative plasticity,* which refers to the ways in which the brain is able to renew, regenerate, and "compensate for losses caused by lesions."[11] This process can be associated with *modulation plasticity* as it relates to memory and learning, but "adult neurogenesis, being the final mechanism of plasticity and one strongly controlled by a subject's personal experience and environmental interactions, very likely constitutes an additional mechanism of individuation—with the major difference that it is operational throughout life."[12] It is this type of development that is central to Mahmood's discussion of the work practices do in cultivating the individual's habitus, as well as Hirschkind's notion of the sedimentation of affective dispositions. I argue that in extending these neural phenomena in this way, Malabou helps develop a model for understanding the processes of subjectivation through plasticity.

According to Malabou, "contemporary subjectivity is being a brain."[13] This statement means that, given the knowledge about how the brain functions, it seems more accurate to think of subjects as plastic. Patterns of thought, emotional and affective dispositions, and modes of behavior characteristic of a particular subject are conditioned through the conscious and nonconscious correlation of neuronal networks and bodily movements, and it is this structuring that endows a particular subject with its individuality. In my view, such a statement is not intended to reduce the subject to its neuronal connections but instead means that plasticity as a neuronal phenomenon accounts for the types of bodily and affective learning and memory described by Mahmood and Hirschkind, and that plasticity as a general philosophical concept provides a way to conceptualize the functioning of the processes involved in the formation of the subject and its relationship to the world.

In *Politics of Piety,* Mahmood takes up a project aimed at exploring the modes of agency that exist within the *da'wa* movement and the ways that the practices associated with this movement are misunderstood and misrepresented as either forms of resistance to modernity or passive submission to the male-dominant norms of Islamic society. I take up the work of Mahmood here in order to highlight some of the important attributes and characteristics of the subject she describes, as well as the processes by which that subject comes to be formed. Her primary argument is that the subject, rather than being the independent autonomous individual endowed with certain universal capacities and tendencies, is actually one with culturally constructed desires and intentions that is formed through *modes of subjectivation*—a term Mahmood borrows from Foucault.[14]

She draws on this in order to show how agency, as a principle of effectivity, is not the product of any innate desire, will, or ghost in the machine. As she argues, these models of agency fail to capture the self-formative power of the subject in cases where the subject's actions are not directed by the normative conceptions of freedom and resistance. Instead, how a person engages with the world and the forms of behavior it enacts as well as the patterns of thought it experiences are conditioned by the techniques of learning, memory, and disciplining that are authorized by processes of power, and agency must be understood within these overriding structures of power.

For Mahmood, "power is to be understood as a strategic relation of force that permeates life and is productive of new forms of desire, objects, relations, and discourses."[15] She goes on to say that "the subject . . . does not precede power relations, in the form of an individuated consciousness, but is produced through these relations, which form the necessary conditions of possibility."[16] What this description illustrates is that the subject for Mahmood has the inherent capacity to be formed by external processes of power, and is not independent and autonomous. The subject is not something that transcends or exists independently of social and political structures, but is instead produced through the interaction of those structures with the internal processes of the subject. It is with this in mind that Mahmood states: "My investigation treats the empirical character of bodily practices as the terrain upon which the topography of the subject comes to be mapped, and I elaborate the architecture of the self through the immanent form bodily practices take—*an analytical move that productively reverses the usual routing from interiority to exteriority in which the unconscious manifests itself in somatic forms.*"[17]

We ought not to be looking to the mysterious "self" to explain the subject, but instead ought to look to embodied practices to see how the subject's internal states are developed through those actions. She also discusses how the internal structures of intentionality, volition, and affect give particular form to behaviors. She states, for example, that "the space of ritual is one among a number of sites where the self comes to *acquire* and *give expression* to its proper form."[18] So the subject is not simply given form, or as Mahmood states, it is not a "repository of tradition and culture"; rather, the subject must be seen as having the additional capacity to give form to itself through particular behaviors and practices. Thus, while she claims that her work reverses the direction of analysis, I would argue that her work allows for both directions of analysis and is actually an illustration of the plasticity of the subject insofar as her subject displays the two primary features of plasticity being discussed: the power to give and to receive form.

It becomes clear in her work that the perceived intention of the members of the *da'wa* movement is not simply to resist norms imposed in present-day Egyptian society, nor is it a project that seeks to liberate its members from oppression or subjugation. Instead, the primary purpose of the movement is seen as the cultivation of the pious Muslim subject that exists in the proper embodiment of actions, as well as the formation of a proper *umma* that serves to orient Muslims in everyday life and to encourage the cultivation of virtues in daily activities. According to Mahmood, "Among mosque participants, individual efforts toward self-realization are aimed not so much at discovering one's *true* desires and feeling, or at establishing a personal relationship with God, but at honing one's rational and emotional capacities so as to approximate the exemplary model of the pious self."[19] Mahmood illustrates this shift in teleology, from freedom to cultivation, through her discussion of Aristotle and Foucault on virtue ethics and uses the account of developing modesty (*al-haya*) in order to "examine the kind of agency that was involved when a novice tried to perfect this virtue, and how its performance problematizes certain aspects of current theorizations within feminist theory about the role embodied behavior plays in the constitution of the subject."[20] Through this discussion she highlights two crucial points: "To begin with, what is striking here is that instead of innate human desires eliciting outward forms of conduct, it is the sequence of practices and actions one is engaged in that determines one's desires and emotions. In other words, action does not issue forth from natural feelings but *creates* them."[21] The second point is that "bodily acts—like wearing the veil or conducting oneself modestly in interactions with men—do not serve as manipulable masks in a game of public presentation, detachable from an essential interiorized self. Rather, they are the *critical markers* of piety as well as the *ineluctable means* by which one trains oneself to be pious."[22] This implies a shift away from looking at behaviors and practices as symbols and representations, and towards looking at the actual "work [practices] do in constituting the individual," a point that I will pick up again through the work of Hirschkind.[23]

With reference to the first point, from her descriptions of the women explaining the cultivation of modesty, it can be seen that the women are conscious of what they are doing and have a particular intention in their actions. Their practices are aimed at cultivating a particular virtue that does not inherently exist in themselves, not at the realization of a universal virtue of self-empowerment. Therefore, from a Western perspective, since these women do not strive for self-empowerment, they are often not considered to possess agency and are thereby stripped of any conscious engagement in the world. Such superficial engagement fails to account for the ways in which traditions themselves come to be shaped through the actions of their participants.

Furthermore, the modes of subjectivation she makes reference to are often referred to as pedagogical processes that are "geared precisely toward making prescribed behavior natural to one's disposition."[24] These prescribed forms of behavior, or "moral virtues (such as modesty, honesty, and fortitude) are acquired through a coordination of outward behaviors . . . with inward dispositions (e.g., emotional states, thoughts, intentions) *through the repeated performance* of acts that entail those particular virtues."[25] In her discussion of these pedagogical processes, she makes reference to the notion of habitus to explain how a set of capacities is acquired through repeated practice, and how that set of capacities becomes "a nondeliberative aspect of one's disposition."[26] Thus, her discussion of modes of subjectivation I believe can be informed and supported by theories of memory and learning, an area of study in which neural plasticity has come to play a crucial role.

In *Biology of Freedom*, the psychologist Pierre Magistretti and the neuroscientist François Ansermet explore the role of plastic processes in human development, particularly with respect to learning and memory. They begin by saying: "The mechanisms of memory are based on an essential property of the nervous system: neuronal plasticity."[27] Furthermore, plasticity "enables the brain to register in a lasting way pieces of information coming from our environment, making it possible for the experiences undergone by each individual to leave a trace in the neuronal circuits."[28] While this has generally been linked with the formal aspects of learning, they state that "it is legitimate to suppose that [traces] may be extended to all of an individual's experiences, especially to what contemporary neuroscientists call emotional memory."[29] For them, the reality of plasticity as a biological phenomenon suggests a mechanism for understanding the individuality and uniqueness of each subject.

Therefore, when Mahmood states that she is interested in "the work [practices] do in constituting the individual," I would argue that the *work* she is referring to is best understood through the processes of learning and memory associated with neural plasticity.[30] The practices of the women she studies have the power to shape them as subjects precisely because their practices and experiences are able to structure neuronal networks and bodily processes in particular ways. Consequently, I believe that what is fundamental to her subject, insofar as it enables the formative processes that she describes, is its plasticity. Again, this is not to say that the subject can be reduced to brain processes, but that those brain processes in conjunction with gestural and disciplinary practices allow for certain modes of subjectivation that give rise to different subjectivities.

However, this type of process should not be seen as only developing desires, or intentional states in general. Such a view would limit our understanding of subjectivity in a way that would center on the role of consciousness. To get beyond this idea, in his introduction to *Genealogies of Religion,* Talal Asad writes, "One does not have to subscribe to a full-blown Freudianism to see that instinctive reaction, the docile body, and the unconscious work, in their different ways, more pervasively and continuously than consciousness does. This is part of the reason why an agent's act is more (and less) than her consciousness of it."[31] The point here seems to be that effectual power, agency, is not necessarily tied to subjectivity through consciousness alone. In other words, it is not solely due to their consciousness that people have agency in the world. Consequently, it seems reasonable to attempt to rethink subjectivity as something more than consciousness insofar as consciousness is not entailed by agency.

Charles Hirschkind in his work *The Ethical Soundscape* offers one approach to rethinking subjectivity from an embodied perspective where mind and body, or the conscious and nonconscious, are synthesized into what he says is "the *human compound,* as Jousse glosses the indivisible unity of body and mind, [that] is the product of a complex dance of rhythmic gestures, or *gesticulations,* the motor actions by which the body *intussuscepts* the world it inhabits, incorporating what is outside within it."[32] This *intussusception,* or the taking within of something, is exemplified in the studies of perception in that there seems to be a very real way in which, in the act of perception, we bring the world into ourselves. The opposite logical movement would be *gesticulations,* which could then be seen as the projection of our selves into the world. Furthermore, it seems these processes are connected at a nonconscious level, where by nonconscious I mean the physical processes of which one cannot be conscious, implying that there is a way in which the individual can interact in a mutually affective manner with the world without the aid of consciousness. I would argue that this movement between *intussusception* and *gesticulation* is one that takes place in the plastic subject.

This interaction is not simply one in which the subject is formed by the environment; instead, it must be seen as a reversible relationship in which the subject also gives form to the environment. For Hirschkind, "Viewed in this light, cassette sermons emerge as more than just a technology of ethical self-fashioning. Such tapes contribute to *the creation of a sensory environment* from which the subject draws its bearings, an environment that nourishes and intensifies the substrate of affective orientations that undergird right reasoning."[33] This practice of listening associated with the cassette sermons does far more *work* than simply the construction of the subject. It also works to construct a public space, or ethical soundscape, which in turn reinforces the cultivation of a particular type of subject, in this case the ethical listener or pious Muslim. Thus, gesture plays an extremely important role in defining Islamic subjectivity in this case, and so it is important to look at these more nonconscious modes of behavior when thinking about the study of the Islamic tradition.

In addition to adding gesture as a level of engagement worth exploring further, he also highlights some alternative views on perception and its role in the tradition. In my view, introducing an *enactive* conception of cognition and perception could help us to see agency through a new lens.[34] Addressing Hirschkind's work as a whole, one of his goals in his account of the practice of listening to cassette sermons is to demonstrate some of the inadequacies of Western models of agency and the assumptions upon which these models are grounded. He states in his introduction that "the analytical standpoint afforded by the notion of democracy is inadequate for grasping the articulations of politics, ethics, and religion in postcolonial contexts like Egypt, and for assessing the possibilities of social and political justice they may enfold."[35] One of the primary reasons for this is that "it is widely recognized that the politics, ethics, and epistemologies that defined the Enlightenment project were deeply entwined with a set of assumptions regarding the relative value of the senses."[36] This hierarchy of senses has rendered truth increasingly abstract, leading to a privileging of text over speech, reading over listening, interpreting over embodying, and inner meaning over outward expression. In the drawing of these distinctions, and by the tying each of the former elements to modernity, progress, and reason, the latter elements become tied to the senses, tradition, and irrationality. According to Hirschkind, "the vision of disembodied reason that undergirds these normative judgments in my view provides an inadequate standpoint from which to think about political practice as sensible activity."[37] His discussion of cassette sermons in Egypt demonstrates how embodied practices can help to shape both political and social spaces in particular contexts.

The sensible activity being discussed in his work, generally understood as ethical listening, is positioned within a larger context of postcolonial Egypt. The approach to listening in the Islamic tradition is significantly different than within the Enlightenment tradition, the latter often characterizing listening as a passive state. "*Samʿ*, in other words, is not a spontaneous and passive receptivity but a particular kind of action itself, a listening that is doing."[38] Thus, ethical listening is an active way of being in the world, a means for constructing the self and the space in which that self exists. Such an active view of perception has also been a conclusion reached by a variety of people working in the field of neuroscience, where it has become clear that visual perception is not an unmediated and passive process that gives us direct access to the world.[39] With this view, I believe it will become possible to see political and social reasoning as sensible activity, rather than strictly cognitive.

This view of listening enables the cassette sermons to orient Muslims in a variety of ways, including strengthening their knowledge of Islam, providing forms of therapeutic relaxation, and constructing an "ethical soundscape" conducive to the cultivation of virtues. In this way, these sermons help to shape a "pious sensorium" that enhances the subject's capacity to experience a close relationship to God in all aspects of life. For Hirschkind, "Listening invests the body with affective potentialities, depositing them in the preconscious folds of kinesthetic and synaesthetic experience and, in doing so, endows it with the receptive capacities of the sensitive heart, the primary organ of moral knowledge and action."[40] The skillful *khatib* is thus one who is able to engage the audience not just on the mental level, but on the physical level as well. Certain emotions are given a physical manifestation, and over time, these associations become a part of the subject's disposition—or way of perceiving the world. Perception, in this sense, should then be seen not as a passive state, but as an active relationship with the world that is conditioned by past experiences. "Memory, in other words, is not built upon ideas, and much less upon visual images, but rather on the reactivation of gestures, understood as the sensory sediments of prior perceptions."[41] This relationship illustrates the importance of an embodied approach not only in studying traditions, but also in studying cognition more generally. It is through research in plasticity and embodied cognition that it will become possible to integrate the body and mind into a more unified subject in which the cognitive models that reduce subjects to thinking machines are replaced by more robust and dynamic models that accommodate the gradations of human behavior and experience in ways that account for their social, historical, and biological roots.

Lastly, it seems to me necessary to ask how we can use the knowledge about the functioning of our brain to analyze the types of subjectivities being formed through various structures of power. Our brain is not a fixed and rigid entity, nor is it infinitely flexible and adaptible. Such distinctions are reminiscent of the classifications of tradition as rigid versus liberalism as progressive, or of religious subjects as resistant and modern subjects as flexible; but I believe these can be overcome through the incorporation of plasticity into our understandings of agency, subjectivity, tradition, public and private space, and temporality. Such a move certainly calls into question the value judgments associated with liberalism and its priviliging of flexibility, adaptability, and hybridity as proper attributes of the modern subject. Consequently, it seems plausible to begin to look at how subjects are being formed through different cultural practices and how those subjects engage with the world. These are some questions explored further by Malabou in her works, and I believe Mahmood and Hirschkind present examples of the often overlooked attributes of subjectivity that demonstrate its plasticity. Such a move enables us to look at the forms subjects take, rather than the types they represent.

Notes

1. Saba Mahmood, *Politics of Piety* (Princeton, N.J.: Princeton, 2005).
2. Charles Hirschkind, *The Ethical Soundscape* (New York: Columbia, 2006).
3. Catherine Malabou, *The Future of Hegel* (New York: Routledge, 2005).
4. Catherine Malabou, *What Should We Do with Our Brain?* (New York: Fordham, 2008).
5. Malabou, *The Future of Hegel*, 8.
6. Ibid., 10.
7. Malabou, *What Should We Do with Our Brain?*, 20.
8. Ibid., 24.
9. Ibid.
10. Ibid., 25.
11. Ibid.
12. Ibid., 27.
13. Catherine Malabou and Clayton Crocket, "Plasticity and the Future of Philosophy and Theology," *Political Theology* 11, no. 1 (2010): 29.
14. Mahmood, *Politics of Piety*, 17.
15. Ibid. 7
16. Ibid.
17. Ibid.; italics mine.
18. Ibid., 121–122.
19. Ibid., 131.
20. Ibid., 31.
21. Ibid., 155.
22. Ibid., 157.
23. Ibid., 158.
24. Ibid., 29.
25. Ibid., 131; italics mine.
26. Ibid., 136.
27. Ibid., 137.
28. François Ansermet and Pierre Magistretti, *Biology of Freedom* (New York: Other, 2007), 18.
29. Ibid., 19.
30. Ibid., 20.
31. Talal Asad, *Genealogies of Religion* (Baltimore: John Hopkins University Press, 1993), 15.
32. Hirschkind, *The Ethical Soundscape*, 77.
33. Ibid., 125.
34. John Stewart, Olivier Gapenne, and Ezeqyiel A. Di Paolo, eds., Enaction: Toward a New Paradigm for Cognitive Science (Cambridge, Mass.: MIT Press, 2010).
35. Hirschkind, *The Ethical Soundscape*, 5.
36. Ibid., 13.
37. Ibid., 31.
38. Ibid., 34.
39. Stewart, Gapenne, and Di Paolo, Enaction: Toward a New Paradigm for Cognitive Science.
40. Hirschkind, *The Ethical Soundscape*, 79.
41. Ibid., 78.

17 From Cosmology to the First Ethical Gesture
Schelling with Irigaray

Lenart Škof

IN THIS ESSAY I want to explore Schelling's cosmological philosophy by comparing it to early Indian philosophy on one hand and the philosophy of Luce Irigaray on the other hand. In the first section I begin with a comparison of Schelling's cosmogonical question from *Ages of the World* and the Indian Vedic cosmogonic hymn "Nasadasiya." The basic question of this section on the "philosophy of beginning" is whence comes the creation of the world. There is no direct textual evidence in Schelling's writings that he read this particular Vedic hymn, but there are striking similarities between Schelling's cosmogonical concepts and Vedic early cosmological thinking that deserve our close attention. In the second section I first elaborate on ancient Indian teaching on the breath (*prana*) and then approach the philosophy of Luce Irigaray as presented in her later works and relate it to Schelling's and Vedic cosmogonical questions. It is important to acknowledge a link in Irigaray's philosophy to Indian thought (such as in her *Between East and West*). By analyzing Irigaray's philosophy of cosmical/natural breath/ing I explore her recently theorized plane of gestures as an intermediate space between microcosmos and macrocosmos. In this endeavour I plea for a new philosophy of the spirit, evolving from the naturalistically understood phenomenon of breath.

Schelling with the *Vedas*

I would like to begin with Indian mythological or cosmological philosophy to see how closely related Schelling's philosophy is to Indian Vedic thought as exemplified in *Rig Veda*. In the so-called cosmogonical or creation hymn of *Rig Veda* (*Rksamhita* 10.129), "Nasadasiya" (or "Bhavavrtam"), we find the most elaborate ancient testimony of the philosophy of beginning, and cosmic breath as a constituent part of primordial creation:

> 1. Then was not non-existent nor existent:
> then was no realm of air, no sky beyond it.
> What covered it? and where? and what gave shelter?
> Was water there, unfathomed depth of water?
> 2. Death was not then, nor was there naught immortal;
> no sign was there, the day's and night's divider.
> That One thing, breathless, breathed by its own nature:
> apart from it was nothing whatsoever.
> 3. Darkness there was: at first concealed in darkness
> this All was indiscriminated chaos.
> All that existed then was void and formless:
> by the great power of Warmth was born that Unit.
> 4. Thereafter rose Desire in the beginning,
> Desire, the primal seed and germ of Spirit.
> Sages who searched with their heart's thought
> Discovered the existent's kinship in the non-existent.
> 5. Transversely was their severing line extended:
> what was above it then, and what below it?
> There were begetters, there were mighty forces,
> free action here and energy up yonder.
> 6. Who verily knows and who can here declare it,
> whence it was born and whence comes this creation?
> The Gods are later than this world's production.
> Who knows whence it first came into being?
> 7. He, the first origin of this creation,
> whether he formed it all or did not form it?
> Whose eye controls this world in highest heaven,
> he verily knows it, or perhaps he knows not.[1]

The Vedic hymn 10.129 on creation is (alongside the hymn 10.121) the most important philosophical hymn of the *Rksamhita*. The hymn is an account given by the Vedic poet and seer about the primordial stage or obscure "ground" of all existence. There was neither being (*sat*) nor nonbeing (*asat*), in the beginning, says the Vedic seer. There "existed" only "That One" (*tad ekam;* Greek *to hen*), which, being beyond "life" and "death" proper, *breathed* and lived from itself. The third and fourth stanzas offer an explanation of the actual beginning of the world from the first two stanzas: if "That One" is the obscure ground, being *alive* (i.e., breath) even before there was a life and a death, then the primeval Warmth or fervor (*tapas*) is the actual force of creation. Later, in the fourth stanza, Desire/Love (*kama;* Greek *eros*) is the germ of Spirit and as such the first sign of life. For some commentators it is the Spirit that precedes Desire. The absolute genitive structure ("Desire, the primal seed and germ of Spirit") verifies both interpretations. However, I wish to follow here the first interpretation. According to Bloomfield, "That One" even breathes "in a higher sense, without breath (literally 'wind') which is physical and material."[2] "That One" is in a neuter case and as such precedes any "personal" identification, except for the breathing. The fourth stanza is crucial for our explanation: *kama*, "the Desire to live,"[3] therefore comes before mind (*manas*), even Spirit. We can say that for the Spirit to arise in its supreme divine nature, there must be longing of That One (God?; cf. stanza 7) for life. For Deussen, this hidden or obscure principle of longing is a possible hint of the unconscious nature of the principle of creation.[4] But later in the process of creation, both feminine and masculine appear: in the fifth stanza we find "begetters" (*retodha*) and "mighty forces" (*mahimana*), male and female cosmogonic principles. The female principle, *mahimana*, literally means "greatness."[5] The hymn ends with a question, casting doubt over whether the creation has "emanated" or rather been created (by a God?). There is no answer.

Let us see how this Vedic hymn is related to Schelling's philosophy of nature.[6] For Schelling there is no contradiction in the paradox that things in nature are mutually dependent and that they coordinately arise from each other and vice versa:

> In the cycle whence all things come, it is no contradiction to say that that which gives birth to the one is, in its turn, produced by it. There is here no first and no last, since everything mutually implies everything else.

But when we have an original cosmogonic situation, the above constellation applies even to God:

> God contains himself in an inner basis of his existence, which, to this extent, precedes him as to his existence, but similarly God is prior to the basis as this basis, as such, could not be if God did not exist in actuality.[7]

Schelling gives one possible philosophical answer to the riddle posited in the Vedic hymn regarding the impossible condition at the beginning of the world. In the "Nasadasiya," we find neither being (existent) nor nonbeing (nonexistent) but at the same time "That One" *breathes* (and lives) with its own nature. In Schelling it is

> the longing which the eternal One feels to give birth to itself... Man is formed in his mother's womb; and only out of the darkness of unreason (out of feeling, out of longing, the sublime mother of understanding) grow clear thoughts.[8]

In the *Ages of the World* Schelling posits the cosmogonical question: "Where has everything come from?"[9] The answer to this riddle, present also in the Vedic hymn, is for Schelling as follows: will finds itself to be "an eternal No that conflicts with the Yes." For the cosmological conflict to be solved, it is only possible to understand the cosmological Will as negating itself in order to reach the essence. Furthermore, the will itself corresponds to the power of Warmth (*tapas*) from the Vedic hymn, an energy leading to two Indian concepts—*kama* and *trishna* (Greek *eros* and *epithymia*). But for Schelling, as for the Vedic hymn, what-is (*sat*) and what-is-not (*asat*) are only "one essence regarded from different sides."[10] The original conflict of both aspects in That One (*tad ekam, to hen*), or will is the revelation of the *eternal* good, which we have to understand as the eternal outpouring of the stream of life itself, a riddle, or revelation of an eternal longing of a *No* for *Yes*. For this reason, "the spirit is not only the unity of the opposites . . . it is at the same time the link between eternity and the life. . . . The entire life, after all, originated in the first place out of the longing of eternity for itself."[11]

There is another riddle that is to be solved for Schelling—namely, the riddle of the relation between the body and the spirit.[12] The whole, for Schelling, is "a spiritual-corporeal essence." In this early stage of the becoming both are again "the two sides of one and the same existence."[13] In Žižek's Lacanian reading of Schelling as the first dialectic materialist, "*there is no spirit without spirits or ghosts,* no 'pure' spirituality without the obscene specter of 'spiritualized matter.'" But rather than follow Žižek's divide or a double surplus (based on a reading of Schelling's dialogue *Clara*) between the *spiritual element of corporeality* on the one hand and the *corporeal element of spirituality* on the other (the so-called subtle corpses or dead animal bodies with their magnetism versus ghosts, living dead, etc.), we could posit another question: is not the opposite also the case, namely that the spirit is primarily related to the emergence of a life rather than to its limit at the opposite side, death? Do we not search for the primordial relation of a *No* to *Yes* in Schelling (and not vice versa) for the spirit as a link between eternity and the life, or nature (the body)? I understand this as emergence of a life precisely in the sense in which Agamben reads Deleuze. For Deleuze, another empiricist in this line, it holds that "we should not enclose life in the single moment when individual life confronts universal death" (this refers to his example of a dying man, a rogue, from one of the Charles Dickens novels, and of respect or love "for his slightest sign of life"). Rather it is present in "very small children [which] all resemble one another and have hardly any individuality, but they have singularities: a smile, a gesture, a funny face—not subjective qualities. Small children, through all their sufferings and weaknesses, are infused with an immanent life that is pure power and even bliss."[14]

I therefore think that the creation, or revelation, for Schelling consists precisely in the inner tension of *nature* itself, namely, the presence of the obscure longing as a sign of an emanation of *spirit/breath/life* from "nature." In *Philosophical Inquiries into the Nature of Human Freedom* we read:

> These forces which are divided but not completely separated in this division [between nature and reason], are the material out of which the body will later

be moulded; while the soul is that living nexus which arises, as the center of these forces in their division, from the depths of nature. Because primal reason elevates the soul as inner reality out of a basis which is independent of reason, the soul, on this account, remains independent of it, a separate and self-maintained being.[15]

The soul as a *living* nexus (and self-maintained being) and a mediator between the realms of "Gods" and "humans" is therefore a key to our understanding of Schelling's concept of nature. As it will follow in the second section, it is also a possible way for us to conceive of a new philosophy of *spirit* and *life* based on the breath.

From Schelling to Irigaray

In my reading of a Vedic cosmogonical hymn, I have pointed to the obscure moment of a birth/emanation/creation of the world from the Warmth (*tapas*) or Desire/Love (*kama*). The spiritual is already present in this moment as a potentiality: but it is not perceptible until the first signs of life (like breathing) are recognizable. It is the longing of "That One," or, the eternal One (Schelling) that is a germ of the Spirit. A transition from *No* to *Yes*, and a breath and the soul as a living nexus are the first signs of *life*.

Let me now present Indian Vedic cosmogonical teaching on the breath. It is in Indian Vedic thought, approximately four centuries before the *Samkhya-Yoga* system (i.e., between 900 and 700 BCE), that we find the most ancient elaborations of the concepts of cosmic wind/breath outside the Semitic area.[16] We find references to wind and breath in the *Samhitas* (the oldest parts of Vedic collections), but the most ancient testimony and elaboration for the so-called Wind-Breath Teaching (Wind-Atem-Lehre)[17] can be found in the philosophy of nature of *Jaiminiya upanishad brahmana 3.2.2.* and *4* (*JUB*). This teaching is an example of a typical Vedic macro-microcosmic analogy between the macrocosmic Wind (*vayu*) and microcosmic breath (*prana*). From the cosmological point of view, the wind is the only "complete" deity since all other deities/gods/elements/phenomena (sun, moon, stars, fire, day, night, waters, etc.) return to him during the enigmatic stillness of the night, while he never stops blowing. But at the most abstract level, it is the difference between the perishable (day, night . . .) and imperishable or "eternal" (Wind) that led to the so-called Wind-Breath Teaching and later to the concepts of *atman* and *brahman* in Indian thought. Analogously, then, breath in (wo)man is the most important of the five vital powers (breathing, thinking, speech, sight, hearing) since it is only breath that is present during deep sleep. Of course, in the moment of death, breath returns to its macrocosmic eternal origin, the Wind. In an idiosyncratic Vedic plural all five vital powers are called *pranas* (i.e., "breaths"; this marks the very beginning of Indian epistemology), named after the first in the series, breath. Breathing as the most important vital power is thus equated with life itself and later with person's self (*atman*). Finally, as a term for life, *prana* is the essence of a living body.

But before proceeding to the ethical consequences of this teaching, it is necessary to introduce the middle term, *mesocosm*, in order to understand the relation between macrocosm and microcosm. *Mesocosm* is expressed in a ritual as a third term of the triangle structure *the ritual–the cosmic realities–the human body/person* in the Vedic-Upanishadic context.[18] I find Michael Witzel's interpretation of Vedic thought extremely useful for understanding what Irigaray would refer to as the process of spiritualization, or coming to the age of the Spirit.[19] Witzel argues for the reconstruction of the term "mesocosm": within the Vedic magical interpretation of the world, we face different analogies or magical "identifications" between the macrocosmic and microcosmic realities or gods (for example Sun-eye, Wind-breath, Earth-body, Waters-semen, Fire-speech, etc.). This way of thinking uses different "mystic" links/correlations and equivalents/identities, some obvious (such as between Sun and the eye or Wind and breath) and some more hidden and esoteric (between Moon and mind). There exists a nexus or a connection (in Sanskrit *bandhu* and *upanishad*) between two single entities in the *Vedas*. In my opinion, it is crucial to understand these ancient magical correlations between the human and divine realms in order to be able to formulate an outline for a contemporary embodied ethics as a new economy of our intersubjective-"mesocosmic" rituals, i.e., of *embodied ethical gestures*, based on breath as vital power.

To accomplish this task I would finally like to turn to Luce Irigaray's philosophy and her ethics of breath. In *Sharing the World* Luce Irigaray wrote that it is "to her, as living nature, that I have to abandon myself in order to preserve my own life." For Irigaray, we have "to seek help in nature" in order to be able to survive.[20] Our past and our future meet in one single moment of a new sensitivity for our Breath and life, two key phenomena to which we need to pay attention in our times. But how is the body related to this economy of ethical gestures? What is an ethical gesture springing from the embedded and embodied life of an individual, man or woman? A gesture, like the ancient rituals, is the presence of a touch, a word, or thought in the space of proximity—the mesocosm. Here there is a co-presence of us and nature. For Irigaray, this proximity is explained as a "communion with the real presence of the living." Furthermore, by "being in nature" I bear the other(s) within me. This is the gesture of "embodying, for a moment, an unlimited life in order to make him present to me, with me. Which is not without the mystery, the enthusiasm and the reserve, but also the risk, that inspire such a human, and more than human, gesture. We were, we are, two."[21] In *Between East and West* we can read that the first and last gesture of both natural and spiritual life is to breathe (by oneself).[22] Elsewhere Irigaray explains how important the role of the mother/woman is in this process:

> The divine appropriate to women, the feminine divine, is first of all related to the breath. To cultivate the divine in herself, the woman, in my opinion, has to attend to her own breathing, her own breath, more even than to love.... Becoming divine is accomplished through a continuous passage from nature to grace, a passage that everyone must realize by oneself, alone.... The feminine breath seems at once more linked with the life of the universe and more interior. It seems to unite the subtlest real of the cosmos with the deepest spiritual real of the soul. Which inspires a woman appears to remain joined with the universe's breath, related to the wind, to the cosmic breathing.... In this way, the woman can welcome the other in her soul.[23]

Woman shares her breath preeminently by keeping it "inside." By a "feminine economy of the breath" she is keeping and cultivating breath inside the body and sheltering in herself the first seed of nature, the Warmth or Love, which is the eternal longing in Nature for Spirit (in Irigaray this is the spiritualization of the body, or nature). The first breath of the world we share, both in nature (macrocosm) and in (wo)man (microcosm) is at the same time the possibility of a space-between, intersubjective or inter*corporeal* (in the widest sense of the term) space/mesocosm where our lives coexist in a community comprised of all differences (culture, sex, age, even species). A *bodily-spiritual* gesture of keeping and sharing the breath is an ethical gesture of respecting the life of the universe, for Irigaray. It is then the opening of a new philosophy of spirit, based on the way of the breath and respect for life, as already indicated in Agamben's reading of Deleuze.

In her essay "Ethical Gestures toward the Other," Irigaray explains in a new context the key feature of the third phase of her work, namely ethical gestures. According to the human body, the first autonomous gesture is breath, air being the very first food of life. In Genesis, it is said that God *breathed into his nostrils the breath of life* (Gn 2:7).[24] For Irigaray, to become spiritual it is necessary to transform this vital breath "into a more subtle breath" (of loving, listening, caressing, etc.) which corresponds to our transformation of natural life into a spiritual life.[25] I find the most important element in Irigaray's third phase of her work in the incipient relation with the other as a woman—a relation based in her respect for life. In our civilization, we forget an ancient teaching, also exemplified in Vedic hymns and later in the Upanishads and transmitted to us also in the form of Schelling's second and third phases of his philosophy, namely that it is from the ground as the primordially *alive* that women and men exist and thrive.

There is yet another important element present in Irigaray's thought: silence. For Irigaray, silence is "the laying out of a space-time that must remain virgin in order for a meeting to happen. It is openness that nothing occupies or preoccupies—no language, no values, no pre-established truth."[26] Silence is a threshold still (or again) to be revealed to us. I understand it as a substratum of a mesocosm, a *pure gesture* of a deserted intercorporeal space-between still to be inhabited by us.[27] This is according to our intersubjective or microcosmic relations. On a macrocosmic level (which corresponds to nature in our world) in the *Vedas* and related cosmogonical accounts (such as Genesis, for example), *silence* is a sign of the primordial potentiality for the Spirit to arise from the primordial creational longing for Nature, or God. We have seen in the *Vedas* and in Schelling's philosophy that the longing for "That One," or, the eternal One is a sign of a transformation from a *No* to a *Yes* (a life).

While we all know and recognize radically the need of others (including animal others, and, in a way, even nature) to take in and give out breath, at each and every moment, we still reside in our life-worlds, in the grip of most elemental fears of losing the ground beneath our feet, constantly protecting ourselves and taking more than we possibly need (of ourselves, of nature) for ourselves, and causing others to suffocate by not getting their food of life—*air*. We always realize too late that there was a life. There is a task still to come and to be realized in ethics: namely, being attuned to the process of a new *spiritual* transformation of humanity in order to become enlightened enough to be able to hear the voices of the other, to discern the signs and gestures inviting us to begin a dialogue with her or him, or with the Nature in one of her beautiful incarnations. And last but not least, it is a task to respond to the call of the other person, or a nonhuman animal and their breathing in an ethical way.

In my essay I have argued that in both Schelling and Irigaray there exists the possibility to approach this new plane of ethics. By pointing to the cosmological question in Schelling and the mesocosm as a space-between (i.e., intercorporeality) I have understood the latter as a newly conceived place (like the ancient rituals, for example) of a mysterious transition from pure gesture to the first ethical gesture of a (wo)man. The economy of ethical gestures, and later the way to embodied ethics, has its origin in the macro/microcosmic awakening of life that comes to us as a breath or is breathed into us. Breath is then the origin of any embodied ethics, claiming to enter into the intercorporeal realm of humans (and the living nature) via gestures. As I have shown in this discussion, our search for the originary embodied ethics requires us to go back to the past ages of the world, where the primordial potentiality of the Spirit arises from the primordial creational longing for Nature, or God. This is a way of silence—as a substratum of a mesocosm and the opening and origin of ethical gestures. Silence is thus understood as a signpost to deserted intercorporeal space-between still to be inhabited by us. And it is only this way that we will be able to open up a new future for us: a future of a coming ethico-spiritual age that Irigaray so aptly refers to as *The Age of the Breath*.

Notes

1. *The Hymns of the Rgveda*, trans. by R. T. H. Griffith (Delhi: Motilal Banarsidass, 1995), 633-634. See also Maurice Bloomfield, *The Religion of the Veda* (New York: G. P. Putnam's Sons, 1908), 235-236: "1. Nor being was there nor non-being; there was no atmosphere and no sky beyond. What covered all, and where, by what protected? Was there a fathomless abyss of the waters? 2. Neither death was there nor immortality; there was not the sheen of night nor light of day. That One breathed, without breath, by inner power; then it truly nothing whatever else existed besides."
2. Bloomfield, *The Religion of the Veda*, 236.
3. Ibid., 237.
4. Cf. Paul Deussen, *Allgemeine Geschichte der Philosophie, Erster Band, Erste Abteilung* (Leipzig: Brockhaus, 1920), 120. Deussen compares this alleged unconscious principle with *Prakriti* (the "material" original stuff, or *Urstoff/Urwesen* of the creation) of the *Samhkya* system.
5. Paul Thieme has pointed to its modern French equivalent in *grossesse* (*Schwangerschaft* in German): Paul Thieme, *Gedichte aus dem Rig-Veda* (Stuttgart: Reclam, 1964), 68.
6. There is no direct textual evidence in Schelling's writings that he read this Vedic hymn. There are numerous references to the *Vedas* in the first part of his *Philosophy of Mythology* (*Einleitung in die Philosophie der Mythologie*) but without the exegetical analysis of any particular hymn. Generally on Schelling and India cf. Jean W. Sedlar, India in the Mind of Germany: Schelling, Schopenhauer, and Their Times (Washington, D.C.: University Press of America, 1982) and W. Halbfass, *India and Europe: An Essay in Understanding* (New York: SUNY Press, 1988), 78. Sedlar rightly observes that for Schelling ancient Indian texts (i.e., Vedas) were "very unsatisfactory reading" (Sedlar, India in the Mind of Germany, 44). In his mythological analyzes on Indian religions Schelling pays no attention to early Indian myths or the religion of Veda—besides many "errors on the subject of India . . . he declined to accept Vedas as 'Indian' at all" (Sedlar, 130-131). But important for our analysis is that he felt that the Vedas "do not contain the 'explanation or the actual secret of the mythology itself'" (131). Halbfass also rightly observes that from Schelling's early positive views and general openness towards India, his later works turn towards more critical and anti-Romantic approach (Halbfass, *India and Europe*, 78). See also chapter 8 in Jason M. Wirth, *The Conspiracy of Life: Meditations on Schelling and His Time* (Albany: SUNY Press, 2003).
7. F. W. J. Schelling, *Philosophical Inquiries into the Nature of Human Freedom*, trans. with critical introduction and notes by J. Gutmann (La Salle, Ill.: Open Court, 1989), 33.
8. Ibid., 34 and 35.
9. F. W. J. Schelling, *The Abyss of Freedom/Ages of the World*, trans. Judith Norman, with an essay by Slavoj Žižek (Ann Arbor: University of Michigan Press, 1997), 134.
10. Ibid., 143. The original conflict of both aspects in That One (*tad ekam, to hen*), or will, is the revelation of the *eternal* good, which we have to understand as the eternal outpouring of the stream of life itself, a riddle, or revelation of an eternal longing of a *No* for *Yes*. For this reason, "the spirit is not only the unity of the opposites . . . it is at the same time the link between eternity and the life. . . . The entire life, after all, originated in the first place out of the longing of eternity for itself."
11. Schelling, *The Abyss of Freedom/Ages of the World*, 143 and 146.
12. For a detailed interpretation of the body in Schopenhauer (including an intercultural or comparative study) see my "Metaphysical Ethics Reconsidered: Schopenhauer, Compassion and World Religions," *Schopenhauer Jahrbuch* 87 (2006): 101-117. Cf. this paper also to polemicize against Žižek, who in his study on Schelling contends that "Schelling's late phi-

losophy should by no means be reduced to a mere 'intermediate' phenomenon, announcing the contours of future thought in the inadequate language of the past. It rather functions as a kind of vanishing mediator, designating a unique constellation, in which, for a brief moment after the disintegration of Absolute Idealism, something became visible that, once so-called post-Hegelian thought settled itself, and found shape in the guise of Schopenhauer, Marx, and Nietzsche, was again lost from sight" (*The Abyss of Freedom/Ages of the World*, 4). I think it is perfectly plausible to believe that Schopenhauer also belongs to the so-called 'disintegration stage' after the Absolute Idealism. See on that aspect also my "'The Second Philosophy' of Arthur Schopenhauer: Schopenhauer and Radical Empiricism," *Schopenhauer Jahrbuch* 91 (2010): 55–64.

13. Schelling, *The Abyss of Freedom/Ages of the World*, 148.

14. Gilles Deleuze, *Pure Immanence: Essays on A Life*, trans. by A. Boyman (New York: Zone Books, 2005), 28–30. For Agamben I refer to his book *Potentialities* (Stanford, Calif.: Stanford University Press, 1999), 230.

15. Schelling, *Philosophical Inquiries into the Nature of Human Freedom*, 37.

16. For a detailed elaboration of Indian concept of breath see my paper "Il ruolo ed il significato degli elementi acqua, aria e terra nell'antica filosofia indiana e greca: uno studio comparativo," *Magazzino di filosofia* 5, no. 13 (2004): 123–137.

17. See M. Boland, *Die Wind-Atem-Lehre in den älteren Upanisaden* (Münster: Ugarit-Verlag, 1997).

18. See *Upanishads, Upanishads*, trans. and intro. P. Ollivele (Oxford: Oxford University Press, 1996), lii (Introduction): "The central concern of all Vedic thinkers, including the authors of the Upanishads, is to discover the connections that bind elements of these three spheres to each other. The assumption then is that the universe constitutes a web of relations, that things that appear to stand alone and apart are, in fact, connected to other things." I should add that a possible contemporary ethical term for mesocosm is a gesture.

19. *Katha Aranyaka*, critical ed. with translation into German and introduction by M. Witzel (Cambridge, Mass.: Harvard University Press, 2004), see n129 on page xl of the Introduction for the history of the usage of "mesocosm." For Irigaray see "The Age of the Breath," in Luce Irigaray, *Key Writings* (London: Continuum, 2004), 168, and related works such as *Sharing the World* and *Between East and West*.

20. Luce Irigaray, *Sharing the World* (London: Continuum, 2008), 42.

21. Luce Irigaray, *Between East and West: From Singularity to Community* (New Delhi: New Age Books, 2005), 5.

22. Irigaray, *Sharing the World*, 43.

23. Irigaray, "The Age of the Breath," 165, 166, and 167.

24. *The Holy Bible* (NRSV) (Nashville: Thomas Nelson Publishers, 1989). For an analysis of Irigaray's elaborations on the Spirit see part 4 of *Teaching*, ed. L. Irigaray and M. Green (London: Continuum, 2008).

25. Luce Irigaray, "Ethical Gestures toward the Other," *Poligrafi* 15, no. 57 (2010): 3–23. See 4.

26. Irigaray, "Ethical Gestures toward the Other," 9.

27. For pure gesture and its relation to *a life* in Agamben, see *Potentialities*, 79 (in his essay on M. Kommerell's criticism "Kommerell, or On Gesture"): "Beyond the gestures of the soul and gestures of nature there is a third sphere, which one may call pure gestures. . . . This 'pure gestures' have given up all claim to reality." According to Kommerell, with Agamben, what is at issue now is to find a way to the profane mystery as an intimacy of living here and now, a new initiation "into life itself" (84).

18 Prolegomenon to Thinking the Reject for the Future of Continental Philosophy of Religion

Irving Goh

IN SEEKING TO outline a future of Continental philosophy of religion, as is the objective of this volume, perhaps we first need to trace the trajectory of the future of Continental philosophy itself. It could be said that the latter endeavor had already been put in place by Jean-Luc Nancy sometime in 1986, when he posed the question of *qui vient après le sujet*, or "who comes after the subject," a question coming in the wake of the dissolution, or the putting to death, of the *subject* by Continental philosophy since the late 1960s. What Nancy's question implies is that any inauguration of a future of Continental philosophy would be marked by a figure of thought otherwise of the *subject*. That future remains to come, since most responses to Nancy's questions have only rearticulated the *subject*, supplementing it with predicates that have been left out in its past theorizations.[1] In other words, as long as thought takes recourse to the *subject*, we still do not have a future of Continental philosophy. To inscribe a future of Continental philosophy, and hence also a future of Continental philosophy of religion, we would need to articulate another figure of thought, and that is the aim of this intervention.

Before we articulate what this figure is, it is perhaps also necessary to contextualize that "future" wherein a Continental philosophy of religion would situate itself and make a critical intervention. I would say that that "future" is not distant from what contemporary intellectual discourse has been calling the "postsecular." According to scholars such as José Casanova, Hent de Vries, and more recently Jürgen Habermas, the postsecular can be characterized by the articulations of local religions on the one hand, and the rearticulations of institutionalized religions on the other, in a supposed secular world.[2]

These same scholars have also observed that what entails from these articulations and rearticulations is but violence: violence between local religions and institutionalized ones as the former contest the domination of the latter; violence among local religions as each group seeks to legitimize itself or gain a stronghold within a society or state; and last but not least, violence arising from the age-old contest between religion or faith and the claim to reason or knowledge. In short, one could say that contemporary postsecular violence springs forth from the inability to accept differences—differences between local and institutionalized forms of religions, differences between local religious groups or denominations, and differences between faith and knowledge. Put another way, that violence is the result of an inability to share space with persons, other beings, objects, or concepts, with whom or with which one disagrees. Given this present postsecular violence, it is not unreasonable to demand that any endeavor to construct a future out of this postsecular world be one that tries to resolve existing postsecular violence. It is also from this critical necessity to engender a less violent postsecular future that I argue we need a new figure of thought.

St. Paul, or more specifically, Badiou's Pauline Subject, which is also Badiou's *subject* par excellence,[3] has seemingly presented itself as such a figure. The recent investment in St. Paul by contemporary scholarship since the publication of Badiou's *Saint Paul—La fondation de l'universalisme* would no doubt give this impression.[4] The conclusion of Badiou's text would even suggest that the *subject* as embodied by St. Paul can lead us toward a less violent postsecular future. To be sure, Badiou does not deploy the term "postsecular" anywhere in *Saint Paul* or in any of his other works. However, in the conclusion, Badiou writes, "For the subject, [the] subjective logic culminates in an indifference to secular nominations."[5] As I would read it, that "indifference to secular nominations" can presuppose a certain disenchantment with present secular situations, which then implies that what Badiou's *subject* works toward, that is, its "subjective logic," is a departure from present secular ways of thinking and living toward some sort of postsecular future. In other words, one may still trace a postsecular trajectory in the Pauline Subject's "indifference to secular nominations."

According to Badiou's philosophy, the work of this Pauline Subject is nothing less than the declaration of his or her fidelity to the truth of the Christ-Event that is the resurrection of Christ, which, in Badiou's reading, is also a project of universalism because this declaration promises salvation to all regardless if one is Jewish or not. That project of universalism, at first glance, seems promising for a future postsecular world, since, as suggested especially by the chapter "Universality and the Traversing of Differences" in *Saint Paul,* it potentially ends all violence between particular differences by demonstrating that it is beyond all particular differences. Certainly, Badiou makes sure in his text to say that particular differences are not to be ignored, disdained, or negated,[6] and that if the

"Christian militantism" of St. Paul "must be a trajectory [*traversée*] indifferent to worldly differences [*différences mondaines*]," then this "indifference" must be "an indifference tolerant of differences."[7] However, there is the sense that an irreducible (and at least symbolic) violence against differences remains with Badiou's Pauline Subject. One can probably sense this from Badiou's rhetoric on his Pauline Subject's "militant tonality," which includes "the appropriation of particularities," the consideration of "the empirical existence of differences" as "essential inexistence," and the too forceful desire to "transcend differences."[8] This is not to mention that there is hardly any consideration if particular differences actually welcome the traversing of the Pauline Subject's "universalist militantism" "across them, in them."[9] The mobilization of the Pauline Subject is therefore not totally immune to violence. In fact, according to Badiou's philosophy, violence is very much an aspect of his conceptualization of the *subject*: after the "subjectivation" by a Truth or an Event, for example, the Christ-Event, the *subject* inaugurates itself within the fabric of the existing world through a certain *forçage* or "forcing"; and in traversing this world, or according to the rhetoric of Badiou's earlier *Théorie du sujet*, in the "subject-process" of the *subject*, the latter typically proceeds via a trajectory of "destruction," tearing apart in its wake all existing manner of living or thinking, as it militantly declares what it sees to be the Truth.

What I am suggesting above is that Badiou's raising of the figure of St. Paul or Pauline Subject is not unproblematic or without problems. It is not the interest, however, of this intervention to further elucidate those problems.[10] Allow me to just say that I disagree with this return or resurrection of the *subject*, just as Continental philosophy, I believe, and also a Continental philosophy of religion, will do too, given Continental philosophy's commitment to the unending project of affirming and respecting differences. Now, Badiou may be correct, especially in *L'Éthique* (where his critique of any philosophy of difference(s) is more forceful, or in other words, less tolerant), to say that today's claims to "multiculturalism" or "the right to differences" is superficial, because it accepts only "good" differences, that is to say, differences that are passive and integrate themselves into the perspective or ideology of the dominant group or the majority. However, that does not mean that there is no endeavor to affirm, accept, or let be the other that disagrees with or is incommensurable to oneself. The recent postsecular texts of Habermas, and Derrida's *Foi et savoir*, are at least works that testify to that endeavor. Furthermore, one in fact hardly finds a space in Badiou's thought for this other that disagrees with oneself, since what follows in Badiou's conceptualization of the *subject* is that one follows this *subject* in his or her fidelity to a truth or event. In other words, what must be in place following this *subject* is an unquestioning adherence to what the *subject* perceives as *the* truth. In all, Badiou's *subject* does not really resolve postsecular violence. One could even say that in the *subject*'s "indifference" to differences, it is still not that distant from the existing postsecular intolerance of differences. In that sense, resurrecting the *subject* is but another form of postsecular violence.

To avoid the trappings of Badiou's *subject* (including the *subject* in the history of philosophy), and for a less violent postsecular future, I reiterate then that we need a figure of thought otherwise of the *subject*. Here, I would like to propose the *reject* as this figure of thought. I understand the *reject* through three turns. The first turn concerns the *reject* as it is conventionally understood, that is to say, a passive figure targeted to be disdained, denigrated, abandoned, banished, or exiled. The *reject*, however, can also be an active figure, rejecting in its turn forces that are oppressing or targeting it. It may even be the case that it *first* rejects others with a force so overwhelming and unbearable that it is subsequently rendered a *reject* by those around it. This active force constitutes the second turn of the *reject*. But I would like to think that the *reject* turns the force of rejection around on itself too. This is not an (auto-)nihilistic gesture, however. As I see it, the *reject* auto-rejects itself only to prevent itself from hypostasizing on a particular thought or disposition. Auto-rejection here must be understood as creative regeneration, allowing the *reject* to think itself anew constantly.[11]

It could be said that the *reject* is no stranger to religion, especially Christian religion. In terms of the passive *reject*, Adam and Eve immediately come to mind, in their banishment from Eden. But before Adam and Eve, one may even be so audacious as to say that God was also some sort of *reject* when Adam and Eve disobeyed his commandment to not eat from the tree of knowledge of good and evil. With regard to the active *reject*, one may turn to Luke 14, where the claim is made that only those who reject their families, and even their own lives, can truly follow Jesus. As for the *auto-reject*, perhaps one can locate it in the *homo tantum* in the Davidean Psalms, the *homo tantum* who accepts the refusal of solidarity or fraternity dealt to him by almost all his fellow human beings and is left only to cry out to God.

For a future (of) Continental philosophy of religion that will chart a less violent postsecular future, I argue that it is not so much the active *reject* that one must put forth. This second turn of the *reject*, when it goes unchecked, can present a possible regression to something like a *subject*. The force of rejecting others is after all borne by the *subject* too, since, as the history of the *subject* since Descartes has shown, it seldom hesitates to negate or denigrate everything else around it in the course of its desire to make a foundation of itself. One must not think, however, that the problem of the *reject* will be solved by the complete denial of this second turn. This turn is in fact necessary at times, for example, in the face of an external force that makes *rejects*—in the sense of passive targets of denigration or denunciation—of others. Here, the active force of the second turn is necessary to project some form of resistance against such repressive or oppressive force, such as that, in the context of the postsecular world, of a dominant religion or reason. Put another way, the active force of the *reject* becomes problematic only when it is projected against others that do not pose any violence against the *reject*. In any case, in thinking the *reject* for the purpose of continuing continental philosophy's project of affirming the differences of each and every being, one must be particularly attentive to its second turn: one must not repress it, nor give it too much force.

For a future where differing differences can coexist, I think it is more critical to foreground the *auto-reject*. Firstly, this third turn of the *reject* potentially counters the excessive expression of the second, since, in making itself a *reject*—which is also to remind itself that one and everyone else are *rejects* in certain ways, or that others share with it the condition of being a *reject*—it might induce the *reject* to stay its will to reject others. Secondly, and more importantly, in refusing any foundation of itself, or any insistence on its point of view, or its religion, the *auto-reject* in that regard opens up a space for the other that disagrees with it to come to presence. It recognizes that the other does not necessarily believe in one's faith or reason; it acknowledges that the other is always free to depart from, or even reject, one's faith or reason. This is perhaps the compassion, if not passion, of the *auto-reject*, which lets the other be: its passivity to receive or accept others in their respective differences, and its passivity to await its acceptance by others. Through such auto-rejection, it also resists making itself a commanding *subject*, resisting the interpellation of others to follow in its tracks (as Badiou's Pauline Subject is wont to do). Here, I would even venture to say that the *auto-reject* lets emerge—even if this will only be for a transient moment as it will be illustrated in the following paragraph[12]—what Nancy has called a *communauté désœuvrée*, commonly translated as "inoperative community," which is to say a community that is *not* predicated on any labor toward a singular totality based on predetermined criteria or ideals, but one that comes to presence precisely through the fact of differences that separate one singularity from another, a fact that "unworks" or resists any project of communitarian fusion. Or, to keep with the postsecular context, perhaps it is with the *auto-reject* that one arrives at the messianic "coming community" of Agamben, a community *not* of (ruling) subjects and (ruled) objects but of "whatever" beings without hierarchy.[13]

Where can one find such an *auto-reject*? I suggest that one can see it by returning to the figure of the *homo tantum*: not so much the *homo tantum* of the Psalms, however, but Deleuze's reinterpretation of that figure in his essay, "Immanence: Une vie . . ." There, Deleuze's *homo tantum* emerges precisely from a *reject*—Mr. Riderhood, the detestable and disdained rogue in Charles Dickens's *Our Mutual Friend*. When this *reject* meets with a near-death drowning incident, the rogue in him is put aside in the eyes of others. What the others see now is a living entity that is *just* or *only human*, that is to say, *homo tantum*. It is this aspect of *homo tantum* that renders Mr. Riderhood a "spark of life,"[14] which outshines his roguishness, and draws others to voluntarily want to save this rogue/ reject. According to Dickens, the rogue here would also have auto-rejected its roguish subjectivity, since "the spark of life within [Mr. Riderhood] is curiously separable from himself [as a rogue] now."[15] In Deleuze's nuanced reading, what is put in effect here is "a life," which is not grounded on any particular *subject* or biological life. Instead, what disseminates here is a sense of singularity, a sense of an almost anonymous or nameless living existence without subjecthood or objecthood, if not simply *a sense* that opens itself to others, and *a sense* through which others approach it out of their own desire to affirm or support it. Nothing binding or final is at work here, though, since all that gather around this sense of "a life" remain free to depart, which the rescuers in Dickens's story do eventually, as they regain their perception of the rogue in Mr. Riderhood. Certainly, everything breaks down at the end in this Dickensian episode, but what remains critical is that a sense of community previously unthinkable or unacceptable has taken place, even if it is only for a very brief moment. And that is what the *homo tantum* as *auto-reject*, or *auto-reject* as *homo tantum*, can bring about.

Evidently, the *auto-reject* as *homo tantum*, regardless if it is the *homo tantum* of the Davidean Psalms or Deleuze's *homo tantum*, is a human figure. Here, I would like to go further with the auto-rejection of the *auto-reject:* I would like to posit the rejection of the anthropocentrism and/or anthropomorphism of the *auto-reject,* and think the *auto-reject* in animal terms. Animals are no less *rejects* in Christian religion. Already in Leviticus 11, one reads of how certain animals are segregated from others, and subsequently categorized as those that one should neither touch nor consume. Hélène Cixous, especially in her "messianic" works of the 1990s,[16] has also noted that animals in biblical narratives are very often marginalized once those narratives proceed to underscore the necessity to obey masculine, biblical laws. That does not erase the fact, however, that animals are still needed in those narratives. As Cixous argues, Abraham's journey up to Mount Moriah would have been infernal and unbearable, if not impossible, without his donkey. In other words, there is a certain need for animals to see religion through. By extension, one could also say that following animals today could lead us to a future (of) Continental philosophy of religion or a less violent postsecular future.

Several Continental philosophers have in fact already suggested such a move. Bataille, in *Théorie de la religion,* has tried to think, through the question of animality, of a religion without sovereignty, that is to say, where no one religion reigns over another. Derrida, in *L'animal que donc je suis,* through what he terms *divinanimalité,* has called for the further affirmation of heterogeneous multiplicities without the need to define the essence of any of the entities that make up these multiplicities, out of respect for the respective secrets of those entities. On her part, Cixous, in reminding us that multiplicities must always include feminine and other beings that have been excluded, if not rejected, in the history of human civilization, will reinscribe the messiah in *Messie* and *Conversation avec l'âne* in terms of a female cat, the animal that is always free to come and go, and whose touch is critical not only to lead the narrators toward the future, but also to enable the narrators to write even the future.[17] Following in the trails of these thinkers, and as a conclusion, I would like to propose to continue thinking the animal, this time in terms of an *auto-reject,* for a future (of) Continental philosophy of religion.

For a future (of) Continental philosophy of religion or a less violent postsecular future, it will not be Abraham's donkey that I will turn to, but to Balaam's in Numbers 22. Numbers 22 begins with Balak, king of Moab, finding his territory surrounded by the Israelites. Fearing that the latter will swarm his land, Balak summons Balaam, known to be successful in his blessings and curses, to curse the Israelites in order to keep them out of his land. Balaam does not agree immediately to the invitation to Moab, but says he would seek counsel with God first. God tells Balaam that the Israelites are blessed and that Balaam shall not curse them nor go with Balak's messengers. Balaam heeds God's counsel and refuses the invitation. But the insistent Balak sends more messengers with more promises of greater honor to convince Balaam to take up the invitation. Balaam seeks counsel with God again, and this time, not without irony no doubt, God says go with the messengers if they call to him, but also "to do only what [God] tell[s] [him] to do." God's irony being completely lost to Balaam, Balaam follows Balak's messengers and sets out on the journey to Moab on his donkey. Furious, God puts a sword-wielding angel before the path of Balaam and his donkey. Balaam does not see this angel, but his donkey does, which then swerves off the intended but now fatal path. Balaam strikes his donkey to get back onto the correct route, but this time the angel stands before them in a vineyard path with a wall on each side. The donkey crashes into one of the walls in order to escape the imminent wrath of the angel, but in this process crushes Balaam's foot against the wall, and consequently suffers Balaam's second wrath. The angel then appears where there is no longer any way to turn; and so the donkey falls to the ground, falling on Balaam this time round. For the third time then, Balaam strikes his donkey and cries out that if he had a sword he would kill it. At this point, God opens Balaam's eyes and Balaam now sees the deathly angel before him and realizes he is wrong.

Many things can be said about this passage, for example the quasi-sacrificial gesture of the donkey,[18] and perhaps especially the part where God gives voice to the donkey (which I have omitted above). However, what I would like to highlight here is that the donkey does *respond* in its way. It responds to the deathly angel standing before it and Balaam, responding in a way that Balaam is too stubborn or even stupid or *bête* to understand. In any case, Balaam's donkey responds in a way that will preserve its own life and Balaam's: contrary to what Heidegger would claim, Balaam's donkey knows what it is to die. And in order to save itself and Balaam, in other words to save differences—the difference of humans and the difference of animals, or to preserve the respective life-force of these differences, Balaam's donkey is willing to *auto-reject* itself, in the sense of willingly suffering Balaam's strikes, and accepting Balaam's treatment of it as a *reject* when Balaam claims he would kill it were he in possession of a sword. Now, animals are still very much a missing figure or concept in current postulations of the postsecular. The episode with Balaam's donkey, however, suggests that the animal *auto-reject* can play a critical role in affirming the life-forces of postsecular differences. For a less violent postsecular world therefore, or a future (of) Continental philosophy of religion, where radical differences—differences between religions, differences between religion and reason, and differences between humans and animals—are not only affirmed, but also where their futures or future *élan vital* are safe-guarded, perhaps the *reject* or *auto-reject* that one should follow is the animal.

Notes

1. See the essays in Eduardo Cadava, Peter Connor, and Jean-Luc Nancy, eds., *Who Comes after the Subject?* (New York: Routledge, 1991). Some of the essays first appeared in the September 1988 special issue, under the same title, of *Topoi*, guest-edited by Nancy.

2. See especially José Casanova, *Public Religions in the Modern World* (Chicago: University of Chicago Press, 1994); Hent de Vries, *Religion and Violence: Philosophical Perspectives from Kant to Derrida* (Stanford, Calif.: Stanford University Press, 2001), and his edited volume with Lawrence E. Sullivan, *Political Theologies: Public Religions in a Post-Secular World* (New York: Fordham University Press, 2006); Ananda Abeysekara, *The Politics of Postsecular Religion: Mourning Secular Futures* (New York: Columbia University Press, 2008); and Jürgen Habermas, "Notes on Post-Secular Society," *New Perspectives Quarterly* 25, no. 4 (2008): 17–29, and his intervention in *An Awareness of What Is Missing: Faith and Reason in a Post-Secular Age*, trans. Ciaran Cronin (Cambridge: Polity, 2010).

3. Badiou calls St. Paul "a subjective figure of first importance" (*Saint Paul—La fondation de l'universalisme* [Paris: Presses Universitaires de France, 1997]), 1; translations from this text mine, unless indicated.

4. See especially John D. Caputo and Linda Martin Alcoff, eds., *St. Paul among the Philosophers* (Bloomington: Indiana University Press, 2009), which is the publication of the interventions given at the first Postmodernism, Culture, and Religion conference, whose subject was Badiou's St. Paul. See also the special issue of *South Atlantic Quarterly* on "Global Christianity, Global Critique," 109, no. 4 (2010). For theoretical critiques of Badiou's Pauline Subject, see Slavoj Žižek, *The Ticklish Subject: The Absent Center of Political Ontology* (New York: Verso, 1999), and Giorgio Agamben, *The Time That Remains: A Commentary on the Letter to the Romans*, trans. Patricia Dailey (Stanford, Calif.: Stanford University Press, 2005).

5. Here, I follow, with slight modifications, Ray Brassier's translation (*Saint Paul: The Foundation of Universalism* [Stanford, Calif.: Stanford University Press, 2003], 110). The quote appears on page 118 of the French original.

6. See Badiou, *Saint Paul*, 105 and 118.

7. Ibid., 107 and 106.

8. Ibid., 106.
9. Ibid.
10. That has been in large part the project of *St. Paul among the Philosophers*.
11. For further discussions on the *reject* in contemporary French thought, see my "Structural Reject," *Theory and Event* 12, no. 1 (2009), "Rejecting Friendship: Towards a Radical Reading of Derrida's *Politics of Friendship* for Today," *Cultural Critique* 79 (2011): 94–124, and my forthcoming *The Reject: From Contemporary French Thought to "Postsecular" and "Posthuman" Futures* (Fordham University Press).
12. As said, the link between the *reject* and community will be seen in the next paragraph. Here, I would like to note too that the question of community is also at the horizon of Nancy's question of "who comes after the subject." Nancy concludes his introduction to the project by positing the possibility of thinking "a community *without subject*" ("Introduction," in *Who Comes after the Subject?*, 8).
13. On a community of "whatever" beings rather than a community of *subjects,* see Agamben's *Coming Community,* trans. Michael Hardt (Minneapolis: University of Minnesota Press, 1993). On the messianic dimension of such a community, see his *Time That Remains*.
14. Charles Dickens, *Our Mutual Friend,* ed. and intro. Adrian Poole (London: Penguin, 1997), 439.
15. Ibid., 439.
16. The prophecy that Cixous's works of the 1990s will be "messianic" is Verena Conley's: see her *Hélène Cixous* (Toronto: University of Toronto Press, 1992).
17. I have discussed the messianic contours of these texts in "The Passion according to Cixous: From Human Blindness to *Animots,*" *MLN* Comparative Literature 125, no. 5 (2010): 1050–1074.
18. On the absence of critique of the sacrifice of animals in biblical narratives such as that of Abraham, where a ram will come in to replace Isaac as the sacrificial offering, as is apparently the case of Derrida's *Donner la mort;* see the chapter "Reopening the Question of the Human and the Animal" in Dominick LaCapra's *History and Its Limits: Human, Animal, Violence* (Ithaca, N.Y.: Cornell University Press, 2009).

19 Entropy

Clayton Crockett

THE FUTURE OF Continental philosophy of religion is entropy.
In 1928 Sir Arthur Eddington wrote the following famous caution:

> If someone points out to you that your pet theory of the universe is in disagreement with Maxwell's equations—then so much the worse for Maxwell's equations. If it is found to be contradicted by observation—well, these experimenters do bungle things sometimes. But if your theory is found to be against the second law of thermodynamics I can give you no hope; there is nothing for it but to collapse in deepest humiliation.[1]

The second law of thermodynamics is the law of entropy. Coined by Rudolf Clausius in 1865, "entropy" is a term that measures the disorder of a system. Entropy is a "turning in" or "turning toward," a transformation that implies a bending toward disorder in any thermodynamic system. The Second Law of Thermodynamics was formalized by Clausius to explain the profound implications of Sadi Carnot's work on steam engines in the early 1800s. The Second Law practically undermines the First Law, the idea that all energy as such is conserved, by claiming that in any system disorder always increases as a result of a tendency toward equilibrium. Entropy provides an arrow of time, from past to future, that suggests a limit for both Newtonian physics and quantum physics, with their emphasis on the reversibility of physical interactions.

In what follows, I want to make two claims. First, I assert that the split between the sciences and the humanities is unfortunate and unproductive, because it separates thinking from power in the contemporary academy. We could say that the sciences, at their limit, cannot think insofar as they are cut off from the most acute and important philosophical questions, whereas the humanities, including philosophy and religious studies, are rendered largely impotent because they are disconnected from real forces and powers in the world today. This hyperspecialization of disciplines serves the interests of neoliberal capital. Although Ilya Prigogine and Isabelle Stengers proposed a "New Alliance" between the humanities and the natural sciences three decades ago, their French title *La nouvel alliance* could not be translated into English, and the book was given the name *Order Out of Chaos*.

As a corollary to this claim, I want to affirm the French context of many of the structuralist and post-structuralist Continentalists, including Jacques Lacan, Gilles Deleuze, Michel Serres, and even Jacques Derrida, whose work is so significant for Continental philosophy of religion. These thinkers were writing out of a context where this gap between the sciences and the humanities or philosophy was not nearly as extreme as it is in the English-speaking world. My second corollary is to note and appreciate the new engagement with the sciences in a philosophical vein, particularly Catherine Malabou's important work on neuroplasticity, some aspects of the philosophy of Alain Badiou, Quentin Meillassoux, and François Laruelle, as well as the Speculative Realism that has recently emerged in the United Kingdom, associated with Graham Harman, Ray Brassier, Levi Bryant, and Iain Hamilton Smith. I will consider Brassier's impressive book *Nihil Unbound* below, although I will also suggest that Brassier is limited by the theoretical framework in which he reads Deleuze and understands entropy.

My second claim is that entropy is incredibly important, but it may not be well understood. Most contemporary understandings of entropy rely on nineteenth-century characterizations, and fail to appreciate or understand twentieth-century developments in non-equilibrium thermodynamics (NET). Thermodynamics and entropy are fundamentally related to energy, and we need better ways to think about energy, which is not simply matter or spirit in any dualistic way. To paraphrase Malabou, theology and Continental philosophy of religion "need to be engaged with a new materialism" (Malabou writes "deconstruction" in *Plasticity at the Dusk of Writing*), but this materialism is neither crudely atomistic nor reductionistic because it is based on energy transformation.[2] I will come back to the issue of energy at the conclusion of my essay.

Here is the problem: the twin legacies of the nineteenth century appear to be diametrically opposed, with physical thermodynamics insisting on a universe that tends toward death, disorder, and decay, culminating in a ubiquitous "heat death" that is inescapable in light of the Second Law of Thermodynamics. But the biological theory of evolution, even if it posits physical and simple origins, affirms a process that some theorists have called negative entropy or neg-entropy, leading from disorder to order, and producing organisms of greater and greater complexity. Generally these two processes are opposed, leading philosophers and theologians who take nature seriously either to see evolutionary complexity as a temporary exception to entropy under highly specific conditions, but nested within a larger entropic context, or to suggest, usually by some recourse to idealism, that there is a higher principle of life that is negentropic, and that entropy itself is a limited physical-material principle that occurs more locally.

My argument is that there are not two principles, but only one, which is entropy. But we have not fully understood entropy itself, which Eric D. Schneider and Dorion Sagan redefine in terms of gradient reduction in their book *Into the Cool*. Nature abhors a gradient. What I find both extraordinary and compelling is that Gilles Deleuze, as opposed to being a metaphysician of the One as Badiou claims, or a pan-psychist as Brassier charges, sketches out a preliminary understanding of non-equilibrium thermodynamics in chapter 5 of *Difference and Repetition*. In what follows I will take up Brassier's critical but flawed reading first and then turn directly to Deleuze.

Nihil Unbound is an impressive work. At the same time, it participates in the return of a certain scientism and objectivism in opposing what it sometimes carelessly reads as a textual linguisticism. So there is a kind of positivism at work in Speculative Realism, and also a certain naiveté in supposing that characterizing elements of the nonhuman world as objects is much better than characterizing them in linguistic terms. From a broader perspective, however, we can see the return of ontology, and specifically ontological questions and concerns, in recent "Continental" philosophy. *Nihil Unbound* represents a thought experiment, which Brassier, following Meillassoux's critique of correlationism in *After Finitude*, tries to "think" a radical extinction that cannot be thought, or at least appropriated by thinking for the purposes of human life.[3] Extinction cannot simply be incorporated by thought; thus the *nihil* is unbound from human subjectivity and floats freely. Of course it then pressures human thinking and living, but in a non-dialectical way.

Brassier's thinking of the nihil consists of a radicalization of the Freudian death drive. Here, "death is . . . the original purposivelessness which compels all purposefulness, whether organic or psychological" (*NU*, 360).[4] "The death-drive," according to Brassier, "is the unbindable excess that makes binding possible." (*NU*, 364) Brassier does not simply affirm the naïve view that the universe will end in heat death, but he does envision an inevitable solar catastrophe for the earth, as contemplated by Jean-Francois Lyotard (*NU*, 342). This solar catastrophe, in which the sun burns up all of its hydrogen and then swells up large enough to swallow the planet, is one way for thought to think the annihilation of thinking. Another way is to consider "the currently inexplicable force called 'dark energy,' which will keep pushing the extinguished universe deeper and deeper into an eternal and unfathomable blackness." (*NU*, 349) This paradox can also be located simply at the individual level where a human being attempts to think her own death, which leads to the cessation of conscious thought. The only difference here is the assumption that the survival of the species provides a certain comfort and amelioration for the death of individual.

Ultimately, what Brassier wants from this extremity of extinction is an unbinding that precedes and makes possible all binding, and this logic also appears strangely Derridean, because it is the impossibility of the determinate conditions of thinking and responding that precedes and makes possible all thinking and all responsibility for Derrida.[5] I also don't think that thinking and existence are simply correlated for Derrida in the way that Speculative Realism charges. Because of his rejection of correlation, however, Brassier claims that the truth of extinction is an adequation without correlation or correspondence. The unbound truth of extinction then leads to philosophy's binding of consciousness of extinction, which is the "identity of entropic indifference and negentropic difference" (*NU*, 364).

Brassier reads Deleuze dualistically, and suggests that Deleuze affirms a psychic neg-entropic intensity that counters physical extensive entropy. In his reading of *Difference and Repetition*, Brassier notes the importance of the third synthesis of time, the eternal return of difference, which is a kind of death, but this death leads to the negentropic production of life. Brassier claims that the death instinct in *Difference and Repetition* is psychic and results from an act of thinking that overcomes bare matter in an idealist way (*NU*, 284). Brassier claims that Deleuze introduces an idealist, psychic principle that is ultimately negentropic and overcomes "the transcendental illusion of entropy." Deleuze privileges the psychic realm, and "psychic life escapes from the entropic domain of physical death" (*NU*, 293). Due to his vitalism, Deleuze privileges "psychic expression" over "its bio-physical location," or negentropic expression over entropic explication (*NU*, 298–299). Then this psychism of organic life is entirely delivered over to the act of thinking, such that vital human thinking overcomes the bare matter of entropic disorder and death. Not only is thinking adequate to thinking death, it transcends and overcomes death; this is the problem with correlationism and its covert idealism.

But this is not Deleuze, even though it is a provocative misreading of Deleuze. Brassier argues for a non-dialectizable duality of entropy and negentropy that cannot be simply recuperated by human thinking. This process is a kind of unilateralization: "determination-in-the-last-instance effectively unilateralizes dialectics. Thus unilateralization cannot be dialectically re-inscribed." (*NU*, 221) Unilateralization is an asymmetric choosing of a path that characterizes the arrow of time of entropy. The problem of time, however, is that Brassier does not know how to conceptualize time apart from human thinking, which is odd insofar as he thinks he does know how to think about logic and death in a non-correlationist or nonhuman manner.

One of the most impressive aspects of Brassier's engagement with Deleuze is his focus on chapter 5 of *Difference and Repetition*. So much attention has been paid to the virtual status of mathematical, biological, and philosophical ideas in chapter 4 that chapter 5 has been somewhat neglected. The asymmetrical synthesis of the sensible means precisely the breaking of symmetry that destroys a gradient. Deleuze says that "every intensity is differential, by itself a difference" (*DR*, 222).[6] Intensity defines an arrow of time that passes "from more to less differenciated, from a productive to a reduced difference" (*DR*, 223). This differential intensity is canceled out in extensity, which hides the intensive difference that produces entropy in its attempt to recover equilibrium. Although Deleuze uses little of the language of physics, his analysis here is entirely biophysical, and does not appropriate entropy in negentropic terms as understood psychically.

The classical model of thermodynamics represents, according to Deleuze, "a strange alliance at the end of the nineteenth century between science, good sense, and philosophy" (*DR*, 223). In classical thermodynamics, philosophy and science are constrained by the good sense of entropy. Good sense, as critiqued in chapter 3 of *DR*, "goes from the side of things to the side of fire: from differences produced to differences reduced. It is thermodynamic" (*DR*, 225). Good sense does not completely do away with difference, but it recognizes difference only insofar as it is canceled out in extensity over time. Differential intensity gives way to entropy and heat death; differences are reduced to a smothering sameness. The distribution of sense seems entropic, based upon the progressive elimination of differences.

Deleuze cites Léon Selme's work on Clausius and Carnot, saying that Selme "wanted to show that the increase of entropy is illusory" (*DR*, 228). Entropy is based on a transcendental illusion because it is a universal presupposition that cannot be directly measured. Entropy is the canceling out of differences, but it loses sight of the intensive differences that drive the process. Deleuze explains the fundamental paradox of the classical conception of entropy:

> Entropy is an intensive factor but, unlike all other extensive factors, it is an extension or "explication" which is implicated as such in intensity, which does not exist outside the implication or except as implicated, and this is because it has the function of making possible the general movement by which that which is implicated explicates itself or is extended. There is thus a transcendental illusion essentially tied to the *qualitas*, Heat, and to the extension, Entropy. [*DR*, 229]

Entropy is both extensity and intensity, but it cannot account for intensity except as canceled out in extensity. Deleuze uses a classical metaphorics of depth (which he later repudiates) in identifying depth with the intensity of being, but he shows how intensity works below and beyond the transcendental illusion of entropy.

Intensive quantity "represents difference in quantity, that which cannot be cancelled in difference in quantity or that which is unequalisable in quantity itself" (*DR*, 232). This means that intensive difference both maintains and cancels out difference in its explication. Deleuze says that "if a type of number cancels its difference, it does so only by explicating it within the extension that it installs. Nevertheless, it maintains this difference in itself in the implicated order in which it is grounded" (DR, 232). Intensity preserves itself as difference at the same time as it reveals itself as extensity. Extensity appears elsewhere, outside of intensity: "Intensity is the uncancellable in difference of quantity, but this difference of quantity is cancelled by extension, extension being precisely the process by which intensive difference is turned inside out and distributed in such a way as to be dispelled, compensated, equalized and suppressed in the extensity which it creates" (DR, 233). The force that drives intensity, which is the differential intensity that produces extension, is called repetition. Or rather, intensity is already a differential force itself, producing extensive identities outside itself. Intensity is a process of infinite fractal iterations, the production of images of space-time that repeat differently. Intensity drives the arrow of time that makes the process irreversible rather than time-reversible in a Newtonian sense.

Intensity affirms itself as difference even as it produces extension. Intensity "makes difference itself an object of affirmation" (DR, 234). Difference can affirm itself only as a series, a number of repetitions. Since "intensity is already difference, it refers to a series of other differences that it affirms by affirming itself" (DR, 234). Intensity for Deleuze is a kind of multiplicity, and Deleuze affirms that there are always at least two forms of multiplicity. There are always two series, one higher and one lower as calculated along a quantitative scale. Deleuze explains that intensity "makes the lowest an object of affirmation" (DR, 234). The asymmetrical synthesis goes from higher to lower, affirming the lower. This synthesis is the reduction of gradient differentials that characterizes non-equilibrium thermodynamics.

The asymmetrical synthesis of gradient reduction is a process of individuation. Individuation "is the act by which intensity determines differential relations to become actualized, along the lines of differenciation and within the qualities and extensities it creates" (DR, 246). Individuation occurs and recurs eternally, that is, an infinite number of discrete quantitative times. Individuation is produced; it is not based on any prior Platonic identity. The eternal return "is said of a world *without identity*, without resemblance, or equality" (DR, 241). Eternal return is the infinite iteration of discrete differences, the productive expansion of time-space images, or what Roger Penrose calls spin networks.

Although I agree with Deleuze's analysis in chapter 5, I suggest that Deleuze follows Selme in criticizing an outmoded conception of entropy and thermodynamics. Deleuze provides theoretical tools to rethink entropy itself, but he is not smuggling in a counterprinciple of negentropy to overcome the problematic effects of entropy, as Brassier claims, and his analysis in chapter 5 is not overdetermined by psychic vitalism. In fact, intensive difference is a kind of unilateralization that is non-dialectizable. And what I am calling entropy here is this intensive difference itself, which is the identity of negentropic expression and entropic explication that Brassier invokes. Let's turn to this non-equilibrium thermodynamics more explicitly.

As already mentioned, the second law of thermodynamics is one of the two major scientific legacies of the nineteenth century. The problem is that it appears to directly conflict with the other, evolution. As the ecologist Rod Swenson explains, this situation gives the impression of "two incommensurable rivers—the river of physics that flows downhill, and the river of biology, psychology and culture that flows uphill."[7] Recent works by Swenson and others have suggested that there is only one river, and evolution is not an exception to but rather a further development of the laws of thermodynamics. Non-equilibrium thermodynamics is very close to Deleuze's ontology in *Difference and Repetition*, which theorizes NET without using these precise terms.

Building on the work of Ilya Prigogine on dissipating systems, as well as Ludwig von Bertalanffy's systems theory, Swenson holds that autocatakinetic systems will select the path or paths "that minimize potential or maximize the entropy at the fastest rate given the constraints," which is the law of maximum entropy production.[8] Given a temperature or pressure differential, the flow of energy that occurs will work to reduce this gradient differential as quickly and efficiently as possible. Swenson give the example of a warm cabin in cold woods. Heat escapes the cabin into the surrounding environment relatively slowly, but if one opens a window or a door, the rate of heat dissipation increases in order to maximize the entropy as quickly as possible. Ordered or organized flow through the window or door is more efficient at reducing potentials than disordered flow, and this is most clearly seen in a vortex, where organized air or water flow empties a container much more quickly than a slow, disorganized system. Swenson draws the conclusion: "the world can be expected to produce order whenever it gets the chance—the world is in the order-production business because ordered flow produces entropy faster than disordered flow."[9] If Swenson is correct, then the production of order is not an exception to the second law, but a consequence of it. The functioning of dissipative, autocatakinetic, or self-organized systems has been analyzed as exceptional structures, but what if these structures are the rule rather than the exception?

Biological evolution is still an incredible event, but it may be a leap in degree rather than in kind in relation to chemical and physical processes. The new science of thermodynamics that has emerged in the last half of the twentieth century does not conform to the stereotypical image of classical thermodynamics from the nineteenth century. In their book *Into the Cool*, Eric D. Schneider and Dorion Sagan examine and recapitulate the emergence of this revised science. Schneider and Sagan reformulate the second law as "nature abhors a gradient."[10] Entropy production is gradient reduction.

The reduction of gradients at the maximum possible rate internally organizes complex processes, such as Bénard cells, Taylor vortices, and chemical cycles.[11] For example, "Taylor vortices are produced in an apparatus that consists of two cylinders, one inside the other, with a fluid filling the gap between the cylinders." When you turn the inner cylinder the resulting "rotation of the cylinders produces lateral pressure gradients across the fluid."[12] Later the fluid dynamist Donald Coles showed that "at a critical point of increased rotation, the fluid assumed one of eight different flow patterns."[13] The point is that these patterns that characterize Taylor flows or Taylor vortices are steady-state organizations that are produced by the rotation that generates a pressure gradient differential, and the flows are the result of the system attempting to reduce the pressure differential as efficiently as possible. A simple rotational gradient produces complex patterns. Furthermore, these non-equilibrium systems display a kind of memory: "in their cyclicity they embody past modes of reaching equilibrium."[14] The system carries short-term memory of past states that helps it reduce a gradient most effectively, given that its direct path to equilibrium is blocked. The interaction of the system and its history—which is the combination of the intensity that drives the system and the extensity that it exhibits, in Deleuzian terms—produces novel patterns. These patterns continue as long as there is a gradient differential that is being generated that fuels it.[15]

Complex patterns are the result of the entropy, not the exception to it. The second law "helps provide the temporal frame for the evolution of new laws." According to Schneider and Sagan, "the second law leads to structure by selecting compounds in low-energy molecular combinations, and in selecting for cyclic networks that continuously degrade energy."[16] Life can be seen as a more complexly ordered, genetically self-replicating process that is made possible by the prior organization of physical and chemical systems. Living systems also cycle complex compounds by means of metabolism, and this is a stable way to degrade energy. Life may have originated from an ancient chemical—sulfide-oxygen—gradient in deep sea thermal vents. Schneider and Sagan speculate that "organic chemicals across a gradient may have been selected for properties of maintenance and stickiness to mineral surfaces that were their original environment."[17] As Dorion Sagan explains in another essay, "nonequilibrium thermodynamics thus deconstructs the line between life and nonlife, much as Darwin deconstructs the barrier between humans and other organisms, by showing our behavioral, morphological, and biochemical continuity to other organisms."[18]

Thermodynamics does not contradict evolution, but entropy explains how all complex processes work.[19] Thermodynamics was developed out of principles concerning the productivity of steam engines, but a broadened "nonequilibrium thermodynamics, as the mother of all sciences of complexity, has practical applications to economics, ecology, evolutionary theory, architecture, origins-of-life research, climate research, art, and NASA's search for extraterrestrial life."[20] In terms of this new non-equilibrium thermodynamics (NET), life and other complex systems are grounded in energy flows, and the directionality of nature toward eliminating gradient differentials.[21] Here heat is one among many gradients, but it is not the only one. What Deleuze suggests in *Difference and Repetition* is that it is the overemphasis on heat that makes thermodynamics so problematic. We need to view thermodynamics more a-thermally. Energy dynamics is certainly entangled with heat, but the reduction of energy dynamics primarily to heat is too classically thermodynamic in nineteenth-century terms.

The future of Continental philosophy of religion, then, is entropy. But entropy is a kind of transformation or gradient reduction that produces new forms of structure under specific non-equilibrium conditions along what is sometimes called the edge of chaos. Under the most general conditions, entropy means a tendency toward equilibrium, a loss of useful energy, and an increase in heat and information as the theoretical innovations are spread across a wider network of scholars and readers. This is why for some younger thinkers, figures like Derrida, Levinas, and Marion have become "stale," even if their work was seen as new and vital for Continental philosophy of religion in the 1990s. So we turn to people like Žižek or Badiou, Brassier or Malabou, for new insights. The transformation variations within the "system" of Continental philosophy of religion mean that different figures get associated with different values and different interpretations, and sometimes what is difficult is to cut across how they are presented and packaged to generate vital new forms of thinking. This too is entropy, because it attends to the intensity that is preserved in the transition from one explicated philosopher to another and then expressed differently.

Entropy implies uncertainty, because it is both dynamic and directional. In philosophical terms, we never get the final or correct interpretation. In physical terms, we cannot completely reduce time to configuration space and we cannot have complete reversibility, even in theory. Entropy names the flow of energy, which runs in the direction of reducing gradient differentials. Being is energy transformation. The New Materialism incorporates a quasi-Deleuzian ontology, but it does not idealize Deleuze.

The New Materialism is consonant with a theological sensibility, but it follows the Death of God theology in its rejection of transcendence, and it is suspicious of idealism or any attempt to flee material reality. Energy is neither ideal nor material in conventional dualistic terms; it is material and spiritual at one and the same time. Perhaps the Chinese word *qi* is an appropriate concept, precisely because it is not dualized. Energy is not restricted to life in the narrow sense of organism, and it is not Life in a vaguely spiritualist New Age manner. We could say that energy is life only if we broaden what we mean by life to mean something like complex organized structure.[22] We could say that energy is God only if we define and specify God as the dynamic matrix of organization, the potentiality for emergent structure. But this God is without consciousness or plan. God is not absolute, but the solvent material khora that gives space-time a chance combined with the entropic intensity that makes a difference.

Notes

1. Arthur Eddington, *The Nature of the Physical World* (Cambridge: Cambridge University Press, 1928), 74.
2. See Catherine Malabou, *Plasticity at the Dusk of Writing: Dialectic, Destruction, Deconstruction,* trans. Carolyn Shread (New York: Columbia University Press, 2009), 61.
3. See Quentin Meillassoux, *After Finitude: An Essay on the Necessity of Contingency,* trans. Ray Brassier (London: Continuum, 2008).
4. Ray Brassier, *Nihil Unbound: Enlightenment and Extinction* (London: Palgrave Macmillan, 2007), 360. Hereafter abbreviated as *NU* with page numbers in parentheses.
5. On this aporia of responsibility, see Jacques Derrida, *The Gift of Death,* trans. David Wills (Chicago: University of Chicago Press, 1995), 68–69.
6. Gilles Deleuze, *Difference and Repetition,* trans. Paul Patton (New York: Columbia University Press, 1994), 222. Hereafter abbreviated as *DR* with page numbers in parentheses.
7. Rod Swenson, "Autocatakinetics, Evolution, and the Law of Maximum Energy Production: A Principled Foundation Towards the Study of Human Ecology," *Advances in Human Ecology* 6 (1997), http://www.spontaneous order.net/humaneco2.html.
8. Ibid.
9. Ibid.
10. Eric D. Schneider and Dorion Sagan, *Into the Cool: Energy Flow, Thermodynamics and Life* (Chicago: University of Chicago Press, 2005), 6.
11. Ibid., 77.
12. Ibid., 126.
13. Ibid., 128.
14. Ibid., 129.
15. See ibid., 130.
16. Ibid., 31.
17. Ibid., 180.
18. Dorion Sagan, "Introduction," in Jakob von Uexküll, *A Foray into the World of Humans and Animals with a Theory of Meaning,* trans. Joseph D. O'Neil (Minneapolis: University of Minnesota Press, 2010), 18.
19. See Schneider and Sagan, *Into the Cool,* 31.
20. Ibid., 138.
21. In this vein, it is significant that Stephen Hawking's major scientific contribution was the discovery of the application of thermodynamic laws to black holes. Black holes can be treated as entropy producers, they dissipate heat as information, and they eventually can disappear given massive time spans far beyond the current scope of the universe. See also the contribution of Ted Jacobson, whose paper shows that Einstein's field equations are convertible into thermodynamic equations: "Thermodynamics of Spacetime: The Einstein Equations of State," *Physical Review Letters* 75 (1995): 1260–1263; also at http://prl.aps.org/abstract/PRL/v75/i7/p1260_1.
22. See Eugene Thacker's treatment of the philosophical concept of life in *After Life* (Chicago: University of Chicago Press, 2010).

Contributors

JOSEPH BALLAN is a doctoral candidate at the University of Chicago Divinity School. He is the translator of Stanislas Breton's *A Radical Philosophy of Saint Paul* (2011), and his publications include essays on Kierkegaard, memorial practices, liturgical time, and theologies of work.

JOHN D. CAPUTO is the Thomas J. Watson Professor Emeritus of Religion at Syracuse University and the David R. Cook Professor Emeritus of Philosophy at Villanova. His most recent books are *The Insistence of God: A Theology of Perhaps* (IUP, 2013) and *Truth* (2013). His major books have attempted to persuade us that hermeneutics goes all the way down (*Radical Hermeneutics*), that Derrida is a thinker to be reckoned with by theology (*The Prayers and Tears of Jacques Derrida*), and that theology is best served by getting over its love affair with power and embracing what Caputo calls *The Weakness of God*, which won the 2006 AAR book award for works in constructive theology. He has also addressed wider-than-academic audiences in *On Religion* and *What Would Jesus Deconstruct?* He has an interest in interacting with church and community activists and has long been interested in the Emergent Church.

CLAYTON CROCKETT is associate professor and director of religious studies at the University of Central Arkansas. He is the author or coauthor of five books, including *Religion, Politics and the Earth: The New Materialism*, with Jeffrey W. Robbins (2012), and most recently *Deleuze Beyond Badiou: Ontology, Multiplicity, and Event* (2013). He is the editor or coeditor of a number of books, including *Hegel and the Infinite*, with Slavoj Žižek and Creston Davis.

IRVING GOH obtained his PhD in comparative literature from Cornell University, where he also serves as research fellow at the Society for the Humanities. He has published on Continental thought in journals such as *diacritics, MLN, differences*, and *Cultural Critique*. He is also coeditor with Verena Conley of a volume of essays on Jean-Luc Nancy, *Nancy Now: Current Perspectives in Nancy Studies* (forthcoming). His book *The Reject: From Contemporary French Thought to "Postsecular" and "Posthuman" Futures* is forthcoming.

PHILIP GOODCHILD is professor of religion and philosophy in the Department of Theology and Religious Studies, University of Nottingham, UK. He is the author of *Gilles Deleuze and the Question of Philosophy* (1996), *Deleuze and Guat-*

tari: An Introduction to the Politics of Desire (1996), Capitalism and Religion: The Price of Piety (2002), and Theology of Money (2009), and editor of On Philosophy as a Spiritual Exercise: A Symposium (2013). He is also currently a senior fellow of the Rethinking Capitalism Initiative, University of California Santa Cruz.

CHRISTINA M. GSCHWANDTNER is associate professor of philosophy at Fordham University. She is the author of *Reading Jean-Luc Marion: Exceeding Metaphysics* (IUP, 2007), *Postmodern Apologetics? Arguments about God in Contemporary Philosophy* (2012) and the forthcoming *Degrees of Givenness: On Saturation in Jean-Luc Marion* (IUP). She has also translated several of Jean-Luc Marion's books and Michel Henry's final work, *Words of Christ*.

GAVIN HYMAN is a senior lecturer in the Department of Politics, Philosophy, and Religion at the University of Lancaster, UK. He is author of *The Predicament of Postmodern Theology* (2001), *A Short History of Atheism* (2010), and *Traversing the Middle: Ethics, Politics, Religion* (2013), and editor of *New Directions in Philosophical Theology* (2004).

RANDALL JOHNSON is a psychiatrist and psychoanalytic psychotherapist in Chapel Hill, North Carolina. He is an avid reader of Continental philosophy and has presented papers at a number of philosophy conferences, including meetings of the International Merleau-Ponty Circle, the International Association for Philosophy and Literature, and the Society for Existential Phenomenology Theory and Culture. A number of these papers have been collected into a working manuscript, *Thinking Liminal Sensibility: Writing between Merleau-Ponty and Others*.

CATHERINE MALABOU is a professor in the Department of Philosophy at the Centre For Modern European Philosophy at Kingston University, UK. A renowned contemporary French philosopher, she is the author of *Self and Emotional Life: Philosophy, Psychoanalysis, and Neuroscience* (with Adrian Johnston, 2013), as well as a number of books translated into English, including *The Future Of Hegel: Plasticity, Temporality And Dialectic*; *What Should We Do With Our Brain?*; *Plasticity at the Dusk of Writing: Dialectic, Destruction, Deconstruction*; and *Changing Difference*.

KATHARINE SARAH MOODY is a research associate at the University of Liverpool, where she is working on the Philosophy and Religious Practice network. Katharine's research is positioned at the intersection of philosophy of religion, radical theology, and religious studies. She is the author of *Radical Theology and Emerging Christianity: Deconstruction, Materialism and Religious Practice* (2014) and *Post-Secular Theology and the Church: A New Kind of Christian Is a New*

Kind of Atheist (2014) and coeditor (with Steven Shakespeare) of *Intensities: Philosophy, Religion and the Affirmation of Life* (2012).

EDWARD F. MOONEY teaches courses in the Religion and Philosophy Departments at Syracuse University. His writings include *On Soren Kierkegaard: Dialogue, Polemic, Lost Intimacy, and Time* (2007), *Lost Intimacy in American Thought: Personal Philosophy from Thoreau to Cavell* (2009); and *Excursions with Kierkegaard: Others, Goods, Death, and Final Faith* (2012).

LEON NIEMOCZYNSKI teaches in the department of philosophy at Immaculata University near Philadelphia, Pennsylvania. He specializes in both the American and Continental philosophical traditions, and his interests include the philosophy of religion, the philosophy of nature, logic and metaphysics, aesthetics, German idealism (Schelling and Hegel), and philosophical ecology. He is the author of *Charles Sanders Peirce and a Religious Metaphysics of Nature* (2011) and is the coeditor of *A Philosophy of Sacred Nature: Prospects for Ecstatic Naturalism* (forthcoming) and *Animal Experience: Consciousness and Emotions in the Natural World* (forthcoming). He previously taught for West Chester University in West Chester, Pennsylvania.

B. KEITH PUTT is professor of philosophy at Samford University. He is the editor of *Gazing through a Prism Darkly: Reflections on Merold Westphal's Hermeneutical Epistemology* (2009), and the author of several articles, including "Learning to Live Up to Death–*Finally*: Ricoeur and Derrida on the Textuality of Immortality," "Rightly Passing beyond New Atheism: Continental Connections and Disconnections," and "*Depravatio Crucis:* The Non-Sovereignty of God in John Caputo's Poetics of the Kingdom."

JEFFREY W. ROBBINS is chair and professor of religion and philosophy, and director of the American studies program at Lebanon Valley College, where he has been named the Thomas Rhys Vickroy Teacher of the Year. He is the author or editor of six books, including most recently *Religion, Politics and the Earth: The New Materialism* (2012) with Clayton Crockett and *Radical Democracy and Political Theology* (2011). He is a contributing editor of the *Journal for Cultural and Religious Theory*.

STEVEN SHAKESPEARE is senior lecturer in philosophy at Liverpool Hope University, UK. He also cofacilitates the Association for Continental Philosophy of Religion (www.hope.ac.uk/acpr). He completed his doctorate on Kierkegaard at Cambridge University, before working on a postdoctoral project on Derrida and Judaism. His books include *Kierkegaard, Language and the Reality of God* (2001);

Radical Orthodoxy: A Critical Introduction (2007); and *Derrida and Theology* (2009). His most recent publications are two collections. The first, coedited with Claire Molloy and Charlie Blake, is entitled *Beyond Human: From Animality to Transhumanism* (2012). The second, coedited with Katharine Sarah Moody, is *Intensities: Philosophy, Religion and the Affirmation of Life* (2012). The latter is the first volume in the series Intensities: Contemporary Continental Philosophy of Religion, of which Steven is joint series editor with Patrice Haynes.

DEVIN SINGH is a Mellon Postdoctoral Fellow in the integrated humanities and a lecturer in the Department of Religious Studies at Yale University, where he received his PhD. His research combines work in theology, religious studies, critical theory, and economic sociology in order to assess theology's impact upon present social arrangements. His current book is a contribution to a theological genealogy of monetary economy in the West, examining points of interchange and influence between money and Christian doctrine. Devin's work has appeared in the *Scottish Journal of Theology, Studia Patristica,* and the *Harvard Theological Review.*

LENART ŠKOF is professor of philosophy and chair of the Institute for Philosophical Studies, University of Primorska (Koper, Slovenia). He is the author of monographs and papers on Continental philosophy (Schelling, Schopenhauer, Feuerbach), American pragmatism, Indian philosophy, and the philosophy of Luce Irigaray. His book *Pragmatist Variations on Ethical and Intercultural Life* was published by Lexington Books in 2012. He is a coeditor of *Breathing with Luce Irigaray* (with Emily Holmes, 2013). Currently his main area of research is the genealogy and the politics of breath in Western philosophical history.

JOHN THIBDEAU received an MA in religious studies from the University of Colorado—Boulder in 2012 and a BS in philosophy from Rensselaer Polytechnic Institute, as well as graduate certificates in cognitive science and critical theory. John taught secondary math and physics in Kuwait for several years before returning to graduate school, and he now attends UC Santa Barbara's religious studies program, working in Islamic studies and cognitive science.

NOËLLE VAHANIAN is associate professor of philosophy at Lebanon Valley College. She is the author of *Language, Desire, and Theology: A Genealogy of the Will to Speak* (2003). Her latest book is *The Rebellious No: Variations on a Secular Theology of Language* (2014).

Index

Abnegation, 157–158, 179, 185, 195
Abraham, 7, 45–46, 59–65, 67–70, 74–76, 78, 80–81, 88–89, 114
Absolute, 3–4, 24, 27, 32, 38, 41, 46, 49, 52–53, 55, 65, 70, 81–89, 92, 95–102, 105, 111, 114, 119, 121–123, 156–159, 175–176, 179–182, 186–188, 190–193, 195, 199, 210–212, 214, 217, 222–224, 226–228, 232, 238, 240, 254, 262, 281
Advent, 93–96, 98–101, 103, 141–142, 144, 157, 210
Agamben, Giorgio, 2, 11, 146–148, 151–153, 177, 236, 240, 256, 259, 262, 267, 270–271
Alienation, 34, 203, 232, 237, 239
Alterity, 2, 4, 35, 46, 77, 118, 175–176, 203, 217
Althusser, Louis, 168–172, 177
Analytic philosophy, 21
Anatheism, 7, 95, 101–102, 104–105, 107, 192, 195
Animal, 16–17, 22, 24, 26, 75, 79, 155, 189, 256, 260, 268–271, 281, 285–286
Aquinas, 25, 37, 45–46, 53, 79, 138, 166
Arche-fossil, 82, 85, 87
Archive, 33, 85–86, 174, 178, 226, 239
Aristotle, 25, 202, 205, 210, 247
Augustine, 28, 34, 36–37, 40, 45–46, 56
Auschwitz, 75

Badiou, Alain, 2, 12, 16, 105, 110, 112, 116, 119, 122, 162, 166, 264–267, 270, 273–274, 280, 283
Bakhtin, Mikhail, 66–67, 70, 77
Balaam, 17, 269, 270
Barth, Karl, 27, 51, 53, 219, 220, 222, 225
Barthes, Roland, 219
Bataille, George, 17, 268
Being, 6, 17, 22, 24–25, 28–31, 43, 46, 53, 56–57, 78, 81, 87, 90, 101, 104–106, 110, 112–114, 118, 143, 147, 157, 165, 170, 172–173, 201–202, 210–213, 217, 224, 227, 231, 250, 254–255, 261, 276, 280
Being-for-nothing, 6, 22, 30
Belief, 5, 10, 16, 27–29, 36, 42, 49, 54, 93, 99, 105, 114, 122, 134, 214, 217, 223, 225, 228, 230, 233, 237–243; disavowal of, 237
Bergson, Henri, 86, 106
Bible, 36, 45–46, 50, 58, 63, 262
Bourdieu, Pierre, 170–172, 177

Brassier, Ray, 5, 7, 22, 28–32, 90, 103, 119, 270, 273–275, 277, 280–281
Breath, 16, 38, 131–132, 135–136, 189, 203–204, 253, 254, 255, 256–262, 286
Bryant, Levi, 7, 32, 90, 273

Camus, Albert, 12, 79, 154–155, 165, 198, 205
Capitalism, 2, 11, 128, 137, 140, 148–150, 178, 228, 283
Caputo, John D., 3–8, 10, 12–13, 15, 17, 21–22, 24, 26, 28, 30, 32–34, 36, 37–45, 48–51, 55–57, 59–60, 76, 81, 89, 93–95, 98–109, 111–122, 158, 166, 181–182, 190–192, 197, 200, 209, 270, 283, 285
Carnivalesque, 63, 67, 77
Carnot, Sadi, 272, 276
Chora, 7, 70–71, 79
Chrétien, Jean-Louis, 4, 180, 185, 190–191, 193
Christianity, 53, 57, 109–110, 115, 117–122, 145, 151, 162, 180–181, 190, 199, 228, 230, 239, 270, 284
Cixous, Hélène, 29, 268, 271
Clausius, Rudolf, 272, 276
Coinage, 141–142, 144, 146, 148, 151–152
Coles, Donald, 279
Community, 56–57, 109–110, 115–118, 162, 174–176, 185–186, 188–189, 194, 236, 240, 242, 259, 262, 267–268, 271, 283
Continental philosophy, 1–11, 13, 15–17, 21–23, 25–27, 29–31, 33–34, 51, 55–56, 59–60, 67, 71–73, 76, 78, 81, 83, 88–90, 92–94, 101, 103–104, 109, 112, 155, 165, 167, 184, 192, 197–198, 201, 204, 230, 263–270, 272–274, 280, 284–286; of religion, 1–8, 10–11, 13, 15–17, 21–22, 33–34, 51, 55, 59–60, 67, 71–73, 89–90, 92–94, 104, 109, 112, 155, 167, 184, 197–198, 201, 204, 230, 263, 265–266, 268–270, 272–273, 280, 285–286
Contingency, 32, 53, 83, 89, 90, 94–101, 103, 105–106, 114, 119, 121, 160–161, 166, 231, 281
Correlation, 23–26, 28, 81–83, 94, 105, 245, 258, 274–275; correlationism, 7, 81–83, 86, 274–275
Cosmology, 16, 21, 23, 253; cosmological, 35–40, 45–46, 51, 54, 253, 255–257, 260
Craighero, Laila, 221, 225
Critchley, Simon, 143, 149, 151

287

Death of God, 21, 55–57, 59, 72–73, 78–79, 102, 107, 114–115, 121–122, 158, 164–165, 199, 230, 236, 241, 280

Decolonization, 2

Deconstruction, 2–8, 13–15, 18, 26, 49, 56, 58, 73, 88, 99–101, 105–106, 108–109, 111, 113–115, 117, 119–121, 123, 143–144, 166, 182, 205, 209–210, 212, 214, 217, 222, 228, 273, 281, 284

Deleuze, Gilles, 1, 16–17, 26, 31, 138, 197, 256, 259, 262, 267–268, 273–278, 280–283

Derrida, Jacques, 1–7, 13, 14–18, 21, 23–26, 29, 32–35, 40, 43–44, 46–51, 53, 55–60, 63–66, 72–73, 75, 76–77, 79, 81–82, 85–86, 88–91, 104, 106, 109, 111–117, 119–122, 143, 197, 209–218, 220, 225, 228, 265, 268, 270–271, 273, 275, 280–281, 283, 285–286; *The Gift of Death*, 7, 57–58, 60, 63–64, 76–77, 91, 281

Descartes, René, 8–9, 77, 231, 266

Desire, 5–6, 11, 23, 28, 35, 40, 43, 45, 71–73, 77, 86, 101, 132–133, 137–138, 150, 155, 175, 179, 182, 193, 197–199, 202, 211, 240, 242, 246–247, 249, 254–255, 257, 265–266, 268, 283

Différance, 1, 26, 35, 38–39, 42, 49, 113, 212

Divine, 6–7, 27, 35–43, 46, 52, 56–57, 62, 69, 71, 76, 83, 87–88, 90, 92–95, 98–99, 101–104, 114, 132, 136, 147–148, 153, 158, 162, 164–165, 179–181, 184, 187, 189, 191, 194–195, 200, 203, 236, 255, 258, 259, 268, 283; divinology, 7, 84, 101–103; feminine divine; 259

Economy, 108, 114, 122, 128–129, 140–141, 143–149, 151–153, 176, 214, 228, 239, 258–260, 286

Eddington, Arthur, 272, 281

Emancipation, 8, 10, 101, 110, 174–175

Embodiment, 31, 68, 231, 247

Emerson, Ralph Waldo, 74, 77, 79

Energy, 11, 17, 26, 128, 131, 224, 240, 254, 256, 272–274, 278–281

Enlightenment, 8–9, 64, 78, 90, 242, 250, 281

Entropy, 6, 17, 28–29, 31, 272–281

Epigenesis, 14–15, 209, 213–216; of reason, 14–15, 214–216

Epistemology, 55, 59, 73, 78, 81–82, 171, 250, 257, 285; epistemological, 5, 25, 27, 38, 41, 102, 148, 169–172, 176, 205

Eucharist, 185–186

Event, 4, 8, 23, 27–28, 31–32, 36–37, 39–40, 43, 46, 52–55, 59, 66, 74–75, 81–85, 88–89, 94–97, 99, 101–102, 104–105, 108–118, 120–122, 134, 136, 162, 175, 178, 180, 182, 184–185, 187–189, 191, 194, 196, 209–215, 232, 235, 240, 264–266, 268, 271, 278, 281, 283

Excess, 3, 12–13, 30–32, 74, 114–115, 117, 143, 175–176, 179–185, 190, 192–194, 267, 274

Experience, 12, 27, 36, 49, 75, 79, 93, 96, 105, 109, 114–115, 128, 133–134, 139, 145, 155–156, 170, 176, 179–195, 200–202, 213–216, 221–222, 225–226, 229, 235, 237–238, 243–246, 248, 251, 285; religious, 12, 93, 176, 179–181, 183–185, 187–188, 192, 194–195, 229, 238

Faith, 3, 5–6, 10–11, 15, 17, 21, 26–30, 33, 36, 39, 41–43, 45–48, 51–52, 56–57, 59–71, 74–78, 81, 83, 102–103, 105, 111–112, 114, 116, 120, 134, 145, 149, 162, 165, 172, 179, 182–185, 192–193, 197, 199–201, 209–210, 214–218, 235, 264, 267, 270, 285

False consciousness, 174, 230–231, 234–235, 237–238

Feuerbach, Ludwig, 13, 16, 43, 49, 57, 170, 193, 199, 200, 205, 229, 232–236, 239–241, 286

Fideism, 5, 10, 15, 21, 23, 26–27, 29, 93–94, 101–103, 105

Foucault, Michel, 1, 24, 66, 79, 113, 121, 146, 152–153, 246–247

Freud, Sigmund, 13, 63, 193, 198, 200, 203, 205, 228, 232, 234–237, 239–240, 249, 274

Future, 1–17, 32–33, 38, 55, 57, 59–60, 65, 71–74, 78, 84, 86, 89, 92–94, 97–104, 109, 127, 131, 140–141, 148, 150, 178, 186, 194, 197–201, 204–205, 209–214, 216–218, 221–225, 227–228, 230, 235, 240, 243, 252, 258, 260, 262–264, 266–272, 280, 284

Gift, 7, 14, 29–31, 57–58, 60, 62–64, 70, 74–77, 79, 91, 100, 114, 137–138, 182, 203, 209, 212, 216, 281

God, 2, 4–5, 7, 10, 21–22, 27–29, 31–74, 76, 78–89, 92–95, 97–118, 120–123, 140, 145–149, 158–159, 162, 164–166, 173, 179–182, 184–185, 188, 191–193, 195, 199, 200–202, 215–217, 229–234, 236, 238–239, 241, 247, 251, 254–255, 257–260, 266, 269, 280–281, 283–285

Government, 128, 136, 141, 149, 152–153

Grace, 6, 22, 28, 29, 30, 31, 32, 33, 46, 62, 91, 139, 259. *See also* nihilism

Goodchild, Philip, 8, 9, 10, 11, 13, 17, 18, 127, 137, 141, 149, 150, 153, 176, 178, 197, 283

Grant, Iain Hamilton, 92, 104–105

Gyges, 144

Hägglund, Martin, 33, 86, 88, 90

Harman, Graham, 7, 32, 82, 87–91, 273

Harrison, Robert Pogue, 67, 76
Hegel, Georg F. W., 5, 10, 14–16, 21–22, 25–27, 32–33, 38, 42, 51–53, 66, 92, 109, 113, 119, 153, 174, 209–213, 216–218, 221, 222–228, 232–233, 235, 237, 239–241, 243–244, 252, 262, 283–285
Heidegger, Martin, 14, 23, 25, 30, 33, 40, 42, 55, 59–60, 66, 77, 87, 90, 120, 128, 130, 138, 179–180, 193–194, 209–212, 217, 269
Henry, Michel, 4, 12, 180–181, 186–187, 190–191, 193, 195, 284
Heraclitus, 141–143, 149, 151
Hermeneutics of suspicion, 27–28, 34–35, 38–39, 41, 46–48, 50, 53, 56, 105, 111–112, 114–115, 120–122, 175, 187–188, 192, 195, 232, 283
Holocaust, 75
Homo tantum, 266–268
Hope, 4, 11, 27, 29–30, 41, 48–49, 65, 68, 71–75, 84, 86, 90, 93–94, 97–103, 111, 113, 118, 121, 127, 134, 143, 150–151, 165, 175, 179, 182, 190, 193, 197, 204, 211, 224, 227, 239, 272
Husserl, Edmund, 14, 26, 33, 68, 179, 186, 188, 193, 194, 200
Hyper-chaos, 82, 84, 86

Idealism, 7, 86, 136, 219, 224, 230, 232, 262, 274–275, 280, 285
Ideology, 12, 168–171, 223, 233, 241, 265
Impossible, 4–6, 14, 23, 29, 31–32, 39, 41–43, 53, 55, 61–62, 64, 72, 74, 76, 80, 88, 103, 105, 113–114, 143, 157, 159, 174, 179–182, 187, 191–192, 199–200, 212, 223, 255, 268
Indisciplinary, indisciplinarity, 12, 167, 170–174, 176–177
Inexistence, 7, 92–95, 98–99, 101–102, 104, 265
Interdisciplinary, 12, 167–172
Irigaray, Luce, 16, 253, 257–260, 262, 286

James, William, 229, 238
Janicaud, Dominique, 4, 17, 105, 179, 186, 190, 205
Joy, 29–30, 41, 60, 64, 71–76, 78–79, 85, 120, 134, 181, 229–230
Justice, 8, 12, 27, 31, 37, 40, 52–53, 57, 81, 84, 93–94, 97–103, 113–116, 118, 122, 127, 133, 143, 154–156, 159–160, 162–164, 172, 182, 185, 210, 217, 234, 250

Kant, Immanuel, 5, 7, 10, 15, 21–23, 26–27, 29, 38, 51, 78, 115, 154, 157, 160, 165, 210, 214–216, 218, 232, 270
Kearney, Richard, 7, 56, 93–95, 101–105, 107, 184–185, 192, 195

Kierkegaard, Soren, 6–7, 27, 38, 51, 57, 59, 61, 63–68, 70–72, 75–79, 84, 86, 90, 114, 122, 130, 136, 138–139, 160, 191, 283, 285; *Fear and Trembling*, 7, 59–62, 64–69, 71–78, 81, 191; indirect communication, 68, 77; knight of faith, 62, 74, 76
Kristeva, Julia, 6–7, 59–60, 66–73, 75, 77–78

Lacan, Jacques, 66, 109–110, 122, 221, 228, 256, 273
Lacoste, Jean-Yves, 180, 185, 190, 192
Laruelle, François, 22, 27, 33, 104, 197, 273
Latour, Bruno, 33, 91–92, 104
Leibniz, 87, 230
Levinas, Emmanuel, 1, 4, 12, 24, 28, 46, 57, 59–60, 63, 76–77, 79, 138, 154–166, 180, 280
Leviticus, 268
Liberation, 1, 3, 8, 10–12, 66, 125, 127, 128–130, 133–134, 151, 227–228
Life, 1, 6, 9–10, 12, 21–22, 24–27, 29–32, 37, 39–40, 46–47, 62–63, 65, 67, 69–75, 78–80, 82, 85–87, 90, 94, 97, 100, 102–103, 108, 112–116, 118, 128, 130–132, 135–136, 138, 142, 145, 148, 154, 172, 175–176, 179, 181–182, 184, 186, 191–195, 198, 201–204, 213, 222, 224–226, 229–230, 234, 239, 244–247, 251, 254–262, 267–270, 274–275, 279–281, 284–286
Liturgy, 12, 117–118, 185–190, 193–195
Luke, 116, 266
Lyotard, Jean-François, 54, 66, 274

Machine, 16, 85–86, 246, 251
Mahmood, Saba, 16, 242–243, 245–248, 251–252
Malabou, Catherine, 13–16, 18, 21, 24, 26, 32, 197, 209, 218–228, 243–245, 251–252, 273, 280–281, 284
Marion, Jean-Luc, 4, 12, 57, 166, 180–182, 184, 186–187, 190–192, 194–195, 280, 284
Marx, Karl, 22, 66, 139, 169–171, 173–174, 177, 203, 217, 226, 232–236, 239, 241, 262
Materialism 2, 5–6, 8, 13–17, 21, 24, 26, 28, 32, 74, 86, 89–90, 92, 94, 103–104, 108–110, 112–113, 115–117, 119, 122, 136, 147, 161–162, 175–176, 189, 199, 203, 209, 213, 219, 220–222, 224–226, 228–240, 256, 273, 280, 283–285; nonreductive, 15, 16, 231
Matter, 16, 24–25, 86–87, 100, 108, 110, 115, 161, 256, 273, 275
McCarthy, Tom, 143, 149, 151
Meillassoux, Quentin, 5, 7, 21, 24–26, 29, 32, 82–84, 86, 90, 92–107, 273–274, 281
Meister Eckhart, 30, 55

Messianic, 3-4, 6-8, 13-15, 19, 38, 93, 95, 98-101, 111, 115, 118, 197, 204, 210, 212-214, 216, 223, 267-268, 271
Metaphysics, 22-24, 40, 56, 66, 86, 90, 92-96, 98, 100, 102-106, 108, 130, 150, 177, 202, 284-285
Milbank, John, 8, 28, 108-112, 115-116, 118-120, 123, 151, 153, 160, 166, 238, 241
Monotheism, 45-46, 145
Money, 2, 10-11, 18, 128, 137, 140-153, 283, 286
Monstrosity, 61, 63, 109, 111, 114, 118-122, 166, 240-241
Mortality, 26-28, 31, 68, 70-71, 82, 261, 285
Mourning, 84, 88, 97, 222, 270

Nancy, Jean-Luc, 13-14, 18, 170, 177, 225, 228, 263, 267, 270-271, 284
Natality, 7, 60, 63, 70-71, 78
Negri, Antonio, 2
Neuroplasticity, 16, 209, 213, 273
Neuroscience, 2, 26, 211-213, 220, 223-225, 227, 231, 250, 284
Nicholas of Cusa, 102
Nietzsche, Friedrich, 13, 21-22, 28-29, 31-33, 59, 72, 74, 78, 102, 112, 114, 130, 135, 138-139, 158, 198-199, 203, 230-232, 236, 241, 262
Nihilism, of grace, 6, 11, 22, 28, 30, 109-110, 161
Nonbeing, 254-255
Numbers, 17, 96, 269, 281

Occasionalism, 87
Ontology, 7-8, 17, 35-37, 40-41, 45-46, 48, 51, 54, 56, 59, 73, 78, 81, 83, 93, 94, 101-102, 104, 106, 110, 113-114, 119, 121-122, 150, 153, 161-163, 166, 179, 197, 211, 222, 228, 232, 270, 274, 278, 280, 283

Paul, 8, 16, 47, 109-110, 116-117, 119, 122, 162, 264-267, 270-271, 283
Penrose, Roger, 277
Perhaps, the, 31-32, 39-40, 104, 283
Phenomenology, 2, 4, 5, 12, 17, 23, 26, 33, 48, 66, 90, 93, 105, 115, 138, 179-180, 183, 185-188, 190-191, 193, 195, 200, 205, 210-211, 217, 220, 222, 226, 231, 284
Phenomenon, 31, 105, 150, 175, 180-181, 191, 193, 242, 245, 248, 253, 262; saturated, 181, 184, 190-191, 195
Physics, and continental philosophy, 22-26, 31-33, 223, 272, 276, 278, 286
Piety, 9, 11, 136, 149, 176, 198, 247

Plasticity, 3, 13-16, 18, 21, 32, 207, 209, 211-214, 216-218, 220-223, 225-226, 228, 242-245, 247-248, 251
Plato, 22-23, 28, 70, 92, 129-130, 142-144, 169-170, 173, 277
Poet, 6, 24, 27, 31, 34-36
political theology, 1, 56, 73, 79, 151, 165, 177, 205, 209, 217-218, 228, 252, 285
Politics, 2, 11-12, 16, 70, 84, 86, 115, 128-129, 135-136, 138, 149, 151-154, 163, 166, 168, 173, 177-178, 217, 227, 242, 245, 250, 252, 270-271, 283-286
Postcolonialism, 2, 79
Post-humanism, 16
Postmodern, 4-6, 8, 17, 21, 27, 33-34, 37, 44, 51, 56, 59, 66, 90, 93-94, 104-105, 119-123, 158, 166, 191, 197, 201, 205, 240, 270, 284
Postsecular, 4, 16-17, 90, 104, 263-271, 284
Prana, 253, 257
Prigogine, Ilya, 273, 278
Promise, 3, 6, 14-15, 27, 37, 40, 42-43, 46, 49, 52, 56, 61, 64, 67, 88-89, 99-102, 111, 113, 117, 150, 157, 163, 172, 180, 190, 193, 204, 212, 235-238, 264, 269
Psychology, 2, 16, 76, 230, 278

Qi, 17, 280

Rabbi, 6, 34-36, 39-42, 45-54, 56, 57, 192
Radical Orthodoxy, 2, 4, 108-109, 118-120, 286
Rancière, Jacques, 12, 167, 169-178
Rationality, 9, 10, 95, 214-215, 231, 237, 250
Realism, 2, 6, 7, 15, 17, 21, 32, 38, 39, 80, 81, 82, 86, 89, 90, 92, 94, 101, 103, 104, 183, 273, 274, 275
Reason, 8-11, 14-15, 24, 69, 83-84, 95-97, 99, 104-105, 109, 119, 128-129, 131, 133-134, 136, 165, 171, 182, 197-200, 210, 214-218, 224, 226-227, 232, 235, 250, 255-257, 264, 267, 270
Reject, 14-17, 37, 42-43, 46-47, 66, 81, 95, 119, 154, 186-187, 190, 197, 231-232, 235, 263, 265-271, 275, 280, 284
Religion, 1-13, 15-17, 21-23, 26-35, 39, 42-45, 51-57, 59-60, 63, 66-67, 71-74, 79, 83, 86-87, 89-90, 92-94, 104, 109, 111-112, 115, 117-122, 129, 135, 137, 140-141, 149-150, 155, 166-168, 172-176, 178-179, 182-184, 186, 191-193, 195, 197-201, 204, 214, 217, 225, 229-243, 249-250, 252, 261, 263-270, 272-273, 280, 283, 284-286
Repetition, 17, 56, 63, 68, 74, 76, 120, 186, 244, 274-275, 277-278, 280-281
Responsibility, 64-65, 77, 112, 114-115, 118, 156-160, 162, 164, 224, 235-236, 275, 281

Ricoeur, Paul, 12, 51, 182–183, 187, 191, 194, 285
Rizzolatti, Giacomo, 138, 221, 225
Rollins, Peter, 8, 109, 117–118, 122
Rorty, Richard, 9, 17
Rousseau, 12, 26, 85, 197–200, 204–205

Sacrifice, 30, 64–65, 69, 103, 118, 136–137, 157, 175, 191, 198–200, 227, 271
Sagan, Dorion, 274, 278–279, 281
Sarah, 64, 81, 89, 191
Saturation, 181, 284
Saussure, Ferdinand de, 68
Schelling, F. W. J., 16, 87, 90, 104–105, 121, 253, 255–257, 259–261, 285–286
Schleiermacher, Friedrich, 232
Schneider, Eric D., 274, 278–279, 281
Science, 5–6, 13, 15–17, 21, 23, 31, 66, 74, 77, 82, 128, 130, 168–170, 172, 174, 177, 179, 213, 220–221, 223, 225, 227–228, 231, 233, 235, 239, 252, 272–273, 276, 278–279, 284, 286
Seaford, Richard, 141–142, 145, 151
Secret, 29, 49, 57, 88, 135, 210, 216, 240, 261, 268
Secular, 10–11, 15, 56, 109–110, 114, 119–120, 136, 140, 148–149, 151, 153, 190, 199–200, 224–225, 235, 263–264, 270, 284, 286
Selme, Léon, 276–277
Serres, Michel, 171, 177, 273
Shell, Marc, 141–144, 151–152
Silence, 35, 39, 43, 61, 78, 81, 190, 210, 259, 260
Smith, Zadie, 74-75, 79
Sovereignty, 2, 11, 56, 69, 74, 94, 98–101, 104, 106, 141, 145–148, 150–151, 155, 161, 210, 217, 268, 285
Spectral Dilemma, 84, 90, 95, 97–98, 104, 106
Speculative Realism, 2, 6, 7, 15, 17, 80, 81–82, 90, 92, 103, 273–275
Spinoza, Baruch, 46, 49, 230–231
Spirit, spirituality, 4, 11, 16–17, 40, 64, 94, 104, 108, 110, 112, 115, 118, 122, 130, 135–138, 147–148, 157, 175, 184, 186, 192–194, 199–200, 203, 210–211, 217, 220, 223, 225, 228, 233–234, 236–237, 243, 253–262, 273, 280, 283
Stengers, Isabelle, 227, 273
Subject, 7, 11, 16–17, 24–26, 28, 37, 39, 49, 61, 64, 66, 68–69, 77, 81–84, 87–88, 101, 103–105, 108, 110, 112–117, 119, 121–122, 135, 144, 146–147, 149–150, 153, 156–159, 164–166, 169, 176, 192, 198–199, 202–203, 211–213, 215, 217, 220, 222, 224, 227–228, 230, 232–233, 236, 241–249, 251, 256, 258–261, 263–268, 270–271, 274
Sublime, 61–63, 66, 74, 76–77, 241, 255
Swenson, Rod, 278, 281

Temporality, 13, 32, 47, 86, 209–213, 216, 218, 225, 243, 251, 284
Theology, 1–2, 5–8, 10–12, 18, 21, 23, 27–28, 32–34, 36–40, 42–43, 46, 49, 54–58, 62, 73, 76, 78–79, 87, 89, 91–93, 95, 98–99, 101–102, 104–105, 108–113, 115–122, 140–141, 143, 146, 149–151, 153, 158, 165, 166–167, 177, 179, 190–191, 194–195, 197, 199–200, 204–205, 209, 217–218, 228, 230, 232, 235–236, 240, 252, 273, 280, 283–286; death of god, 21, 55–57, 59, 72–73, 78–79, 102, 107, 114–115, 121–122, 158, 164–165, 199, 230, 236, 241, 280; process, 7; radical, 4–5, 22, 27–28, 33, 36, 119, 122, 228, 284
Theophany, 12, 31, 188–189, 196
Thermodynamics, 17, 272–274, 276–281
Thoreau, Henry David, 72–73, 78, 285
Time, 1–5, 6, 10, 13–15, 22, 24, 29–30, 33, 52, 76, 78, 83, 85–86, 90, 96–97, 101–106, 164, 177, 185–189, 209–218, 221–222, 232, 259, 272, 275–277, 280–281, 283, 285
Tillich, Paul, 6, 26, 34–40, 45–46, 48, 51–56, 201
Trace, 7, 60, 66–67, 70–71, 80–81, 86–90, 117, 248
Transcendence, 4, 38, 46, 52, 53, 56–57, 102, 108, 143, 158, 175, 179, 191, 213, 223, 226, 228, 230, 238, 280
Translation, 40, 49, 76, 82, 87–88, 95, 152, 191, 214, 262, 270; translatable, 39, 43, 49, 88, 111–112, 118
Trauma, 28, 67–69, 112, 114, 118
Tyranny, 142, 144–145, 150–152

Universal, 8–9, 12, 64–65, 85, 101, 104, 110, 115–119, 121, 129–130, 141–144, 154–165, 198, 220, 222, 224, 242–243, 246–247, 256, 264–265, 270, 276

Vásquez, Manuel, 230–233, 238, 240
Vattimo, Gianni, 2, 17, 56–57, 107, 122, 200
Vedas, 253, 258, 260–261
Violence, 10, 12, 56, 63, 76, 79, 89, 99, 103, 110, 111, 120, 146, 160–163, 192, 195, 234, 264–267, 270–271
Vorstellungen, 27–29, 52–54

Westphal, Merold, 6, 34, 36–45, 47, 51, 53, 55–57, 197, 285
Without, 2, 4–7, 15, 17, 22, 24–25, 27, 29–31, 40, 42, 44, 46, 48–49, 52, 56–57, 59, 64, 69, 74, 79, 83–84, 86, 88, 90, 94–95, 97–100, 103–106, 108, 112, 115–120, 127–129, 132, 137, 139, 149, 156–158, 162, 165, 168, 170, 173, 175, 181, 184,

192, 194, 199, 201, 203–204, 210, 212, 214, 219, 223, 226–227, 234, 238–240, 249, 255–256, 258, 261, 265, 267–269, 271, 275, 277, 278, 281

Why, 2, 4, 21, 24–26, 29–30, 46, 48, 51, 55, 59, 61, 71, 73, 75, 80, 84, 96, 111–112, 115–117, 119, 127, 135, 158, 161, 172, 182, 186, 194, 198, 212, 214, 221, 249, 280

Xenophanes, 145

Žižek, Slavoj, 2, 8, 12, 16, 24–25, 108–123, 151, 153–157, 159–166, 226, 229–230, 235–238, 240–241, 256, 261, 270, 280, 283; and Christian atheism, 8, 115, 199

www.ingramcontent.com/pod-product-compliance
Lightning Source LLC
Chambersburg PA
CBHW021347300426
44114CB00012B/1117